The Dell War Series

The Dell War Series takes you onto the battlefield, into the jungles, and beneath the oceans with unforgettable stories that offer a new look at the terrors and triumphs of America's war experience. Many of these books are eyewitness accounts of the duty-bound fighting man. From the intrepid foot soldiers, sailors, pilots, and commanders, to the elite warriors of the Special Forces, here are stories of men who fight because their lives depend on it.

DEATH ON HIGHWAY 1!

Captain Batcheller of Alpha Company stepped out from behind the protection of the lead tank and ran to the wounded man. He bent to grab the man by the shoulders of his flak jacket and started pulling him sideways toward the tank, but a solid burst of gunfire ended the effort. The wounded man was killed; Batcheller was hit in both legs and his right forearm. The impact of the bullets threw him against the base of a tree, entangling him in a coil of concertina wire, unable to move.

Batcheller twisted his head around to see what he could see. He was directly in the line of fire. Fearful that his Marines would sacrifice themselves to rescue him, he yelled to those on the right side of the highway to stay down, to leave him be. Gunnery Sergeant J. L. Canley came up abreast of Batcheller, across the roadway, and Batcheller passed command to him with orders to carry out the mission. It was now up to the company gunny to get Alpha 1/1 to Hue.

There was nothing left for Gordon Batcheller to do. He looked up through the branches of the tree and saw the beautiful blue sky. Then he began to pray.

QUANTITY SALES

INDIVIDUAL SALES

FIRE IN THE STREETS

STREETS

THE BATTLE FOR HUE, TET 1968

ERIC HAMMEL

A DELL BOOK

*To all the men, women, and children who died
in the battle for Hue, and to all who still suffer
the wounds they sustained there*

Published by
Dell Publishing
a division of
Bantam Doubleday Dell Publishing Group, Inc.
666 Fifth Avenue
New York, New York 10103

ISBN: 0-440-21174-3

Reprinted by arrangement with Contemporary Books, Inc.

Printed in the United States of America

Published simultaneously in Canada

April 1992

10 9 8 7 6 5 4 3 2 1

OPM

Contents

No city or town or civil population in either of the Vietnams was fated to experience as much violent bloodshed and destruction for so many days as were Hue and her 140,000 citizens.

Guide to Terms and Abbreviations

I Corps	Military Region I (pronounced "eye cor")
III MAF	Third Marine Amphibious Force
A-1	Douglas Skyraider piston-engine attack bomber
A-4	Douglas Skyhawk jet attack bomber
AK-47	Soviet-pattern 7.62mm assault rifle
APC	U.S.-made M-113 armored personnel carrier
ARA	Aerial Rocket Artillery
ARVN	Army of the Republic of Vietnam
B-40	Soviet-pattern rocket-propelled grenade/launcher
C4	plastic explosive (plastique)
Cal	caliber
CAP	Combined Action Platoon
Cav	cavalry
Charlie	Viet Cong (from Victor Charlie, VC)
Chicom	Chinese Communist (used for NVA hand grenade)
CH-46	Boeing Sea Knight medium cargo helicopter
CIA	U.S. Central Intelligence Agency
CO	commanding officer
CORDS	U.S. Civil Operations and Revolutionary Development Support
CP	command post
CS	tear gas
DMZ	Demilitarized Zone
Doc	any U.S. Navy medical corpsman
Duster	U.S. Army M-42 tracked dual-40mm gun carrier
E-8	U.S. pack-mounted 35mm tear-gas grenade launcher

Exec	executive officer
F-4B	McDonnell Phantom jet fighter–bomber
Gunny	gunnery sergeant
GVN	Government of Vietnam
H&S	Headquarters-and-Service
Huey	Bell UH-1E light attack/transport helicopter
JGS	Joint General Staff (South Vietnam)
KIA	Killed in Action
Kit Carson	ARVN scout, formerly an NVA or VC soldier
LAAW	U.S. M-72 light antitank assault weapon
LCU	U.S. Navy Landing Craft, Utility
Log	logistics
LRRP	U.S. Army Long-Range Reconnaissance Patrol
LZ	landing zone
M-1	U.S.-made .30-caliber semiautomatic carbine
M-2	U.S.-made .30-caliber automatic carbine
M-3	U.S.-made .45-caliber submachine gun (grease gun)
M-14	U.S. 7.62mm assault rifle
M-16	U.S. 5.56mm assault rifle
M-41	U.S.-made Walker 76mm light tank
M-42	U.S. Army tracked dual-40mm gun carrier (Duster)
M-48	U.S. Patton 90mm main battle tank
M-50	U.S. Marine Ontos tracked six–106mm recoilless rifle carrier
M-55	U.S. Army quadruple-.50-caliber machine-gun truck
M-60	U.S. 7.62mm medium machine gun
M-72	U.S. LAAW light antitank assault weapon

M-79	U.S. 40mm grenade launcher
M-113	U.S.-made armored personnel carrier (APC)
MACV	Military Assistance Command, Vietnam
MAF	Marine Amphibious Force
Mechanical Mule	cargo transporter
Medcap	Medical Combined Action Program
Medevac	Medical Evacuation
Mighty Mite	cargo transporter
NLF	National Liberation Front (Viet Cong)
NVA	North Vietnam Army
O-1	U.S. Bird Dog light observation airplane
OH-13S	U.S. Sioux two-seat light observation helicopter
Ontos	U.S. Marine M-50 tracked six–106mm recoilless rifle carrier
PBR	U.S. Navy Patrol Boat, Riverine
PF	South Vietnam Popular Forces
Phantom	McDonnell F-4B jet fighter–bomber
quad-.50	quadruple-.50-caliber machine gun
R and R	rest and rehabilitation (leave)
RF	Regional Forces (South Vietnam)
RPD	Soviet-pattern 7.62mm light machine gun
RPG	Soviet-pattern rocket-propelled grenade
SKS	Soviet-pattern 7.62mm bolt-action carbine
Skyhawk	Douglas A-4 jet attack bomber
Skyraider	Douglas A-1 piston-engine attack bomber
Snakeye	U.S. high-explosive aerial bomb
TCK-TKN	*Tong Kong Kich–Tong Khoi Nghia*; General Offensive–General Uprising; Communist Tet Offensive

TOC	Tactical Operations Center
UH-1E	Bell Huey light attack/transport helicopter
USAID	U.S. Agency for International Development
USIS	U.S. Information Service
USMC	United States Marine Corps
VC	Viet Cong
VNAF	Vietnam Air Force
VNMC	Vietnam Marine Corps
WIA	Wounded in Action

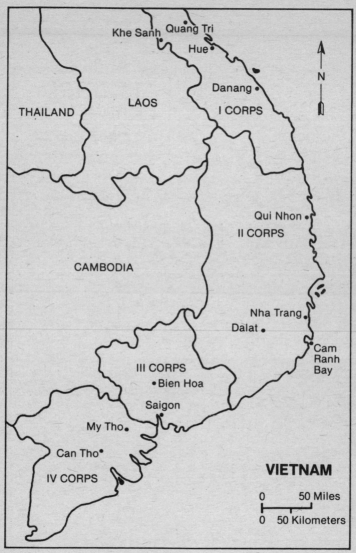

THAILAND

LAOS

Khe Sanh • Quang Tri
• Hue

Danang •

I CORPS

N

Qui Nhon •

II CORPS

CAMBODIA

Nha Trang •
Dalat •

Cam
Ranh
Bay

III CORPS
• Bien Hoa

Saigon •

My Tho •

Can Tho •

IV CORPS

VIETNAM

0   50 Miles

0   50 Kilometers

© F. F. Parry (used with permission)

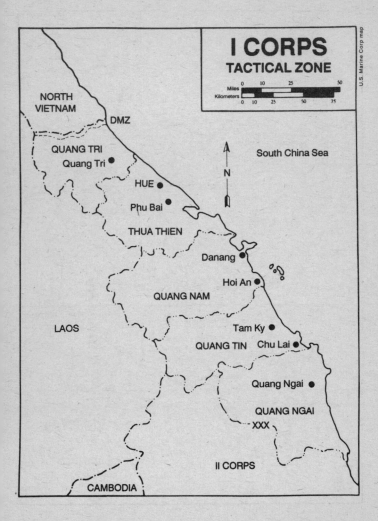

I CORPS
TACTICAL ZONE

U.S. Marine Corp map

Miles 0 10 25 50
Kilometers 0 10 25 50 75

NORTH VIETNAM

DMZ

QUANG TRI
Quang Tri ●

South China Sea

N

HUE ●

Phu Bai ●

THUA THIEN

Danang ●

Hoi An ●

QUANG NAM

LAOS

Tam Ky ●

QUANG TIN   Chu Lai ●

Quang Ngai ●

QUANG NGAI

XXX

II CORPS

CAMBODIA

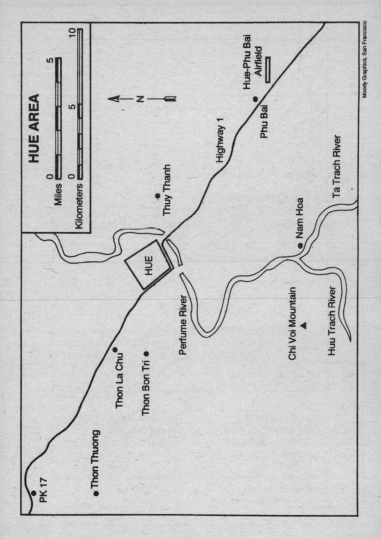

HUE AREA

Miles
0   5
Kilometers
0   5   10

N

• Thuy Thanh

Hue-Phu Bai
Airfield

• Phu Bai

Highway 1

HUE

Perfume River

• Nam Hoa

Ta Trach River

Chi Voi Mountain ▲

Huu Trach River

• Thon La Chu

• Thon Bon Tri

• Thon Thuong

• PK 17

Moody Graphics, San Francisco

xvii

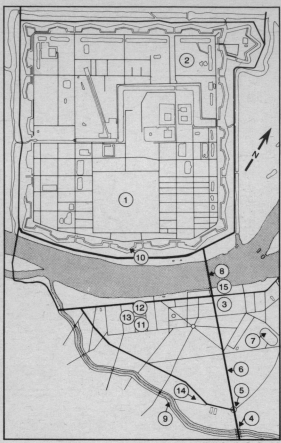

Moody Graphics, San Francisco

HUE

1. Imperial Palace
2. 1st ARVN Division CP
3. MACV Compound
4. An Cuu Bridge
5. Traffic Circle
6. Cane Field Causeway
7. Tu Do Stadium
8. Nguyen Hoang Bridge
9. Phu Cam Canal
10. Citadel Flagpole
11. Thua Thien Provinicial Prison
12. Thua Thien Provincial Admin. Center
13. Hue Municipal Power Station
14. Hue Cathedral
15. Doc Lao Park

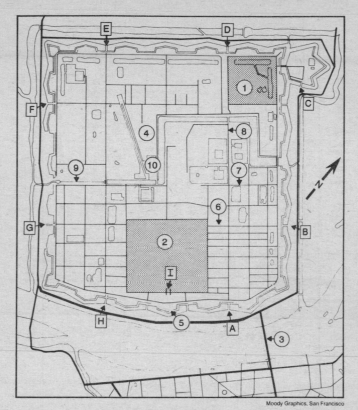

Moody Graphics, San Francisco

THE CITADEL

1. 1st ARVN Division CP Compound
2. Imperial Palace
3. Nguyen Hoang Bridge
4. Tay Loc Airfield
5. Citadel Flagpole
6. Mai Thuc Loan Street
7. Tinh Tam Street
8. Dinh Bo Linh Street
9. Thuy Quan Canal
10. 1st ARVN Ordnance Company Armory

A. Thuong Tu Gate
B. Dong Ba Gate
C. Truong Dinh Gate
D. Hau Gate
E. An Hoa Gate
F. Chanh Tay Gate
G. Huu Gate
H. Nha Do Gate
I. Ngo Mon Gate

DOWNTOWN HUE

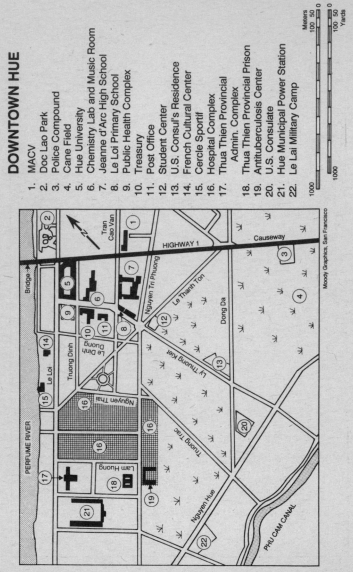

1. MACV
2. Doc Lao Park
3. Police Compound
4. Cane Field
5. Hue University
6. Chemistry Lab and Music Room
7. Jeanne d'Arc High School
8. Le Loi Primary School
9. Public Health Complex
10. Treasury
11. Post Office
12. Student Center
13. U.S. Consul's Residence
14. French Cultural Center
15. Cercle Sportif
16. Hospital Complex
17. Thua Thien Provincial Admin. Complex
18. Thua Thien Provincial Prison
19. Antituberculosis Center
20. U.S. Consulate
21. Hue Municipal Power Station
22. Le Lai Military Camp

Moody Graphics, San Francisco

THON LA CHU AREA

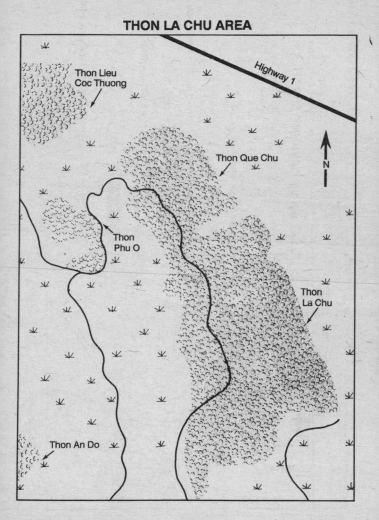

Thon Lieu Coc Thuong

Highway 1

Thon Que Chu

N

Thon Phu O

Thon La Chu

Thon An Do

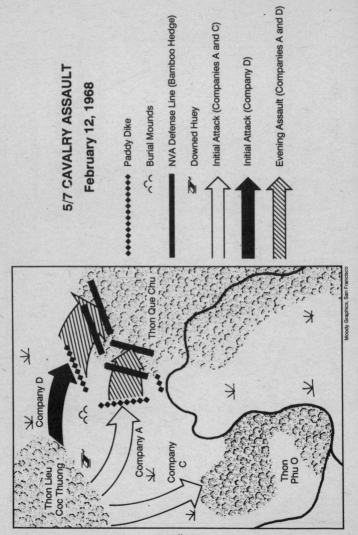

5/7 CAVALRY ASSAULT
February 12, 1968

◆◆◆ Paddy Dike

⌢⌢ Burial Mounds

▬ NVA Defense Line (Bamboo Hedge)

Downed Huey

⇧ Initial Attack (Companies A and C)

⬆ Initial Attack (Company D)

⬈ Evening Assault (Companies A and D)

Thon Lieu
Coc Thuong

Company D

Company A

Company C

Thon Que Chu

Thon
Phu O

Moody Graphics, San Francisco

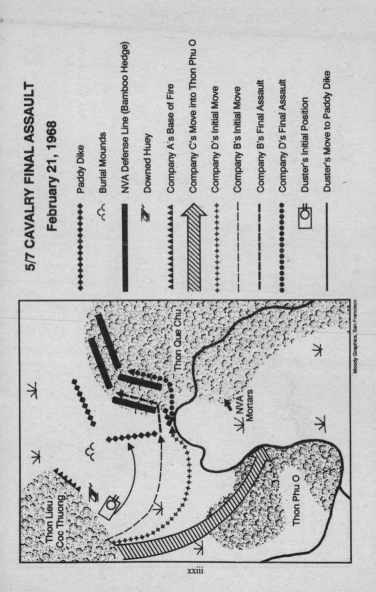

5/7 CAVALRY FINAL ASSAULT
February 21, 1968

Symbol	Description
Paddy Dike
Burial Mounds
NVA Defense Line (Bamboo Hedge)
Downed Huey
Company A's Base of Fire
Company C's Move into Thon Phu O
Company D's Initial Move
Company B's Initial Move
Company B's Final Assault
Company D's Final Assault
Duster's Initial Position
Duster's Move to Paddy Dike

Thon Lieu
Coc Thuong
Thon Que Chu
NVA Mortars
Thon Phu O

Moody Graphics, San Francisco

xxiii

Phonetic Alphabet

Alpha	November
Bravo	Oscar
Charlie	Papa
Delta	Quebec
Echo	Romeo
Foxtrot	Sierra
Golf	Tango
Hotel	Uniform
India	Victor
Juliet	Whiskey
Kilo	X-Ray
Lima	Yankee
Mike	Zulu

Prologue

Sergeant Jack Lofland, USMC
Combined Action Platoon Alpha-2
Thuy Thanh Village, Thua Thien Province

Thuy Thanh was to the northwest of Phu Bai. In late 1967 Thuy Thanh had a population of about 5,000 people. It was almost entirely a farming community. The only industry that existed was the selling of beer, Cokes, and rice to the dozen or so Marines of my combined action platoon (CAP). The villagers were apathetic toward the then-current conflict and, I am sure, toward those that preceded it. They didn't give a damn about us, the Viet Cong (VC), or the North Vietnamese Army (NVA). They said to me more than once, "We just want to be left alone."

My CAP consisted of seven or eight Marines and one Navy corpsman. It and a platoon of about thirty South Vietnamese Popular Force (PF) troops executed daylight patrols, night patrols, and ambushes; provided security for Thuy Thanh; and kept an eye on the political infrastructure of the village.

Early in December 1967 some of the villagers started asking me to give them sandbags. This was a new one. When I asked them what they needed with sandbags, they giggled and made some inane comments, but they never came right out and told me. Not wanting to function within a fog of ignorance, I changed the program of daylight patrols, to find out what was going on.

The daylight patrol was a public relations stunt that we executed almost daily. As the corpsman worked his medcap—tending to the sores, colds, and assorted illnesses of the villagers—the rest of us sipped Cokes and moved along, visiting with the people. In response to the request for sandbags, I changed the routine by going into some of the houses. I was quivering to learn what was going on with my sandbags. The house patrols provided the answer: Not only were the sandbags being filled and used within the houses, but the villagers were actually digging in. In every house I checked, bunkers had been dug and reinforced. The bunkers were large enough to provide shelter and protection for the entire family.

I asked why they were building bunkers, but I wasn't getting any answers. Not having just fallen off a turnip truck, I knew we were due for some visitors. I had a gut feeling that there were going to be many visitors. Our proximity to the large Marine combat base at Phu Bai made us a likely target. We were Phu Bai's distant eyes and ears on our side of the combat base.

The new year, 1968, began with a noticeable increase in enemy activity. I was making contact two or three times a week. These were not major contacts, just patrols of five to seven VC. On occasion there would be an NVA soldier along as an advisor. These contacts were quick, violent firefights that were over in a matter of minutes—or seconds.

Because of the increase in enemy activity, I initiated the killer-team concept to provide added security for the CAP compound. When my regular night activity went out on patrol or ambush, three Marines followed it and moved out to an area no more than 300 meters from the compound. The three were heavily armed and had pyrotechnics for communication. They knew the night activity's route. The killer team usually stayed in place for several hours or until it made contact. The reactionary force, if it was needed, consisted of the one or two Marines left behind in the compound and whatever PFs were available.

By the first week of January, my Marines and I were moving at night in black pajamas and rubber-soled sandals. Our jungle boots left distinctive marks in the dirt, but our sandals were the same as the VC's. They were better at tracking than we were, but I knew we had the potential of being better in combat than they were. We just needed to use the correct tools.

On occasion the VC visited me at night. They called, "*Trung Si* [Sergeant] Jack!" and left notes wrapped in an NVA flag. The notes almost always said the same thing: "The Marines are all going to die in seven days. The PFs will be spared if they put down their arms and return to their homes."

Sometimes I called artillery fire missions from my compound. Phu Bai had 105mm artillery batteries that could send shells around the river that ran along the eastern side of Thuy Thanh. The river was the boundary between our land and the VC's. The VC might play on our side, but before too long they would retreat to their side. Whenever I detected movement of any size on the other side of the river, I called a fire mission from Phu Bai. Occasionally there would be a secondary explosion, indicating that our artillery guys had hit an ammo dump. We would go over by boat the following day to try to get a damage assessment for the artillery folks. They always liked to know what kind of disaster they had caused.

I had called a fire mission on the night of January 11, so, on the morning of January 12, we went across the river to look for anything that might have been hit. In my group were five Marines and five PFs. My CAP's call sign was Motor-2. Since we were the daylight activity, we were Motor-2-Alpha.

Once across, our movement to the impact area took us inland a couple of hundred meters. Then we turned parallel to a treeline. It was a beautiful, cloudless day. The sky was a brilliant blue. The rice paddy we were moving through was dark yellow, which contrasted sharply with the full green of the treeline.

Suddenly machine-gun fire broke out on our right and our left.

We dove for the back side of the nearest paddy dike. I heard mortars. The sound of the machine guns was the distinctive bark of .51-calibers. The mortar rounds fell to our rear. They were white phosphorous. We were pinned down in a .51-cal crossfire, and the mortars to our rear prevented us from pulling back.

One of my Marines took a bullet through his forehead. My radioman took a round in the foot that shattered his leg. The PFs jumped up and began to run, but they were cut down.

I took the handset from my radioman and made the textbook call for fire: "Motor-2. This is Motor-2-Alpha. Give me artillery. Give me gunships. Give me air support." I knew the Marines in the compound could see our location because of the white puffs of the mortar rounds, and they could hear the gunfire.

Throughout all this, we were making a game effort to return rifle fire over the rim of the paddy dike. I could see the enemy. They were NVA regulars. They were wearing khaki uniforms and pith helmets. They started walking out of the treeline, firing from the hip. There seemed to be hundreds of them! They seemed pretty confident. I guess they had reason to be. It was a little like they were swatting a fly with a 1,000-pound bomb.

The Marine carrying our LAAW rocket rolled over, cocked the LAAW, and raised up to fire at the approaching troops. As he raised himself, a round caught him in the back of the neck. It severed his spinal cord. He was already dead when he stood straight up and fired the LAAW into the front rank of the NVA. Then he fell face first into the paddy.

Suddenly, friendly artillery fire came over. It landed about 400 meters to our right. It was not on target, but the fact that it was coming in at all was enough to pull the NVA back into the treeline. The artillery fire stopped, and the NVA started coming out of the treeline again.

Two Huey gunship helicopters came up on the radio net and requested the enemy position. It turned out that the artillery had lifted to give the Hueys access. I told the Hueys that one machine gun was at the base of a white church on my left and that the treeline was alive with NVA. Each Huey made two passes with rocket pods and guns firing.

As the Hueys pulled up and away, I got a strange call on the radio: "Motor-2-Alpha. This is Niner Dash Two. Over." I didn't want to talk to any NVA, so I asked for identification.

"Motor-2-Alpha. This is Niner Dash Two. Look up in the sky."

I looked up and saw two silver dots. They were Marine F-4B fighters out of Danang. I gave them the same information I had given to the Hueys. Then we put our heads down. The fighters came in low and hot and napalmed everything in front of us. As they did, the Hueys came in and took us out.

About a week later, I received the intelligence report on our January 12 action. It said that the unit that hit us was an NVA regiment new to the area.

PART I

GENERAL OFFENSIVE— GENERAL UPRISING

— 1 —

Intelligence "coups" are almost invariably the products of days and weeks and months of exhausting work by dozens, scores, and hundreds of people, most of whom have little or no sense of the depth or breadth of the project in which they are involved. Most often there is no "project" per se, just baskets, and reams, and rooms full of odd snippets of information that overworked analysts might or might not connect to form a single, cogent package. And, once connected, there is no way of knowing until after the fact if the right information, or enough of it, has been tied together.

An experienced intelligence specialist knows that an entire enemy plan might fall into his lap maybe once in a lifetime. And if one does, it only sets off alarms, for it is always best to assume that the enemy himself is at the source of the coup, that he has fed your side plausible but bad information as a means of misdirecting your attention and resources. If there is intelligence, then there must be counterintelligence.

In September 1967 the intelligence-gathering team headed by Robert Brewer, the senior U.S. intelligence advisor assigned to the Government of Vietnam's (GVN's) Quang Tri Provincial Headquarters, unmasked a Communist secret agent and immediately doubled him back on his superiors. The double agent, who was dubbed X-1, handed Brewer's team a coup of the first magnitude: a document called Resolution 13. One look set Robert Brewer's heart aquiver, for he knew that Ho Chi Minh, the Vietnamese Communist supreme leader, had promulgated Resolution 1 in 1919, and that only eleven other such resolutions had been set forth in the nearly fifty intervening years.

Resolution 13 was the product of the Thirteenth Plenum of the North Vietnamese Central Committee. The resolution was an audacious blueprint aimed at attaining a swift victory to a war whose character had taken on the agony of a slow death.

At the time the Thirteenth Plenum was convened, in March or April 1967, the Communists were losing the Second Indochina War, as they called it. Simply put, the reinvigorated Army of the Republic of Vietnam (ARVN) and the growing U.S. combat force in South Vietnam were killing, maiming, or capturing more Viet Cong and NVA fighters each month than the VC could recruit or the NVA could infiltrate from the North. Moreover, the North itself was under costly siege as a result of the U.S. Air Force's and U.S. Navy's massively destructive Rolling Thunder bombing program. In the political arena, one of North Vietnam's two chief sponsors, the Soviet Union, was pushing for a negotiated settlement to the expensive and inconclusive war. And, even more ominous, there were signs that the National Liberation Front (NLF), the South Vietnamese Communist party organization, was actively engaged in prenegotiation talks with the United States.

In spite of the hard evidence indicating an eventual and perhaps imminent Communist collapse in the South, the Thirteenth Plenum concluded that victory was attainable if they continued to use the strategies of the First Indochina War, by which the hated French colonialists had been humiliated and driven out.

An old saying has it that wars are controlled by old men seeking to relive past glories. The truth of this is nowhere more evident than in North Vietnam's great Tet Offensive of 1968.

Briefly, Hanoi's Politburo perceived North Vietnam's independence and Communist existence as being based upon a triple foundation. To these old men, the foundation consisted of a Communist general uprising in August 1945, the victory over 10,000 French Army soldiers at Dien Bien Phu in May 1954, and the immediate resultant collapse of French political will to wage war in Indochina.

The evidence now suggests that the aging architects of the Tet Offensive sought to re-create the triple foundation of Communist Vietnamese nationhood. They thought the time was ripe to seize power over the southern portion of partitioned Vietnam by means of a popular insurrection—another general uprising—against the GVN. They felt also that they could achieve a significant and perhaps decisive military victory over U.S. and ARVN forces, thereby destroying or at least impairing their will to continue the war. All was aimed at achieving a military victory that would lead to a decisive political victory.

The Communists dubbed their plan *Tong Kong Kich-Tong Khoi Nghia* (TCK-TKN)—General Offensive-General Uprising.

TCK-TKN was a long time in reaching fruition, but Phase I was put into action in the summer of 1967 at Con Thien. Con Thien was a U.S. Marine-held hilltop position overlooking the Demilitarized Zone (DMZ), the putative boundary between the two Vietnams. The so-called Con Thien siege and similar NVA-initiated events through the autumn of 1967—chiefly at Loc Ninh, Song Be, and Dak To—had two purposes: to test the mettle of U.S. and ARVN units and to draw the enemy to the periphery of South Vietnam—away from the major cities and political centers that were to be the objectives of Phase II.

Phase I was a bloody debacle for the NVA and VC; they were repulsed at every turn. Though the Communists learned important tactical lessons and were successful in diverting the enemy's attention to the periphery, both the NVA and VC lost many irreplaceable combat veterans and hard-to-replace weapons.

Of the lessons learned from Phase I, the most important was that it was imperative to avoid U.S. combat units whenever possible. The strength and mobility of the U.S. units were a threat to the success of TCK-TKN as a whole. Senior General Vo Nguyen Giap, the chief military architect of TCK-TKN, changed the military plan: henceforth, the NVA and VC were to concentrate their attacks on ARVN combat units, which were weaker than American units. The only U.S. installations that were to be engaged directly were senior command-and-control headquarters and key air bases from which American relief forces could be mounted. Giap assumed—accurately, as it turned out—that American senior commanders would rush U.S. combat units to aid their own endangered headquarters rather than relieve GVN political centers, which were the real targets of the general offensive.

On the political side of the plan, the North Vietnamese and their southern Communist allies believed that the people of

South Vietnam were ready to rise up against the so-called puppet regime in Saigon. It had long been a delusion of the aging Politburo that the August 1945 Communist coup against the French had been wholeheartedly supported—if not actively advanced—by the majority of Vietnamese and other Indochinese peoples. By mid-1967, the Hanoi government was certain that South Vietnam's common citizens were prepared to join in the reunification of their nation under the Communist banner. At the very least, the northerners believed, the peoples of South Vietnam so hated the American occupiers and their openly corrupt puppet regime that they would rise up simply to reassert their freedom and independence. Once the NVA and VC and their political cadres had invested the South's political centers, the Communists thought the majority of the people would turn out to take up arms and build barricades to prevent the return of the capitalist oppressors. The Politburo hoped that large portions of the ARVN rank and file, softened up in advance by anti-GVN and anti-American propaganda, would mutiny and perhaps even rally to the Communists.

Phase II of Resolution 13 called for an assault on the major cities and political centers of the South. Phase III was to be an all-out attack on the Khe Sanh Combat Base, which was to be besieged just prior to the Phase II assault. The operation against isolated Khe Sanh was designed to be a replica of the victory at Dien Bien Phu. In 1954 the French had agreed to negotiate before Dien Bien Phu fell, but the loss of that isolated base so appalled the French public that the political will of the French government collapsed. The Politburo believed that the 1968 Phase II attacks on the cities would convince the American public that the war could not be won; the fall of Khe Sanh would end the Americans' ability to negotiate realistically over the reunification of Vietnam. This was the strategy that had brought victory in the First Indochina War, and the Politburo thought it could be made to work again.

In actuality the negotiation phase of TCK-TKN was kicked off in advance of the others. On December 30, 1967, North Vietnamese Foreign Minister Nguyen Duy Trinh stated publicly that the Communists were ready to negotiate a peace settlement immediately upon the cessation of the American bombing of the North. Trinh's was the first definite statement out of Hanoi to that effect; previously the Communists had said only that peace talks *could* begin if the bombing ceased. In the context of TCK-TKN, Trinh's announcement was the first assault on American political motivation to remain in the war.

Robert Brewer's double agent, X-1, was not, of course, to be totally trusted. For one thing, his Resolution 13 was much more specific about targets and timetables than most Communist plans that had fallen into U.S. or South Vietnamese hands. More-over, it was not written in the usual Communist jargon. To test the resolution's validity, Brewer drew up a long list of indicators that, if they surfaced between September 1967 and January 1968, would validate X-1's version of Resolution 13.

Throughout December and January the Communists tripped off the indicators on Brewer's list, one after another. For example, Brewer felt that if the Communists were really going to mount TCK-TKN, they would precede it with reconnaissance by higher-ranking officers than had previously been involved in such missions. Sure enough, several NVA captains were killed near Thrieu Phong District Headquarters. And, on the night of January 1-2, 1968, an NVA regimental commander and four other officers were killed by U.S. Marines in the wire at Khe Sanh. Brewer and his staff felt also that, if the Communists were planning to attack Quang Tri City with the seven battalions indicated in Resolution 13, they would probably use the assembly areas they had used in the past, booby-trapping them in advance to keep ARVN and U.S. Marine patrols out. On schedule, the assembly areas blossomed with booby traps.

As Robert Brewer and scores of other intelligence types throughout South Vietnam were to learn, they did not know the half of it. But they knew something, enough to prepare them-selves and such of their countrymen and allies as could be per-suaded to listen. For the vast majority of South Vietnam's 14,000,000 citizens and the 500,000 Western troops based in South Vietnam, TCK-TKN would be delivered in the dark of night, an utterly devastating surprise.

— 2 —

Hue, to the Western eye, where the civilizations of Vietnam and France merged to form a unique culture reminiscent of and yet distinct from both, the embodiment of the old catchphrase "where East meets West." A city outwardly both Buddhist and Catholic, both Vietnamese and French, both ancient and modern, both progressive and conservative. Hue of the broad, tree-lined European boulevards and the thronging Asian marketplace. Hue, the Imperial City, golden relic of Vietnam's faded glories; Hue, the university city, hopeful symbol of Vietnam's modern future.

A city uneasily at peace in a nation totally at war, Hue was now at the tranquil eye of the hurricane, but was soon to reap the whirlwind.

The Christian year turned from 1967 to 1968; Tet Nguyen Dan—the Buddhist Lunar New Year, the Year of the Monkey— approached. Hue had been so long untouched by the war that it was virtually unguarded, and unprepared for the special fate Resolution 13 had fashioned for it.

In all their bloody history, the Vietnamese never forgot Tet, never stinted in its celebration. In all of Vietnam, nowhere was the annual week-long festival celebrated as intensely as it was in Hue. Think of Tet week as all your cherished religious holidays and favorite patriotic festivals rolled into one. If you can do that, you can perhaps begin to understand the reverence and joy with which Tet is celebrated in Vietnam. But you cannot begin to experience the thrill and sense of renewal of Tet in Hue.

To top-ranked officials in both Vietnams, Tet 1968 probably offered new hope, new light. Certainly, to the Communists who had planned Phase II of the General Offensive–General Uprising to coincide with the Lunar New Year, Tet 1968 held a bold hope for the future. And to the highly placed optimists in Saigon and their American allies, it seemed possible that the Year of the Monkey might bring a favorable peace, for the Communists appeared to be in decline: Communist battlefield casualties had been extremely high in recent months; the NLF was making peaceable noises, and the North Vietnamese foreign minister had

recently proposed a quid pro quo that could lead to direct nego-
tiations.

As for the common folk—the farmers and soldiers, civil
servants and shopkeepers on whose shoulders the blows of war
fell most heavily—most felt as the people of Thuy Thanh Village
felt: they wanted only to be left alone.

To be left alone: as Tet 1968 approached, fate and Vo
Nguyen Giap had already ensured that the people of Hue would
not realize that hope. No city in Vietnam was to experience as
much violent bloodshed and destruction for so many days as was
Hue and her 140,000 citizens.

The largest, most obvious symbol of Hue's dual past—the
Vietnamese imperial past and the French imperialist past—was
the hulking Imperial Citadel, copied from the Imperial City in
Peking and adapted by French military architects. Emperor Gia
Long began work on the Citadel in 1802, upon his ascension to
the throne. His ascension followed years of bloody civil war,
which began when his family, the Nguyen dynasty, was deposed
and murdered and ended when the usurper's son was executed.
When the Citadel was completed in 1820, its French architects
adjudged it to be impregnable by any Asian army of the day.
Defended by a moat and six-meter-high earth-filled masonry
walls, its four corners aligned in the cardinal directions, the
Citadel measured 2,500 meters on each of its sides. Over the years
the ramparts were strengthened, so in some places they were
seventy-five meters thick. Behind these walls was an entire city:
streets, parks, moats, homes, villas, shops, and government buildings. Within this city was a second walled city, the Imperial
Palace. The palace walls were two to five meters high, and they
measured 700 meters to a side. In all, the Citadel encompassed
more than six square kilometers.

The Citadel dominated all of Hue from its position on the
northern bank of Song Huong, the River of Perfumes. In late
1967 a modern European-style city nearly as large as the Citadel
spread along the Perfume River's south bank, directly opposite
the Citadel. Between rice paddies and the numerous streams and
canals were patches of dry ground that formed Hue's distinctive

neighborhoods. During the war years, when the city's population swelled from the influx of peasants from the countryside, unsightly shantytowns and squatters' villages sprang up, ringing the city on valuable land traditionally kept under intense cultivation.

Hue rested on the generally flat coastal plain, between the South China Sea, only three kilometers to the east, and the impinging Annamite Cordillera, only three kilometers to the west. Situated in this flat, narrow passage directly astride National Route 1 (Highway 1), Vietnam's main north-south coastal highway, it is strange that Hue was not seriously molested by the Viet Cong prior to 1968. This peace was perhaps a measure of her special place in the hearts of the South Vietnamese of both camps.

Few ARVN units were based in or around Hue, though the very competent 1st ARVN Division was headquartered in a corner of the Citadel along with one of its infantry battalions. And the city's ample port facilities and railroad and road junctions made it a natural location for support units and some of the 1st ARVN Division's cantonments and training facilities.

There was no U.S. combat unit based within miles of Hue in late 1967. The main American facility in Hue was the MACV Compound, headquarters of Advisory Team 3 of the Military Assistance Command, Vietnam (MACV, pronounced "mackvee"). From this sparsely fortified former hotel, hard against Highway 1 and just a little more than a block south of the Perfume River, U.S. Army officers and specialists and a few U.S. Marine and Australian trainers traveled out to advise the 1st ARVN Division. The MACV Compound was hardly more than it had been in its former life: a hotel for transient advisors supported by some permanently billeted administrative personnel.

The nearest large American base to Hue was at Phu Bai, which was astride Highway 1 about eleven kilometers south of the Perfume River. The Phu Bai Combat Base, as it was somewhat grandiloquently titled, was a major American headquarters and support facility. For the moment, overseeing Phu Bai and several U.S. Marine combat units working out of it was Task Force X-Ray, a subheadquarters of the 1st U.S. Marine Division. The Hue–Phu Bai airfield—a field run by the U.S. Air Force, just north of the combat base—was the largest facility of its kind in the region.

North of Hue, on Highway 1 exactly seventeen kilometers from the Imperial Palace, was a former French Army base called PK 17 (Post Kilometer 17). The site was now the headquarters of the 1st ARVN Division's 3rd Infantry Regiment and, usually, a reinforced battalion or two. Still farther north along Highway 1 was Camp Evans, a major base operated under the aegis of the 3rd U.S. Marine Division but soon to be turned over to freshly transferred U.S. Army units.

Though Hue could be reinforced easily from nearby Phu Bai, PK 17, and Camp Evans, the truth was that at the end of January 1968 no one in Hue or any of the nearby bases was giving any thought to the looming Communist threat. No one knew there was a threat. The ARVN infantry battalion assigned to the city consisted mostly of new conscripts undergoing the first stages of basic training. All the other battalions of the 1st ARVN Division were in the field, spread across Quang Tri and Thua Thien provinces, South Vietnam's two northernmost states.

If the 1st ARVN Division was tactically unprepared to defend Hue because of pressing business elsewhere, the civilian population, in no way inured to the war that had reached other southern cities, was equally unready to meet an attack. There were thousands of war-experienced refugees in Hue, but that is exactly the point—Hue had always been the perfect refuge because it was so utterly untouched by the war. Indeed, the only violence Hue had seen in the decade of the 1960s had been during protest demonstrations by Hue's devout, politically active Buddhists. The first of these, in 1963, had been directed against favoritism by the Catholic president, Ngo Dinh Diem, on behalf of Catholics. The 1963 Buddhist uprising had been a major factor in Diem's downfall, and a similar Buddhist insurrection in 1966 had nearly led to the ouster of the military junta in power at that time. The second Buddhist insurrection was quelled and the junta saved by direct U.S. military intervention in Hue.

It was a telling measure of Hue's secure and peaceful status that high-ranking ARVN officers paid large bribes to win assignment to the various military and civil agencies headquartered there.

The American military situation in the far northern reaches of South Vietnam's Military Region I (I Corps) was in a state of flux. The American presence in I Corps was doubling and perhaps trebling.

Before 1968, I Corps was the realm of the I ARVN Corps (the 1st and 2nd ARVN divisions and 51st ARVN Infantry Regiment) and the III U.S. Marine Amphibious Force (III MAF—the 1st and 3rd Marine divisions, the 23rd "American" Infantry Division, and the 2nd Republic of Korea Marine Brigade). As 1967 gave way to 1968, several new units were deployed to I Corps: the 1st Cavalry Division and the newly arrived airmobile 101st Airborne Division. The Americal Division was to remain in the southern I Corps area, alongside the 2nd ARVN Division, 51st ARVN Regiment, and 2nd Korean Marine Brigade. The 1st Marine Division—an experienced, first-rate combat unit—was to move into northern I Corps to fight beside the 1st ARVN and 3rd Marine divisions. At the same time, the U.S. Army's innovative, highly mobile, and brilliantly successful 1st Cavalry Division—the Air Cav—was moving, one brigade at a time, into northern I Corps to help the 1st ARVN and 3rd Marine divisions counter increased NVA activity. Indeed, the NVA threat was deemed so serious—and the potential for a sweeping American victory so great—that northern I Corps was slated to receive more American combat troops than any other region of the country, including the strategically vital III Corps region around Saigon.

A new subheadquarters of the Saigon-based MACV was to oversee all the combat forces in I Corps. First announced on January 27, 1968, the name of the new jointly staffed headquarters was MACV Forward, a clear indication of its importance in the future scheme of things. After taking up residence at Phu Bai, in the same building that housed the 3rd Marine Division rear command post, MACV Forward was to directly oversee III MAF and the new U.S. Army corps (which would soon emerge as the Provisional Corps, Vietnam, and then as XXIV Corps). MACV Forward's focus would be operations in Quang Tri and Thua Thien provinces.

The massive growth of the American military presence in northern I Corps was not without its difficulties. From early January 1968, the road net encompassing Highway 1 through Phu Bai, Hue, PK 17, and Camp Evans was choked with the men and equipment of the 1st Marine, 101st Airborne, and 1st Cavalry divisions. The larger encampments, Phu Bai and Camp Evans, were particularly busy, crowded with transient infantry and support units waiting overnight or for up to a week for their marching orders.

January was a time of extreme confusion for the burgeoning American commands in I Corps. The existing base facilities, already stretched to sustain three and then four U.S. combat divisions, simply were not up to handling the massive influx of troops and supplies. Two brigades of the Air Cav were temporarily without most of their helicopters because fuel-storage and fuel-handling facilities at their new bases were inadequate. The first fresh brigade of the 101st Airborne Division assigned to northern I Corps was brand-new in-country, and it had to gain experience from largely unproductive patrolling aimed at acclimating the troops to local conditions and combat fieldcraft in general.

The 3rd Marine Division, whose forward command post moved north from Phu Bai to Dong Ha in late January, was to tighten its tactical area of responsibility northward to cover only northern Quang Tri Province. As such, it was the least affected of the four U.S. divisions. On the other hand, the 1st Marine Division had to shift its entire strength northward into Thua Thien and southern Quang Tri provinces, an area very different from its former domain, which had been centered on the huge northern base at Danang. The division had to uproot its base facilities; move them across the forbidding Hai Van Pass; reassemble them; and follow, a battalion at a time, as its old hunting ground was turned over piecemeal to the still-forming Americal Division. Unlike the Air Cav or even the 101st Airborne Division, which could call on air transport, the 1st Marine Division was obliged to move almost everything on trucks. Thus, it faced the trickiest, nastiest move of all.

Though the command post of the 1st Marine Division's 1st Marine Regiment (1st Marines) and the forward divisional subheadquarters (Task Force X-Ray) had already moved north to Phu Bai, it was expected that the division would be only partially effective in its new tactical area of responsibility by the middle of February. It was not expected to be completely effective before mid-March.

Any sustained movement of roadbound convoys in Vietnam was likely to provoke enemy attack. Road patrols and guard detachments at vital bridges were beefed up, but there was only so much that could be done. Patrolling Highway 1 and guarding its numerous chokepoints tied down troops and reduced the combat effectiveness of the infantry battalions involved. The isolated guard outposts also provided VC and NVA units in the region with many small targets that could be easily pinned down and overrun.

The section of Highway 1 between Phu Bai and Camp Evans, including the section through Hue, was to be the most heavily traveled of all. This was because the main bodies of three of the four U.S. divisions slated for duty in northern I Corps would be based at or north of Phu Bai. Some of the men involved in planning and implementing the huge military migration saw Hue as a potentially hazardous obstruction. For several miles in the city, Highway 1 ran between rows of dominating multistory buildings, and there were also many bridges, including a very long one across the Perfume River. But there was no practical way to bypass the city, so an attitude of fatalism prevailed. Besides, the local VC cadres had never before violated Hue's tacitly recognized sanctity. If the VC were going to harass the convoys, they were likely to do so in the countryside.

On the night of January 20, 1968, the attack on Khe Sanh began. The attention of those in the American and ARVN senior headquarters in I Corps was naturally attracted in that direction, away from the cities and towns in eastern I Corps and even along the previously heavily embattled strip between National Route 9 and the DMZ.

Commentators who have attempted after the fact to divine Communist intentions regarding Khe Sanh have emphatically pointed out that there is nothing in the captured Communist records, nor in any public statements since, to indicate that Khe Sanh was a feint devised to draw combat troops to the far north-western corner of South Vietnam. This might be true; indeed, no public statements have ever revealed Khe Sanh as a feint. But the fact is that the attention of America's military leaders, including Lyndon Johnson's almost total concentration, was instantly riveted on Khe Sanh. Plans were immediately drawn to relieve the besieged base by using most of the two newly arrived brigades of the 1st Cavalry Division. Even as the new Air Cav divisional command post was being prepared to open at Phu Bai on January 27, Lieutenant General Robert Cushman, the commanding general of III MAF, directed Major General John Tolson of the 1st Cavalry Division to prepare a contingency plan for the relief or reinforcement of the Khe Sanh Combat Base. Thus, intentionally or not, the Communists at Khe Sanh came close to drawing the U.S. Army's most mobile combat division away from the center of the Tet action just before the action was set to commence.

Other factors conspired to focus attention on Khe Sanh. For many months, U.S. intelligence agencies had been picking up rumors of a large-scale Communist offensive. The rumblings seemed to indicate that the blow would fall just before the annual week-long Tet holiday.

General William Westmoreland, MACV commanding general, had become convinced that the NVA and VC were about to launch a major offensive in Quang Tri Province, along the DMZ. Westmoreland's conviction—a reasonable but incorrect assessment of the Communist summer offensive along the DMZ—was the driving force behind the buildup of U.S. divisions in northern I Corps and the plan to establish MACV Forward there.

Notwithstanding General Westmoreland's opinion, intelligence analysts at III MAF headquarters in Danang felt that the main pre-Tet target would be Danang. Thus the Marines hatched an elaborate scheme aimed at getting the enemy to launch the attack prematurely. When no attack fell on Danang and Khe Sanh came under siege, III MAF analysts assumed that Khe Sanh had been the object of the rumblings all along.

At the same time that Khe Sanh was becoming *the* focal point, other indications suggested that a major blow would fall along Highway 1 somewhere north of Danang and south of Hai Van Pass. An attack around Phu Loc would have made sense in light of the 1st Marine Division's heavy use of the highway. Though analysts gave no date for this potential pre-Tet effort, prudent countermeasures were set in place—even though doing so slowed the 1st Marine Division's move into northern I Corps.

At 0130, January 26, the command post of Task Force X-Ray, at Phu Bai, was struck by a barrage of fifty 82mm mortar rounds. There was no follow-up, so the blow was interpreted as a routine though unusually protracted harassment by a local VC unit. When no significant blow had fallen by 1800, January 29—the hour the annual Tet truce went into effect—the alert along Highway 1 was marginally relaxed.

No one dreamed that the Communists would launch a major assault anywhere in South Vietnam during the Tet truce. It was well known that something might happen just before or just after the three-day truce, but the Communists had never seriously violated Tet.

Weeks of intelligence gathering indicated that the 4th and 6th NVA regiments were, respectively, ten kilometers south and twenty kilometers north of Hue—a day's march. The two NVA units had both been in evidence for some weeks and had not directly engaged any ARVN or U.S. units except Sergeant Jack Lofland's tiny CAP patrol. Elements of the 5th NVA Regiment, which was hiding in the hills west of Hue, were not detected at all.

No one seemed to know why two crack regiments had suddenly appeared in the vicinity of Hue, nor how or when they had arrived. But they were not bothering anyone or even making threatening moves. The NVA regiments were tracked, but they were not molested. The 1st ARVN Division was spread too thin to challenge the NVA, and all the American combat units anywhere near Hue were too busy with moving-in problems to take decisive action.

That no special precautions—much less active attacks—were undertaken despite strong evidence pinpointing two elite NVA regiments violated one of warfare's most enduring tenets: One must never base actions on what the enemy's *intentions* might be; all action must be based upon the enemy's *capabilities*. No one guessed what the 4th and 6th NVA regiments might be doing near Hue, but no one posited, either, what they could accomplish if they went into action. A mild report about the NVA regiments was issued to local military agencies, but neither ARVN nor any U.S. headquarters overseeing the sector promulgated an alert.

— 3 —

A week before Tet MACV commander General William Westmoreland urgently recommended that the three-day Tet truce be cancelled. General Earle Wheeler, chairman of the U.S. Joint Chiefs of Staff, had concurred, and South Vietnamese President Nguyen Van Thieu agreed to cancel the truce on the morning of January 29, half a day before it was to go into effect. However, a major communications foul-up in Saigon on January 29 prevented announcement of the cancellation. President Thieu and most of the GVN's senior officials scattered for the holidays, before the problem could be corrected. Thus, on January 29 no Tet combat alert was issued by MACV, the ARVN, or any GVN agency.

Acting without authority, completely on his own, Brigadier General Ngo Quang Truong was the only senior field commander, ARVN or American, to prepare any sort of defense before the onset of the Tet offensive in the Hue area. Truong, who had assumed command of the 1st ARVN Division during the Buddhist insurrection in 1966, was a canny, battle-wise thirty-eight-year-old. A 1954 graduate of Dalat Military Academy, he had served for twelve action-packed years as a front-line commander with the ARVN Airborne Division. Completely self-reliant, self-confident, and inner-directed, a self-starter with a wonderfully disciplined mind and an iron will to win, he was one of the best senior combat commanders the ARVN had ever fielded.

At dawn on New Year's morning, January 30, General Truong, his senior staff officers, and the 1st ARVN Division's three regimental commanders helped the mayor of Hue at the annual flag-raising ceremony at Hue Citadel's southeastern wall, overlooking the Imperial Palace and the Perfume River. At the close of the ceremony, Truong and his senior officers returned to the division command post (CP), a large former French Foreign Legion compound occupying the northern corner of the Citadel. Truong planned to stand down his division CP and send all but a skeleton watch of his staff officers and headquarters troops on leave for the first three days of Tet. The division's infantry units were engaged in the regional pacification program; thus they could not be stood down even for Tet. The regimental commanders were to return to their own CPs.

Just prior to joining his family at home, which was south of the Perfume River, General Truong took a few moments to glance through fresh reports that had reached his desk since he had departed for the flag ceremony. Several of the reports outlined extremely serious violations of the day-old Tet truce by very large Communist units operating in central South Vietnam, in Kontum, Pleiku, Binh Dinh, Khanh Hoa, and Darlac provinces.

As Truong read the reports, something clicked. Several divergent thoughts came together: In a U.S.-supported heliborne assault in the mountains west of Hue in mid January, 1st ARVN Division troops had uncovered an unoccupied but superbly equipped 500-bed military hospital; in the two weeks since, two elite NVA regiments had been pinpointed in the immediate neighborhood north and west of Hue; and, within the past twelve hours, many NVA and VC combat units had been attacking ARVN and other GVN posts in five central provinces despite the Tet truce.

Despite Truong's intuition that a Communist offensive was about to be launched in and around Hue and other northern I Corps cities, it was difficult for the general to reach the necessary decision to rescind holiday leaves. Tet was too important an event to cancel on the basis of mere speculation. The division staff worked brutally long hours throughout the rest of the year, and its morale depended greatly upon the Tet reprieve. If Truong rescinded leaves and was right in his assessment, no harm would be done and much good could be accomplished. If he was wrong, however, staff cohesion might be shattered. Truong had a feeling, an instinct, but he had no hard intelligence that the attacks in the south would spill over into his division's zone of responsibility. No higher headquarters had alerted him. Everything he saw was in his mind's eye. There was no hard analysis, no confirmation from on high. Then the young commander's instincts—finely honed in his career of constant action—assumed control of his racing thoughts.

Truong decided to go for broke. He ordered regimental commanders and all staff officers still on duty in the 1st ARVN Division CP to meet with him. As soon as the senior officers had assembled, Truong ordered his entire division to full alert. The division staff officers and headquarters troops were to remain at their posts. The regimental commanders were to return to their CPs, as planned, to place all their battalions on full alert. All divisional staff officers and headquarters troops who had already departed for Tet leave and could be reached were to return to the CP without delay.

The order came as a major blow to the division staff. However, all the senior officers had been handpicked by Truong; he trusted them and, perhaps more important, they trusted him. There was a moment of stunned silence followed by unanimous obedience.

General Truong contacted the commander of his elite all-volunteer personal guard, the Hoc Bao (Black Panther) Company, and ordered him to remain at full alert within the Citadel. Finally, Truong ordered the commander of the elite thirty-six-man 1st Division Reconnaissance Company to patrol the western approaches to the city aggressively. If there was to be an attack that night, the division commander was certain it would come from the hills to the west.

For all his prescience, even General Truong fell into the age-old trap of trying to divine the enemy's intentions rather than reacting to his capabilities. Truong later reported, "I suspected the enemy had the will to attack. I did not think they had the capability." Still, in time of war, it is often better to do the right thing for the wrong reasons than the wrong thing for the right reasons.

Only after Truong issued his orders did he receive belated official word that the truce had been canceled by his government. The result of Truong's timely insight, flawed though it was, saved his life, the lives of his wife and their children, and the lives of many of his staff officers and their families. Indeed, in reestablishing the war footing of his division early enough to do some good, Ngo Quang Truong probably saved the city of Hue and most of her 140,000 citizens from an outcome far worse than the horrid fate they did suffer.

Marine Major Frank Breth, the 3rd Marine Division liaison officer to the 1st ARVN Division, spent the morning of January 30 at the 3rd Marine Division rear CP, at Phu Bai, getting caught up on local events following a week's leave. As Breth was on his way back to Hue's MACV Compound, Lieutenant Colonel Ed LaMontagne, 3rd Marine Division embarkation officer, approached him. LaMontagne was an old friend, former commanding officer, and the man responsible for getting all his division's heavy equipment from Phu Bai up to Dong Ha. LaMontagne told Breth he planned to be in Hue the next day to oversee the movement of some heavy rolling stock by way of the Navy LCU (landing craft) ramp on the Perfume River. Since the LCU ramp was only a few blocks from the MACV Compound, LaMontagne asked if he could stop by for lunch. Realizing that LaMontagne was as interested in a good lunch as in visiting with an old friend, Breth said he would save him a place. Then Breth jumped into his jeep to buck the eleven kilometers of solid military and civilian traffic snaking up Highway 1 from the Phu Bai gate to Hue.

When Major Breth checked into his office at MACV later in the day, the compound was crowded with advisors on holiday because their ARVN units had stood down for the truce. There was nothing much going on; no one at MACV had heard of General Truong's full-scale alert. Frank Breth figured he would get caught up on a week's worth of paperwork in plenty of time to have a leisurely lunch the next day with Lieutenant Colonel LaMontagne.

Marine 2nd Lieutenant Terry Charbonneau's platoon of

Charlie Company, 1st Motor Transport Battalion, was in Phu Bai on the morning of January 30. The enormous task of moving the entire 1st Marine Division into northern I Corps was falling mainly upon the shoulders of the 1st Motor Transport Battalion, and the work was unremitting—by far the most exasperating Lieutenant Charbonneau had seen since his arrival in Vietnam in November 1967. To make matters worse, the last days of January were being frittered away moving divisional units already in Quang Tri City and Camp Evans south—*back* to Phu Bai.

The Marine infantrymen were as pleased as Charbonneau about their return trip south. They deliberately took their time in loading their gear and themselves aboard trucks. In fact, they had been so slow on the afternoon of January 29 that the convoy had set off after dark. Charbonneau's impatience had raised a few eyebrows among the infantry officers, but Charbonneau was more concerned about what an overnight stay in Camp Evans would do to the schedule than he was about the remote possibility of action along Highway 1.

On January 30, Charbonneau's platoon was joined by a platoon from Alpha Company, 1st Motor Transport Battalion, for yet another quick trip to Camp Evans to pick up another element of the same uncooperative infantry battalion. The plan was to be back in Phu Bai that evening, then on the road back to Camp Evans again on the morning of January 31.

While the January 30 convoy was forming up in Gia Le, the 1st Motor Transport Battalion's camp north of Phu Bai, senior officers explicitly warned of possible Communist attacks along Highway 1 before or possibly even during the Tet festivities. Already the veteran of several ambushes around Hai Van Pass, Terry Charbonneau was as ready as he would ever be to fight for his life if he was attacked while on the road. But he was too busy, too tired, and too harried to give serious thought to all the weird what-if situations a worried mind could conjure up in the middle of a war.

During a brief stop along the road into Hue, Charbonneau allowed an Army Long-Range Reconnaissance Patrol (LRRP, pronounced "lurp") team to hitch a ride to their unit in Camp Evans. He was glad to have the LRRPs along, because no other convoy guards were available. In fact, because of personnel short-ages, the convoy lacked assistant drivers, who could have been pressed into a combat role in the event the convoy was ambushed. The LRRPs were a welcome addition, indeed.

As the convoy passed through villages and market areas south of Hue, the usual crowds of Vietnamese kids were out, but there was a big change from the usual roadside scenes. The countryside was celebrating Tet, so, instead of begging from the Marines, the kids were throwing rice candy at them. Though he sensed the special spirit behind the gesture, Terry Charbonneau would not eat the candy out of fear the local VC had poisoned it or laced it with ground glass. Finally, however, the LRRP team's Kit Carson scout—a former NVA soldier who had rallied to the GVN—explained that Tet was a time of giving, and that it was doubtful the candy was booby-trapped. The scout tried a few pieces to prove the point, and then everyone sampled the candy.

Hue was packed with foot traffic and vehicles of every de-scription. In addition to the teeming military traffic involved in moving four U.S. combat divisions, the city was filled with Tet pilgrims, who overfilled the narrow roadways, causing gridlock at bridges and other chokepoints along Highway 1. Terry Char-bonneau's convoy was halted, permanently it seemed, right at the southern edge of the city, directly opposite the modernistic Hue Cathedral.

The LRRPs were amazed at what they saw in their first look at Hue. A few had been in Vietnam for several years, but none had ever been in Hue. They told Charbonneau that Hue was less affected by war than any Vietnamese city they had seen. It seemed to be downright prosperous despite the war. They pointed out that most of Hue's houses seemed to have been improved over time, a sight they had not seen in other Vietnamese cities, where it was fortunate if a house was rebuilt after combat. Hue, they all proclaimed, seemed to be leading a charmed existence.

When it looked like the delay was going to last quite a bit longer, the LRRP team leader asked Lieutenant Charbonneau for permission to go buy some beer. Charbonneau was at first reluc-tant to grant permission; he did not want to leave the soldiers behind if the road was suddenly cleared. But he gave the sergeant fair warning and told him to do what he wanted. The LRRPs were gone in a flash.

Many minutes later, when the beer party re-emerged from the teeming neighborhood, the convoy had advanced only a few yards. The LRRP team leader climbed into Charbonneau's jeep and told the lieutenant that he and his men had not found any stalls open but that they had come upon a courtyard in which several generations of a large Vietnamese family were celebrating the Lunar New Year. The LRRPs had asked if they could buy some of the beer the family had on its food-and-drink-laden tables, but the patriarch had firmly refused to sell it. Instead, he had invited the LRRPs in for a round of good French wine—two large tumblers for each of the soldiers.

Shortly after the LRRPs rejoined the convoy, the traffic jam dissipated and the trucks rolled forward in fits and starts. The trip north out of Hue was as it had been going into Hue: the villagers along the way were outwardly friendly, and the kids tossed rice candy into the passing trucks. The only sour note that registered on Terry Charbonneau was the hate-filled glare of a young man who, in hindsight, was probably counting the trucks and noting their contents as they passed through a large village north of Hue.

The convoy finally arrived in Camp Evans well after noon. Once again, the Marine infantrymen who were to be transported back to Phu Bai were very lax in their outlook, and the entire afternoon was frittered away in desultory loading. Another convoy, from Dong Ha to Phu Bai, passed through Camp Evans late in the afternoon, but, unlike the previous afternoon, Charbonneau was forbidden to return to Phu Bai that evening.

It was good that Charbonneau was ordered to stay off the road. No one in Camp Evans knew it, but after dusk Highway 1 south to Hue was due to close.

Jim Bullington, a U.S. foreign service officer on loan to the Agency for International Development (AID), spent most of January 30 at his office in Quang Tri City, tidying up his desk and exchanging a final round of information with his boss, Robert Brewer, the Quang Tri Province senior advisor. Bullington was on his second tour in Vietnam. His first had been in 1965 and 1966, as vice consul in Hue—until the consulate was burned to the ground by rioting Buddhists. This Tet, Jim Bullington was on his way to Hue for family business—to share the holidays with his fiancée and her family. The Than-Trong clan's Tet banquet was set for that evening, and Bullington was going early, to settle in with the friend who had offered to put him up.

Jim Bullington had access to the latest intelligence reports. He knew that an NVA attack in northern Quang Tri or Thua Thien provinces appeared imminent. He had been hearing similar reports for some time, but he did not dream they would reach fruition during Tet. If the NVA and VC did not kick off their attacks before Tet, he felt, then it was certain they would not do so until after Tet's important initial three days. For all that, however, Bullington and his comrades in Quang Tri received early notification of Communist attacks in central South Vietnam, and they had early news that the GVN and MACV had canceled the Tet truce.

Despite the forbidding news, Jim Bullington decided to proceed with his holiday plans. He felt he could not let his fiancée or her family down. He boarded the Air America afternoon shuttle to Hue and, as soon as it landed, checked in with the Civil Operations and Revolutionary Development Support (CORDS) office for the latest intelligence update. An attack was imminent, but, as one CORDS official declared, "We looked for it before Tet, but it didn't come. So now we expect it after Tet. But," the official concluded, "today there seem to be indications that it just might come as early as tonight." Jim Bullington sensed no tinge of urgency in the official's voice and manner, and he noted that no extraordinary preparations were in force. Conditions in Hue appeared to be calmer than they had been in Quang Tri, so he went to his friend's house.

Bullington's fiancée, Tuy-Cam, had left work at the United States Consulate in Danang the previous day, January 29, to take the bus home to Hue. There had been no untoward incidents on the 105-kilometer journey, but the trip was typically tense because no one knew what the VC might have in mind from moment to moment. Though Tuy-Cam worked for the consul, she had heard nothing about Communist intentions.

The Than-Trong clan was gathering for the holidays at their compound in a wealthy suburb south of the Perfume River and west of the Phu Cam Canal. Late news arrived that Tuy-Cam's middle brother, Long, an Air Force cadet, would be missing the banquet because he was getting ready to attend flight school in Texas. However, Tuy-Cam's older brother, An, an ARVN first lieutenant, would be released from duty at Thua Thien Province Headquarters in time for the evening banquet. In fact, during the day An stopped by the house with a load of beer and whiskey.

As the final preparations for the banquet were getting under way, Long arrived home unexpectedly. He had been able to take a few days' leave after all. Shortly thereafter, Jim Bullington arrived with two other American guests—Steve Haukness, an associate of Tuy-Cam's from Danang, and Steve Miller, a Foreign Service School classmate of Bullington's, now a U.S. Information Service (USIS) official based in Hue. Haukness told Tuy-Cam that another of her American coworkers who had been invited to the banquet had been unable to get out of Danang in the wake of a Communist attack in the city the previous night.

During the meal, Tuy-Cam's elderly uncle asked Jim Bullington if he was afraid because "many people say that the VC will attack tonight." Bullington assured the uncle that he was not afraid because "we hear these reports all the time in Quang Tri, and I've sort of gotten used to them. Besides, where I'm staying, they could never find me." For all that, however, Bullington was feeling nervous.

The party broke up about an hour before midnight. While Tuy-Cam and her sisters retired to a back room to play traditional Tet card games, Steve Miller drove Jim Bullington to the Hue municipal power station, where Albert Istvie, a Franco-Vietnamese who worked for the power company, was putting Bullington up in the company guest house. Miller then drove to his own home with Steve Haukness, who would be staying over with him. The three Americans noted no untoward activity on Hue's streets during the drive, and all turned in without a thought about the dire predictions to which they had become inured.

In the hours after midnight, Hue seemed to be settling down following the day's revelries, but scores of people were still out and about. Many were innocent Tet revelers, but many others were men and women of extremely sinister intent.

PART II

ASSAULT ON HUE

The first shots of the Hue offensive were fired at 2200 on January 30. The unwitting culprits were members of the South Vietnamese Regional Forces (RF) company defending a pontoon span at Nam Hoa, south of Hue, where the Ta Trach and Huu Trach rivers join to form the Perfume River. It is doubtful the typically jumpy RFs actually saw any Communist troops on their way toward Hue. They probably opened fire on shadows or images from their worst nightmares.

Lieutenant Nguyen Thi Tan's 1st ARVN Division Reconnaissance Company was patrolling an area several kilometers west of Hue. Tan heard the shooting and routinely deployed to search the immediate area. This was fortuitous, because the reconnaissance troops discovered immediately that they were directly in the path of a large-scale military migration. As Lieutenant Tan and his Australian Army advisor crouched in the scrub growth, scores of dark forms filtered silently past them toward the city. Tan instantly warned his thirty-five ARVN soldiers to stay under cover and remain still and silent. Then he radioed the 1st ARVN Division CP and whispered his report of the contact and every detail he could make out. Before long, two enemy battalions had passed the reconnaissance company's position.

The Communists' contemplated seizure of Hue was only one part of Resolution 13's nationwide "decisive victory," but it was a major part. Except for the massive assault scheduled to take place in and around Saigon, no attack on any city in South Vietnam would involve more Communist troops than the attack on Hue. Bright jewel of Vietnam's briefly glorious past, Hue bore a symbolic importance greater than its size. The lightning victory the Communists expected to win there would be memorialized by special victory celebrations, including a triumphal parade by crack NVA regiments. They would march and celebrate and receive the accolade of the "risen" masses.

The Communists planned to seize Hue in one blow, a bluntly straightforward coup de main. To this end, they had gathered a force of over 5,000 crack NVA and VC soldiers under the direct leadership of the commanding general of the Communist Tri-Thien-Hue Military Region (encompassing Quang Tri and Thua Thien provinces). The Hue assault and occupation force comprised the elite, independent 4th, 5th, and 6th NVA regiments; the 12th NVA Sapper (engineer assault) Battalion; at least one other unidentified NVA sapper battalion; one NVA rocket battalion; local VC combat units of various types and sizes; and the VC's crack Hue City Sapper Battalion. Elements of all these units were to take part in the initial assault on the city, following a precise tactical plan developed from close study of a scale model of Hue painstakingly constructed from cast-off American ration boxes. The eight-foot-square model was so detailed that even replicas of major radio antennas were included.

By the evening of January 30, VC spearhead companies had already slipped into the city in the guise of civilian pilgrims. They were to re-form at designated meeting sites, and, together with NVA units scheduled to slip into the city en masse during the night, attack and overrun a stunning variety of military and civil objectives. There were 314 immediate objectives in all, from the 1st ARVN Division CP to the home of Hoang Huu Pha, a schoolteacher and member of the Vietnamese Nationalist Party.

The planning, thorough to the last detail, had been the work of many weeks. Hundreds of infantry weapons—including .51-caliber heavy machine guns and perhaps hundreds of tons of ammunition, demolitions, and supplies—had been smuggled into Hue disguised as civilian goods or, at the last minute, in gift-wrapped parcels.

The initial attacks were timed to create maximum confusion and prevent mutual support by city-based GVN National Police and ARVN units. As the military and civil targets fell, VC political cadres supported by NVA infantry units were to fan out through the city, arresting political figures and civil workers and calling on the people of Hue to rally to the Communist cause. Once the city was completely subdued, the victorious VC and NVA units would have their glorious victory parade, after which they would help fortify the entire city to stand off possible counterattacks.

Because the seizure of Hue was to be part of a huge matrix of Communist assaults that same night, outside support was expected to be minimal inasmuch as all ARVN and American military units in the area would be under attack at once. The large U.S. and ARVN bases north and south of Hue would be heavily bombarded, and ARVN and American checkpoints and choke-points along Highway 1, such as passes and bridges, would be directly attacked or bombarded to sow maximum confusion and delay counterattacks.

Each section of Hue was literally an island isolated by the waters of the Perfume River, its complex of feeder streams and canals. Therefore Hue was an ideal military target. Each section could be isolated with great ease by attacking and holding the limited number of bridges. Efforts by surviving ARVN or National Police units inside Hue to reinforce one part of the city from another could be stopped by defensive positions at any of these obligatory crossing points. In the event of outside attack, each of Hue's islands could be separately fortified and, because most of the waterways were narrow, supported by infantry weapons fired from adjacent islands. Moreover, except for in the wartime shantytowns, nearly all the buildings inside the Citadel and in the modern city were of stout concrete or masonry construction. Each building was a potential pillbox or bunker that could be fortified to withstand direct assault by even the most heavily equipped modern infantry.

But the Communists never really expected that they would have to defend Hue against a threat from the outside. Throughout South Vietnam, large components of the ARVN were expected to mutiny—many might even rally to the Communists. In swift course the hated Americans would be herded toward Vietnam's ports, whence they would be free to sail away forever, as had the French in 1954. TCK-TKN would culminate in decisive victory, the reunification of Vietnam under the Communist banner. The Communists had no doubt about it.

Because the Hue City Sapper Battalion had to cross especially rugged terrain, it was the first of the Communist combat units staged on the outskirts of Hue to begin its move into the city. The battalion left its jungle camps on the morning of January 29. The unit had to be broken up into very small groups so it could be safely ferried across the deep Ta Trach River, south of Hue, that night. The crossing went according to plan.

That same night the crack VC sapper unit was followed to the Ta Trach ferries by elements of an NVA sapper battalion and the 4th NVA Regiment's 804th NVA Battalion, which were slated to attack and overrun the MACV Compound. These units also crossed the Ta Trach without incident. They followed the Hue City Sapper Battalion toward the southern outskirts of the city.

The 4th NVA Regiment's plan and timetable came a cropper on the afternoon of January 29, when troops of the NVA sapper battalion and the K4C NVA Battalion were detected on the south bank of the Ta Trach. Though this component was bombarded by artillery for two hours, no ARVN or American infantry force was dispatched to investigate. The NVA dragged their casualties back into the jungle, regrouped, and waited until the next afternoon, January 30, to resume the crossing operation. A full day behind schedule, this major assault force did not have a prayer of attacking its objective in concert with the rest of the Tet assault forces. Thus the main body of the 7th ARVN Armored Cavalry Battalion, south of Hue, would be spared an early disabling blow.

Despite the discovery of one NVA force, ARVN and American units completely missed the next NVA arrival. The K4B NVA Battalion and an NVA sapper battalion, which were charged with seizing the heart of the modern city, moved into a village on the south bank of the Ta Trach and remained there under cover through January 30. They began crossing the Ta Trach and advancing on Hue at dusk.

The 810th NVA Battalion, a component of the 4th NVA Regiment, was apparently not slated to enter Hue until around noon on January 31. At any rate, it was not detected in Hue until then.

The four-battalion composition of the 4th NVA Regiment was strange, and it gives some credence to reports that the K4B and K4C battalions were actually amalgams of NVA and VC main-force companies. Indeed, the unit designations are more in line with the VC order of battle. It is possible that the amalgams were conceived to present the appearance of a general uprising—that is, to suggest that southern troops were involved in the liberation of Hue. Alas, what the NVA and VC did in 1968 to obscure their orders of battle from U.S. and ARVN intelligence also obscures it from historians.

(Though it confuses the issue, it must be said that all NVA battalion designations given here are somewhat speculative. To mask their true order of battle and the battlefield situation, VC and NVA regularly relabeled their units when identifying them in documents or broadcasts. It is virtually certain, however, that four battalion-size infantry units and two sapper battalions were employed to invest the city south of the Perfume River, and that all were operating under the 4th NVA Regiment.)

To the north and west of Hue, the 6th NVA Regiment began moving out of its jungle camps at 1000, January 30, about the time Brigadier General Ngo Quang Truong was putting his intuitive alert into effect. By 1800, shortly after dark, the lead element of the 6th NVA Regiment left the cover of the jungle and proceeded in orderly columns toward the city. The lead unit stopped on a high hill at 2000 and prepared the evening meal: a special Tet treat of dumplings, Tet cakes, dried meat, and gluten-ous rice mixed with sugar. After the meal the soldiers received one canteen of tea apiece, and the officers checked the troops' gear. Many soldiers took the opportunity to change from their jungle clothing into fresh khakis, complete with unit tabs and decorations—a sign of their confidence that they would meet little opposition before the planned victory parade.

As soon as all preparations had been completed, the 6th NVA Regiment broke up into three assault groups. The first, composed of forty crack troops and a hand-picked infantry company, crossed Highway 1, passed through a large village, waded across a stream, and approached the northwest wall of the Cit-adel. When the general attack commenced, this force was to penetrate directly into the ARVN CP compound by way of an old water gate that ran through the center of the compound's north-east wall.

The 6th NVA Regiment's second element, the 806th NVA Battalion, crossed Highway 1 and prepared to attack and occupy an ARVN checkpoint and highway bridge at the western corner of the Citadel. Once its objectives had been seized, this force could fend off counterattacks from the direction of PK 17.

The battle plan called for the 806th NVA Battalion to attack the temporary camp of the 2nd ARVN Airborne Battalion also. This camp was just northwest of the Citadel. But on January 29 the crack ARVN airborne unit had been routinely transferred to another location, out of reach to the north of the city. The Communists were unable to alter their plans on such short notice. Consequently the 2nd ARVN Airborne Battalion and the accompanying 3rd Company, 7th ARVN Armored Cavalry Battalion, remained a potentially dangerous mobile force that would have to be countered if it moved on the city.

The 6th NVA Regiment's main body, composed of the 800th and 802nd NVA battalions, waded across a wide creek due west of the Citadel. This was the force that had nearly walked over Lieutenant Tan's 1st ARVN Division Reconnaissance Company. It was the only Communist force that any ARVN or American unit had pinpointed in advance. However, no action was taken to prevent it from reaching its jump-off positions.

After crossing the creek the 800th and 802nd NVA battalions proceeded to Ke Van Creek, which formed the Citadel's southwestern moat. They crossed this barrier without incident and went to ground in the shadow of the Citadel wall. As soon as NVA and VC units opened the Hue offensive inside the Citadel, the 800th and 802nd NVA battalions were to fan out and seize the Chanh Tay and Huu gates, which were in the southwestern wall; attack Tay Loc Airfield; and then secure the Dong Ba and Thuong Tu gates, at the Citadel's eastern corner.

As the 6th NVA Regiment's infantry and sapper units moved toward the Citadel, an 82mm medium-mortar company veered off in the direction of PK 17. When the attack began inside Hue, this unit was to pin down the 3rd ARVN Regiment's CP, thus preventing a coordinated counterattack by unengaged 3rd ARVN Regiment units before the city was fully in Communist hands.

As the 4th and 6th NVA regiments and other NVA and VC units tightened the rings around their objectives, the senior command group of the Tri-Thien-Hue Military Region broke out special treats at its command post, high atop Chi Voi Mountain, about twelve kilometers southeast of the Citadel. A special Tet message from Ho Chi Minh was read. Then the senior commanders convened in the operations room to monitor the kickoff of the assault.

— 5 —

By 0115, January 31, the entire 6th NVA Regiment and 12th NVA Sapper Battalion, the Communist force assigned to seize the Citadel and the northern approaches to Hue, were poised to launch simultaneous assaults. Spearhead elements had already penetrated the Citadel by climbing the northwest Citadel wall directly opposite the 1st ARVN Division CP compound. The village of An Hoa, right outside the western corner of the Citadel, had been quietly and completely occupied by the 806th NVA Battalion. And the 800th and 802nd NVA battalions, approaching the Citadel's southwestern wall from the west, had stopped in front of Ke Van Creek to reorganize and deploy.

At 0130, January 31, a small NVA sapper detachment crossed Ke Van Creek and advanced across Highway 1 to occupy a bridge across a sluice about halfway along the Citadel's southwestern wall. At the point where the sluice breached the wall, members of the sapper detachment moved up to cut several strands of barbed wire, the only barrier.

North and south of the Perfume River, all the NVA and VC units that could reach their attack positions on time were settled in by 0310, awaiting the signal to attack. The signal was to be a sheaf of rockets fired at Hue from the western hills at 0330.

G hour, as the Communists had dubbed the assault kickoff, came and went. Nothing happened. No rockets were fired; no assaults were launched.

As a thick fog covered the approaches to Hue and parts of the city itself, the commander of the Tri-Thien-Hue Front waited at his observation post atop Chi Voi Mountain. Another minute passed in dead silence. And then another. At 0333, a staff officer called the 6th NVA Regiment commander by radio and asked if he had seen the signal yet. The regimental commander, Lieutenant Colonel Nguyen Trong Dan, gave a tense, nervous response indicating that he had seen nothing. The front staff officer called an observation post and received this reply: "I am awake; I am looking down at Hue. The lights of the city are still on; the sky is quiet. Nothing is happening."

Silence returned to the Tri-Thien-Hue Front command post, where everyone waited anxiously. What could have gone wrong?

After entering the Citadel through the sluice in the southwestern wall, four Communist soldiers—two members of a local VC unit and two NVA sappers—approached the Chanh Tay Gate, the northernmost entrance along the Citadel's southwestern wall. The four, who were dressed in ARVN uniforms, were to overwhelm the gate guards and, from inside, open the way for the assault battalion lying in wait right outside the wall.

The team leader, Comrade Thanh, had scouted the guard post during the day, when twenty civil guardsmen had been on duty. Now, less than a handful would be there. As the four neared their jump-off position opposite the guard post, Comrade Thanh ordered the others to put out their cigarettes and stand in the shadows to await the signal to attack.

In his bedroom in the MACV Compound, Colonel George Adkisson, commander of MACV Advisory Team 3, awoke with a start. Alerted by some subconscious signal, he sat up in bed and fumbled for his field telephone, but the line was dead. Agitated now by an unremitting internal alarm, Colonel Adkisson put on his trousers, combat boots, and pistol belt. Then he started out the door of his room.

At 0340, January 31, 1968, the NVA 122mm rocket battalion—burrowed in firing positions in the hills west of Hue—launched the first salvo. Before the first rockets even landed, NVA mortars south of the Perfume River and east of Highway 1 opened fire at multiple targets.

Colonel Adkisson stepped briskly through the door of his bungalow. At that instant, two or three 82mm mortar rounds fired from within nearby Tu Do Stadium detonated directly on the tile roof of a building nearby. Seconds later, several 122mm rockets detonated in the MACV courtyard. Colonel Adkisson stepped back into the doorway just as several more rockets fell. His first thought was that Hue Sector Headquarters, directly across a back street from MACV, was under attack.

The *whump-whump-whump* of the first salvo of NVA rockets woke Jim Bullington from a deep sleep. Bullington listened to the rockets and mortar rounds fall for a few minutes, but none was even close to his guest house in the power plant. Further reflection convinced Bullington that there was nothing he could do to influence events. So, cool war veteran that he was, he drifted back to sleep.

Meanwhile, a short distance to the west of Bullington's guest cottage, his fiancée—Tuy-Cam—was startled awake by shrieking, crying, and pleading in the darkness outside her parents' home. One of her three sisters shrieked, "Oh, God! VC!" and rushed into the adjacent bedroom to wake her other two sisters.

In a moment the household was in a turmoil as the family worked together to hide Tuy-Cam's two brothers, An and Long, who were both home on leave from the service. Quickly the two young men, together with every shred of evidence that might give away their presence, were shoved into the attic. An and Long barricaded the door from within.

Outside the house, VC and NVA were running through the neighborhood, their boots thudding on the pavement. Closer to home, two refugees Tuy-Cam's grandmother had allowed to camp in the backyard were questioned by several VC and then led away. Everyone in the house slipped into the family's bombproof bunker. At length, Tuy-Cam's mother exclaimed, "So, here they are!"

As Tuy-Cam's mother prayed, the sounds of detonations and gunfire continued.

At the first flash of the first salvo of incoming rockets, Comrade Thanh and his three companions opened fire and threw grenades into the guard post at the Chanh Tay Gate. Several of the stunned civil guardsmen who stood at the base of the Citadel wall were mowed down. Others turned and fled. Realizing they were under attack, ARVN soldiers patrolling the bridge across the Citadel moat pulled a few strands of barbed wire across the roadway. They were immediately pinned down by fire from Comrade Thanh's team.

At that moment one of Thanh's men signaled with a flashlight, and the 800th NVA Battalion regulars waiting outside the Chanh Tay Gate poured into the Citadel. The soldiers swept over the ARVN bridge guards and the surviving civil guardsmen. The NVA soldiers and Thanh's men exchanged revolutionary slogans as the 800th Battalion fanned out to seize objectives throughout the western Citadel.

The forty handpicked NVA sappers assigned the task of infiltrating the 1st ARVN Division CP compound via the water gate were thwarted when they discovered that the gate bridge had collapsed into the moat and had been replaced by a stout barbed-wire barrier. After milling about for several crucial minutes, the sappers and an accompanying company of the 802nd NVA Battalion felt their way southwestward along the Citadel's northwestern wall. Finally, under cover of mortar rounds fired from the south, they launched an unrehearsed attack on the ARVN post guarding the Hau Gate. The four guard bunkers were quickly overrun, but the element of surprise had been lost. The spearhead force barely cleared the Hau Gate in time to link up with the balance of the 802nd NVA Battalion, which was driving eastward along the northwestern wall from the An Hoa Gate.

Under cover of nearly a hundred 82mm mortar rounds, the combined NVA assault force pushed a dozen ARVN soldiers out of their post on the southwestern side of the 1st ARVN Division's CP compound, but other ARVN troops were attracted instantly by the sounds of gunfire. As the NVA crossed the compound's southwestern wall and attacked the ARVN division's medical center, Lieutenant Nguyen Ai, an ARVN intelligence officer, counterattacked at the head of a scratch platoon of thirty ARVN clerks, medics, and several hospital patients.

Only sixty feet from the NVA's forwardmost element, Brigadier General Ngo Quang Truong looked up from his desk in time to see his aide, at the window, empty his pistol at the attackers. Truong wondered whether he, a brigadier general, would be leading infantry before the night was over. He quickly forced himself back to the business of running his entire division while his troops held the enemy at bay.

Lieutenant Ai was shot through the shoulder, but he continued to lead the counterattack in the medical center. Within minutes five NVA soldiers were shot to death inside the compound and another forty were mowed down as the vastly superior but profoundly shocked NVA force pulled back to the west.

A subsidiary attack, possibly incorporating some VC units, moved on the CP's main gate, in the compound's south wall. The attack drew immediate defensive fire, and an ad hoc reaction force stopped the attackers cold.

A second serious setback was dealt to the 6th NVA Regiment at 0400, as a company each from the 800th NVA and 12th NVA Sapper battalions were converging to seize Tay Loc Airfield. An unreported wire barrier forced the NVA units to diverge from their direct route onto the runway. At 0350, as the force sought a way around the barrier, it ran smack into a depot manned by the 1st ARVN Ordnance Company, which conducted a spirited defense of its small compound and forced the NVA soldiers to recoil. Though the NVA companies succeeded in setting fire to an ammunition warehouse, fuel tanks, and quarters, they could not force their way through the ARVN ordnancemen. At 0400, as the NVA companies were trying to muster a flanking push across the runway itself, Captain Tran Ngoc Hue's 250-man ARVN Hoc Bao Company swept in from the east in the nick of time. The skilled Hoc Bao troopers fired their rifles and volleys of M-72 LAAW antitank rockets directly into the leading NVA files just as the NVA soldiers reached the center of the runway. The shocked NVA soldiers quickly retreated and called for help. Another company of the 800th NVA Battalion was diverted from its objectives east of the Chanh Tay Gate, but it arrived too late to have any impact. Several buildings in the airfield complex remained in NVA hands, but the NVA offensive in the northwestern Citadel was effectively blocked.

As soon as the pressure on the airfield appeared to lift, Captain Hue led his Hoc Bao troops in a long, curving path back to the 1st ARVN Division compound. The stymied NVA apparently never knew that the Hoc Bao soldiers had gone, for they did not renew their attempts to capture the airfield or the ordnance depot.

With the return of the Hoc Bao Company, the 1st ARVN Division headquarters units were able to launch an effective counterattack that drove the 802nd NVA Battalion completely out of the division CP compound. Thus, in the northwestern half of the Citadel, there remained two widely separated ARVN enclaves manned by less than 600 ARVN soldiers, most of whom were noncombatants. Directly facing them were the complete 802nd NVA Battalion, part of the 800th NVA Battalion, and most of the 12th NVA Sapper Battalion—in all, an enemy force numbering as many as 700 crack combatants.

Awakened suddenly from a deep sleep, Marine Major Frank Breth, the 3rd Marine Division liaison officer to the 1st ARVN Division, counted three distinct rocket detonations outside the MACV Compound. Then, as Breth was shrugging into his war belt and grabbing his M-16 rifle, the fourth 122mm rocket blew up the province advisor's house, inside the compound itself, right behind Breth's room. As Breth sought shelter in the tiny shower stall in his room, another 122mm rocket hit a nearby jeep; its gas tank exploded. The roof over Major Breth's head fell right in on him. As a company commander and infantry battalion staff officer along the DMZ throughout the latter half of 1967, Breth had endured countless rocket attacks. This time, he thought he was dead. It took precious moments for him to figure out he was okay. His worst wound was a gouge in the head, a throbbing inconvenience he decided to ignore.

Though thoroughly taken in by the NVA surprise mortar and rocket attack, Colonel George Adkisson's MACV advisors and headquarters troops reacted superbly to the first detonations inside their compound. Provided with an incredible five-minute respite between the end of the bombardment and the onset of the 804th NVA Battalion's planned sapper-and-infantry assault, the

officers and men who had been assigned to defensive positions in
bunkers and guard towers throughout the compound leaped to
action, as did many volunteers. Everyone else headed for shelters
to await the outcome or orders from above.

The shelling had a negligible effect, and the first of the NVA
assaults against the compound gate and various points around
the outer wall facing Highway 1 ran directly into vigorous defensive fire. The main assault, on the main gate, ran smack into the
fire of three specially trained Marine security guards who had
been sent to Hue several months earlier by the U.S. embassy in
Saigon. The Marines were on post in a bunker at the southwest
corner of the compound before the initial bombardment ended—
ready, willing, and able to blunt the NVA attack coming straight
up Highway 1 from the south.

Another key factor in the defense was an M-60 machine-gun
post in a tower overlooking all the approaches to the compound.
The M-60 gunner, Specialist 4th Class Frank Doezma, was the
first to fire at the NVA main assault group, and he temporarily
stopped the attackers dead in their tracks. The NVA reacted by
firing a B-40 rocket-propelled grenade (RPG) into the six-meter-
high tower. The M-60 was knocked out and Doezma's legs were
shredded in the blast. The first man to reach the smoking tower
was Marine Captain Jim Coolican, who was off duty that night
from his advisory job with the Hoc Bao Company. Doezma was
Coolican's regular jeep driver. As soon as Coolican deposited
Doezma on the ground, he climbed back into the tower to slam
40mm high-explosive grenades at the NVA with the M-79 grenade launcher he had looted from the open MACV armory.

By the time Coolican opened fire, Major Frank Breth had
climbed onto the roof of the main building. From there he looked
out on a scene of total chaos—people yelling, gunfire and detonations, a maelstrom of noise and confusion. As the veteran
Marine major tried to shut out the noise and look for clear
targets, he saw the remnant of an NVA sapper platoon moving
north along Highway 1, directly toward the compound's front
gate. As they approached, many of the NVA were cut down,
principally by the three Marine security guards and Captain Jim
Coolican. However, about fifteen of the enemy kept on coming.

The Marines manning the southwest guard post shot down about half of the remaining NVA, but one of the NVA stuffed a grenade into the bunker's firing aperture, killing all three Marines. Taking careful aim at a figure carrying what seemed to be a satchel charge, Major Breth fired his M-16 and dropped him to the ground. But other NVA quickly followed. Breth continued to fire his M-16 on full automatic. Then it seemed like everyone was yelling, "Shoot! Shoot! They're coming down the road! Shoot!" Breth and another Marine major began hurling grenades from the roof, right down on the NVA survivors. The NVA turned and ran. The assault on the front gate of the MACV Compound was over.

The NVA platoon had little room in which to maneuver, and all their routes of attack were obvious and easy to seal off. After a series of futile attacks on the eastern and southern compound walls, the 804th NVA Battalion backed off. From then on, the greatest danger the Americans inside MACV faced was from the wild shooting of the thoroughly panicked men in the adjacent central station of the GVN National Police. In fact, an Australian Army advisor was probably killed by fire from the police station.

As the RPG and small-arms fire directed against MACV died down, the advisors could hear shooting from all around the city, mainly from AK-47s. Hue seemed to be under attack everywhere at once.

Elsewhere south of the Perfume, the K4B NVA Battalion appeared to have achieved success in its zone—the triangle formed by the Perfume River to the northwest, Highway 1 to the northeast, and the Phu Cam Canal to the south. At any rate, a large number of isolated civil objectives in that sector were seized, and VC cadres were soon moving in to set up a civil government of their own. However, a small number of thinly manned ARVN posts on the south bank of the Perfume could not be taken by the widely dispersed K4B NVA Battalion, and, strangely, a number of small, isolated ARVN camps and facilities in its zone were left undisturbed throughout the night.

The Communists later claimed that all three assault battalions in the 4th NVA Regiment zone, south of the Perfume River, were in position to attack their objectives in advance of the initial rocket volley. They even claimed that the K4C NVA Battalion and an attached sapper unit—the force that had been pinpointed, bombarded, and delayed by artillery fire on the afternoon of January 29—had completed a forced march from the Ta Trach ferry sites during the evening of January 30. However, the K4C NVA Battalion's main objective, the cantonment of the 7th ARVN Armored Cavalry Battalion, was not seriously molested during the night. Certainly it was not attacked by the reinforced K4C NVA Battalion.

No Communist unit attacked the 1st ARVN Engineer Battalion compound, on the southern edge of the city, nor the U.S. Navy's Hue LCU ramp, on the Perfume River. If, as they later claimed, the Communists reduced all the civil targets on their long list of objectives, they nevertheless did a spotty job of reducing military targets.

To the Communists, clearing the military opposition was a means to an end. That end was the civil objectives, because of what they symbolized. The Communists were seeking the general uprising. Ultimately, however, passing up or wasting opportunities to destroy military targets was their undoing.

— 6 —

It is an axiom of night battle that things are never as bad as they seem. Daylight invariably chases away the deepest of fears and the wildest of speculations shared by combatants on both sides. No matter how bad things really are, they are never as bad as they seem to be at night.

Long before dawn offered Hue's beleaguered defenders the first glimmer of hope, Brigadier General Ngo Quang Truong was at work planning and ordering the relief of the city. Heavy fighting seemed to be raging everywhere in Hue at once, and the reports General Truong was receiving at the 1st ARVN Division CP were vague, often bordering on panic, and thus of little use beyond establishing the scale of the Communist plan. But Truong intuitively grasped what there was to grasp, gathered what information there was to gather, and acted while there was still time to act. Above all, he knew, it was vital to launch some form of counterattack before the Communists reduced all their objectives and consolidated all their gains. Blooded warrior that he was, Truong knew for a certainty that the Communists could not have seized all their objectives without error or setback. He knew from bitter experience that fluid situations tended to work to the advantage of the defender. The sounds of gunfire from all directions and the reports Truong was able to gather on his radio told him the situation remained extremely fluid and that, probably, the Communist timetable was a shambles. Moreover, he quickly learned that he still had the means for knocking the Communist plan further askew and, hopefully, defeating it in short order.

General Truong was quite right. The Communists had only come near to winning a swift victory. But they had failed to do so, and time definitely was not on their side.

The 6th NVA Regiment continued to battle mightily for key objectives within the Citadel, but the situation around General Truong's CP seemed to have stabilized. Even though Truong's troops were unable to attack out of the compound, at least the Communists seemed unable to attack into it. On the south bank of the Perfume River, the 4th NVA Regiment appeared to have conceded several key objectives. The MACV Compound was no longer under direct pressure, and the cantonments of the 7th ARVN Armored Cavalry Battalion and the 1st ARVN Engineer Battalion, both on the southern fringe of the south bank of the Perfume, had never been molested at all.

Unfortunately for Hue's defenders, the axiom that dawn imposes reality and presents new opportunities cuts in both directions.

At G hour, the handpicked 3rd Company of the 6th NVA Regiment's 800th NVA Battalion had made its way from the Huu Gate, on the southeastern end of the Citadel's southwestern wall, toward the Ngo Mon Gate, the southeastern entrance into the Imperial Palace. However, before getting very far, this company had been diverted to help two other NVA companies that were stalled in their bid to overrun Tay Loc Airfield. The 3rd Company did not get back on the track for several hours.

At about 0500, shortly after the Hoc Bao Company was ordered back from Tay Loc Airfield to help defend the 1st ARVN Division CP, General Truong ordered the 1st ARVN Ordnance Company to abandon its depot beside the airfield and withdraw to the 1st ARVN Division CP compound. The way things seemed to be going in the Citadel, conceding the depot and the airfield to the Communists was preferable to losing the ordnance troops or being forced to fritter away assets in rescuing or supporting them. Soon the 800th NVA Battalion renewed its attack on the recently abandoned airfield and secured it without further loss. The NVA soldiers destroyed the light observation airplanes they found parked near the runway and looted the ordnance depot of its stores, including many weapons.

Far behind schedule, the 800th NVA Battalion's 3rd Company set out again to seize the Imperial Palace and the huge flag platform on the southeastern wall of the Citadel, opposite the Ngo Mon Gate. However, the company was delayed again by Lieutenant Nguyen Thi Tan's 1st ARVN Division Reconnaissance Company. Following its evening scouting mission west of the city, the company had infiltrated Citadel streets by way of the 1st ARVN Division CP compound. Lieutenant Tan's troops, skilled at moving without detection, launched tiny hit-and-run delaying actions against the NVA infantry company. However, at 0600 a platoon of NVA sappers the ARVN scouts apparently did not engage seized the Ngo Mon Gate from an eight-man squad of sentries.

As soon as the Ngo Mon Gate was seized, the main body of the long-delayed 3rd Company side-slipped Lieutenant Tan's tiny blocking force and poured into the palace compound. It routed or took prisoner all the GVN civil guardsmen and national policemen within. Then, to underscore the deeply symbolic victory, each of the NVA liberators took his turn sitting on the imperial throne.

A platoon from the 800th NVA Battalion's 3rd Company seized the flag platform in the center of the Citadel's southeastern wall at the same moment the Ngo Mon Gate fell. The Communist soldiers swiftly pulled down the gold-and-red GVN flag—the same banner General Truong's troops had raised the previous morning. For the moment, nothing more was done, but the fact that the GVN flag was not flying was obvious to all who could see the flagpole in the dawn's early light.

General Truong's first priority was to plan the relief of his own CP compound, with its vital command-and-control communications links, not to mention the 1st ARVN Division's brain trust. (It must be said that, in addition to directly overseeing the battle for Hue, Truong and his staff officers remained in control of the rest of the 1st ARVN Division, which was engaged to the hilt in heavy fighting from the DMZ to south of Hue.) One of Truong's first acts was to contact Lieutenant General Hoang Xuan Lam, the I ARVN Corps commander. Though Lam's own CP was under siege in the NVA's all-out attack on Quang Tri City, the corps commander hastily contacted his superiors in Saigon—also under Communist attack—and convinced them to transfer the 1st ARVN Airborne Task Force to Truong's direct control.

Then General Truong radioed the commander of the 2nd ARVN Airborne Battalion and asked if that crack strategic-reserve unit had been molested during the night in its temporary bivouac north of the city. No, the battalion was safely beyond the cordon the Communists had thrown around the city. It was fully intact and awaiting orders.

General Truong ordered the 2nd ARVN Airborne Battalion, numbering around 300 troops, to proceed to the 1st ARVN Division CP by the most expedient route, rolling up Communist units if they could be swiftly overrun, but bypassing them if they could not. It was essential to the plan emerging in Truong's racing mind that at least one strong, competent combat unit reach the division CP as soon as possible, intact and ready to launch a counterassault.

The 2nd ARVN Airborne Battalion swiftly left its bivouac and marched directly toward the Citadel. However, as soon as the lead paratroop company reached the built-up area—at about sunup—it ran into a company of the 806th NVA Battalion deeply entrenched within stout civilian buildings. The thrust instantly bogged down as all the paratroop companies were sucked into bloody, time-consuming house-to-house firefights.

In addition, General Truong had ordered the 7th ARVN Airborne Battalion and the 3rd Company, 7th ARVN Armored Cavalry Battalion, to attack together from PK 17. Their objective was the western corner of the Citadel. Directly overseen by the 1st ARVN Airborne Task Force headquarters, these fresh units proceeded rapidly along Highway 1. But, like the paratroopers, they also ran afoul of the waiting 806th NVA Battalion. Outside An Hoa village, just to the northwest of the Citadel, this second relief force became bogged down in bloody, painstakingly slow house-to-house fighting against the superbly entrenched NVA battalion.

Ongoing radio inquiries revealed to General Truong that about half the 7th ARVN Armored Cavalry Battalion was in the battalion cantonment south of the enemy cordon. This force seemed quite capable of securing the southern route into the city. Truong ordered the battalion commander, Lieutenant Colonel Phan Huu Chi, to attack north along Highway 1 with everything he had. Truong hoped Chi could get as far as the Nguyen Hoang Bridge, which carried Highway 1 across the Perfume River. If Chi could get across the bridge, he was to fight his way into the Citadel.

Lieutenant Colonel Chi's armored unit was equipped with eleven 26-ton M-41 light tanks armed with 76mm guns and several M-113 armored personnel carriers (APCs) armed with .50- and .30-caliber machine guns. These weapons would have been more than adequate in many situations in the bush, but they were not up to attacking directly up a narrow highway into the teeth of NVA soldiers emplaced in masonry buildings and equipped with a seemingly inexhaustible supply of lethal B-40 RPGs. Three successive armored attacks were beaten back, each with heavy losses for absolutely no gains.

Though the 3rd ARVN Regiment CP was at PK 17, itself under indirect bombardment through the night of January 30, all four infantry battalions of the 3rd ARVN had been arrayed in or around Hue. The 1st and 4th battalions—which had been conducting sweep operations near the coast east and southeast of the city—awoke to find that their separate bivouacs were surrounded by elements of the 4th NVA Regiment's 804th NVA Battalion. The 4th Battalion, 3rd ARVN Regiment, was pinned throughout the day on January 31, but continuous counterattacks finally carried the 1st Battalion, 3rd ARVN Regiment, through the encirclement and to the east, toward the coast.

The 2nd Battalion, 3rd ARVN Regiment, had been on a routine sweep west of the city on January 30. Like its sister battalions to the east, it had been in a bivouac in the field when the attack started. It was not directly attacked during the night, nor did it find any Communist forces in its immediate vicinity at dawn. However, when this 250-man unit attempted to move eastward along the north bank of the Perfume River, it was unable to breach the Communist cordon around the west side of the Citadel.

The 3rd Battalion, 3rd ARVN Regiment, had been at the 1st ARVN Division training center, a camp on the north bank of the Perfume River, a short distance west of the Citadel. The battalion was an asset of dubious value, however. Though it was the only battalion in the 1st ARVN Division that was nominally at full strength with 700 officers and men, its size was due to the recent intake of a large number of new conscripts. The battalion was not very far along in its training syllabus when the battle erupted. General Truong undoubtedly wished he had a more experienced unit emplaced so close to the Citadel, but it is another immutable law of battle that, when you must go, you must go with what you have. The Communist force that lay in the unskilled ARVN battalion's path to the Citadel was apparently neither very strong nor very well consolidated, but the half-trained government troops were not up to breasting even that weak tide. Nothing much happened. The ARVN battalion was unable to advance, and the weak Communist force was unable to counterattack.

The Communists were doing extremely well around the periphery of the urban battlefield. Small, well-rehearsed VC commando units staged swift predawn assaults on suburbs and neighborhoods to the east and northeast of the Citadel, seizing without serious opposition many police stations and civil buildings. Farther out, hard-hitting VC main-force units seized one village and hamlet after another. Among the many outlying villages that fell that night was Thuy Thanh, from which Marine Sergeant Jack Lofland's CAP Alpha-2 was ejected during a bloody battle.

Several so-called fortified hamlets along Highway 1 north of Hue were attacked by elements of the reinforced 5th NVA Regiment. The GVN Regional Forces (RF) and Popular Forces (PF) units in these hamlets were easily destroyed or booted out. Chief among the lost hamlets west of Hue, on the west side of Highway 1, was Thon La Chu, in which a multistory American-built concrete bunker was converted for use as the command post of the Tri-Thien-Hue Front headquarters.

Even senior NVA field commanders candidly concede that the seeds of the eventual and costly Communist defeat in Hue were sown by the 4th NVA Regiment's inability to capture the MACV Compound and the 6th NVA Regiment's inability to reduce the strategically vital 1st ARVN Division CP. In fact, aside from Tay Loc Airfield and the 1st ARVN Ordnance Company depot inside the Citadel—positions relinquished at General Truong's order—the Communist infantry and sapper battalions did not turn ARVN or American military units out of even one position within the city limits.

Despite the Communists' singular military failure inside Hue, the appearance of victory that first day was theirs. At 0800, January 31, triumphant NVA soldiers raised a 54-square-meter blue-and-red NLF flag from the pole on the Citadel's massive flag platform. This symbolic act signaled to the world that Vietnam's ancient imperial center had fallen. Indeed, the Communist commanders hoped that the huge banner would serve as a beacon, drawing in all of Hue's citizens who wanted to throw off the yoke of capitalist oppression.

The NLF flag became a beacon, all right. From January 31 until it was taken down on February 26, the best efforts of the

Army of the Republic of Vietnam, half the Vietnamese Marine Corps, and portions of ten U.S. Marine and U.S. Army infantry battalions would be aimed at tearing down that huge, defiant NVA banner and replacing it once again with the gold and red of the Republic of Vietnam. It would be done, but on the ruins of eight of every ten of Hue's buildings and at the expense of thousands of Vietnamese and hundreds of American lives.

— 7 —

Although the 4th and 6th NVA regiments and their attached NVA and VC sapper battalions were having mixed luck seizing military objectives within the Citadel and south of the Perfume River, VC commando units had seized control of most of the GVN, provincial-, and municipal-government apparatus by sunup. Most GVN National Police, Thua Thien Provincial Police, and Hue Municipal Police barracks, stations, and outposts were swiftly overrun, as were government offices of every type.

As NVA and VC military units struggled to reduce military targets, VC "insurrection" units spread out to arrest the hundreds of Hue citizens whose names and addresses appeared on Communist hit lists. One of the most-wanted targets was Lieutenant Colonel Pham Van Khoa, the Thua Thien Province chief. When the Communists finally blew up his stoutly defended residence at 0800, January 31, they learned that Khoa had flown the coop before they had even surrounded the building. A political sycophant who had risen to authority under the old Diem regime, Khoa had left his wife and children at home at the first report of gunfire and fled on foot six blocks to the sprawling city hospital complex. There the province chief hid out in an attic. In the morning, a Communist military unit set up a headquarters in the room below his hideout.

Though the roundup was aimed at civil servants and politically prominent South Vietnamese civilians, Americans and Europeans in Hue were by no means spared. American businesspeople and European residents of Hue were not immediately molested, but all American civil servants were targeted for swift arrest on the basis of the not altogether farfetched notion that they were intelligence operatives.

Steve Miller, the U.S. Information Service official who had joined Jim Bullington and the Than-Trong clan for dinner the night before, was warned in the early hours that thirty VC had occupied the building next door to his home. Neighbors offered to conceal Miller and escort him to the hoped-for sanctuary of Hue Cathedral, but Miller opted to remain at home to see how the situation developed. Possibly, he did not want to endanger the neighbors in the event he was discovered among them. Whatever his reason for staying at home, Miller paid with his life. When his body was discovered weeks later, his arms were bound behind him and he had been shot in the head.

Jim Bullington did not work in Hue and was therefore not on any of the Communist hit lists. Asleep in the guest house on the grounds of the Hue municipal power station, he had been awakened by the sound of mortar rounds detonating at the start of the Communist assault, but he had gone back to sleep because he knew there was nothing he could contribute to the defense of the city.

Bullington awoke again at 0730, this time to the sound of scattered small-arms fire. "The police must still be a little nervous about the attack," he thought as he knotted his tie. "Or maybe they've cornered a sniper somewhere." He decided to check in at MACV to see what the situation was before he drove across the Phu Cam Canal to see his fiancée, Tuy-Cam.

As Bullington walked out the door of the power-station guest house, he saw his host, Albert Istvie, a Franco-Vietnamese who managed the Hue power company. Istvie, who was in a building about twenty meters away, across a courtyard, looked authentically shocked when he noticed Bullington. He said nothing, but the meaning of his gestures was perfectly clear: get the hell back inside the house and be quick about it.

Bullington knew nothing and could only sit in the guest house and imagine what might be going on. He had been in a few close situations before, however, and decided that there was no reason to be unduly alarmed. Still, the continuing small-arms fire became worrisome, so Bullington took his pistol out of his suitcase, just in case.

The waiting grew unbearable. Bullington's curiosity finally got the better of his prudence, and, at about 1030, he ventured out again. This time, he walked all the way across the courtyard to the building where he had seen Istvie. Istvie, who did not see Bullington until he was already nearing the building, ran to the door and whispered, "What are you doing here? I told you to stay in the house. They're here; the North Vietnamese are right here. They're all around us! Now get back, quick."

"They're right here?" Bullington asked.

"Yes, dammit, right here! In this building. Now go."

Bullington returned to the guest house. For the first time, he began to realize the gravity of the situation.

As dire thoughts echoed in Bullington's head, he chambered a round in his pistol. It was a Chinese 9mm automatic, given to him a month earlier by the district chief in Quang Tri, who had taken it from the body of a high-level VC political cadre. Bullington had never fired it. In fact, he had never fired any pistol before, so he spent a few minutes figuring out how it worked, a simple enough matter. He had brought it along chiefly for its trophy value, to show some friends who valued such things. He had never considered the prospect of actually using it.

For many interminable hours, Jim Bullington sat in the guest house and waited. And worried. Finally, at about 1500, there was a quiet knock on the door. For a moment, Bullington was terrified, but then he reasoned that the NVA probably wouldn't bother to knock. However, he was still terrified. "Is that you, Albert?" His voice came out in a croak, from the fear.

It was indeed Albert Istvie. He had brought Bullington a ham sandwich and a warm bottle of beer. "You are a very lucky man," Istvie said. He explained that an NVA company had occupied the large compound, which was composed of the guest house, the courtyard, the building where Istvie had been, and several other structures. It was a major miracle, he noted, that Bullington had not been spotted on either of his two ventures out of the guest house. Istvie guessed that the North Vietnamese had apparently invested the entire city and intended to hold it.

The thought suddenly struck Jim Bullington that his life was completely in Istvie's hands. Istvie wasn't a government employee or a member of an anti-Communist political party, and he didn't work for the Americans. Bullington reasoned, therefore, that Istvie was not a target of the Communist assassination teams that had already begun their work. But if it were discovered that Istvie was hiding Bullington, they both knew, he and his family would immediately become targets.

Bullington had known Istvie for several months and considered him to be a friend. But was his friendship strong enough to protect Bullington when to do so meant risking his own life and the safety of his family? Bullington could only pray that it was.

Istvie returned at about 1730. He had arranged a special signal—four knocks—so Bullington was spared the terror of his first arrival. He said that it wasn't safe for Bullington to stay where he was—no startling revelation, since Bullington could hear the NVA soldiers who had moved into a building only fifteen meters away. It was best, both men decided, for Bullington to flee the power station altogether. The NVA were sure to search the guest house sooner or later. Istvie explained that a pair of French priests he considered to be good friends lived two houses down the street. He thought that it would be much safer for Bullington there, and the priests had agreed to take him in. Bullington was to leave the power station at 1800, when the NVA would most likely be occupied with their dinners.

Before Istvie left, he looked at Bullington's pistol and said, "You'd better hide that. It wouldn't do you any good against more than a hundred of them. And if something goes wrong and they find it on you, that would make it much worse for both of us." That seemed to make sense, so Bullington hid the firearm.

At the agreed hour, Istvie rapped on the door. By the time Bullington cracked it, his friend was walking quickly across the courtyard. Istvie looked up at one of the NVA-occupied buildings, then moved away without signaling Bullington to follow him. Something had gone wrong. Bullington closed the door and considered once again just how risky the movement operation was.

Istvie returned in about thirty minutes. He explained that

one of the NVA soldiers in the house across the way had been looking out the window at the start of the previous attempt. Bullington and Istvie agreed to try again.

On the second attempt, none of the NVA seemed to be looking, so Istvie motioned for Bullington to come ahead. Bullington walked across the courtyard unobserved, then ducked through the gate in the wall behind Istvie's home. He waited briefly in the family's outhouse while Istvie scouted ahead. At Istvie's direction he crawled through a side window and jumped down into the yard of the house next door.

A stranger met Bullington at the door and escorted him quickly indoors. He introduced himself as Father Marie Cressonier and presented Bullington to Father Pierre Poncet, a fellow missionary who had been evacuated from Khe Sanh and was staying with him.

Bullington spoke good French, but he knew that it would be obvious to any Frenchman—though not necessarily to an NVA soldier—that he was not a native speaker. After discussing several options, Father Cressonier gave Bullington a black clerical gown and other priestly garb. In the event the NVA spotted Bullington, the Frenchmen decided to try to pass him off as a visiting Canadian priest.

"You're welcome here as long as you need to hide," Father Cressonier said at length. "But I'm sure your Marines will retake the city by tomorrow or the next day, and you will be safe." Jim Bullington shared Father Cressonier's unfounded optimism, little thinking that the many shocks of January 31 were only the beginning of his ordeal.

After staying up all night to the sound of running feet and shouted voices with northern accents outside their lavish home, the Than-Trong family's worst fears began coming true. At daybreak, the four sisters again heard people running outside. Someone cried in a northern accent, "Stop or I'll shoot! You are the enemy of the people!"

Next, the sisters heard what sounded like a lot of people walking and running in the street. "It is here, this house," someone said.

"Are you sure?" another voice asked.

"No, I'm not sure."

"He does not live here?" a northern-accented voice asked.

"No, I don't think so."

"Maybe this will help you recognize the house!" Then the sisters heard a man moaning.

At about 0800, soldiers in NVA uniforms banged on the door. "Open up or we'll shoot," one of them demanded. "Hurry!"

"Yes, yes, I'm opening the door," Tuy-Cam's mother replied. But she dawdled a bit to allow Tuy-Cam to shepherd her aged grandmother into the family bunker. Tuy-Cam's two military-officer brothers, An and Long, had already been hiding in the attic for several hours. When Tuy-Cam's mother finally opened the door, several of the uniformed men rushed in, their rifles leveled at the family.

"Where are the men?" the soldiers asked.

"Here they are," Tuy-Cam's mother replied, and she pointed to her youngest son, Dung; the houseboy, Chuong; and Tuy-Cam's cousin, Sy, who lived with the family. They were all boys, barely teenagers.

The NVA soldiers stared at the youngsters in open disbelief. As one of them searched the house, he found Tuy-Cam in the family bunker with her aged grandmother. "Get out! Get out of there," he ordered. "Is there anyone else?"

"No," Tuy-Cam replied. But the soldier stuck his head into the bunker to make sure. "Is there anyone up there?" he asked, pointing at the attic.

"No," Tuy-Cam's mother replied emphatically, "there is no one there."

The soldier made no move to check the attic, but he warned, "Later, when we come back, if we find people in there, we will shoot you."

With that, the entire family was herded with rifle butts out into the street, where thousands of people were already on the march. When the throng reached a span across the Phu Cam Canal, it joined an even larger throng. Tuy-Cam saw many relatives, friends, and neighbors, but no one spoke to anyone else. Everyone just looked at each other and kept silent.

"Your fingers are red!" an angry female VC cried into Tuy-Cam's face. She was referring to Tuy-Cam's nail polish. Then, to everyone the VC announced: "This kind of woman could not even lift a stick, much less fight the American imperialists."

"Is there anyone here who speaks English?" an NVA soldier asked. "These people," he said, pointing to a pair of men who stood by a tree, "are not Vietnamese."

"They are Filipinos," someone said.

Tuy-Cam was afraid she would be denounced by someone who knew she worked for the Americans in Danang. Fortunately, no one gave her away. Extremely fearful, she clung to her grandmother, who clung to her like a baby.

An airplane, apparently on a reconnaissance mission, appeared high over the city. The female VC stood in plain view and opened fire at it. Other VC followed suit, but with no apparent effect. The airplane circled for a few minutes, then quickly disappeared.

Well past noon, an ARVN jeep pulled up. An NVA soldier got out of the jeep, signaled for the leader of the VC unit, and talked to him in a very low voice. Tuy-Cam could not make out what they were saying. Then the NVA soldier jumped back into the jeep, which departed.

"Listen carefully," the VC commander said. "You are allowed to go home." Everyone instantly stood up, ready to leave, but the Communist officer yelled, "Sit down again! I mean only the women and small children. All the men, go over there." He pointed in the direction of a vacant lot. Immediately, soldiers began pushing all the men to the lot. Tuy-Cam's mother started to cry when an NVA grabbed brother Dung, houseboy Chuong, and cousin Sy by their shirts and pulled them roughly toward the men's group. Then the women and children were allowed to leave.

Tuy-Cam and her family's women were barely home before a squad of NVA soldiers arrived at the front door. "Mother," one of them called politely to Tuy-Cam's mother, "we have not eaten since the day before yesterday. Do you have anything to eat?"

The NVA consumed a big meal—almost everything left over from the previous night's banquet. Then they sat down and simultaneously interrogated and propagandized the family. For nearly two hours, they asked questions about everything and everyone. Then they adjourned to the rear of the Than-Trong compound and searched for picks and shovels in the two thatch huts there. With the implements they found, the NVA dug a trench along the bamboo fence. By the time the trench had been completed, Dung, Chuong, and Sy were home.

After a time, Tuy-Cam's brothers, An and Long, signaled from the attic. One of Tuy-Cam's sisters was posted by the back door and another sister was posted by another door—to make sure no NVA soldiers were in sight. Then Tuy-Cam and her mother answered the signal. The brothers wanted to go to the bathroom. Chuong, the houseboy, found an empty kerosene can, and the women managed to pass it up to the brothers. Then the family sat down and tried to eat what little food the NVA soldiers had left in the kitchen. No one could swallow anything. Tuy-Cam's mother looked up at the attic and down at the food, but no one made a move. No one had the nerve to try to pass food to An and Long.

PART III

INTO THE FOG

The first help the Americans sent to embattled Hue from the outside came in the form of a strange fighter-bomber sortie. Major Tom Johnson was a six-month combat veteran flying with Marine Attack Squadron 311 out of Chu Lai, which was about 170 kilometers southeast of Hue. The first two missions Johnson had flown in response to the Tet emergency had been undertaken in the dead of night with the aid of his A-4 bomber's on-board radar bombing-guidance system. In essence, he had lugged his bombs to a point in space, presumably over a target of value, and had dropped blind when the radar system cued him to drop. His mission over Hue would require a little more of his flying skills.

Johnson was ordered to fly his A-4 jet to Hue on the wing of another A-4. At daylight, as they approached the target area, they were turned over to a Marine O-1 Bird Dog spotter-plane pilot, which was to be their airborne controller. The aerial observer aboard the O-1 told the A-4 pilots that he had "some VC" and that the target was beneath an overcast five-hundred to six-hundred feet thick. The observer also said that he had come in under the cloud deck from the southeast and had found the visibility good underneath.

Johnson and the other jet pilot slowed their A-4s to 250 to 300 knots and carefully let down through a break in the overcast. They scooted along beneath the clouds and returned to the vicinity of the O-1. There, they encountered several tall radio masts that poked up into the overcast. The A-4 jocks knew that there would be guy wires between the masts and the ground, so they stayed clear until they could actually see the cables. Major Johnson realized that it would be a real challenge to fly below the overcast, avoid the O-1 and the guy wires, locate the target, get into position to roll in, track the target, pickle the bombs, and pull off without making a mistake.

Fortunately, the A-4s were carrying 250-pound delay-action Snakeye bombs, which could be released at a very low altitude without blowing the A-4s out of the air. However, at the speeds

involved, the limited altitude would prevent the pilots from tracking the target for as many seconds as they would like before they
had to pickle their bombs. Also, the dive angle was much shal-
lower than Johnson wanted it; he and the other A-4 pilot could
not ensure the accuracy they could have guaranteed had the
ceiling been higher. The two pilots took deep breaths, flew in,
and unloaded the Snakeyes. All things considered, Johnson felt
the A-4s had done well.

The next task was a napalm drop, which generated more
worries. The A-4s would be able to lay the incendiary canisters
right on the target, but Johnson knew from bitter experience that
the napalm bombs might not ignite if they were dropped from
too low. If the napalm did not ignite, the A-4s would have to
make another pass to set it off with tracer rounds from their
20mm cannon. Fortunately, the napalm ignited when it was
dropped, so the A-4 pilots did not have to risk a strafing pass.

As the two A-4s departed the area, the aerial observer gave
them a bomb-damage assessment, passed the word that the
ground troops thanked them, and said that everyone was impressed with their performance in the overcast. He told Johnson
and the other A-4 pilot that theirs was the only flight he had ever
directed under those conditions.

"Those conditions" were the reason the battle for Hue was to
be waged with virtually no air support. The low overcast that
greeted fixed-wing airmen on January 31 hovered over the city
for the next three weeks. On January 31, in addition to Major
Tom Johnson's mission, the only known aerial sorties over Hue
were undertaken by Vietnamese Air Force (VNAF) A-1 Skyraider
propeller-driven attack bombers, by spotter planes like the one
that guided Johnson, and by the reconnaissance plane Tuy-Cam
saw early in the afternoon.

Following their wild defensive reaction to the 804th NVA
Battalion's assault, the few authentic combat veterans in the
MACV Compound worked to cobble together as strong a defense
as their numbers and the available weapons and ammunition
allowed. There were nowhere near enough weapons to go around,
but, then, many advisors and clerical workers opted to take refuge
in bunkers.

The sound of gunfire could be heard throughout the city, and there was no information to dispel the wildest rumors. The breaking dawn did little to banish gloomy outlooks, for the portents were everywhere enmeshed in the foreboding gray mist of the day.

A quick assessment of the damage caused by the initial volley of NVA rockets revealed extensive breaches in the compound's outer wall. Fortunately, however, the wall was not in danger of collapsing.

Communications with the outside world were intact, but the state of confusion at MACV was so complete that there were no cogent reports to send to potential rescuers. The radio room sent out the details that were known, but no assessments. As the morning wore on, this lack of cogency in reporting resulted in an Armed Forces Radio broadcast from Saigon that stated that the situation in Hue was well in hand. To the men who had endured the terror-filled night at MACV, the broadcast from Saigon was downright infuriating. At first, they yelled and cursed the radio announcer, but they changed their tune markedly as the magnitude of the nationwide offensive emerging from ongoing radio reports put their plight, however awful, in proper perspective. They, at least, had not been overrun.

Sporadic shooting continued throughout the morning, but at about 1300 the tired and frightened MACV defenders heard the sound of heavy firing to the south. There were the distinctive roars of American .50-caliber and Communist .51-caliber machine guns, the yammering of American M-60 machine guns, the high-pitched chatter of AK-47s, and the slower *pop-pop-pop* of M-16s. No one at MACV knew what it meant. No one at MACV even dared to guess aloud.

The persistent fog that hung over Hue was a literal fog; the metaphorical fog that hung over Phu Bai and other major military bases within supporting distance of Hue was even less permeable to human senses. It was the fog of war. Piercing it was to be an extremely costly enterprise.

No one in the busy, sprawling Phu Bai Combat Base could tell what was going on inside Hue. If anyone knew anything about the Communist Tet Offensive, it was local knowledge, the result of sketchy information from around Phu Bai and its satellite camps. The sum of the sketchy reports appeared to indicate that there was some Communist activity at the fringes, out along Highway 1. Maybe—maybe—there was some small excitement in Hue.

Lieutenant Colonel Marcus (Mark) Gravel's 1st Battalion, 1st Marine Regiment (1/1, pronounced "One One"), was usually assigned to southern I Corps. At this point, however, it was just coming off a two-month tour along the DMZ and displacing from Quang Tri to Phu Bai. The last of Gravel's four infantry companies scheduled to reach Phu Bai was Captain Gordon Batcheller's Alpha Company (Alpha/1/1, or "Alpha One One"). In fact, by nightfall on January 30, only a little over three-quarters of the company had actually reached Phu Bai. Captain Batcheller and his executive officer (exec) were the only company officers to arrive; two platoon commanders and about forty Marines had missed the last helilift of the evening, and one of the company's lieutenants had been nabbed to attend, of all things, a divisional leadership school.

For Alpha/1/1, January 31 was supposed to be a day off to rest and reequip. Then, on February 1, it was to be trucked to Hue to guard the Navy LCU ramp on the Perfume River—the first time any Marine infantry unit had been assigned a job inside Hue.

After settling his troops in on the evening of January 30, Captain Batcheller was informed by a member of the 1/1 staff that his truncated company was the Phu Bai "reaction force." No specific concern was identified at that time. Very early on the morning of January 31, Batcheller was ordered to move Alpha/1/1 south along Highway 1 at first light. The company was to meet an ARVN guide who would lead it to reinforce his unit, which was between Highway 1 and the nearby coast.

In short order, the main body of Alpha/1/1 mounted several 6 × 6 trucks inside the base wire. Two U.S. Army M-55 antiaircraft machine-gun trucks, each carrying a beastly quadruple-.50-caliber machine gun, joined up. The convoy headed south along Highway 1. A moderately thick ground fog hampered visibility beyond the edge of the roadway. No one in the convoy knew of any alerts.

This was new territory for Alpha/1/1; no one knew where the best ambush ground lay, and no one could see anything through the fog. Members of Marine CAP units encountered along the way told Captain Batcheller that local Vietnamese had reported numerous enemy units moving in a northerly direction. However, they added, they were unable to confirm the civilian reports about "*beaucoup* VC."

The convoy arrived at the rendezvous point, but there was no sign of the promised ARVN guide. After reporting to the 1/1 CP by radio, Captain Batcheller was ordered to reverse direction and head north along Highway 1 to link up with a unit of the U.S. Army's 1st Cavalry Division, which was north of Hue. When Batcheller consulted his map to gauge the distance, he learned that Highway 1 ran off the edge of his map sheet at Hue. In-country since late August 1967 and the Alpha/1/1 commander since Christmas Day, the twenty-eight-year-old Bostonian assumed he would be able to sort the matter out on the way.

At the time Alpha/1/1 turned north, the morning fog had not yet lifted and the Marines were as engulfed in the fog of war as ever. The journey past Phu Bai was relatively swift, but the men noted something eerie: Vietnamese highways were always abustle with commerce and travelers and kids begging for food; this morning, hardly a soul was afoot.

Shortly after the small convoy passed Phu Bai, a radio call from the 1/1 CP changed Alpha/1/1's mission once again. Instead of proceeding through Hue to find the 1st Cavalry Division, the company was to stop off just south of the Perfume River to reinforce the MACV Compound. The radio call registered concern about trouble in and around Hue, but there was no specific information. Captain Batcheller's orders were simply to relieve the Advisory Team 3 compound.

It was still hazy at about 1030, when the Alpha/1/1 convoy approached a bridge across a creek about three kilometers southeast of the MACV Compound. Just past the bridge, Alpha/1/1 could see the rear of five Marine M-48 tanks that were halted on the roadway. A brief conversation with a Marine major accompanying the tanks revealed that this was a platoon of Alpha Company, 3rd Tank Battalion, a 3rd Marine Division unit on its way to the Hue LCU ramp for transshipment to northern Quang Tri Province. The tanks had unlimbered their guns. Crewmen were peering from turret hatches into the fog, obviously looking for signs of enemy activity. The tankers' heightened state of alert was undoubtedly motivated by the nearby wreckage of a single ARVN M-41 tank, in which the gruesomely burned body of a crewman leaned out from a turret hatch. There were other obvious signs of recent enemy activity in the immediate vicinity.

The major in charge of the little tank convoy had just been in contact with Phu Bai to ask what was going on ahead. The tanks had been proceeding out of Phu Bai on the assumption that Highway 1 was clear and secure. The response the major received from Phu Bai was ambiguous to the point that he had asked for permission to return to the base or that infantry supports be sent ahead. (For all their armor, tanks are distinctly vulnerable to infantry attack unless they are accompanied by friendly infantry.) Phu Bai had just told him to return when Alpha/1/1 arrived.

Captain Batcheller and the tank major quickly agreed that the tanks should support Alpha/1/1 and continue north to MACV. Without further ado, Batcheller ordered his infantrymen to dismount from the trucks and advance on foot, sweeping both sides of the road as they went.

Several minutes after the tank-infantry column jumped off, Captain Batcheller was contacted on the company radio by Sergeant Alfredo Gonzalez, the 3rd Platoon's twenty-one-year-old acting commander. Gonzalez informed Batcheller that, as the 3rd Platoon was clearing the buildings on the right side of the highway, he could see a walled compound out in the center of a large field. There appeared to be uniformed people moving around inside the compound, but Gonzalez could not see what uniforms they were wearing. Batcheller ordered Gonzalez to set up a base of fire with his M-60 machine guns and advance across the open area. If the people in the compound opened fire, the Marines were to destroy them. A short time later, Gonzalez reported that the uniformed people were ARVN soldiers.

Meantime, Staff Sergeant Curtis Godfrey's 2nd Platoon was

advancing up the left side of Highway 1, cautiously peering into every building. There was no one there. Suddenly, the 2nd Platoon was taken under fire from fifty meters away by several NVA soldiers manning a building at a fork in the road. Staff Sergeant Godfrey was shot in the right leg and thrown into the muck-filled drainage ditch bordering the highway. A minute later, the firing ceased as abruptly as it had begun. As Staff Sergeant Godfrey looked on, Sergeant Alfredo Gonzalez emerged from between two buildings across the highway. He was carrying an armload of four AK-47s. It was obvious from the triumphant expression on Gonzalez's face that he had had a hand in silencing the bushwhackers. A moment later, Godfrey was loaded aboard a truck with two other wounded Marines and sent back to Phu Bai.

The reinforced infantry company continued to advance at a slow walking pace through sporadic small-arms fire. About 700 meters north of where Alpha/1/1 had first seen the tanks, the head of the column passed through the T-shaped intersection at which Provincial Route 546 branched off to the west and Highway 1 made a hard right turn to continue almost due north toward Hue. About 100 meters beyond the intersection, the point of the column reached the edge of a built-up area that appeared to Captain Batcheller to be a Wild West town's Main Street. The buildings, which closely bordered the roadway, featured high facades of wood-lathe construction. The road ahead looked more like a constricted alleyway than South Vietnam's premier national highway.

As the Alpha/1/1 vanguard was preparing to enter the built-up area, a convoy composed entirely of Marine work vehicles approached from the rear. Soon Lieutenant Colonel Ed LaMontagne, the 3rd Marine Division embarkation officer who had decided to accompany the work vehicles from Phu Bai to the Hue LCU ramp, sought out Captain Batcheller. After the two briefly discussed the situation on the road and what might be going on at MACV, LaMontagne said that he thought Alpha/1/1 was moving too slowly. Captain Batcheller agreed, and he ordered his infantrymen to mount the tanks and trucks.

The loss of Staff Sergeant Godfrey, earlier, had left Alpha/

1/1's already overtaxed command echelon severely strained. Captain Batcheller was the only company officer in attendance, and he had only one staff noncommissioned officer left to help control the troops—Gunnery Sergeant J L Canley, the company gunny. Canley was an exceptional veteran troop leader, but—with the infantry company command group, tanks, trucks, work vehicles, and two quad-.50 trucks to keep track of—he was spread too thin. The rifle platoons were commanded by junior sergeants. Captain Batcheller noticed that the sergeant leading the forward platoon—Staff Sergeant Godfrey's 2nd Platoon—was obviously anxious about his increased responsibilities, so the captain joined him atop the lead tank with his two radiomen and a corpsman. Batcheller wanted to be on hand to steady the novice platoon leader. The captain knew that the point was not the best place for the company commander to be, but he felt he had no choice.

As the column proceeded into the built-up area, Captain Batcheller directed his infantrymen to fire their weapons ahead and to the flanks to preempt or suppress potential ambushes. Even so, the lead portion of the convoy was struck by light small-arms fire. Then a volley of B-40 RPGs streaked out from nowhere. The lead tank's upper works were struck. Captain Batcheller was untouched, but the senior corpsman was killed instantly and the battalion radioman sustained mortal injuries. Despite the incoming gunfire and RPGs, the convoy plunged forward and crossed the Phu Cam Canal over the An Cuu Bridge. Surprisingly, this vital span was not even outposted by enemy snipers.

About 100 meters north of the An Cuu Bridge, the lead tank emerged from the 600-meter-long gauntlet into a large, open intersection with a traffic circle in the center. Though Batcheller had not seen them, as many as six ARVN M-41 tanks and at least one APC were arrayed around the traffic circle. These had been destroyed during the last of the 7th ARVN Armored Cavalry Battalion's four unsuccessful attempts to relieve the Citadel by attacking straight up Highway 1. In the last attempt, shortly after noon—less than an hour before Alpha/1/1 arrived—the ARVN battalion commander, Lieutenant Colonel Phan Huu Chi, had been killed when his command APC was gutted by a direct hit, probably from a B-40 rocket.

As the column debouched into the intersection, the tanks, trucks, quad-.50 trucks, and work vehicles dispersed, and the company corpsmen went to work on the casualties. Captain Batcheller jumped down from the lead tank to assess the situation and reorganize Alpha/1/1.

About fifty meters beyond the traffic circle, a huge sugarcane field stretched out on both sides of the highway. Highway 1, which bisected the cane field in a straight line from southeast to northwest, was completely exposed atop a tree-lined causeway built upon a meter-and-a-half-high berm. A full kilometer away, on the other side of the field, was the southern edge of a heavily built-up area, the beginning of downtown Hue.

As Captain Batcheller supervised the movement of casualties to cover and tried to establish radio contact with the 1/1 CP and various supporting-arms agencies, the commander of the lead tank asked if it would be okay to fire the tank's 90mm main gun. When Batcheller peered northward, he could see what looked like ARVN soldiers moving around in two small compounds beside the causeway, about halfway across the cane field. Figures that appeared to be Vietnamese civilians were moving on foot from west to east across the cane field. Batcheller cautioned the tanker to avoid shooting into the two compounds or at the civilians; otherwise, he didn't care what the tank fired at, and he allowed it to just pick out targets and erase them. The tank commander gave the captain a huge grin and ordered his gunner to commence firing. Meanwhile, Lieutenant Colonel Ed LaMontagne had taken charge of the quad-.50 trucks and deployed them forward so they, with their awesome firepower, also could engage targets in the cane field. Batcheller was not sure if the tank and quad-.50 gunners had clear targets or if they were just engaging likely enemy firing positions, but, either way, it was okay with him. The loud noise of the outgoing fire was music to his ears, and the incoming small-arms fire seemed to subside. Several mortar rounds detonated in the cane field and around the halted Marine column, but their source could not be determined.

By then, most of the fog had lifted, and visibility had improved significantly. Captain Batcheller tried to call for air and artillery support, but, except for other radios on the Alpha/1/1 tactical net, all the nets to which he had access were clogged with Vietnamese-language traffic. Finally, using the radios in the lead tank, Batcheller made contact with Lieutenant Colonel Mark Gravel, the 1/1 battalion commander. Gravel said he was coming forward from Phu Bai and expected to catch up with Alpha/1/1 soon.

After Gravel and Batcheller discussed the lack of specific information concerning enemy activity around Hue, Batcheller ordered his infantrymen and the tanks to advance to MACV. The infantrymen were to hug the right side of the tree-lined causeway berm, and the widely separated tanks were to advance on the roadway while the quad-.50 trucks remained in position near the traffic circle to cover the advance with their fire.

Captain Batcheller and his company radioman stayed on the roadway, slightly behind the lead tank. From there, Batcheller could see fairly well and talk to the tank crew through the intercom phone mounted on the tank's rear fender. From there, also, the company radioman stood the best chance of talking with the platoons or switching frequencies to contact Lieutenant Colonel Gravel or supporting-arms agencies.

The tanks had advanced well down the causeway, with the infantry keeping pace below and to the right, when Captain Batcheller heard the impact of a round to his left rear. He turned and saw that a Navy officer who had been accompanying LaMontagne's heavy-equipment convoy had been shot in the leg.

After hesitating for a split second, Batcheller stepped out from behind the protection of the lead tank and ran to the wounded man. He bent to grab the man by the shoulders of his flak jacket and started pulling him sideways toward the tank, but a solid burst of gunfire ended the effort. The wounded man was killed; Batcheller was hit in both legs and his right forearm. The impact of the bullets threw Batcheller across the roadway, and he came to rest against the base of a tree.

Batcheller was on his right side, entangled in a coil of concertina wire, unable to move. His back was to the main source of incoming fire—to the north—and bullets were occasionally hitting close to him. His right forearm was open from wrist to elbow, and there was a gaping hole in his right thigh. He did not know it yet, but his right femur was shattered.

After assessing his wounds, Batcheller twisted his head around to see what he could see. He realized that he was directly in the line of fire. Fearful that his Marines would sacrifice themselves to rescue him, he yelled to those on the right side of the causeway to stay down, to leave him be. A short time later, Gunnery Sergeant J L Canley came up abreast of Batcheller, across the roadway, and Batcheller passed command of the company to him with orders to carry out the mission. It was now up to the company gunny to get Alpha/1/1 to MACV. Canley wished Batcheller well and moved forward.

There was nothing left for Gordon Batcheller to do except wait for the firing to subside and hope someone would eventually come back and rescue him. He looked up through the branches of the tree and saw the beautiful blue sky. Then he began to pray.

— 9 —

Captain Chuck Meadows's Golf Company, 2nd Battalion, 5th Marines (Golf/2/5), was the temporary "palace guard" in Phu Bai on the afternoon of January 30—it was the only fully organized infantry company in the combat base. The rest of 2/5 was stretched out in company-size packets south of Phu Bai, along Highway 1, as far south as Hai Van Pass. The entire battalion was new to northern I Corps; mainly, it had lived and fought for about a year in Quang Nam Province, to the south of Thua Thien Province.

The confused state of affairs brought on by the mass migration of 1st Marine Division units into northern I Corps resulted on January 30 in the transfer of Golf/2/5 to the temporary operational control of the newly arrived headquarters of the 1st Marine Regiment (1st Marines). Thus, as the only fully manned infantry company in Phu Bai, Golf/2/5 became the 1st Marines palace guard.

At 1645, January 30, Captain Meadows was ordered by the 1st Marines CP to conduct a night march out of Phu Bai to a hill about a kilometer to the west. Regiment did not tell Meadows what he was supposed to do out on the hill, but Meadows assumed that higher headquarters had reason to expect an enemy effort—probably a rocket or mortar raid—from that direction. Golf/2/5 left Phu Bai at midnight and marched to the hill without incident. The troops, who were veterans of scores of similar precautions, expertly set in and manned routine 50 percent watches—that is, half the men were on duty at all times.

Sure enough, at about 0330, January 31, several rockets streaked directly over Golf/2/5's hill and detonated inside the Phu Bai wire. Captain Meadows shot an azimuth toward the apparent source of the rockets and radioed the numbers to the 1st Marines CP. No one asked Golf/2/5 to do anything to follow up, and, at daybreak, the company returned to its tent camp inside the Phu Bai base. The troops grounded their gear and went to eat breakfast.

The rumor making the rounds of Golf/2/5 at breakfast was that the company's former operating area in Quang Nam Province was the scene of a big battle and that the company was flying out to fight there. No one was glad to hear the news, for that area of Quang Nam was a booby trap-infested region in which scores of Marines had been maimed for no apparent gain.

While Golf/2/5 was eating breakfast, Chuck Meadows was called to the 1st Marines CP and told that the company was being attached to Lieutenant Colonel Mark Gravel's 1/1. Meadows walked away from the regimental CP with the vague understanding that there was some sort of trouble in Hue and that Golf/2/5 and the 1/1 CP group were to head north to the 1st ARVN Division CP compound to escort the ARVN commanding general back to Phu Bai. No one at Regiment or the 1/1 CP had told Captain Meadows of the mayhem sweeping most of South Vietnam that morning. The mission sounded so routine that Meadows allowed his Marines to leave their packs in Phu Bai in the care of a small fire watch. Meadows naturally expected to be back inside the Phu Bai wire well before dusk. The only special gear the Marines took with them were their rain suits, for it was a misty, drizzly morning.

The scuttlebutt that reached Meadows's troops in advance of the official word accurately predicted that the company was on its way north, to Hue; this was deemed vastly preferable to the rumored rush south to Quang Nam Province. Talking among themselves, the Golf/2/5 Marines built up a sort of ecstasy over the trip to Hue. Everyone who had been in-country for more than a few weeks had heard that Hue was a garden spot of clean prostitutes, decent food, and friendly people. The consistent rumor making the rounds of Golf/2/5 as it waited in the mist was that a few VC were making nuisances of themselves, and the company, which was on quick-reaction duty, was heading north to quell the disruption.

There appeared to be no hurry getting the mission under-way. Seven or eight trucks had to be conjured up from the busy motor-transport units at neighboring Gia Le, and that took time. While they were waiting, most of the 160 Marines and Navy corpsmen in Golf/2/5 simply crapped out in the open, catching up on sleep or huddling together to ward off the cold winter mist.

The transport assignment fell to 2nd Lieutenant Jerry Nadolski, a platoon commander with Charlie Company, 1st Motor Transport Battalion. As soon as Lieutenant Nadolski's mixed bag of 6 × 6 trucks had been assembled, the lightly equipped Marines and corpsmen hopped aboard. Captain Meadows introduced himself to Lieutenant Colonel Gravel and several of Gravel's staff officers, and at 1030 everyone headed north. Lieutenant Colonel Gravel's jeep was at the head of the column, Lieutenant Nadolski was riding in the cab of the lead truck, and Captain Meadows was in the cab of the second truck.

The troops treated the trip as a holiday outing. Phu Bai was as far north as Golf/2/5 had ever been, so the sights were new. Despite the cold mist that whipped over them, there was laughing and joking aplenty as the Marines leaned back and took in the sights. Unknown to any of them, one of the two men in the lead jeep had a pretty good idea that there was going to be action ahead. Lieutenant Colonel Mark Gravel had been in intermittent contact with Captain Gordon Batcheller before and during the early part of the drive; he knew that Alpha/1/1 had gotten into a fight, and he sensed that something terrible had happened. However, most of the trip from Phu Bai was made in silence; there was no radio contact with Alpha/1/1 for many long minutes.

Something was wrong. The convoy was well along the road to Hue when Chuck Meadows suddenly realized that no people were out and about. In fact, there weren't even any chickens scratching alongside the roadway. There was *nothing* going on.

Private First Class Bill Tant was oblivious to the first signs of danger. Tant had been in Vietnam since Christmas, but he had yet to experience any real action. He still retained the new guy's rosy, heroic view of the war. In fact, Tant was eagerly asking his squad leader, Corporal Glenn Lucas, if Lucas thought Golf/2/5 was going to see any enemy soldiers this trip when the convoy nosed past the southernmost wrecked ARVN M-41 tank. Corporal Lucas, who had only ten days left to serve in Vietnam, pointed at the destroyed tank, with the charred crewmen hanging out of a turret hatch. He answered, "You'll probably see more action than you want to."

The Golf/2/5 convoy proceeded into the market-area shantytown that stretched about 500 meters alongside Highway 1. From his vantage point in the lead truck, Lieutenant Nadolski noticed that a number of the tin-roofed shanties in the market area had been shot up, but he didn't dwell on the matter. Shot-up buildings were a common enough sight on the roads Nadolski traveled for a living.

The Golf/2/5 convoy crossed the An Cuu Bridge, went around the traffic circle, passed through the northern section of the market area, and nosed onto the causeway across the kilometer-wide cane field. There were no signs yet of Alpha/1/1's fight. That unit had surged across the causeway only an hour earlier but was by then completely out of sight within the southern edge of the city proper.

Suddenly, light small-arms fire reached out at the convoy from dead ahead. The lead trucks—Lieutenant Nadolski's and Captain Meadows's—swerved to a halt, and all the rest of the trucks along the column followed suit. Lieutenant Colonel Gravel's jeep, which was well into the open area when the shooting started, also swerved to a halt, blocking both lanes of the causeway. The battalion commander and his driver, the only men riding in the jeep, bailed out with alacrity and took cover on the right side of the berm. From his vantage point Gravel could see khaki-uniformed figures to the northwest, jogging and marching in the open alongside the southern edge of the city.

Even before Captain Meadows had hurtled out of his truck, he had seen the muzzle flash of a machine gun set in just in front of a large walled compound at the southwestern corner of the cane field. The NVA machine gun was about 200 meters to the left of the roadway and well ahead of Golf/2/5's position, about 700 meters away altogether.

Meadows and his rain-suited Marines clambered to the mist-damp ground, brought their weapons to the ready, and moved to the right, away from the fire, down behind the causeway berm. Meadows ordered the nearest M-60 machine-gun team to set up at the head of the column and return fire at the enemy machine gun. Then he started trying to find out what the hell was going on. Since Lieutenant Colonel Gravel was out of his jeep and without a radio, Chuck Meadows was on his own, a turn of events he liked just fine despite the confusion and danger of the moment.

While Golf/2/5 was getting itself organized to advance on foot, Captain Meadows ducked into a Texaco gas station he thought would be a good initial observation post. During his brief stay inside, he scavenged a city map of Hue he chanced to find taped to a wall. It wasn't a particularly good map, Meadows noted—most of the major structures were keyed to a list on the back of the sheet. But it was drawn at half the scale of his military map. It even had half-assed military grid markings, which might be a big asset if artillery fire or air support could be arranged.

By the time Meadows had inspected the Texaco map, the company was set to move out on foot. Lieutenant Nadolski and his trucks were left behind the protection of the abandoned buildings. They could not advance because of the gunfire and because Lieutenant Colonel Gravel's jeep and trailer were blocking the causeway. They would be called ahead when the road was clear and safe.

Golf/2/5 encountered no difficulty in crossing the cane field behind the protection of the causeway berm. However, as the Marines advanced farther north, several of them spotted knots of khaki-clad NVA soldiers way off to the left, at the southwestern edge of the cane field, in the vicinity of the now-silent NVA machine gun. Slowly, the picture resolved itself. A large NVA unit—the 4th NVA Regiment's fresh 810th NVA Battalion—was moving north into the city, paralleling Golf/2/5's route. Every once in a while, a burst of gunfire whistled over the heads of the Marines. Presumably, the shots were idle gestures on the part of individual NVA soldiers who wanted the Marines to know their side was full of fight. When Captain Meadows got wind of the NVA migration, he decided to ignore it. The NVA column was a tempting target, and Meadows figured Golf/2/5 could lick the enemy soldiers in a stand-up fight, but his mission was to get to MACV and on up to the 1st ARVN Division CP compound. Lieutenant Colonel Mark Gravel had reached exactly the same conclusion. Gravel had never seen so many NVA troops in the open, but this was not the occasion to take them on.

As Golf/2/5 proceeded north, the first hard evidence of Alpha/1/1's fight became apparent. Here and there, wounded Marines were being treated by corpsmen and fellow Marines. Chuck Meadows learned that the wounded Americans were members of Alpha/1/1 and got a quick rundown on their unit's situation.

By happenstance, Lieutenant Colonel Gravel spotted a wounded Marine entangled in a roll of concertina wire bordering the left side of the road. It was Captain Gordon Batcheller. Gravel was awed by the size of the wound in Batcheller's right thigh. He knelt down to see if the blood-covered company commander was still alive. He was, but he was really tangled up in the wire. For his part, Batcheller was extremely surprised to see that his battalion commander had arrived on the scene so soon after their last radio conversation. (Batcheller was lucid, but he had apparently lost his sense of time.) There was still sporadic fire coming from the NVA infantry column to the southwest, so Gravel ordered his driver to retrieve their jeep and maneuver it to the left edge of the roadway to form a protective barrier. When it was in place, a

Golf/2/5 corpsman gave Captain Batcheller cursory medical treatment, and several Marines extricated him from the wire. As soon as the captain was free, a Marine tried to splint his shattered right leg with the handle of a shovel scavenged from Gravel's jeep. Before the splint could be secured, however, the Good Samaritan was shot through the foot.

At the time Captain Batcheller was being extricated from the barbed wire, Lieutenant Jerry Nadolski started easing his empty 6 × 6 trucks forward from the southeast. As Nadolski got out onto the raised roadway, he could see the many khaki-clad NVA soldiers moving northwestward along the far edge of the cane field. Individual NVA soldiers were firing at the trucks, which Nadolski took to be a warning. When the trucks reached Lieutenant Colonel Gravel's position, Gravel commandeered one of them and ordered the driver to turn it around. Then several wounded men, including Captain Batcheller, were hoisted aboard. While the rest of the convoy headed northwest, the casualty truck raced southeast at top speed. Gordon Batcheller was operated on in Phu Bai that afternoon. He was out of danger and would emerge whole, but he faced ten months in a Stateside hospital.

As the Golf/2/5 Marines entered the outskirts of the built-up area, they were at the height of wariness, but the battle in the area was over. There was still the odd round zinging between buildings, but the danger was minimal. When Captain Meadows noted that the Alpha/1/1 Marines in the area were still collecting their casualties, he ordered his platoons to advance quickly but cautiously to MACV, which was about 350 meters northeast of the edge of the built-up area.

Signs of a moving fight abounded. As Golf/2/5 advanced up Highway 1, it ran into more Alpha/1/1 casualties. However, the street remained reasonably quiet, and the Alpha/1/1 Marines and corpsmen appeared to have the situation well in hand. As Meadows glanced down one major side street, to the left, he saw the backside of a tank, which was on station guarding the Alpha/1/1 casualty evacuation.

Major Frank Breth and another Marine, Major Wayne Swenson, were checking in with the Marine security guards in the bunker at the MACV Compound's southeast corner when a nearby group of Army advisors erupted in cheers and shouts of "Hey, Marines, here comes the Army!" Breth looked down the street and, to his everlasting amazement and joy, saw his lunch date, cigar-chewing Lieutenant Colonel Ed LaMontagne, leading a pair of Marine M-48 tanks right up the middle of Highway 1. "Take another look," Breth shouted back at his Army colleagues, "Those are U.S. Marine tanks!"

As soon as Lieutenant Colonel LaMontagne could break away from a covey of proud, back-slapping fellow Marines, he reported to Colonel George Adkisson, the MACV Advisory Team 3 commander. LaMontagne filled the Army colonel in on the progress of the moving fight involving Alpha/1/1. He urgently requested that Adkisson dispatch trucks to help evacuate the Marine infantry company's many casualties. Adkisson, who had been under enormous strain all night, briefly hesitated. Before he could recover, a handful of Marine officers—Major Breth, Major Swenson, Captain Jim Coolican, and two or three others— simply commandeered two trucks, including a Navy stake-bed truck that happened to be parked near the MACV gate.

Accompanied by one of the Marine tanks, the Marines drove hell-bent down Highway 1 to the southeastern edge of the built-up area, where Marines from Alpha/1/1 and Golf/2/5 were still engaged in sporadic exchanges with unseen NVA soldiers. There were wounded and dead Marines all over the place, but mainly in a roadside ditch at the northeastern edge of the cane field. Someone called out that there were wounded Marines around a walled compound halfway out in the cane field. The stake-bed truck, with most of the Marine officers aboard, plunged into the open and roared down the exposed causeway.

The rescuers found a knot of leaderless, bypassed Alpha/ 1/1 riflemen in the ditch beside the compound—the Thua Thien Provincial Police headquarters—about halfway back along the exposed causeway. As the officers jumped down to the roadway, Major Frank Breth, who had commanded a Marine infantry company at Con Thien during the height of the siege, noticed how jumpy the Marine riflemen were; he had never seen troops as jumpy. Before Breth could say anything, Lieutenant Colonel LaMontagne pointed at the men in the ditch and said to Breth, "You get those guys together." At that instant, NVA soldiers, hunkered down along the southwestern edge of the cane field, opened fire. "Shit," LaMontagne bellowed. Breth looked at LaMontagne's outstretched arm and saw where a bullet had grazed along the pointing finger. "Holy shit," the normally sanguine LaMontagne screeched, "they're shooting at us!"

Under dwindling fire, the officers got the trucks turned around and helped the Marines in the ditch load their wounded comrades aboard. Then everyone headed northwest, to the built-up area. There the Marine infantrymen went their own way, to help their comrades establish a base of fire and collect, treat, and protect even more casualties. The two trucks with the wounded men aboard drove straight through to the MACV dispensary, where Advisory Team 3's only surgeon, Captain Steve Bernie, and his medics were already hard-pressed in the battle to save lives.

It is probable that the last Americans to leave the causeway were Lieutenant Colonel Mark Gravel and his jeep driver. After getting Captain Gordon Batcheller and several other casualties on their way toward Phu Bai, the two worked slowly northwestward on foot, searching both sides of the road for more hidden men. They found no one else, and, eventually, Gravel realized that there was no one behind him. He thought of going back with his driver to fetch their abandoned jeep, but, on quick reflection, that seemed like a really lousy idea. Fearful that his powerful battalion radio might fall into the wrong hands, Gravel found a Marine who was carrying an M-72 LAAW antitank missile and ordered him to blow up the jeep. This was done.

Gravel next set out to find Gunnery Sergeant J L Canley, the acting Alpha/1/1 commander. On the way up the street, Gravel encountered Sergeant Alfredo Gonzalez, who was grinning widely over the outcome of several wild encounters in which he had prevailed. Eventually, Gravel found Gunny Canley. The huge noncom was standing in the middle of the roadway, oblivious to the bullets that spattered all around him, directing the clearing of an NVA-occupied building. Gravel and Canley were among the last Marines to close on the MACV Compound.

The failure of the 804th NVA Battalion to press its advantage in numbers on MACV in the predawn January 31 assault was understandable. The NVA unit had simply been outfought. What seems incomprehensible is that the commander of the 4th NVA Regiment, Lieutenant Colonel Nguyen Van, did not reinforce the 804th NVA Battalion or, at least, order the battalion commander to isolate the compound from the outside. Seemingly more incomprehensible is the NVA's failure to close Highway 1, an eminently easy task. After all, the 810th NVA Battalion was on hand to observe and harass Alpha/1/1 and Golf/2/5 as they entered the city. Why did the NVA take no measures to seal Highway 1? Because doing so had not been part of the 810th NVA Battalion's mission.

As if the battlefield failures were not enough, the vaunted Communist intelligence-gathering assets had completely overlooked an isolated and unprotected U.S. Army cryptocommunications relay center south of MACV and west of Highway 1. As a result, MACV and the 1st ARVN Division CP never lost contact with outside agencies, an extremely important advantage in the long run.

The twin failures to seize MACV and close off Highway 1 were crucial. They point to the greatest weakness of the Communist plan: its unyielding rigidity. Once rebuffed, the 804th NVA Battalion's commander apparently was unable to grasp that the next best action would have been to isolate MACV from outside reinforcement. The same is true of the 4th NVA Regiment's commander, and the 810th NVA Battalion's commander. These ultimately decisive early battlefield errors were symptoms of an across-the-board failing in the way the NVA trained its officers and selected them for promotion. All plans were promulgated from the top; midlevel initiative was not so much frowned on as forbidden. In Hue, these were fatal flaws.

Despite the damage the NVA inflicted on Alpha/1/1, the company reached MACV at about 1445, as did the 1/1 CP group and Golf/2/5, which had sustained only minimal casualties. So, nearly 300 Marine infantrymen, five Marine M-48 tanks, two U.S. Army M-55 quad-.50 trucks, and at least two straggling 7th ARVN Armored Cavalry Battalion M-41 light tanks were now on hand to meet the renewed efforts of 4th NVA Regiment's four infantry and two sapper battalions to secure southern Hue.

— 10 —

As soon as Golf/2/5, Alpha/1/1, the 1/1 CP group, and the Marine convoys had fully closed on the MACV Compound, an ad hoc group of Marine, Army, and Australian officers led by Lieutenant Colonel Ed LaMontagne began fashioning a viable defensive outlook for the MACV Compound and several neighboring installations. The brain trust for the committee included Major Frank Breth, Captain Jim Coolican, and Major Wayne Swenson, the 1st Marine Division liaison officer assigned to the 1st ARVN Division. The three Marine officers were old friends who had trained Marine lieutenants together at The Basic School, in Quantico, Virginia, before being ordered to Vietnam the previous summer. As such, they constituted a well-oiled team, tactically competent and immensely combat-experienced. Falling in with this group was Major Walt Murphy, the 1/1 operations officer, who had accompanied Golf/2/5 into the city. As luck would have it, the extremely talented Murphy had served as a tactics instructor at Quantico with Breth, Swenson, and Coolican.

As raw materials, the brain trust had Gunnery Sergeant J L Canley's hastily reorganized Alpha/1/1; five Marine M-48 tanks; two ARVN M-41 tanks; two Army M-55 quad-.50 trucks; and a hodgepodge of MACV advisors, administrators, clerks, and Marine security guards. How could these elements be melded into a tactically sound fighting force occupying tactically sound defensive positions? The first strategic decision was to expand MACV's holdings as far north as the southeastern ramp of the Nguyen Hoang Bridge across the Perfume River.

A particularly important addition to MACV's holdings was Doc Lao Park, an open area on the bank of the Perfume River beside the Nguyen Hoang Bridge. Though the park was exposed to fire from Communist positions along the north bank, it provided an otherwise perfect helicopter landing zone (LZ) from which many wounded could eventually be evacuated.

As MACV troops in Doc Lao Park engaged in a desultory and inconclusive exchange of fire with NVA troops holed up in multistory buildings on the north bank of the Perfume, the first medevac bird to reach Hue arrived overhead. It was a Marine CH-46 cargo helicopter out of Hue–Phu Bai Airfield. While the CH-46 circled out of range above the clouds, several of the most serious emergency medevac cases were rushed up from the MACV dispensary bunker. When the wounded had been staged in the park, the helicopter was called in. As it settled down amidst a cloud of dust thrown up by its rotors, the rear ramp was lowered and the crew chief began heaving out boxes of ammunition. Under no enemy fire whatsoever, a handful of litters were loaded into the CH-46. Then, as onlookers yelled to the crew chief to tell him there were many more wounded still to be evacuated, the helicopter rose swiftly into the afternoon sky.

For long minutes after the CH-46 lifted off, neither side fired. It was dead quiet. After a long lull, the Marine brain trust gathered in the open, right behind a Marine M-48 tank, hoping to see what was happening on the other side of the river. No one had a clue.

Major Frank Breth was staring hard, scanning the foot of the Nguyen Hoang Bridge, when, all of a sudden, he saw a huge cloud of dust and debris emerge from right beneath the northeastern bridge ramp. This was the backblast of a recoilless rifle. Unbelievably, Breth even saw the round that was heading across the river directly toward him. The 57mm recoilless rifle round blew a tremendous hole in a massive stone wall directly behind the M-48 tank, and the thirty or so NVA soldiers in the riverfront buildings once again peppered the park with small-arms fire.

As soon as Breth shook off the effects of the blast, he saw that the Marine M-48 tank was engaging the enemy soldiers on the far bank with its turret-mounted .50-caliber machine gun. Though Marines and MACV troops in the park spiritedly returned the enemy fire, their M-16s and M-60s lacked the range and hitting power to have much effect on the buildings the NVA were using for cover. They were just wasting valuable ammunition.

In a few moments, Breth noticed that there was an ARVN M-41 tank directly to his left, at the foot of the bridge ramp. But the tank was doing nothing. Breth immediately ordered Army 2nd Lieutenant Fred Drew, a scrappy young advisor, to accompany him to the ARVN tank to learn why it was not returning fire.

The two officers ran across an open stretch and clambered up onto the M-41's rear deck, in relative safety behind the turret. Both began hammering on the turret hatch with their rifles, hoping to rouse the tank commander. Nothing; there was no response. At that, Major Breth noticed that the .50-caliber machine gun mounted on the turret had a full box of ammo affixed to it. "Hey, Drew," Breth yelled above the din of gunfire, "how about loading for me?" Lieutenant Drew nodded, so Breth stood up, yanked back the machine gun's charging handle, and opened fire.

As Major Breth fired across the river, he could see chunks of riverfront buildings 300 meters away being tossed into the air wherever he laid the stream of .50-caliber tracer. But just as his fire was becoming effective, Breth ran out of ammunition. Again he banged on the turret, but there was no sign of life within the twenty-six-ton tank. By then, however, it was quiet again.

Moments after the heavy exchange ended, a second Marine CH-46 arrived over Doc Lao Park. As soon as the helicopter began descending through the cloud base, the NVA resumed firing, this time with at least one .51-caliber heavy machine gun, an ideal antiaircraft weapon. Once again, the M-48 tank opened fire with its .50-caliber cupola machine gun, and the Marines and MACV troops joined in with their ineffective M-16s and M-60s. The NVA had fire superiority, however, and there seemed to be no way to overcome it so the CH-46 could set down.

The cavalry arrived. Two Navy riverine patrol boats (PBRs) stationed at the nearby Navy LCU ramp dashed out into the stream and hurled a devastating fire with their dual .50-caliber machine guns. Within moments the PBR gunners were tearing the riverfront buildings apart. The NVA .51-caliber fire was completely shut off, and most of the NVA infantry weapons became quiet once again.

As soon as the NVA fire was cut off by the roving PBRs, the CH-46 set down. Casualties were loaded aboard. As it lifted away into the clouds, another CH-46 set down, and the rush to get wounded men aboard was repeated.

For most of the emergency medevacs, the Navy PBRs saved the day. For several of the wounded Marines and soldiers, however, help came too late. Among the latter group was Specialist 4th Class Frank Doezma, who had been seriously wounded in both legs while manning the machine gun on MACV's watchtower at the outset of the night attack. Though Dr. Steve Bernie and his MACV medics kept him alive for over twelve hours, Doezma died from shock and blood loss before his medevac bird reached the triage center at Phu Bai.

— 11 —

Golf/2/5 was not directly involved in the new MACV defensive picture because it still had to get to the 1st ARVN Division CP compound. While many Golf/2/5 Marines temporarily beefed up various new defensive posts outside the compound, Captain Chuck Meadows strode deeper into the embattled enclave to find out what was going on. The battle he had fought and the signs of other battles he had seen along the way from the An Cuu Bridge simply did not jibe with any of the information Meadows had ever received about Hue. Clearly, he had stepped into something very soft and very deep.

After checking on the wounded Alpha/1/1 and Golf/2/5 Marines, Captain Meadows quickly found his way to the MACV tactical operations center (TOC), a sandbagged bunker near the center of the compound. The first person Meadows saw inside the TOC bunker was Lieutenant Colonel Mark Gravel, who was arguing with a tall, distinguished-looking Army colonel—the MACV Advisory Team 3 commander, Colonel George Adkisson.

As Captain Meadows eavesdropped, Gravel picked up a radio handset and continued what appeared to be an ongoing argument with someone in Phu Bai, at the Task Force X-Ray CP. Gravel was asking why he and Golf/2/5 needed to continue on to the Citadel. More than Gravel's words, the tone of Gravel's voice signaled to Captain Meadows that events were running completely counter to any understanding he had of the situation in Hue. As Gravel continued to argue with Task Force X-Ray, Meadows stood silently at the margin of a small crowd, taking it all in. Meadows was struck by how emotionally wrung out Gravel appeared.

Captain Meadows concluded that Adkisson was trying to dissuade Gravel from continuing his mission across the Perfume, and that Gravel was trying to convey this to Task Force X-Ray. For his part, Colonel Adkisson felt he could do no more than marshal the arguments; he had no authority to order Gravel to remain at MACV.

Gravel did not understand that Adkisson was trying to persuade him not to cross the river; he had reached the same conclusion on his own and was explaining why to Task Force X-Ray. Whatever was going on between Adkisson and Gravel did not matter; Task Force X-Ray was arguing against aborting the mission. When an unseen, unknown Marine general at distant Phu Bai turned aside the arguments he thought he was presenting via Lieutenant Colonel Gravel, Colonel Adkisson stopped arguing.

Apparently, Task Force X-Ray's commander, Brigadier General Foster LaHue, was receiving his orders direct from III Marine Amphibious Force (III MAF) Headquarters, in faraway Danang. Gravel remained under firm orders to continue with his mission. What's more, Task Force X-Ray had added the stricture that Golf/2/5 was to conduct its mission without using its mortars and without the aid of air or artillery support. When Lieutenant Colonel Gravel blurted an objection in an incredulous tone, he was told that he was not to destroy or even damage Vietnamese property, particularly the Citadel's historic structures. Task Force X-Ray did not identify the source of this stricture, but Gravel had the distinct impression that it came from high up, perhaps as high as the White House.

Although Colonel Adkisson felt that Gravel's mission was

unreasonable and perhaps suicidal, he provided directions to guide Golf/2/5 into the Citadel by the route least likely to be massively defended.

Acting on Colonel Adkisson's advice, Chuck Meadows planned to follow Highway 1 across the 400-meter-long Nguyen Hoang Bridge; turn left on the first big street (still Highway 1); and proceed about 300 meters to the turnoff to the Thuong Tu Gate, which led into the south corner of the Citadel. Once through the gate, the company would have a straight two-kilometer run into the 1st ARVN Division CP compound. This route from MACV into the Citadel was thought to be lightly defended, and it was. But that was relative; it was very well defended where it mattered.

The Marine company left the vicinity of the MACV Compound at 1610, January 31. At the southeastern end of the bridge, just two blocks north of MACV, Captain Meadows left two of his three 60mm mortars and one of his rifle platoons in reserve.

Lance Corporal Barney Barnes, whose squad of 2nd Lieutenant Steve Hancock's 2nd Platoon was to be the company point, found two ARVN M-41 tanks at the foot of the bridge's southeastern ramp. Barnes tried to get the tanks to lead the way, but he was firmly rebuffed by the ARVN crewmen. Their tanks were all that remained of the main body of the 7th ARVN Armored Cavalry Battalion, and they had had enough war for one day. Lance Corporal Barnes was infuriated but could do nothing more.

As the Golf/2/5 mortars were being set in beside the bridge ramp, Lance Corporal Barnes's squad pointman stepped out onto the span. The rest of Lieutenant Hancock's platoon scattered right and left along the walkways bordering the roadway, and the Golf/2/5 CP group and 2nd Lieutenant Mike McNeil's 1st Platoon followed Barnes's squad. Behind them were Lieutenant Colonel Gravel, a radioman, and a Marine interpreter—all on foot.

The bridge was so long that none of the cautiously advancing Marines could see over the crest of the arched roadway. There was nothing to be seen ahead but sky and the top of the looming wall of the Citadel. There was the sound of distant gunfire to keep the troops alert, but no sign of the enemy anywhere near the bridge.

The moment the lead fire team of Lance Corporal Barnes's lead squad crested the arch, it was fired on by an NVA machine gun set inside an open-topped guard bunker at the northwestern end of the bridge. From the path of the green tracer rounds, it was easy to see that the grazing fire was initially unable to strike any of the Marines. However, ricochets caroming off the steel trusses endangered everyone. From his vantage point in Doc Lao Park, on the south bank, Major Frank Breth saw a spectacular cascade of sparks as hundreds of bullets and ricochets struck the steel trusses.

The 2nd Platoon halted, and Chuck Meadows made his way forward to Lance Corporal Barnes's position. When he arrived, Barnes was trying to get an M-60 machine gun set up to counter the NVA .51-caliber fire. Meadows concentrated on trying to get a feel for what his platoons were facing. It was doubtful that Golf/2/5 could move forward.

The first casualties were being treated, and the main body of the company was still out of sight of the NVA machine-gun team. The M-60 team opened fire, but in a matter of seconds the machine-gun team leader was shot dead. At that point, the leader of the 2nd Platoon's next squad, Corporal Lester Tully, took matters into his own hands.

While the NVA machine gun was concentrating on the M-60, Corporal Tully ran up the walkway and reduced the NVA machine-gun position with a hand grenade. Five NVA soldiers were killed in the blast, and several others were seriously wounded. As soon as the NVA machine gun was silenced, Lieutenant Hancock's entire platoon rapidly crossed to the north bank. There, the platoon set up a hasty defensive perimeter and began gathering and treating its casualties.

Lieutenant Colonel Gravel arrived on the north bank of the river only moments after the main body of Golf/2/5. When he got there, several seriously wounded NVA soldiers were still flopping around inside the grenaded guard bunker. Coldly,

Gravel instructed his Marine interpreter to interrogate the ones who were still able to talk. Though none of the NVA were of sufficient rank to know much about the NVA plan or order of battle, the details they provided went a long way toward clarifying the picture and bolstering Gravel's opinion that he and Golf/ 2/5 were definitely in the wrong place at the wrong time.

While the interrogations were proceeding, Gravel personally radioed back to Colonel Adkisson's TOC to request that vehicles be sent across the bridge to evacuate the wounded and the enemy prisoners. To his amazement, the request was denied. Furious, Gravel immediately set out, back across the bridge, to find vehicles and volunteer drivers.

In short order Gravel returned from his angry hike to MACV with several trucks—at least one Marine 6 × 6 truck and the Navy stake-bed truck that had accompanied the earlier rescue effort to the causeway. Also accompanying him were several civilian vehicles that had been hot-wired and commandeered on the spot. In addition, on its own, one of the Army M-55 quad-.50 trucks made its way across the bridge. Like Lance Corporal Barnes before him, however, Gravel had been unable to activate the crews of the two ARVN tanks deployed beside the south bridge ramp.

As Major Walt Murphy, the 1/1 operations officer, and several other volunteers from the 1/1 operations section jumped off the 6 × 6 truck, Marines from the 2nd Platoon of Golf/2/5 began loading their dead and wounded comrades onto the vehicle. Suddenly, there was a large explosion in the midst of the riflemen and the battalion staffers. Several onlookers thought it was a B-40 blast, and someone even reported the cause as a satchel charge tossed into the crowd by an NVA sapper. Lieutenant Colonel Gravel thought it was a hand grenade that had fallen from the body of a dead or wounded Marine. Whatever the source, the result was devastating. Many Marines were wounded, Major Murphy the most seriously of all. A spray of shrapnel had erupted upward beneath the bottom edge of his flak jacket.

Long before the dust of the blast had settled, the quad-.50 gunner began dismantling the nearest buildings with his hideously effective antiaircraft weapon. Whatever NVA soldiers remained in those structures certainly died in the hail of half-inch bullets.

Another fierce response came from the driver of the 6 × 6, Private First Class Nolan Lala, a Marine whose irreverent attitude toward authority was legendary in the 1st Motor Transport Battalion. Lala, who had had several close calls in ambushes along Highway 1 in previous weeks, had been in continuous danger since picking up part of Alpha/1/1 at Phu Bai that morning. Though Lala's nerves were about shot—he had requested relief from driving duties earlier in the week—he had acquiesced that morning to taking one last trip because of the critical shortage of lead drivers. And he had volunteered to accompany Lieutenant Colonel Gravel back across the bridge to rescue fellow Marines. When the blast erupted beside his truck on the afternoon of January 31, Lala erupted back. He fearlessly stood up in the truck's vacant .50-caliber ring mount—there were not enough drivers to provide the luxury of assistant drivers or gunners—and added his fire to that of the quad-.50 truck. Then, when someone told Lala that a full load of wounded and dead Marines was aboard his truck, he sat down in the driver's seat and drove back across the exposed 500-meter span—in reverse.

While Mark Gravel had been arguing fruitlessly with the TOC for trucks to take out Golf/2/5's wounded, Captain Chuck Meadows had ordered Lieutenant Mike McNeil's 1st Platoon to take over the company lead. McNeil's platoon turned left at the end of the bridge and proceeded up Highway 1, right in the shadow of the massive wall of the Citadel. In the first block McNeil's platoon passed a movie theater that was showing *Gone with the Wind*. Back at the bridge ramp, Chuck Meadows, still shaken from the challenge at the bridge, was looking over the casualties and taking reports. It was quiet—a condition Meadows was learning to dread as a portent of violence.

Private First Class Bill Tant, who had been thirsting for his first action earlier in the day, was about to get a bellyful of it. Tant's squad, led by Corporal Glenn Lucas, was the vanguard of McNeil's platoon when it reached an intersection with a tiny alley leading through some buildings fronting the Citadel wall. Corporal Lucas turned to Tant, who was the point fire-team leader, and told him to wait until he, Lucas, could check out the passage. Tant was in awe of Lucas's calm bravery. Though Lucas had only ten days left in Vietnam, he was still taking mortal chances.

No sooner had Corporal Lucas disappeared from view than Tant heard an AK-47 burst to life. Then an M-16 fired. Then Corporal Lucas ran into sight. He had a flesh wound and a story. An NVA soldier had fired at him, and he had fired back. He said he thought the NVA soldier had been killed. With that, Lucas resumed the lead and moved up Highway 1 again. The next street up was the Thuong Tu Gate road, a pretty little commercial intersection with a pharmacy on one corner.

When Corporal Lucas's squad turned right at the intersection, it was confronted by the intimidating Citadel wall; the massive gate; and, of all things, a bridged moat. For the first time Bill Tant could see the huge NLF banner flying on the Citadel flagpole. It was an awesome sight for Tant and his comrades, who had not begun to overcome the multiple shocks of the day.

Just as Corporal Lucas's vanguard squad reached a point about fifty meters north of the Highway 1 intersection, the entire company came under intense fire from atop the Citadel wall and particularly from positions within the gate. From the bridge ramp, Chuck Meadows could see what he presumed to be enemy soldiers moving across Highway 1 southwest of his position. But—despite the evidence of the intense fire—he could not detect any NVA closer in.

The enemy soldiers nearest to Bill Tant's position outside the gate were only thirty to forty meters away. In a flash, four or five Marines behind Tant and on the same side of the street were bowled over. About the same number were shot as they advanced toward the gate on the other side of the street. Tant tried to enter the nearest building to get out of the line of fire, but found that the door and windows had been nailed shut. All the doors and windows of all the buildings fronting the gate road had been sealed. As more and more of his comrades went down, Tant stepped behind a tree, which provided adequate cover from the sheets of bullets that were flying down the narrow road. Corporal Lucas leaped for the same tree, but he did not make it. As Tant looked on, Lucas fell to the roadway. Tant could not see where Lucas had been hit, but it was obvious that the squad leader had been wounded seriously. Tant wanted to rescue Lucas, to pull him behind the tree, but the enemy fire was literally chipping away at his cover on both sides. There was no way to move safely. To his rear, Tant heard someone yelling to Lieutenant McNeil, telling the platoon commander that the point squad was getting cut to pieces.

Captain Meadows and his CP group—the company gunny and several radiomen and forward-observer teams—dashed up the highway to the intersection of the gate road. To be closer to the action, Meadows went forward to a big tree right in front of the pharmacy. From there, he could see into the Thuong Tu Gate during lulls in the shooting. At first glance he ordered Lieutenant McNeil to send several Marines up to the pharmacy roof so they could get better observation and firing positions. McNeil sent an M-60 team and several riflemen to the roof, and they began dueling with the NVA inside the gate.

Even a cursory assessment consisting of quick peeks was enough to convince Captain Meadows that it was time to abort the mission. With over two kilometers of narrow streets separating his lead riflemen from the 1st ARVN Division CP compound, there was no way anyone was going through the Thuong Tu Gate that day.

Golf/2/5 could not advance, but it remained to be seen if the remnants of Corporal Lucas's squad could withdraw from the gate road. As Bill Tant stared at Corporal Lucas's inert form, calculating the odds of a rescue attempt, Hospitalman Donald Kirkham, one of the 1st Platoon's two Navy corpsmen, inched his way up the sidewalk, taking care of each of the wounded Marines he encountered along the way. After many minutes, Kirkham reached a point opposite Corporal Lucas. Just as he was about to move away from the relative safety of the wall to grab the wounded squad leader, Lucas, who had not moved a muscle before Kirkham arrived, motioned violently for the corpsman to stay back. But Doc Kirkham made his move anyway—and was shot in the throat.

Chuck Meadows was on his second tour in Vietnam, as a

combat company commander. He had been in dangerous situations before, but he had never been in a mess like the one he was facing now. His company was being systematically chewed to pieces, and there was no guarantee it was going to be able to withdraw without losing most of a platoon. Slowly, as Lieutenant McNeil's rear squads painstakingly built up the tempo of their return fire, several survivors toward the rear of the pinned squad were able to extricate themselves. But there were still dead and wounded Marines caught in the crossfire pouring out of the gate and up the narrow, sheer-sided gate road. A good deal of the limited vista Captain Meadows had enjoyed at the start of the fight was now obscured by dust and gunsmoke. Nevertheless, he was able to direct the fire of the M-60 machine gun from the pharmacy roof. The M-60 seemed to be having some effect on the hottest NVA positions inside the gate. With the aid of smoke grenades effectively laid down by grenadiers firing M-79 grenade launchers, several more of the Marines who were pinned down along the street were extricated.

After a head count Lieutenant McNeil reported that he was still five men short. A great deal of shouting brought forth a clue as to the whereabouts of the missing men. Corporal Glenn Lucas, Private First Class Bill Tant, Lance Corporal Patrick Lucas, Private First Class Gerald Kinny, and Hospitalman Donald Kirkham were arrayed around Tant's tree, which was about fifty meters from Captain Meadows's tree.

Someone hot-wired a Vietnamese flatbed rice truck. As Meadows ordered his men to heave or fire smoke grenades through the gate, the truck ran forward to act as a moving shield for those who were still trapped in the street.

As soon as Bill Tant was able to leave the cover of his bullet-riddled tree, he reached out to grab Corporal Glenn Lucas. At the same moment, Lance Corporal Patrick Lucas also grabbed the wounded corporal, and he and Tant dragged him to safety. Two Marines who had come forward with the truck grabbed Doc Kirkham, but the corpsman had already bled to death from the gaping bullet hole in his throat. The extrication was nearly flawless and resulted in no new casualties. However, Private First Class Gerald Kinny was not among the evacuees.

Chuck Meadows momentarily ran out of the special brand of nerve it takes to order other men into mortal danger. He laid down his M-16 behind the tree that had served as his cover and ran forward into the smoky haze that enshrouded the gate road. He found Kinny fifty meters forward, on the right side of the street. With one hand, Meadows heaved Kinny up by his belt buckle, and, with Kinny's M-16 in his other hand, he began running back toward the intersection. Halfway back, Meadows ran into his battalion radioman, Corporal William Peterson, who helped drag Kinny the rest of the way behind Meadows's tree in the Highway 1 intersection. Unfortunately, Private First Class Gerald Kinny was dead on arrival.

With Lieutenant McNeil's entire platoon accounted for, Captain Meadows radioed Lieutenant Colonel Gravel and gave his assessment of Golf/2/5's situation. By then, Meadows could tell the 1/1 battalion commander that his company had sustained five killed and forty-four wounded—losses of about 35 percent—since first being fired on north of the An Cuu Bridge. Meadows told Gravel that, on his own authority, he was pulling back to the Nguyen Hoang Bridge. He asked that trucks be made available to evacuate the dead and wounded. A few minutes later Gravel called back to approve Meadows's plan.

As the main body of Golf/2/5 re-formed around the northwestern bridge ramp, the NVA in the area ceased firing. As soon as it was relatively safe, a Vietnamese man emerged from the rubble of a nearby building. He was wearing an ARVN uniform and a red beret—the symbol of the elite ARVN airborne battalions—and identified himself as 1st Lieutenant Doan Van Ba, a medical doctor. Doctor Ba was hustled aboard one of the last trucks on the north side of the bridge and driven to MACV. He had some difficulty establishing himself as a bona fide physician in the eyes of some spooked MACV staffers. But, to Dr. Steve Bernie, hitherto the only doctor at MACV, *Bac Si* [Doctor] Ba quickly established himself as a competent surgeon and a real godsend.

The withdrawal across the Nguyen Hoang Bridge to MACV was completed around 1900, nearly three hours after the doomed move on the Citadel had commenced. After the withdrawal, Lieutenant Colonel Gravel led a squad from Alpha/1/1, two Marine tanks, and several MACV volunteers on an attempt to rescue an unknown number of American civilians from the CORDS building, which was two blocks south and several blocks west of MACV. The ragtag force nearly penetrated to the objective, but it was turned back by an extremely strong NVA response.

As the stymied rescue force was preparing to return to MACV, scores of civilian refugees, many of them children, emerged from the rubble of several nearby buildings. The NVA did not pursue, so the refugees followed the American force back toward the MACV Compound. The Americans were glad to save some lives, but the refugees constituted a security nightmare. The wounded civilians were taken to the overworked MACV dispensary; the others were bedded down in an adjacent ARVN compound.

On January 31, the last fruitful act mounted from MACV was a late-night helicopter medevac from Doc Lao Park engineered by Lieutenant Colonel Mark Gravel. In addition to the eight wounded evacuees who were carried up from MACV and lifted out, four of the rescuers had to be medevacked because of wounds they suffered on the way to the LZ. From this Gravel learned an important if costly lesson: Never again did he send his men into an unsecured area by way of city streets, which the NVA obviously knew well enough to stake out. After January 31, Gravel always took a tank along to make new streets, right through buildings and walled compounds. The method destroyed a lot of Hue, but it saved lives.

For the first Marines to arrive in Hue from Phu Bai, January 31 was a bloody day. In the two infantry companies, a combat force of about 300 men, approximately eighty Americans had been killed or wounded, though twenty of the wounded were treated and returned to duty on the spot. For all that, however, MACV was relatively secure, and, more important, higher American headquarters knew for a certainty that Communist forces now held most of the city and apparently were there to stay. The fog of war was far from dissipating, but it had been penetrated.

The problem thus became less a matter of determining what was going on than of figuring out a way to deal with it.

— 12 —

By means of radio conversations during the night of January 31, I ARVN Corps and III Marine Amphibious Force (III MAF) established some broad policy guidelines regarding clearing operations in and around Hue. Codifying reality, the two senior headquarters agreed that the Communist forces inside Hue would have to be subdued and driven out under the separate but broadly coordinated efforts of the two local combat commands— Brigadier General Ngo Quang Truong's 1st ARVN Division and Brigadier General Foster LaHue's Task Force X-Ray. The north bank of the Perfume River was declared the boundary between the two commands. That is, Truong's ARVN battalions would be responsible for clearing the Citadel and the approaches to it, while LaHue's yet-to-be-constituted task force would clear the southern city and the approaches to it.

Since I ARVN Corps and III MAF were extremely busy dealing with multiple emergencies in an unprecedented situation that had not begun to attain focus, there was little more either could do beyond informing the subordinate commanders on the scene about the overall agreement. The senior commanders conditionally approved in advance whatever Truong and LaHue did with whatever combat units they could muster. With that, the senior commanders turned their attention to pressing matters nearer to their respective headquarters (Quang Tri City and Danang) and left Hue to Truong and LaHue.

As the situation inside Hue slowly crystalized, higher headquarters continued to respond to the Communist challenge by establishing increasingly lengthy lines of command. At 1123, Task Force X-Ray handed the task of liberating southern Hue over to the 1st Marines. Almost immediately, the 1st Marines CP promulgated an operations order naming the clearing effort Operation Hue City and assigning 1/1 "the mission of conduct-

ing sweep and clear operations in [the] assigned area of operations to destroy enemy forces, protect U.S. nationals, and restore
[the southern portion] of the city to U.S. control."

On the Communist side of the command equation, the Tri-
Thien-Hue Front headquarters was moved out of the hills overlooking Hue to Thon La Chu, a prosperous agricultural hamlet
about four kilometers northwest of the Citadel's north corner,
immediately south of Highway 1. The front headquarters was
an American-built concrete-and-steel multistory bunker. The
5th NVA Regiment set in to guard the new base, and the commanders got back to work coordinating the mayhem Communist
forces were wreaking throughout Quang Tri and Thua Thien
provinces.

South of the Perfume River, the Communists used February
1 as a day of consolidation and stocktaking. Except for a dogged,
indecisive battle that continued to rage at the Thua Thien Provincial Prison, the battalions of the 4th NVA Regiment sat back on
what they had gained and pretty much ignored the objectives that
had eluded their grasp. They continued to pluck minor prizes
they had overlooked or had deliberately bypassed on January 31,
but, on February 1, they made no significant moves against the
apparently unperceived thorn in their side—the MACV Compound. Also on February 1, while elements of the 4th and 6th
NVA regiments were engaged in mopping up GVN outposts and
rounding up "criminal elements" throughout Hue, NVA infantry
and sapper units began overseeing the erection of field fortifications around the southern city and east of the Citadel. The work
was accomplished mainly by civilians who were impressed into ad
hoc labor battalions.

The Communist battalions inside Hue had attained most of
their military goals and had seized most of their key military
objectives by 0800, January 31, the hour at which they raised the
NLF flag over the Citadel. However, beginning exactly 24 hours
later—at 0800, February 1—the 1st ARVN Airborne Battle
Group—composed of the 2nd and 7th ARVN Airborne battalions; bolstered by the 3rd Company, 7th ARVN Armored Cav-

alry Battalion; and supported by an ARVN 105mm artillery battery at PK 17—breached the 806th NVA Battalion's defenses north and northeast of the Citadel and sprang into the 1st ARVN Division CP compound. These reinforcing units, particularly the cavalry troop, had sustained heavy losses in the full day of fighting they had weathered to reach the Citadel. Their arrival, however, meant that General Truong not only had the means for holding his CP compound indefinitely, but that he had a powerful, able combat force with which to begin serious counterattacks. And, Truong was informed that the 9th ARVN Airborne Battalion would be airlifted from Saigon to PK 17 the next day. In addition, he learned that on February 2 the U.S. Marines would helilift the entire 4th Battalion, 2nd ARVN Regiment, from Quang Tri City directly into the Citadel.

While the airborne units were consolidating inside the 1st ARVN Division CP compound, all four infantry battalions of the 3rd ARVN Regiment were still involved in separate actions in which they had become enmeshed throughout January 31. Continuing their loosely coordinated attacks from west of the Citadel along the north bank of the Perfume, the 3rd ARVN Regiment's 2nd and 3rd battalions managed to reach the southwestern Citadel wall. However, neither battalion could muster the momentum required to carry on through either of the southwestern gates, which were held by the 12th NVA Sapper Battalion. As the day wore on, the best either ARVN battalion could manage was to clear narrow enclaves hard against the wall and set in for more bitter fighting. The two ARVN infantry battalions had run out of steam and were, for all practical purposes, trapped.

To the east of the city, the 3rd ARVN Regiment's 1st and 4th battalions found themselves unable to even begin counterattacks against Hue. Throughout January 31, the 1st Battalion had fought to break out of an encirclement and maneuver eastward to an ARVN outpost on the coast of the South China Sea. On February 1, this battalion boarded a small flotilla of motorized junks and was transported up the Perfume River to a spot east of the Citadel. From there, it battled its way toward the 1st ARVN Division CP compound, where it arrived at 1500, an important addition to General Truong's burgeoning force.

The 4th Battalion, 3rd ARVN Regiment, remained hard-pressed. It had been encircled by elements of the 804th NVA Battalion at the outset of the Tet attacks, and throughout February 1 it remained so—fighting for its life.

During the night of January 31, Tuy-Cam heard the ominous sound of digging behind the family house. She strained her ears to pick up the faint sound of human voices, but the NVA soldiers outside were inhumanly quiet. Even the sandals they wore, which were made of tires, did not squeak when they walked.

Toward dawn, Tuy-Cam heard raindrops on banana leaves. As she listened, Chuong, the houseboy, came in from the kitchen and said he had seen big gun positions and a newly dug trench, all camouflaged with branches and leaves, along the bamboo fence at the rear of the family compound.

Soon the NVA soldiers came in to beg for tea, but they lingered for breakfast. It was fascinating for Tuy-Cam to watch them use their chopsticks. One of the two ends was used to shovel food inside their mouths, but the other end was used to pick up food from serving dishes. "It is more sanitary this way," they explained. "You will not get your saliva into the food you share with others."

Suddenly, as the NVA soldiers ate, a large group of VC barged into the house. It was making the rounds of all the local households. The same questions the family had endured the day before were asked again, and the same answers were given. One of the VC checked all the rooms on the first floor, and then the group left.

Soon the NVA squad finished eating, thanked the family, and also departed up the street. Tuy-Cam's mother waited a long moment and then looked up at the attic, where her two sons were hiding. "Do you need anything?" she asked loudly. The brothers replied that they were hungry and thirsty. She sent several bottles of water up to them—quickly, in case some NVA soldiers came back. She told the brothers, who had not eaten for two days, that she hoped to send up some food by dinnertime. The NVA soldiers returned to their gun position a few minutes later.

Around noon, a small group of NVA soldiers came in and

started propagandizing the family. They asked if everyone knew who "Uncle Ho" was. The family members said they did. The NVA said the family "must not side with the government of the lackeys," but instead "must fight against the American aggressors." They should "stand up and join the National Liberation Front to fight for the liberty of the country [and] join the movement to fight for 'independence, freedom, and happiness' "—the motto of the Communist Party. Then the political cadre gave the family a small NLF flag and asked that it be displayed. "When the country is independent again," one of them promised, "we will be back to teach you Communism and what it did to bring prosperity to the people." Finally, the VC asked for some tea, drank it, and departed with the promise that they would be back later. "We want to see some improvement in your attitude," one of them cautioned.

There was no electricity for the lights, and the days were short at that time of year, so the women decided to prepare dinner before dark. As they worked, a heavy rain started falling. Chuong, the houseboy, had reported earlier that the water pressure from the tap was very low. The idea of collecting rainwater struck everyone at once, so they gathered all the containers they could find and set them outside.

After the rainwater had been brought in, Tuy-Cam's mother posted the sisters at the doors to make sure no one was in sight. Then she sent some food up to An and Long. The container came down with a message for Tuy-Cam: "We could be wrong, but we think Big Sister is safe with her friend," they wrote. Their message calmed Tuy-Cam's fears. She looked up and said, "Thanks."

"Big Sister"—Tuy-Cam's fiancé, Jim Bullington—was indeed safe. He spent February 1 in the home of Father Cressonier and Father Poncet, trying to relax and wait out the storm. In the afternoon, through binoculars borrowed from the French priests, Bullington watched two VNAF A-1 Skyraiders as they bombed and strafed targets within the Citadel. That was his first indication that the Communists had occupied the imperial seat. Next, he spotted the giant NLF flag atop the Citadel wall. Mostly, that day, Jim Bullington worried about Tuy-Cam.

During the wee hours of February 1, Task Force X-Ray ordered Lieutenant Colonel Mark Gravel's thinly stretched ad hoc battalion to jump off at first light to relieve the GVN force still holding out in the Thua Thien Provincial Prison. While they were at it, they were to liberate the adjacent Thua Thien Province Adminstration complex, which Marines had mistakenly identified as the Provincial Headquarters. The order caused considerable consternation among Gravel's harried senior officers, who had weathered a day of trying to crack city defenses.

To Task Force X-Ray, the prison was a mere 1,200 meters from MACV, a distance any competent battalion should be able to fight through in the bush. To Mark Gravel and Captain Chuck Meadows, however, the prison was eight long city blocks from MACV—a distance twice the one Gravel had failed to negotiate on his way to the CORDS building on January 31 and four times the one that had cost Gravel's convoy four casualties in the night medevac. Gravel and Meadows were beginning to realize that they had been lucky to get into Hue at all the previous day, before the Communists had begun setting in their defenses. To both officers—though not to their superiors—it was obvious that the resistance was stiffening. Indeed, by then both Gravel and Meadows realized that getting to the prison—or any fighting inside Hue—involved a kind of experience that neither possessed. Nor had any of their young troops ever been trained in city fighting.

The last time Marines had fought in a built-up area had been in September 1950, in the liberation of Seoul, Korea. At that time Marines had faced a beaten foe fighting a ragged rearguard action of short duration. Gravel had served in the Korean War, but he had not fought in Seoul. Meadows had entered the Marine Corps in the early 1960s; he had been trained to fight in built-up areas, but that was years before he arrived in Hue. He had seen no city combat in his first tour as a company commander nor on his current tour with Golf/2/5. In fact, no one in 1/1 or Golf/2/5 had ever fought in a built-up area; the Marine Corps had virtually cut city-combat tactics from its wartime infantry-training program.

Lieutenant Colonel Gravel protested the order to secure the prison and the administration complex, but he was told to carry

on. In response, Lieutenant Mike McNeil's 1st Platoon of Golf/
2/5, the Golf/2/5 CP group, and an ad hoc squad of MACV
volunteers jumped off from MACV at 0700.

The NVA were out in force. Initially, McNeil's platoon was
unable even to fight its way across Highway 1—to the other side
of the street. Even the pair of Marine M-48 tanks assigned to the
effort were unable to breast the enemy fire. If anything, the M-
48s were a liability, for they drew an inordinate amount of fire,
including volleys of B-40 rockets, from the masonry buildings
overlooking the highway. In no time, the tanks' antennas had
been clipped, and all the gear stowed outside the hulls was shot
away. Clearly, the NVA had drawn a line along the western edge
of Highway 1.

After hours of pressing, the inadequate assault force managed to advance one block southeast along Highway 1. From
there, it was to turn southwest onto the first cross street, Tran
Cao Van. It was only six more blocks to the prison.

Specialist 4th Class Jim Mueller was a MACV clerk who felt
he owed his life to the Marines of Golf/2/5. When a call for
volunteers had gone out that morning, Mueller, an Army brat,
had volunteered to help them. Though Mueller was a clerk who
had received only rudimentary infantry training, he felt he could
handle house-to-house fighting as well as the battle-hardened
Marines, who were openly expressing trepidation at the prospect
of more city combat.

Specialist 4th Class Mueller followed the Golf/2/5 Marines
to the intersection of Highway 1 and Tran Cao Van and joined a
long line of men who were standing with their backs against a
wall of the corner house. A tank was in front of them, preparing
to round the corner onto Tran Cao Van. As everyone waited for
the tank to make its move, an NVA soldier fired several rounds
from a top-floor window of the house the Americans were using
for cover. The bullets struck close to Jim Mueller, but Mueller
could not return fire without permission from his sergeant.

"Sarge," Mueller called, "there's someone up there shooting
at me."

"Where?"

"There." Mueller pointed at the window.

"Well," the sergeant observed, "there's no one shooting at you now."

"Well, no, but do I have permission to shoot?"

"If he starts shooting again, call me and then shoot."

Mueller could not believe what he had just heard. He had to have permission to defend himself! If someone tried to kill him, he had to have permission to shoot back.

As Mueller was mulling over the absurdity of this directive, the Marine M-48 tank nosed around the corner and started down Tran Cao Van Street. A squad of Marines advanced behind the tank, but the MACV soldiers and other Marines stayed behind the wall, back on Highway 1. The tank immediately drew heavy small-arms fire from a steeple atop the chapel of the Jeanne d'Arc Private Girls' High School, hitting one of the Marines following the tank. The tank fired its 90mm main gun right at the steeple, and the whole structure toppled over into the street.

With that, the MACV soldiers were ordered to sweep through the house to the back courtyard. For all Specialist 4th Class Mueller knew, the NVA soldier who had fired at him a few minutes earlier was still inside the house. Nevertheless, the entire MACV squad and several Marines went inside and began checking all the rooms. In the process, one of Mueller's companions almost got killed. The man had gone into a room, and an NVA soldier threw a grenade in through a window. Out of instinct, the Marine turned and started shooting. Luckily, he hit the grenade, and it bounced outside and blew up.

The Marines and MACV soldiers searched the entire house. Jim Mueller was scared the whole time. At one point, several of the Americans stepped into what appeared to be a hospital room. There was a bed with a sheet hanging around it. Someone ordered Mueller to make sure there was no one in the bed. Mueller wondered, "Do I shoot first and ask questions later? Do I wait until one of my partners opens up the sheet and, in that split second, decide to kill the person who is there?" His mind was racing as he approached the bed, ready to shoot. When one of the other soldiers parted the sheet, Mueller saw there was no one behind it. Jim Mueller had to take a deep breath; he knew then that he did not want to kill anybody.

The soldiers and Marines eventually worked their way

through the house and out into the courtyard. Word was that the NVA were moving back, giving the Americans some room. For all that, the Marines and soldiers were unable to fight their way over the courtyard wall. Every time someone stuck his head above the top of the wall, the NVA poured heavy fire at him. At length, the stymied Americans called up a second M-48 tank, and, with its main gun, it blew a hole right through the wall. All hands charged through the breach, firing blindly as they went to keep the NVA down and prevent them from firing back.

As the NVA were prodded a short distance up Tran Cao Van, dozens of civilians emerged from the buildings they passed and ran toward Highway 1. After that, Lieutenant Mike McNeil's platoon advanced all of fifteen meters against resistance that grew steadily fiercer. The Marines vainly tried to advance, and the volunteer Army squad escorted the civilians back to MACV.

While the attack toward the prison inched forward up Tran Cao Van Street, Lieutenant Steve Hancock's 2nd Platoon of Golf/2/5 headed south on Highway 1 to the edge of the kilometer-wide cane field. Its mission was to try to locate the home of a pair of U.S. State Department officials in the neighborhood west of the highway. Miraculously, the two American civilians emerged alive and unscathed following an hours-long search.

Early in the afternoon of February 1, Task Force X-Ray asked that all the transportation trucks that had carried Alpha/1/1 and Golf/2/5 to MACV on January 31 be sent back to Phu Bai, where they were sorely needed to carry more combat troops and supplies to Hue. Mark Gravel concurred with the request; there was no way to maintain or fuel the trucks adequately at MACV. The trucks were loaded with all the killed and all but the most seriously wounded. A day and night of battle around MACV had proven that helicopter medevacs could not keep pace with the toll of casualties. Moreover, the dead were presenting an increasing health risk and a threat to morale.

Mindful that Highway 1 might be cut at any of the many chokepoints between Hue and Phu Bai, Mark Gravel and Chuck Meadows decided between them to send a reinforced platoon back as convoy escort. Meadows selected Golf/2/5's 3rd Platoon, commanded by 2nd Lieutenant Bill Rogers. The 3rd Platoon had not been seriously engaged and had suffered no casualties on January 31, so it was the strongest unit. Also, as the most experienced of Golf/2/5's platoon commanders, Lieutenant Rogers was deemed the most capable of leading this dangerous leap into the unknown.

Not only was Rogers's platoon to guard the trucks, it was, in effect, to escort Lieutenant Rogers himself, who was to act as an officer-messenger to the colonel commanding the 1st Marines in Phu Bai. Assuming he survived the trip, Rogers was to describe the situation at Hue in candid detail so that the off-the-scene commanders would have a better understanding of what the tiny combat force at MACV was facing. So important was it that Rogers's report be believed and understood, that it was deemed worth sending nearly forty precious combat infantrymen along to ensure the lieutenant's safe arrival. Both Army M-55 quad-.50 trucks were to accompany the infantry platoon and act as additional convoy escort. Sending these valuable resources was another reflection of the importance the commanders placed on getting Lieutenant Rogers through to the regimental CP. As soon as the message had been delivered, Rogers's platoon was to head back to Hue with supplies and reinforcements. If Highway 1 was interdicted or if any of the bridges had been blown, everyone was to return to MACV.

Just before the trucks left MACV, the convoy commander, 2nd Lieutenant Jerry Nadolski, was directed to proceed all the way to Phu Bai at the best speed the trucks could make, about forty miles per hour. He was to abandon any vehicles that were disabled along the way and, if possible, to barge through any roadblocks.

The beds of all Marine trucks operating in Vietnam were routinely covered with layers of sandbags, a crude but effective shield against mines. Anticipating steady sniper fire along the way, all the troops were ordered to lie facedown on the sandbagged truck beds. One infantryman was placed in the cab of each truck, alongside the driver, to ride shotgun or man a ring-mounted .50-caliber machine gun—if that truck had one.

The convoy's speed and the boldness of the mission apparently caught the NVA by surprise. All the bridges were intact, and the convoy encountered only desultory, disorganized resistance. Only one truck was lost along the way, just south of the Phu Cam Canal, the result of a direct RPG hit. Fortunately, there were no casualties, and the Marines who had been riding in that truck jumped aboard the next few trucks without appreciably slowing the convoy. The convoy raced into the open cultivated area to the south.

Miraculously, without further loss of vehicles and with no casualties whatever, the convoy reached Phu Bai at around dusk. As 2nd Lieutenant Nadolski shepherded the trucks into the Gia Le camp, Lieutenant Rogers reported to the regimental CP. There, though he was nervous in the presence of so many field-grade officers, Lieutenant Rogers told his compelling tale. As soon as he was released from the regimental CP, Lieutenant Rogers was free to begin worrying about a return trip to Hue.

Lieutenant Rogers's message apparently got through to the field-grade officers assembled in the 1st Marines CP, for wheels began turning and important results would follow.

— 13 —

Lieutenant Bill Rogers's advice reached Phu Bai too late to help another infantry company of the 2nd Battalion, 5th Marines. At noon, February 1—hours before Lieutenant Rogers left MACV—Task Force X-Ray assigned Fox/2/5 to the 1st Marines for duty with 1/1 in Hue.

On the afternoon of January 31, 2/5 had been undertaking a coordinated three-company effort to clear an NVA battalion out of the area around the vital twin-span Troi Bridge complex, eight kilometers south of Phu Bai. Suddenly, with no warning, the 5th Marines CP ordered Fox/2/5 to break contact with the enemy and report to Phu Bai immediately. The order was peremptory and nonnegotiable; Fox/2/5 pulled out of the battalion line and assembled in a field for the drive north to Phu Bai.

At the moment the order arrived, 2/5 was on the brink of defeating the NVA battalion, which had begun threatening the Troi Bridge complex during the previous night. In a twinkling the Marine battalion lost its superior position, its superior fire-power, and its ability to win. When Lieutenant Colonel Ernie Cheatham, the 2/5 commander, asked 5th Marines how he, with only two remaining companies, was supposed to carry off the destruction of the NVA battalion, the answer was, in effect, "Carry on." But the NVA cannily divined 2/5's disadvantage and disengaged from what minutes earlier had been a deadly encircle-ment. As the NVA unit evaporated into the countryside, Lieuten-ant Colonel Cheatham silently thanked his lucky stars; if the NVA commander had been more alert, he would have realized that the rump of 2/5 remaining on the field could have been defeated in detail by the suddenly superior NVA force.

As soon as the smoke cleared at Troi Bridge that evening, January 31, Lieutenant Colonel Cheatham got on the radio to the regimental CP and started raising holy hell. Cheatham's experi-ence in Vietnam had imbued him with an intense disdain for the propensity of higher headquarters to commit units to multiple events piecemeal and attach out infantry companies willy-nilly to strange battalions. He received no satisfaction. The regimental commander, who might have gone to bat for him or at least calmed him down, was out of the country on R and R. The regimental exec replied that the order detaching Fox/2/5 had come from Task Force X-Ray, and that there was nothing 5th Marines could do.

Fox/2/5 was in terrific shape when it left Troi Bridge for Phu Bai. Though the unit had sustained several losses around the bridge on January 31, hardly anyone was on R and R; all the men who had been lightly wounded, injured, or sick had been returned to duty; and the few replacements required had arrived. Thus Fox/2/5 was nearly at full strength, well rested, and well inte-grated. It had its full complement of lieutenants and staff non-commissioned officers, and all the squads were led by sergeants or seasoned corporals.

When Fox/2/5 reached Phu Bai by truck late in the afternoon, the company commander, Captain Mike Downs, was ordered to report to the Task Force X-Ray CP. There Downs met with the task force operations officer and his assistant, both lieutenant colonels. Though Downs knew nothing of the situation in Hue or even around Phu Bai, he could not imagine why the CP was in a state of confusion bordering on panic. Following a useless briefing, Downs was sent over to the 1st Marines CP, where the regimental operations officer told him that Fox/2/5 would be flying up to Hue the next day to operate with Lieutenant Colonel Mark Gravel's 1/1. Once again, Captain Downs emerged from a sketchy briefing with only the vaguest sense of what was going on in Hue. As far as Downs could figure it, there were enemy troops inside Hue, and Fox/2/5 was needed to push them out. The impression Downs had was that his company would be back in Phu Bai pretty quickly, in a few days at most.

Like Golf/2/5 before it, Fox/2/5 was going to Hue without its packs. The troops had grounded their personal possessions before going into the attack at Troi Bridge, and there had not been time to retrieve them when the call came to report to Phu Bai. All they had was ammunition, weapons, web gear, and whatever they had had the foresight to cram into their pockets.

The troops received a hot meal that evening, and everyone slept under canvas that night. On the morning of February 1, the troops learned through unofficial channels that they were bound for Hue. None of them had ever spent any time in Hue, but virtually all of them were glad to be going. Fox/2/5 had been months in the bush, had taken casualties, and had very little besides its corporate bitterness to show for the experience. Word had it that the NVA was standing and fighting in Hue—something neither the NVA nor its VC allies had ever done in the bush Fox/2/5 had tromped. Word was, Hue was the place to "get some," the ideal venue in which to exact payback for all the unavenged casualties Fox/2/5 had sustained in the bush.

Reinforced with a pair of 81mm mortars and two 106mm recoilless rifles, Fox/2/5 began lifting out of Phu Bai at 1458, February 1, aboard a small number of CH-46 transport helicopters. They were bound for the Doc Lao Park LZ. In addition to lifting out Fox/2/5, the Marine helicopters were charged with carrying a significant resupply of ammunition and other goods for 1/1 and the two Marine companies already in Hue.

The Fox/2/5 Marines and their officers were unprepared for the sporadic fire that greeted most of the helicopters as they set down on the Doc Lao Park LZ. In a few cases, the helicopters were struck by small-arms fire, which penetrated the thin metal skin and terrorized the unwitting troops inside. Fortunately, no one was injured, but the Marines charged off the helicopters' rear ramps with serious intent, certain the LZ itself was under ground assault.

Among the many terrorized by the incoming fire was a load of American news reporters who had hitched a ride into Hue aboard Mike Downs's CH-46. Shortly after landing, the company commander could account for only two of the reporters, a United Press International team. Downs surmised that the other newspeople had returned to Phu Bai, without ever leaving the helicopter.

There were not enough helicopters to fly the reinforced company the short distance to Hue in one lift, so the last squads did not arrive until 1705. By then, the leading elements of Fox/2/5 were already in a bloody fight.

Lieutenant Mike McNeil's platoon of Golf/2/5 had been battling the entire day in an effort to relieve the GVN force in the Provincial Prison, six long blocks southwest of MACV. A dogged effort had carried Captain Meadows's tired troops across the highway and about fifteen meters up the first block of Tran Cao Van Street, but the NVA's resistance had steadily stiffened. The attack had ground to a standstill. As the hours wore on, the mission was scaled back. All Meadows's and McNeil's platoon had to do was reach a small compound housing a U.S. Air Force communications contingent. The hostel was only a few blocks southwest of Highway 1, half the distance to the prison. Three blocks or six blocks, it didn't matter: Golf/2/5 remained bogged down less than a half block from its line of departure.

The eye-opener of the day for Chuck Meadows and his Marines was how many men it took to secure a row of buildings. In order to achieve this, Golf/2/5 was learning, a unit had to secure every room in every one of the structures; it had to fight a war in three dimensions rather than the usual two.

As soon as two platoons of Fox/2/5 were assembled at MACV, Lieutenant Colonel Gravel decided to send them to restore some momentum to the drive on the Air Force hostel. Captain Downs had hardly reported to Mark Gravel's CP, at MACV, before an Air Force sergeant who had lived in the hostel was attached to the company as a guide. Then Captain Downs's company marched one block southeast on Highway 1 and turned right—southwest—up Tran Cao Van, the first cross street. The entire route looked like a cyclone—or a war—had hit it.

Just before reaching Tran Cao Van, Mike Downs had met Chuck Meadows and Captain Jim Gallagher, 1/1's new operations officer. Gallagher, a communicator by trade, had recently extended his tour of duty in Vietnam to take a crack at commanding an infantry company. He had barely taken over Delta/1/1 when news of Major Walt Murphy's death had reached him. As 1/1's senior captain, he had felt obliged, despite his lack of hard infantry experience, to fly to Hue to assume Murphy's duties until a more suitable replacement could be found. Captain Gallagher had arrived aboard one of the night medevac choppers and had assumed his new duties as soon as he reached MACV. He had been up front with Chuck Meadows all day, learning on the run.

Learning on the run was Fox/2/5's operative mode, just as it had been Golf/2/5's from the beginning of duty in Hue. Learning to deal with defended urban terrain had cost Golf/2/5 two killed and five wounded on February 1—that made a total of seven killed and fifty-seven wounded in twenty-four hours. Now it was Fox/2/5's turn to pay the price of experience.

Corporal Chris Brown's squad of 2nd Lieutenant Rich Horner's 2nd Platoon took the Fox/2/5 point as soon as Chuck Meadows and Mike Downs had completed the formal turnover. At word from Lieutenant Horner, Brown's squad was to turn the corner from Highway 1 onto Tran Cao Van and attack down the right sidewalk. Another squad from Horner's platoon would follow and then peel off to attack up the left side of the treelined residential thoroughfare. The officers had already told everyone that every building on both sides of the street had to be completely secured from bottom to top before anyone could go on to the next building and that units on both sides of the street had to advance apace to avoid NVA flanking fire from second-story windows.

The Air Force sergeant–guide joined Brown's squad a few moments before the Marines were to turn the corner. The first thing he told Chris Brown was that Golf/2/5 had been trying to fight its way up the street since around sunup and that the men had had their "butts beat every time." He went on to render his opinion that the mission was "suicidal." Corporal Brown went over to Lieutenant Horner to convey the Air Force sergeant's sentiments, but Horner just shrugged his shoulders and said, "Let's move out."

Horner's platoon advanced about fifteen meters up Tran Cao Van with two squads abreast and one in reserve, a classic infantry formation. After passing through Golf/2/5, the two Marines constituting the lead fire team of Corporal Brown's squad set up behind a shoulder-high masonry wall to provide cover. This was another classic infantry maneuver, strictly by the book. Though Fox/2/5 had never fought in a town and the junior troops had never been adequately trained to undertake house-to-house combat, the troop leaders knew very well how to feel their way into hostile terrain. It was about then, however, that Corporal Brown, Lieutenant Horner, and Captain Downs went beyond the knowledge that had been keeping them and large numbers of Marines like them alive in the bush. It was then that Fox/2/5 learned what the term *mean streets* really signifies.

Private First Class Louis Gasbarrini moved out first. He stepped from behind the wall and scuttled down the sidewalk to the nearest tree. Lance Corporal Charles Campbell went next, up and over the wall. Before Campbell had hit the ground, Gasbarrini had been seriously wounded in the arm by a burst of AK-47 fire that could have come from anywhere. Someone yelled, "Corpsman, up!" and Hospital Corpsman 3rd Class James Gosselin, a twenty-six-year-old former Green Beret, charged into the open from behind the wall. He was halfway to Gasbarrini when he was shot dead in his tracks, Fox/2/5's first fatality in Hue.

No sooner had Doc Gosselin fallen than the NVA trained their fire on Corporal Brown; the Air Force sergeant; and Private

Stanley Murdock, Brown's radioman. No doubt the NVA were drawn to the whip antenna on Murdock's squad radio. Lance Corporal Carnell Poole was a few steps behind the three men when the automatic-weapons fire reached out at them. Poole distinctly saw the stream of bullets pin Murdock to a wall at his back; the sheer force of the bullets held the radioman on his feet. The firing stopped, but Murdock just stood there, holding his M-16 loosely at his side, gasping for air every few seconds. In extreme slow motion, before Lance Corporal Poole or any of the other shocked onlookers could act, Private Murdock's eyes glazed over and the gasping stopped. Fox/2/5 had sustained its second death in a matter of seconds. The Air Force sergeant was seriously wounded by the same burst.

Despite the gunfire spraying the back side of the wall—or because of it—several members of Brown's squad streaked into the street, intent upon reaching the apparently safer left side. Most of the men made it to cover, but Corporal David Collins, Private First Class William Henschel, and Private First Class Cristobal Figueroa-Perez were shot off their feet. When the dust settled, none of them was moving.

As Chris Brown shrugged off the shock of near sudden death, Lieutenant Horner's piercing yell reached him: "Move it out!" Brown looked up, but there was no one around him. For a second, the squad leader didn't know what to do. Then he went into automatic overdrive—he moved on training and instinct. Brown whipped out from behind the wall and zigzagged down the sidewalk. When it seemed the right time to dive in, he landed next to Lance Corporal Campbell, who told Brown that, every time he tried to fire back at the NVA in the buildings, bullets kicked cement dust into his face.

Corporal Brown yelled to Private First Class Gasbarrini, who was in front of everyone. Gasbarrini yelled back that he had been hit in the arm and that he was playing dead because he was afraid to move behind the nearest cover.

Corporal Brown's squad was stymied. If anyone made a move, NVA soldiers in the buildings overlooking the street fired into Tran Cao Van. Brown sent word back to Lieutenant Horner that Gasbarrini was wounded and beyond reach. Horner sent word forward to Brown that he was trying to get a tank up to cover a rescue effort. Brown ordered everyone who could to withdraw back behind the wall. Then Fox/2/5 settled in to wait. There wasn't anything else anyone could do. Minutes later, Lieutenant Colonel Gravel ordered Fox/2/5 to call it a day and return to MACV as soon as the company could police up its casualties.

It seemed to Chris Brown that hours passed before two Marine M-48 tanks turned into Tran Cao Van and chugged toward Private First Class Gasbarrini. When the lead tank pulled up even with the wall Brown was using as a sanctuary, he gingerly stepped out behind the armored vehicle and followed it warily down the right side of the street. The tank passed Gasbarrini and stopped, a steel wall to protect the evacuation. When Chris Brown leaned down to help the wounded man, a stream of bullets reached out toward them. Brown felt warm fluid streak over his outstretched hands; he was certain Gasbarrini had been wounded again, but it was only water. A round had gone through Gasbarrini's canteen. Brown pulled the wounded man behind the tank, and other members of the squad helped Gasbarrini toward the rear.

As the lead tank stood guard and probed the surrounding buildings with fire from its .50-caliber cupola machine gun, members of Brown's squad warily convened in the street to lift their wounded and dead comrades onto the flat rear deck of the second tank. Four of the men—Doc Gosselin, Private Murdock, Corporal Collins, and Private First Class Henschel—appeared to be dead. A fifth, Private First Class Figueroa-Perez, appeared to be seriously injured.

As the rear tank, which was also firing its .50-caliber machine gun, pulled back, a B-40 rocket streaked out from a second-story window and struck it squarely on the side of the engine compartment. Two of the bodies on the rear deck, which was over the engine, were thrown to the street. Immediately, piercing screams erupted from one of the bodies. Several Marines ventured back to the tank to see who it was and why.

The screaming man was Private First Class William Henschel. He had been shot in the head in his bid to cross Tran Cao Van, and knocked unconscious. It was no wonder his spooked comrades had mistaken him for dead; his gruesome head wound had looked fatal, and there had been no time to conduct an adequate check in the middle of bullet-swept Tran Cao Van. When the B-40 blew Henschel off the tank, the shock of the blast apparently roused him. A closer inspection revealed that Henschel's left leg was missing below the knee. No one could tell if it had been blown off by the B-40 or if the tank had backed over it. It didn't matter; the leg was gone. Henschel was known in Fox/2/5 as the "Marine Doc." Though he had no formal first-aid training, he carried a Unit One aid pack, just like the Navy corpsmen. He still had it when his shocked and dazed comrades peeled him off the surface of Tran Cao Van. Its contents were used to affix a tourniquet and control the bleeding of his leg. The head wound turned out to be superficial.

After the tanks pulled back around the corner to Highway 1, one more absolutely motionless Marine still lay in an exposed position about twenty meters down Tran Cao Van. A nose count revealed that he was Private Roberto de la Riva-Vara. Every effort had been made to reach de la Riva-Vara's body, but the tanks had been unable to shield the rescuers, and the NVA had staked it out, certain they could kill any rescuers who ventured out after it. Lieutenant Horner had had enough. With nothing to show for it, Fox/2/5's 2nd Platoon had suffered fifteen casualties, of whom three were known dead, one (Figueroa-Perez) was expected to die, and one (de la Riva-Vara) was presumed dead. The lieutenant asked Captain Downs to please call it a day; there was no sense losing more men to rescue de la Riva-Vara's body.

Mike Downs was not going to leave anyone behind. After the wounded and dead were unloaded from the tank and sent on their way to MACV, Downs ordered both tanks back up Tran Cao Van to cover Lieutenant Horner's recovery of de la Riva-Vara's body. Firing their machine guns as they went, the tanks advanced cautiously past the spot at which one of them had already been hit by a B-40. Nothing much happened. The NVA fired their AK-47s at the tanks, but no more B-40s were fired. The tanks moved forward, and the infantrymen followed them. As they reached de la Riva-Vara, he waved his arms a little. He had been shot in both legs and had been cannily playing dead. On the way back, Lieutenant Horner was wounded.

The Fox/2/5 casualties were taken back to MACV without further incident. Later that night, all the serious casualties of the day, including Lieutenant Horner, were medevacked off the LZ in Doc Lao Park. Unlike the bloody medevac effort of the previous night, the convoy to the LZ was led by one of the M-48 tanks, which simply drove through houses and courtyards along a path the NVA snipers could never have staked out in advance.

Before dawn, news arrived that Private First Class Cristobal Figueroa-Perez had died of his wounds in Phu Bai's triage center. This good and popular Marine's death was keenly felt, but the part that really set everyone on edge was knowing that his wife was going to get the proceeds of his $10,000 life-insurance policy. A week earlier Figueroa-Perez had received a Dear John letter from her; she had moved in with another man.

Lieutenant Colonel Ernie Cheatham was still at Troi Bridge with the 2/5 CP group and two infantry companies when, late in the afternoon of February 1, Task Force X-Ray ordered him to lead his CP group and Hotel/2/5 to Phu Bai for eventual duty in Hue. With enormous reluctance Cheatham turned operational control of Echo/2/5 over to 5th Marines and left it alone to guard Troi Bridge. He could only hope that the NVA battalion that 2/5 had chased off the day before did not tumble to the fact that the tables had been turned and that the Troi Bridge's twin highway and railroad spans were again ripe for the plucking.

Upon his arrival at Phu Bai, Cheatham was appalled by the level of confusion and panic he found. Internal guard posts had been set out throughout the sprawling camp, and it seemed to the battalion commander that he was challenged by panicky sentries every five to ten meters. Though damage from rocket detonations was apparent here and there throughout the camp, Cheatham did not feel the level of danger at Phu Bai was much higher than normal.

Ernie Cheatham had assumed that he was going to accompany Hotel/2/5 to Hue in the morning, but he discovered, to his chagrin, that the infantry company had been assigned to 1st Marines for service with 1/1. There was no word as to what Cheatham or his headquarters elements were to do. Cheatham

couldn't believe what was going on. Unfortunately, he didn't
know the half of it.

After Fox/2/5 bedded down for the night in an ARVN
compound adjacent to MACV, Captain Mike Downs was sum-
moned to the 1/1 CP and told that Task Force X-Ray wanted
1/1 to launch a night attack to relieve the Thua Thien Provincial
Prison. Since Fox/2/5 was in better shape than Alpha/1/1 or
Golf/2/5, Lieutenant Colonel Mark Gravel wanted Fox/2/5 to
carry out the order. Downs had no idea that Golf/2/5 had tried
and failed to reach the prison during the day, so he asked where
the objective was and how he could reach it. As soon as Lieutenant Colonel Gravel pointed it out on his map, Downs commented
that the folks at Task Force X-Ray were absolutely crazy. Gravel
replied that orders were orders, so the company commander asked
the battalion staff officers what they thought lay between MACV
and the prison. On reflection, it was agreed that Fox/2/5 would
attack directly down Le Loi Street, the broad boulevard fronting
the Perfume River. To do the job, Gravel was willing to attach
two of his Marine M-48 tanks to Fox/2/5. However, under
orders from very high authority, Fox/2/5 would not be permitted to call for indirect fire from organic 60mm or 81mm mortars, and certainly not from any friendly artillery batteries in
range of Hue. The more Downs heard, the worse things looked.

The maps were vague and there were no aerial photos of the
prison—no way to plan a break-in. When Captain Downs asked
what the best approach was, someone said he should break in by
way of the adjacent Provincial Administration complex. When
Downs naively asked if anyone had contacted the province chief
for advice, a MACV advisor revealed there were NVA .51-caliber
machine guns on the roof and an NLF flag flying in front of the
building. Downs's temper erupted, but he nonetheless called the
Fox/2/5 CP and told his company gunny to get the troops
saddled up.

Before Mike Downs left the 1/1 CP, he asked Mark Gravel
if he could write a message to Task Force X-Ray to try to explain
the situation around the prison. Gravel agreed. Downs then
hooked up with the Marine major who had accompanied the

Marine tanks into Hue on January 31, and the major agreed to help him draft the message and to send it out over his signature. The two ironed out the wording and sent a lengthy, detailed, and blunt message via the 1/1 CP. In the message Captain Downs and the major explained that the prison was six blocks from MACV; that the NVA controlled all the streets on the southwest side of Highway 1; that Golf/2/5 and Fox/2/5 had been unable to fight their way a half block southwest of the highway in bloody, day-long attacks; and that no one at 1/1 or MACV even knew if there were any prisoners left in the prison. Shortly after this message was sent, Task Force X-Ray canceled the night attack.

When Mike Downs returned to his CP, he ordered Gunnery Sergeant Ed Van Valkenburgh to stand the troops down for the night. The company gunny was so relieved that he admitted to the company commander, "I don't think I could've gone down that street again, Sir." Downs thought for a moment and replied, "Gunny, the way they wanted us to go tonight would have made the fight we had this afternoon seem like a walk in the sun."

Sometime after Fox/2/5 stood down, Task Force X-Ray once again ordered 1/1 to launch a coordinated attack toward the prison at dawn, seizing intermediate objectives along the way. If the prison could not be taken in one fell swoop, it would be the object of Task Force X-Ray's long-term plan. The fixation of Task Force X-Ray—or perhaps higher headquarters—on relieving the prison ultimately shaped the course of the battle south of the Perfume.

— 14 —

The ARVN position inside the Citadel improved dramatically on February 2. While U.S. Marine helicopters were ferrying the 9th ARVN Airborne Battalion directly into the 1st ARVN Division CP compound, the Hoc Bao Company and the 2nd and 7th ARVN Airborne battalions attacked to the southwest and seized Tay Loc Airfield from the 802nd NVA Battalion. As the day went by, the rear echelon of the 4th Battalion, 2nd ARVN Regiment, and a company of the 3rd Battalion, 1st ARVN Regiment, were helilifted into the 1st ARVN Division CP compound. The 1st Battalion, 3rd ARVN Regiment, went into action clearing NVA troops off the northwestern Citadel wall itself.

The effect of the ARVN reinforcements and their multiple attacks was perceptible and profound. It was evident as the day's fighting wore on that the main body of the reinforced 6th NVA Regiment was going to ground inside the Citadel wall, which was honeycombed with bunkers built by the Japanese during World War II, and in the stoutly built and easily defended masonry buildings throughout the Citadel. Brigadier General Ngo Quang Truong sensed that the fight to liberate the Citadel would be long and costly, but he felt in his bones that his troops had the initiative and the upper hand. He believed the 6th NVA Regiment had allowed itself to become entangled in a losing rearguard display that was more of a political gesture than a solid military threat.

In other action involving ARVN units based around Hue, the 4th NVA Regiment finally began moving on the 1st ARVN Engineer Battalion cantonment, south of the city. The engineers hung on through the day, but they considered their situation precarious. The 4th NVA Regiment's 804th NVA Battalion also continued to press in on the encircled 4th Battalion, 3rd ARVN Regiment, east of the city, but the ARVN battalion grimly held out despite a rising toll of dead and wounded.

South of the Perfume, February 2 was largely a day of consolidation. At 0950 a platoon of Golf/2/5 set out from the MACV Compound to rescue a handful of U.S. servicemen manning the MACV radio station. This vital communications link, on the northern edge of the cane field east of Highway 1, had not been molested by the NVA. Indeed, it is probable the NVA had not targeted it despite its unmistakable antenna array.

An NVA unit staked out along Highway 1 south of MACV fired several thousand AK-47 rounds and at least a dozen 60mm mortar rounds at the Golf/2/5 platoon. The Marines answered in kind and easily pierced the NVA blocking positions, though three Americans were superficially wounded. The relief force reached the radio station and escorted the technicians back to MACV after the facility was disabled.

From noon on, Captain Chuck Meadows and his two Golf/ 2/5 platoons were involved in a battle royal over possession of the massive main building of Hue University. On the south corner of Highway 1 and Le Loi Street and dominating most of the neighborhood and the nearby riverbank, the huge structure was the first objective assigned to 1/1 in Task Force X-Ray's desired push to the Thua Thien Provincial Prison and the Provincial Administration complex. After crossing Highway 1, Golf/ 2/5 waded directly into intense NVA small-arms fire, intermittent mortar fire, .51-caliber machine-gun fire from the Citadel wall, and even recoilless rifle fire from farther up Le Loi Street. The Marines responded with every weapon they could bring to bear—including 81mm mortars, in use for the first time in Hue. However, though higher headquarters offered to send Marine air to support the attack, Hue remained closed in and no air attacks could be launched. At length, around 1445, Meadows's cut-down infantry company managed to enter the masonry structure, which had two-and-a-half stories and was built around a huge courtyard. The company began a room-by-room clearing operation.

Captain Mike Downs's Fox/2/5 spent most of February 2 widening the perimeter around MACV—clearing and securing several ARVN and government buildings that butted against the southeast, northwest, and northeast sides of the MACV Compound.

One of the buildings that the 3rd Platoon of Fox/2/5 had secured was the Hue Directorate of Police. As Lance Corporal Forrest Towe was searching the second floor, he heard a faint noise from over his head. The day before, when he had heard he was going to Hue, Towe had been one ecstatic Marine. Though a dental appointment had caused him to miss the one-day street-fighting course Vietnam-bound Marines at that time received, he was up for "some house-to-house" after seven months of literally beating the bush for an enemy that never stood and fought. Towe still liked tossing live hand grenades through doorways, but only one day after landing in Doc Lao Park he was a little less enamored of stepping into smoke-filled rooms to spray their interiors with his M-16. Combat in a built-up area was proving to be extremely nerve-racking even after a day in which no enemy soldiers had been encountered. So now there was that rustling going on over his head, and it could not be ignored.

Over Towe's head was a hole in the ceiling, and a charred rafter beam lay wedged against the second floor of the police building, through the hole, and into the half-story attic. "What the hell," Towe thought, and he shinnied up the rafter beam. As Towe's head came level with the attic floor, he saw two men standing over a Soviet-pattern RPD light machine gun that was aimed out a calf-high ventilation hole. The two men, who were dressed in civilian clothing, were Vietnamese. When they heard Towe, they turned in unison and held up their hands. "Friend! Friend!" they yelled in unison. "Sure," Towe thought, "Everyone's a friend when you have the drop on him." Next the two men started shouting, "Police! Police! Police!" Towe yelled back, "Get away from the gun," and motioned for them to back away from the RPD. The two were a little slow on the uptake, so Lance Corporal Towe fired a few M-16 rounds into the RPD's receiver assembly. That got the two Vietnamese men moving! It turned out that one of the men had been literally sitting on a .38-caliber Smith and Wesson revolver, which Towe stuck into his belt. By now there was a Marine fire team rummaging through the room below, so Towe called down to warn them that he was sending down a couple of NVA suspects. Then he prodded the men down the rafter beam.

When Lance Corporal Towe's prisoners reached MACV, the two claimed to be policemen and explained away their civilian dress as an attempt to blend into the populace in the event they were captured by the NVA. In due course the identities they claimed were confirmed.

Early in the morning of February 2, 1st Marines arranged to send a five-truck resupply convoy to Hue. Captain Ron Christmas's Hotel/2/5, which had spent the night in Phu Bai after being dispatched from Troi Bridge, was designated as the convoy escort. It would ride in seven 6 × 6 trucks. In addition to his infantry company, Captain Christmas would have at his disposal the two Army M-55 quad-.50 trucks that had gone up to Hue on January 31 and returned to Phu Bai on February 1. Finally, hitching a ride on the ammunition and supply trucks would be two officers and about two dozen Marines from Alpha/1/1 who had been stranded in Quang Tri on January 31 and who had arrived at Phu Bai at first light.

The twelve-truck convoy was supposed to get under way at 1000, but it was delayed indefinitely because of the many reports concerning the enemy's control of the approaches to Hue. Moreover, aerial observers continued to report that the cloud ceiling was too low for air support. The decision was to wait and see if the cloud ceiling lifted.

At 1100, 1st Marines was given direct control of two Marine Ontos from the 1st Tank Battalion and a pair of Army M-42 tracked dual-40mm gun carriers (known as Dusters). Though these potent weapons were added to Captain Christmas's force, the convoy continued to wait for a clearer sky. Finally, at 1417, Christmas received the order to leave Phu Bai.

Corporal Herbert Watkins, a squad leader with Alpha/1/1's 1st Platoon, wasn't sure where Hue was or what he would be facing once he got there. All Watkins had heard was that Alpha/1/1 was catching hell in Hue. Watkins was aboard the lead truck with two fellow 1st Platoon squad leaders, Corporal Bill Stubbs and Corporal Richard Pettit, and 1st Lieutenant Donald Perkins, the artillery forward observer assigned to Alpha/1/1. Corporal Watkins was reasonably eager to get up to Hue, but Corporal Stubbs was not eager at all. Stubbs had only a few days left to serve in Vietnam, and he was understandably unhappy to be going into a big battle. But the company first sergeant, who was remaining in Phu Bai to help run the rear CP, said everyone had to go, including Corporal Stubbs.

Corporal Bob Meadows, a Hotel/2/5 squad leader, had received the word that there were "a few snipers loose" in Hue and that his platoon was going up there to clear them out. Meadows had gotten into a conversation with the Army sergeant in command of the dual-40mm Dusters, and the sergeant had said that he had heard on his tactical radio that most of Hue was in NVA hands. Corporal Meadows didn't know what to think.

When Captain Ron Christmas had received the order to mount out to Hue, he hadn't known much more about the situation there than Corporal Meadows and Corporal Watkins, and he had known very little about conditions along Highway 1. Fortunately, the morning delay had afforded Christmas an opportunity to pick up some information. Though he somehow missed connecting with Lieutenant Bill Rogers of Golf/2/5, he did speak with several wounded Fox/2/5 and Golf/2/5 Marines who were passing through Phu Bai. From them he learned that any convoy going up Highway 1 might come under fire from NVA or VC units, and Christmas decided to act on the assumption that he and his Marines would be facing a running fight. Extra ammunition was issued to all hands, and every Marine was ordered to face outboard, ready to fire at any structure or position from which enemy soldiers fired at the convoy. Also, the Alpha/1/1 Marines, who were interspersed among the supply trucks, were loaded for bear. They each carried 400 or 500 rounds for an M-16, all the grenades they could manage, and three or four M-72 LAAW rockets. Corporal Herbert Watkins had twenty-one magazines for his M-16, plus three or four bandoleers of 5.56mm ammunition.

As the long delay continued, Captain Christmas formulated a concrete plan for dealing with ambushes. Doing so was typical of this twenty-seven-year-old professional officer. A picture-perfect Marine who had served at Marine Barracks, Washington, D.C., before assignment to Vietnam, Ron Christmas was deservedly known as a comer—a young officer marked by his superiors early in his career for eventual high command. Christmas's response to the troubling information he heard from men who had been to Hue and back was an immediate-action plan: If the convoy was fired on, it was to try to run the gauntlet while everyone returned the fire; if a vehicle was disabled, the vehicles ahead and behind would stop just long enough to pick up the men from the damaged vehicle, which was to be abandoned. If the convoy was stopped altogether by an obstruction or blown bridge, everyone was to disembark, form a perimeter, and attack and clear any enemy positions. As soon as the plan was promulgated, Christmas used the remainder of the delay to rehearse everyone for the various eventualities.

Just before the convoy got rolling, Corporal Herbert Watkins looked around at the faces of the Marines in the trucks. Everyone looked anxious.

The trucks started rolling, and all hands locked and loaded their weapons. As the lead truck rolled through the gate onto Highway 1, Marines by the road called, "Give 'em hell."

A short distance up Highway 1, the convoy passed an ARVN cantonment on the right side of the road. Many of the ARVN soldiers were standing behind an immense barbed-wire fence, watching the convoy go by. To Corporal Watkins, they looked like "a bunch of chickens in a henhouse, just staring at the trucks." It didn't seem right that they were there and Watkins was heading toward Hue.

Soon, the trucks were passing blown-up buildings in the string of roadside villages north of Phu Bai. The people were back. Many of the villagers were standing in the doorways of their ruined homes, sullenly watching the convoy pass along the highway.

Several kilometers along Highway 1, the convoy crossed a small bridge. There were signs that someone had tried and failed to drop the structure into the creek it spanned. Just beyond the bridge, at the spot where the main body of Alpha/1/1 had met the Marine tanks on January 31—only two days ago—the convoy stopped briefly beside the destroyed ARVN M-41 tank. The charred crewman was still leaning out of the turret hatch. A sniper plinked a few rounds out at the convoy, but the trucks got rolling again. No one was hit, and the vehicles quickly outran the gunfire.

The convoy entered the built-up area south of the Phu Cam Canal, sped across the An Cuu Bridge, passed the traffic circle, and rolled most of the way across the cane-field causeway without taking serious fire. As it neared the southeastern edge of the built-up area, only 320 meters from MACV, Corporal Bob Meadows felt the pressure lift from his shoulders. A superb bush Marine, Meadows instinctively equated cities with safety. He had been sure the convoy was going to get hit as it crossed the cane field, but that had not happened; Meadows was starting to feel at ease. That was when NVA soldiers, in the houses and beyond the treeline, unleashed a withering fire on the convoy.

In compliance with Captain Christmas's orders, the lead truck barreled off the causeway and straight up the highway, between a long row of two- and three-story buildings. Marines in all the trucks fired into the masonry structures, which loomed over their heads all along the highway. Corporal Meadows saw an NVA machine gun firing from the roof of a gas station and ordered the men in his truck to fire at it. At that moment, one of the Army Dusters started up the right side of the column from the rear, forcing the truck drivers to pull to the left. The farther up the street the trucks penetrated, the more intense the enemy fire became. NVA soldiers were hanging out of the windows, firing down on the trucks. Glancing ahead from his place in the second truck in the column, Corporal Meadows saw a huge pillar of smoke and debris rise from the roadway. Apparently, NVA sappers had set off a command-detonated mine. Fortunately, the detonation was premature; the lead truck was still short of the explosion.

In the lead truck, Corporal Herbert Watkins missed seeing or hearing the mine detonation. He had climbed up on top of the ammo boxes and was lying on his back, firing his M-16 up at the NVA. His attention was totally focused on the AK-47 bursts that were chewing up the ammo boxes beneath him. The next thing Watkins knew, he was flying through the air. As he landed in a large crater, he thought the truck had hit a mine. However, the crater had been there already when the panicky driver had plowed right into it at top speed. Watkins crawled over to the truck and saw that Lieutenant Donald Perkins, the forward observer, was pinned in the crater. The truck's rear wheel was on his chest. Watkins told the lieutenant that everything would be all right, but the corporal knew better. Perkins's chest was crushed, and there was no way to extricate him short of driving or towing the truck out of the crater.

The truck driver was long gone. As soon as the vehicle had stopped, he had run for it. Under heavy fire, Corporal Richard

Pettit ran around to the driver's side, hopped in, and tried to move the truck. No luck; it wouldn't move. Corporal Watkins and Corporal Bill Stubbs stayed with Lieutenant Perkins, firing back at the NVA in the houses across from them. At length, since the truck was not moving, Watkins got up on the running board on the protected passenger's side of the cab and told Pettit that the truck was just sinking deeper into the crater. Pettit climbed out through the passenger's door just as a burst of gunfire engulfed the driver's side.

While Corporal Pettit had been trying to move the truck, Marines in the trucks to the rear reacted as they had rehearsed. Hotel/2/5 hurtled from its vehicles and set up a base of fire, suppressing by gunfire every NVA position it was possible to reach.

The moment the convoy halted, Corporal Bob Meadows had led his squad off the second truck and started advancing up the right side of the street, which seemed to be taking less fire than the left side. The Duster that had been trying to pass Meadows's truck when the mine detonated had squeezed past that truck and advanced beyond the lead truck. As Meadows and his squad followed the Duster, the Army antiaircraft gunners had all but taken down a three-story building. On the way past the crater, Corporal Meadows had glanced in and saw Lieutenant Perkins. The rear wheel of the truck was on the officer's chest, and only his head and one arm were showing. In spite of himself, Meadows thought, "You're a dead man."

As the Dusters, Ontos, quad-.50 trucks, and truck-mounted .50-caliber machine guns virtually demolished several buildings, squads of Hotel/2/5 Marines launched assaults directly into two or three of the buildings overlooking the stalled vehicles. Most of the NVA fled. When the buildings had been cleared, everyone behind the crater converged on the trucks, mounted up, and continued to fire into the buildings. Corporal Meadows's squad and several others had by then advanced on foot about half the distance to MACV. It was as risky to return as it was to advance, so they kept going.

When Corporal Watkins and Corporal Pettit returned from the cab of their truck to the crater, Lieutenant Perkins was dead.

Unaware of what was going on behind them, they and Corporal Bill Stubbs kept blasting away at the NVA in the houses on the left side of the street. Watkins thought it was like fighting a hive of bees. Plenty of fire still came from buildings overlooking the lead truck and from other buildings farther up the street. To Watkins, it looked like NVA were all over the place.

Suddenly, without warning, the rest of the convoy careened around the stalled lead truck and ran the rest of the way to MACV. It is doubtful anyone knew the three corporals were still manning the crater because a dead officer was pinned beneath their truck. Captain Christmas assumed the men in the lead truck had obeyed orders and climbed aboard another vehicle.

Watkins, Pettit, and Stubbs remained marooned beside the truck and Lieutenant Perkins's body for many minutes—none of them knew how long. The incoming fire was intense, and just the three of them were left there. There was no way they could get the lieutenant's body out. None of them had ever been to Hue; none of them knew where they were. They only knew that MACV was somewhere farther up the bullet-swept street.

All three corporals were slightly injured, and they were all shaken by their predicament—Stubbs most of all, because that street at that moment was no place to be with less than a week left in Vietnam. Watkins had a gash in his foot and a painful hematoma on his back, where he had landed when the truck hit the crater. It didn't help their outlook when they remembered that they were hiding behind an ammunition truck.

They made one last effort to free Lieutenant Perkins's body. When that failed, they left. Their only possible course of action was to fight their way up Highway 1 to MACV, however far it might be. The three were experienced bush fighters; they made the most of the ample cover and wriggled along houses and walls, block by interminable block. The NVA were everywhere, behind cover, firing from unseen positions at ground level and from upper-story windows and roofs.

It seemed to take forever for the three corporals to get to MACV, but they did it, and without being shot. When they got inside the friendly compound, they reported that Lieutenant Perkins was still back at the truck and that another truck or a tank would be needed to move the stalled vehicle. Corporal Pettit went back with a tank and a Hotel/2/5 fire team, Corporal Stubbs was sent to rejoin Alpha/1/1, and Corporal Watkins was sent to the MACV dispensary to have the gash in his foot bandaged. When he got there, the dispensary was full of dead and seriously wounded people. An Army medic was just tying off the bandage when Pettit returned with Lieutenant Perkins's body. As soon as Watkins and Pettit officially identified the lieutenant, they also returned to Alpha/1/1.

At about 1600, Hotel/2/5 and the Alpha/1/1 stragglers crossed Highway 1 to join the main body of Alpha/1/1 at Hue University. By then, the NVA resistance in the massive structure had been subdued by Golf/2/5, and Alpha/1/1 was mopping up and setting in its own defenses. When the Alpha/1/1 stragglers reached the university, command of their company passed from Gunnery Sergeant J L Canley to 2nd Lieutenant Ray Smith, who had arrived with the day's convoy. Though Lieutenant Smith had only been in-country for a short time, he was Alpha/1/1's senior lieutenant. The company executive officer had been sent home the day before, at the conclusion of his tour.

Hotel/2/5 relieved Alpha/1/1 of responsibility for securing the university. The new arrivals filtered through the classrooms, looking for NVA stragglers and locating the upper-story windows with the best vistas. Though the Hotel/2/5 Marines were told that the enormous building had been cleared already, their first experience in city fighting had taught them to take no chances, and they grenaded or shot up every room they passed. The company's 60mm mortar section set up in the courtyard in the center of the university block and immediately began firing at suspected NVA strongholds to the southwest while observers in the upper-story windows called the shots. As Hotel/2/5 was clearing rooms and setting in at the university, Alpha/1/1 crossed Le Loi Street to clear several small government buildings along the south bank of the Perfume River, southwest of the Nguyen Hoang Bridge.

At 1815 the NVA attacked the Alpha/1/1–Hotel/2/5 perimeter around Hue University and Doc Lao Park. The Communists delivered intense fire from across the river and from the southwest, down Le Loi Street. One of the Marine M-48 tanks that had been in continuous action since noon on January 31 was struck and disabled, though not destroyed, by a 75mm recoilless rifle round. Alpha/1/1 and Hotel/2/5 Marines blew off 4,300 M-16 rounds, 2,000 M-60 machine-gun rounds, ninety-five M-79 grenades, eighty-five 90mm tank rounds, and twenty-five 81mm mortar rounds. When the exchange finally subsided around 2200, no one could guess what damage all that fire had caused, but one Marine was dead, eight needed to be mede-vacked, and thirteen were treated for minor wounds and returned to duty. Intermittent sniper fire from across the river continued to strike Alpha/1/1's riverfront positions all night. The Marines returned fire in kind, though probably without much effect.

February 2 was Fox/2/5's first chance to look around the "big city," and most of the troops felt out of place after weeks and months of tromping the bush. When Lance Corporal Ernie Weiss unexpectedly stepped into a pharmacy on a street just east of MACV, he remembered that he had lost his toothbrush a week before his arrival in Hue; his mouth felt cruddy. Though everyone had been warned against looting, Lance Corporal Weiss could not overcome the impulse to replace his lost toothbrush at the expense of the missing pharmacist whose shop Weiss felt he was liberating. The way Weiss was thinking, the toothbrush was the most important thing in the world. When he finally went to use it for the first time that night, it was missing. No wonder. By then, Ernie Weiss had had a terrible day.

After Lance Corporal Weiss liberated the pharmacy, his platoon was sent back to MACV. Then, toward evening, the entire company was called out. Unbelievably, on direct orders from Task Force X-Ray, Captain Mike Downs had again been ordered to attack toward the Thua Thien Provincial Prison and eject the NVA and VC who were holding it and the Provincial Administra-tion complex.

Captain Downs left his 2nd Platoon at MACV as the com-pany reserve and crossed Highway 1 with his company CP group and Fox/2/5's 1st and 3rd platoons. The assigned route was southwest along Truong Dinh Street, the treelined thoroughfare along the edge of Hue University, between Le Loi and Tran Cao Van streets.

By the time the 3rd Platoon, which was leading, had slowly made its way down the first block of Truong Dinh, directly across from Hue University's southeastern wall, one of the squad leaders, Sergeant John Maloney, had somehow wound up on the point. As Maloney was rounding the next corner, the Marine right behind Gunnery Sergeant Ed Van Valkenburgh saw something that upset him, and he unloaded a whole M-16 magazine into a building across the intersection. Right away, an NVA across the intersection fired most of an AK-47 magazine into Sergeant Maloney, who went down hard beside a courtyard wall. However, all the Marines behind him were spared from walking into what Gunny Van Valkenburgh immediately recognized as a carefully plotted ambush.

The instant the shooting started, the tank that was accompanying the two Marine platoons had been hit by a B-40, and a small sliver had struck Captain Mike Downs, albeit without much effect. As soon as the tank was hit, the driver had gone bonkers and started backing up, out of any possible line of fire. The barely controlled monster machine lurched into a telephone pole, and, in no time, all the phone cable that had been strung above the street was wound into the wheel assembly, as was a roll of barbed wire that had been lining one side of the street.

As soon as Sergeant Maloney went down, Sergeant Willard Scott, the 3rd Platoon right guide, ordered the lead fire-team leader, Lance Corporal Jim Yates, to take over the squad and get Maloney out of the line of fire. Yates was scared half to death, but he moved up. From another location overlooking the intersection, an NVA soldier opened fire. A bullet that ricocheted off the wall struck Yates in the neck, and he went down. Yates felt around in his neck and found the bullet lodged next to his windpipe. He crawled backwards out of the line of fire and ducked through the courtyard gate, where several other Marines had gone to ground. A moment later, another Marine rolled through the courtyard gate. He had a bullet wound in the shoulder.

The firing was less than a minute old, and the entire 3rd

Platoon was under cover except for Sergeant Maloney, who still lay where he had fallen. The platoon commander, 2nd Lieutenant Donald Hausrath, moved up to the courtyard and assessed the situation. Then he turned to Lance Corporal John Griswold and said, "Griswold, you take your fire team out there on the street and bring Sergeant Maloney back." Griswold was a veteran, as experienced a bush Marine as Fox/2/5 had. Nevertheless, the order caught him short. He stared at the lieutenant for a moment and asked, "You mean by ourselves?" He was incredulous. "Yeah," Lieutenant Hausrath rejoined, "by yourselves. We'll give you support." Griswold looked at the other two members of his fire team—Lance Corporal Ernie Weiss and Private First Class Mike Sowards—and said, "You gotta be shitting me." But Griswold went back out into the street, leading Weiss and Sowards toward the intersection.

Lance Corporal Griswold's team had almost inched up to Sergeant Maloney's body when the NVA cut loose again. There was so much fire going *crack-crack-crack-crack-crack* right over their heads that Lance Corporal Weiss could not even hear himself shout, and the rounds were striking the street so close to him that puffs of dirt were constantly thrown into his face. Many of the AK-47 rounds ricocheting off the compound wall, to their left, ricocheted again off Weiss's helmet—*ping-ping-ping-ping-ping*.

Lance Corporal Griswold finally reached the corner and grabbed a handful of Sergeant Maloney's clothing. Maloney was dead, and the prone fire-team leader found that he was impossible to budge. Griswold got up on his knees and started yelling at Sowards and Weiss, "Get your asses up here and help me!" Sowards, who was right behind Griswold, looked back over his shoulder at Weiss, who said, "Go ahead, Mike. Go ahead." Neither of them jumped right in to help, but it quickly came to the point that Griswold was yelling and screaming so violently that they were more afraid of him than they were of the NVA fire. The two lurched forward, and Sowards grabbed a handful of Sergeant Maloney's clothing while Weiss started firing his M-16 at anything that even looked threatening. It wasn't good enough. In desperation Weiss yelled at Sowards, "Mike, throw me your rifle." Sowards complied with alacrity, and Weiss simultaneously fired both M-16s while Griswold and Sowards hauled the dead squad leader out of the intersection.

As Ernie Weiss fired both M-16s into a building on the opposite corner, he thought of a Marine he had once seen who had been shot in the face. Involuntarily he twisted his head to the right so the same thing wouldn't happen to him, but he never stopped firing. Bullets continued to strike the ground around him, and he knew he was going to die. That's when he lost his fear. Defiant now, Weiss turned his face toward the enemy, coolly reloaded both M-16s, and coldly fired into the window from which he was certain one or more NVA were firing at him. Weiss was livid with an unreasonable, unquenchable rage by the time a Marine armed with an M-79 appeared in front of him and began pumping 40mm fragmentation grenades into the window with which Weiss had been dueling. Weiss reloaded and fired one of his M-16s from right beside the grenadier's head. The grenadier turned and bleated, "Hey! What're you doing?" Weiss replied, "Well, get outta the way. I was here first!"

Then Captain Downs called the night attack off and ordered everyone back to MACV. When Downs left Truong Dinh Street, he was carrying a wounded Marine in his arms.

Lance Corporal Ernie Weiss helped to carry Sergeant Maloney's body back to MACV. He wouldn't have had it any other way. That evening, he cried for John Maloney.

Ironically, the Thua Thien Provincial Prison finally fell to NVA and VC forces on the night of February 2. Guided by one of the few ARVN soldiers known to have gone over to their side, the Communist troops managed to sneak into a key guard post and overwhelm the occupants. After that, the entire prison fell in short order, and 2,200 inmates—criminals and political prisoners—were freed from their cells and escorted to the Tu Dam Pagoda, south of the Phu Cam Canal. Following a political exhortation, anyone who wanted a weapon was given one. Many of the political prisoners naturally joined VC militia units, but many of the criminals disappeared into the night to ply their trades and, while they were at it, sow additional confusion and dismay among the citizens of Hue and their would-be liberators.

On February 2, Fox/2/5 sustained one Marine killed and sixteen Marines wounded. That night, a Fox/2/5 veteran of about two weeks in the bush cracked up. He lay on a bed, hallucinating, whimpering, and talking to himself, until members of his squad tied him down and one of the docs dosed him with morphine. In the morning, he was carried—babbling and raving—down to the MACV dispensary on a stretcher. Many of his fellow Marines cursed the man out loud, but many others wondered who would be the next to crack.

PART IV

THE TREASURY

Inside the Citadel on February 12, the multibattalion ARVN sweep from the 1st ARVN Division CP compound continued, but at a severely restricted pace. Outnumbered by Brigadier General Truong's ARVN battalions, the reinforced 6th NVA Regiment had lost the initiative and gone over to the defensive, but the NVA were dug in and apparently willing to fight to the last man.

Outside the Citadel, the 4th Battalion, 3rd ARVN Regiment, remained surrounded by elements of the 4th NVA Regiment's 804th NVA Battalion. In spite of heavy casualties, however, the ARVN battalion was edging closer to U.S. Marine-held positions east of MACV. The 2nd and 3rd battalions of the 3rd ARVN Regiment remained pinned against the south corner of the Citadel, unable to advance or withdraw.

Throughout the first three days of the Communist occupation of Hue, VC cadres backed by NVA units had picked up scores and then hundreds of South Vietnamese citizens who worked for or were thought to openly support the GVN. There was no end of potential victims because Hue was the major government center in the north—South Vietnam's third largest city, a provincial capital, and the seat of both district and municipal governments. Like such cities in the United States, Hue was jam-packed with politicians and bureaucrats of all ranks and stations, and all of them—and their families—were potential grist for the Communist mill.

In 1971 the official Communist chronicler of the battle for Hue went to great lengths to describe the breadth of the general uprising in Hue. However, no such uprising took place. Hundreds—perhaps thousands—of Hue's citizens who were Communists or committed anti-GVN activists did rally openly to the NLF banner. But the vast majority of Hue's men and women stayed home or fled for their lives. By 1100, February 3, some 1,900 civilians had found their way into U.S. Marine lines and were being cared for at the liberated District Headquarters compound, adjacent to MACV. On the other hand, perhaps several thousand civilians who were not able to reach friendly lines had been impressed into Communist labor battalions and forced at gunpoint to dig trenches and other field fortifications.

From the start, VC political teams had been rounding up American civilian officials and checking on Hue's many non-American foreign guests—mostly medical workers and missionaries. A number of the Europeans were taken into custody while, for unfathomable motives, others were not. Americans, including bona fide civilians with no ties to any government program or agency, were invariably led away into captivity when they could be found. A number of them were executed, but others, including at least one senior CIA official, were not. No pattern seems to have been in effect with regard to the killings.

Fortunately for Jim Bullington, the Communists had no reason to suspect that he was even in town, so his name did not appear on any of their lists. If they had known he was in Hue, they certainly would have tried to capture him because of his work in the city during his previous tour in South Vietnam. Bullington had gone to ground in the home of two French priests, whose identities certainly were known to the local Communists. Though many priests—particularly Frenchmen—were being rounded up or at least visited by the Communists, Bullington's hosts were not even visited.

Bullington had had little to do for two days except worry and look out a window from time to time to see what he could see. The incessant sound of gunfire told him that battles continued to ebb and flow in other parts of the city. But, except for an air raid over the Citadel on February 1, he had seen no signs of fighting or even occupation. On the morning of February 3, Bullington looked out a second-story window of the priests' home and saw four NVA soldiers in the courtyard of the power station, two compounds away. The soldiers were dressed in neat khaki uniforms and each carried an AK-47. Except for the soldiers, the area was absolutely deserted that morning. Later in the day, from time to time, Bullington could see civilians carrying huge bundles of belongings down the main street behind his safe haven.

The high point of the day came when Bullington and the priests heard a rumbling that could only have been a tank. The low point came minutes later, when the three saw the source of their highest hopes: it was an ARVN M-41 tank all right, but it was manned by several men clad in black pajamas.

On February 3, Bullington's fiancée, Tuy-Cam, heard artillery fire rumbling in the distance. No one in the Than-Trong compound could begin to guess what that might portend, but for the moment the artillery was the least of their problems. Absolutely no water was to be had from the taps, and the supply the clan had saved in containers had run out. It seemed as though the streets in the area were filled with armed men in civilian clothes and that the quiet, courteous young NVA soldiers who had been billeted in the area had gone elsewhere.

The soldiers certainly had gone elsewhere. On February 3, the U.S. Marines around MACV took several giant steps in their bid to get an organized offensive under way south of the Perfume. It took the Marines most of the day to get set, but the two or three battalions of the 4th NVA Regiment southwest of Highway 1 certainly were feeling the pressure—had been feeling it for two whole days—and it was no wonder the NVA regimental commander had begun redeploying his assets.

Throughout the morning of February 3, the fighting northeast of Highway 1 involved nickel-and-dime killings, mostly. At sunup, one NVA soldier who was trying to maneuver a satchel charge toward a building on the northeast side of the MACV Compound was shot dead by a Fox/2/5 platoon sergeant. At 0800, Hotel/2/5 Marines manning an upper-story window in Hue University spotted a squad of NVA in the street below. The Marines fired their weapons and four LAAW rockets, and claimed six NVA killed. An adventurous soul even went out into the street and recovered an AK-47 from one of the dead NVA. At 0900, the commander of one of the M-48 tanks saw three NVA soldiers dart into the open, and he killed all three with thirty rounds from his .50-caliber cupola machine gun. And so it went.

The big news of February 3 was that the 1st Marines forward CP group and the 2/5 CP group had been ordered to Hue from Phu Bai. No one in the world was happier to hear that news than Lieutenant Colonel Mark Gravel.

The situation Lieutenant Colonel Ernie Cheatham, the 2/5 commander, had found at Phu Bai on his arrival on the afternoon of February 2 had been sheer chaos bordering on panic. There had been no end of hand wringing among senior Marine officers as far up the chain as III MAF headquarters, at Danang. In the space of a very few hours, Cheatham had heard that Danang was under attack—and that it wasn't; that Hue was in the throes of a full-scale Communist offensive—and that only a few Communist snipers were loose in the city; that the only road into Hue had been severed—and that it was open; that the 1st Marine Division CP had been overrun—and that it hadn't even been attacked. When Cheatham was alerted that he was going to Hue the next day, he went over to the 5th Marines CP and asked the regimental operations officer what was really going on there. The major, who had been Cheatham's assistant when Cheatham had occupied the billet, admitted, "Ernie, I don't know what's happening, but it appears that we are fighting in the city and the only communication we have is with the MACV Compound." Lieutenant Colonel Cheatham had not even begun to penetrate the fog of war when, late in the evening of February 2, he was informed that 2/5 was going to be attached to the 1st Marines next day and that the battalion and regimental CPs were to mount out for Hue.

Until the warning order to mount out to Hue had been transmitted to the 1st Marines, the regimental staff had been putting out fires in a large area of operations that was entirely alien to them. The long night of waiting was fortuitous in that it allowed the 1st Marines' harried commander, Colonel Stan Hughes, and his brilliant but equally harried operations officer, Major Ernie Cook, to focus exclusively on Hue. During the night of February 2, in anticipation of 1st Marines' move to Hue, Task Force X-Ray ordered 5th Marines to assume tactical responsibility for all ongoing operations other than Hue. Guided by Task Force X-Ray's unexplained but evident priority on liberating the Thua Thien Provincial Prison, Major Cook wrote a regimental operations plan by which 1/1 and 2/5 would mount a coordinated attack to the southwest from Highway 1 to the prison. As soon as that objective fell, the battalions were to clear NVA and VC troops out of the entire southern portion of the city.

The long hours of waiting that night at Phu Bai also allowed Ernie Cheatham and his battalion operations officer, Major Luke Youngman, to get as firm a grip as possible on the situation that would be facing 2/5. This was a luxury the exhausted Lieutenant Colonel Mark Gravel and his intensely harried staff had not yet been afforded. Major Youngman spent most of the night fashioning a classic operations order aimed at imposing a clear set of goals and attainable objectives on the battalion. His plan was to take effect just as soon as the command group resumed control of the three companies already in Hue.

As soon as Lieutenant Colonel Cheatham was able to leave the planning in Major Youngman's able hands, he had time to focus on the challenge that was awaiting him in Hue. In perhaps the only period of reflection circumstances would allow him in the next few weeks, Cheatham realized that he had received no training in city fighting since he had been a newly minted second lieutenant preparing to depart for the Korean War. Cheatham had never fought in a built-up area, and he had never sent any other Marine to fight in one. Cheatham's battalion would certainly be called upon to clear terrain measured in square meters and in three dimensions. Hard work on his memory produced a vague recollection of a British Army training film he had seen before being shipped to Korea. All he could recall was that the Brits had done a lot of yelling as they lobbed grenades into rooms, and when they stepped into the rooms they had just grenaded, they fired their weapons for all they were worth.

Somewhere in the 5th Marines' regimental CP, Cheatham knew, were several footlockers filled with field manuals on tactics. He managed to find the 5th Marines' cache and quickly reviewed the slim haul of materials devoted to combat in a built-up area—manuals entitled *Combat in Built-Up Areas* and *Attack on a Fortified Position*. What it all boiled down to was that the best way to fight through a city was to gas the enemy, blow things up, and then clear out the ruins.

Armed with the information gleaned from the field manuals,

Lieutenant Colonel Cheatham ordered his battalion's 106mm Platoon to ready the remaining six of its eight recoilless rifles—two had been flown to Hue with Fox/2/5—and as much ammunition as the gunners could beg, borrow, or steal. Next Cheatham sent his armorers out to scrounge every loose CS tear-gas grenade and gas mask they could find in Phu Bai. He ordered them to stock up on C4 plastique explosive compound and every M-79 grenade and hand grenade they could locate—even obsolescent rifle grenades. Speaking of obsolescent weapons, Cheatham decided to unearth the battalion's flamethrowers and, more important, its 3.5-inch rocket launchers—World War II–vintage bazookas—which had recently been turned in for M-72 LAAW rockets. Cheatham knew that his troops would have to punch man-size holes in thick masonry walls and that there was a lot more bang for the buck in the big rocket warheads than in the lighter, more convenient, but less destructive LAAWs.

As soon as 2/5's commander had listed his needs, he turned the task of gathering all the weapons and munitions over to his can-do executive officer, Major John Salvati. Then Cheatham holed up in a quiet place to spend the hours he had left in Phu Bai poring over the field manuals so he could glean every shred of priceless information.

In his zeal, Major Salvati unearthed a number of 3.5-inch rocket launchers other Marine battalions had stored at Phu Bai, and he scrounged plenty of munitions. However, he quickly learned that there was a temporary countrywide shortage of hand grenades, and that no amount of fast talking, begging, or threats could set it right in the allotted time. Though Major Salvati had persuaded the battalion commander to allow him to accompany the convoy into Hue—Salvati was nearing the end of his field tour and had seen no direct combat as yet—he agreed to remain in Phu Bai an extra day, so he could scrounge more hand grenades and whatever else he thought the battalion would need.

While Major Cook and Major Youngman were piecing together their operations orders, the regimental and battalion personnel officers, the first sergeant of Alpha/1/1, and the four company first sergeants of 2/5 were hard at work scrounging up the first contingent of replacements for the scores of infantrymen who had been killed or wounded in Hue since January 31. As it had in numerous emergencies in the past, the adage that "every Marine is a rifleman" held true at Phu Bai. So, in addition to Marines who were reaching the end of the normal manpower pipeline from the States, the replacement contingent bound for Hue on February 3 would include many motor-transport mechanics, drivers, cooks, bakers, clerks, and rear-area technicians of every variety, and—not to be forgotten—volunteers of every stripe. The levy of rear-echelon technicians was particularly brutal in 1/1, whose CP group was scheduled to turn the three attached companies of 2/5 back to the 2/5 command group that afternoon. Once that was accomplished, 1/1 would be down to just one company—Alpha/1/1—in Hue. Since none of Mark Gravel's other three infantry companies could be spared from their duties elsewhere, a thinly manned new company called Bravo/1/1 was almost wholly constituted from part of the real Bravo/1/1 command group, casual replacements, small levies from 1/1's other three infantry companies, and mainly from Headquarters-and-Service Company, 1/1.

Numerous delays mounted up through the morning. It was not until 1220 that 1st Marines officially assumed operational control of 2/5. Also at 1220 the 1st Marines and 2/5 command groups left Phu Bai in the company of Bravo/1/1, the last dozen Alpha/1/1 stragglers, Lieutenant Bill Rogers's platoon of Golf/2/5, several 6 × 6 trucks filled with replacements, a huge lowboy cargo truck carrying 2/5's six mule-mounted 106mm recoilless rifles, and two Army M-42 Dusters.

The drive to Hue along Highway 1 was rapid and without delays. Though the convoy was cumbersome and vulnerable, the only measures the enemy took against it were in the form of sporadic sniper fire and several mortar rounds that landed far off target.

Somehow, as the convoy was rounding the traffic circle southeast of the cane field, fire discipline came unglued. From his position near the front of the column, Lieutenant Colonel Cheatham realized that the convoy vanguard, composed of Lieutenant Rogers's Golf/2/5 platoon and the two Dusters, was not firing;

virtually all the shooting was coming from the many rear-area troops, unattached individuals, and uncohesive fragments of ad hoc units farther back in the column. The malefactors—who were largely in the hands of officers and noncommissioned officers whom they did not know and would not obey—managed to blow off a huge amount of ammunition in a disproportionate response to the light fire from unseen sources.

Realizing that there was no real enemy threat but that the column was in danger of grinding to a halt, Cheatham ordered the vanguard drivers to increase the speed of their vehicles. When the vanguard started pulling ahead of the rest of the column, drivers to the rear naturally increased their speed to keep up with it. Thanks to Cheatham's quick thinking, the column simply roared across the exposed causeway, into the urban area, and to MACV. The convoy's trail jeep pulled in at 1258.

At 1300, February 3, 2/5 officially resumed operational control of Fox, Golf, and Hotel companies, and 1/1 officially resumed operational control of Bravo/1/1. The regimental CP moved into the MACV Compound, the 1/1 CP remained at MACV, and the 2/5 CP set up in Hue University.

At 1330, the battalion commanders received their orders from Regiment. The upshot of the formal operations order was that the 1st Marines regimental assault southwest of Highway 1 was to commence as soon as all five Marine infantry companies and their supports could close on the line of departure—in other words, later that very afternoon. The unofficial word Ernie Cheatham received direct from the regimental commander was a good deal saltier.

Colonel Stan Hughes was a rough-hewn warrior who said little and did much. He had earned a Navy Cross as a young lieutenant at Cape Gloucester in 1943, then a Silver Star at Peleliu in 1944, and he had commanded Marines in Korea. Colonel Hughes left the official language to his erstwhile operations officer, Major Ernie Cook. Speaking for himself, he told Ernie Cheatham, simply, to go dig the enemy out and to call on Regiment for any help he thought was needed. That was typical of Stan Hughes. In a very few words—and the only time throughout the Hue ordeal he even approximated giving an order to Cheatham—the regimental commander told the attached battalion commander to do whatever needed to be done and that Regiment would take care of the rest: sparring with higher headquarters, obtaining supplies and replacements, and arranging for supporting arms.

The three basic rules for conducting combat in a built-up area are to isolate the battlefield, seize footholds, and conduct a systematic clearing operation.

The Marine and ARVN units in Hue had no control over the first "must"; isolating the battlefield was in the hands of headquarters at a regional level. By February 3, the senior ARVN and U.S. headquarters and the divisions they controlled in I Corps were not yet sufficiently recovered from the onset of Tet to commit the forces that would be needed to isolate Hue from the outside. However, the NVA's apparent ignorance of step 1 had allowed the 1st ARVN Division and Task Force X-Ray to go directly to step 2 on January 31.

The NVA certainly had not isolated Hue. The combination of the 4th NVA Regiment's failure to seize MACV and interdict Highway 1 south of Hue had allowed a U.S. Marine combat force—initially a very weak one—to enter the heart of the city. Precisely the same type of failures on the part of the 6th NVA Regiment along Highway 1 north of Hue and in the Citadel had left the 1st ARVN Division CP compound intact and had allowed three ARVN airborne battalions and elements of three ARVN infantry battalions to beef up General Truong's position. Also, the NVA had never closed the Perfume River, an important potential supply line into the heart of the city. Thus, even though Hue had not been isolated from the outside, the ARVN and the Marines had been allowed to retain and reinforce their footholds within the NVA defensive zone.

The systematic clearing operation had begun inside the Citadel on February 2, with the seizure of Tay Loc Airfield. Around MACV, 1/1's ongoing company-size battles from the afternoon of January 31 through the forenoon of February 3 were still part of step 2—the consolidation of the foothold. The proposed attack by 1st Marines southwest of Highway 1, set to begin on the afternoon of February 3, was to be the beginning of the systematic clearing operation south of the Perfume. Both north and south of the river, the ARVN and the Marines would be mounting clearing operations before their senior headquarters had had an opportunity to isolate the city from the outside. It remained to be seen if this scenario would be successful, for the NVA retained the option—if they still had the capability—of isolating the city from the outside by cutting the unsecured lifelines: Highway 1 between PK 17 and the Citadel, Highway 1 between Phu Bai and MACV, and the Perfume River from the South China Sea to the heart of the city.

As preparations for the afternoon attack mounted, Task Force X-Ray informed Colonel Hughes that the I ARVN Corps commander, Lieutenant General Hoang Xuan Lam, had done what might have been the next best thing to sending large units of combat troops to isolate Hue from the outside. On the afternoon of February 3, General Lam had lifted all restrictions on fire support south of the Perfume River. Hughes's Marines were at last free to call upon any available supporting-arms agency, no matter how destructive its output. This opened the way for on-call support by all manner of artillery up to 8-inch howitzers; naval gunfire; and, if the weather cleared, tactical aircraft.

— 16 —

At 1345, February 3, Lieutenant Colonel Ernie Cheatham received his attack order from Colonel Stan Hughes at MACV. Cheatham proceeded to Hue University to look over 2/5's immediate objectives and map out a tactical plan for seizing them before sunset. The three company commanders reported in, as did the commanders of the battalion's 81mm mortar and 106mm Recoilless Rifle platoons. In sum, Cheatham learned that his cutdown battalion numbered approximately 700 well-armed Marines, most of whom had by then become acclimated to the special rigors of city fighting.

From an upper-story window in the university's short south-western wall, Cheatham got his first look at the type of terrain his battalion was expected to reduce. It looked like hundreds of solid bunkers had been stacked across the landscape, and he was certain each of the formidable masonry buildings was fully manned by tough, professional NVA infantry. On the plus side, Cheatham noted that the university was only a half block inland from the Perfume River, and all that seemed to occupy that half block were several small, low buildings set into a wooded park. If there were NVA in the woods or in the low buildings, they would be easy pickings. The important point was that his battalion's right flank would rest on the river, so he did not need to expend troops to screen that flank. Cheatham knew also that Lieutenant Colonel Mark Gravel's two-company 1/1 was to come up on 2/5's left flank the next morning, February 4. When it did, Tran Cao Van Street would be the battalion boundary. Gravel and Cheatham were old friends and communicated well, a definite advantage. At any rate, beginning the next morning, screening the left flank would be Gravel's job, which meant that 2/5 had to attack straight ahead only, another definite plus.

Cheatham issued his orders to the company commanders and heavy-weapons platoons at 1345. First, Fox/2/5 was to move up even with the university's southwest wall, right through the buildings occupying the block between Tran Cao Van and Truong Dinh streets. That would create a two-company front, with Fox/2/5 on the left and Hotel/2/5 on the right. To implement the orders, Golf/2/5, which was to be the battalion reserve, moved into the university courtyard. The 81mm mortar platoon also moved its six tubes—two were back with Echo/2/5, at Troi Bridge—into the university courtyard, as did Golf/2/5's and Hotel/2/5's three-gun 60mm mortar sections. The battalion's six 106mm recoilless rifles, each mounted on a Mechanical Mule, were brought up behind Fox/2/5 and Hotel/2/5, but no one had quite figured out how to employ them in the close quarters of the city. The problem with recoilless rifles was the enormous backblast they produced. It was a danger in the open, and presumably an even bigger danger in a built-up area, where maneuver space was at a premium. Two M-48 tanks were moved halfway up

Truong Dinh Street, to be used as required. And the two Ontos that had accompanied Hotel/2/5 to Hue the day before were moved forward to positions well out of the line of fire. Each Ontos carried six 106mm recoilless rifles and a .50-caliber machine gun. An Ontos looked like a formidable weapon on paper, but its drawbacks nearly outweighed its advantages. The 106s were mounted externally on an extremely vulnerable, unarmored tracked chassis that was powered by a gasoline engine. Bullets of almost any caliber could penetrate the hull of an Ontos; the gasoline that fueled it was extremely flammable; and the gunner had to stand in the open to reload the six tubes, a time-consuming process under the best of conditions and a tedious, deadly gamble under any form of enemy fire.

The initial phase of 2/5's assault would go off from right to left. In all its details, the plan was a classic scheme for attacking into a fortified area. The only problem was that no one present had ever undertaken such an attack in as intimidating a built-up area as that faced by the battalion that afternoon.

For several good reasons, Captain Ron Christmas's Hotel/2/5 was slated to launch the first attack. The company had been inside the university overnight, and, presumably, the troops and their leaders had had an opportunity to study the buildings immediately to the southwest, chiefly the Provincial Public Health Complex, which was centered on a stoutly built two-story main building standing behind a row of lower buildings. The complex was across Ly Thuong Kiet Street, the northwest-southeast thoroughfare to 2/5's immediate front. Covering fire could be effectively placed on the objectives by Hotel/2/5 weapons and riflemen occupying upper-story rooms overlooking the objective.

In Lieutenant Colonel Cheatham's studies of the night before, he had learned that the way to move through urban terrain was to seize one building at a time through a rigorous application of cover-and-search tactics—a combination of target suppression from a base of fire and swift assault of the objective by a maneuver element. Thus, in the classic manner of infantry attacks, one platoon of Hotel/2/5, operating within the university, was to suppress the enemy fire while another platoon attacked at street level, clearing one building at a time until all the day's objectives had been seized. The third platoon would be held in reserve, for use as needed in target suppression or exploitation of the assault.

Captain Mike Downs's Fox/2/5, which needed some time to infiltrate and blast its way through the buildings between Highway 1 and Ly Thuong Kiet Street, was initially to support Hotel/2/5's attack. The plan called for Fox/2/5 to place flanking fire on Hotel/2/5's objectives and suppress enemy fire from the formidable building that it would be facing directly across Ly Thuong Kiet: the National Treasury. When Hotel/2/5 had taken its initial objectives—the low buildings fronting Ly Thuong Kiet—Fox/2/5 was to attack straight across the street and seize the treasury.

If there was a flaw in the scheme, it was that no provision had been made to secure the buildings to Fox/2/5's left. The failure of repeated attacks down Tran Cao Van Street by Golf/2/5 and Fox/2/5 on February 1 had left the NVA in possession of the city block bounded by Highway 1, Ly Thuong Kiet Street, Tran Cao Van Street, and Nguyen Tri Phuong Street. The two main building complexes occupying that block were the Jeanne d' Arc Private Girls' High School and Le Loi Primary School. The latter, which bordered Ly Thuong Kiet Street, was filled with NVA and commanded a clear field of fire to the northwest, right across 2/5's front. This block was to be 1/1's initial objective, but Mark Gravel's two-company battalion was not scheduled to sally out of MACV until the next morning.

It took two hours for Fox/2/5 to get into position opposite the treasury and the post office, which was next door to the treasury. In that time, the 3.5-inch rocket launchers were distributed to Marines who knew how to fire them, and everyone received a gas mask. Ammunition of all types was distributed, and all hands received a fair share of the limited supply of hand grenades, including CS tear-gas grenades.

At 1545 the lead fire team of Hotel/2/5's 2nd Platoon jumped off against the low structures fronting the Public Health complex. Captain Ron Christmas, who was a very sharp thinker, had reasoned that the best way to get troops across a street that was under enemy observation was to fill the street with smoke, thus obscuring the enemy's vista. So, the first thing the attacking platoons and Hotel/2/5's 60mm mortars did was "pop smoke"—heave smoke grenades and fire smoke rounds into Ly Thuong Kiet Street. Since there was a steady breeze off the river, to the right, the smoke tended to blow toward the left, across the front of the treasury and post office and more or less into the faces of the NVA in Le Loi Primary School. That should have done the job, but the NVA were not slackers. They saw the smoke billow up from the street, and they fired into it—blindly, to be sure, but quite effectively. Everyone in Hotel/2/5's lead fire team piled back into the university building.

The 81mm and 60mm mortars set in around the university courtyard were put into action, albeit against targets beyond the enemy front line, which was only just across the street. Even so, the 81mm mortar gunners had to employ extraordinary skill to fire at ranges far less than those their weapons were designed to reach.

Not all the NVA positions could be covered from the university windows, so Captain Christmas ordered Corporal Bob Meadows's squad of the 1st Platoon to get up on the roof and fire down into the NVA-held buildings that dominated Ly Thuong Kiet Street. As Meadows rousted his squad out of the upper-story rooms it was occupying, Captain Christmas sent three two-man 3.5-inch rocket teams and two two-man M-60 machine-gun teams to join him.

Many rungs of the fire-escape ladder to the roof had been torn out, so the heavily burdened Marines had to shinny up part of the 25-foot ladder. When they got to the roof, they found a huge open area, covered with ceramic tiles and devoid of any cover except for a calf-high cement perimeter wall.

Immediately, Corporal Meadows started the rocket teams and M-60s to work against known targets directly across the street, around the company's objective. For all the height the reinforced squad had gained, however, there were NVA weapons aplenty that were able to reach them. This forced Meadows to keep the weapons teams and all his riflemen and grenadiers on the move, evading fire as well as taking on more targets than there were Marines to cover.

After only a few minutes on the university roof, Bob Meadows saw three enemy RPG teams climb onto a roof across the way. Before he could get any of his men to bear on the new danger, the NVA rocketmen had hidden themselves.

About five minutes into the exchange, Corporal Meadows leaned out over the concrete railing in time to see a man dart across the street and take cover behind a wrecked Volkswagen truck. Meadows fired several M-16 rounds into the truck, coaxing the man back into the open. As the Kentucky-raised game hunter was drawing a bead on the man, he saw that his target sported a long white beard. Just in time, Meadows eased the pressure on the trigger and allowed the civilian elder to enter the university compound.

After about ten lucky minutes of running his reinforced squad back and forth across the roof without sustaining any casualties, Corporal Meadows lay down behind the low concrete fence. On either side, riflemen were firing into one of the tall buildings across the way. Meadows, who had just armed himself with an M-79 grenade launcher, was about to fire at the same building when he saw out of the corner of his eye that a civilian news cameraman had appeared in the open behind him. As the squad leader turned to go toward the newsman—he had warned the man off the fire-swept roof twice already—a B-40 rocket detonated right against the concrete railing. Equally as dangerous as the shrapnel from the RPG were the shards of cement and ceramic roofing tile the explosives had blasted into the air.

Corporal Meadows was facing the cameraman, so he was not touched, but he saw that one of the riflemen who had been lying beside him had a faceful of bloody shrapnel wounds. A glance at the other Marine revealed that he, too, had been badly wounded. In fact, his throat had been cut by shrapnel. Instantly, Meadows leaned down to close the gaping throat wound and called "Corpsman, up!" Then he started dragging the Marine with the throat wound out of the line of fire. Plenty of helping hands arrived, the two Marines were quickly treated on the roof, and both were gingerly lowered by rope down the wrecked ladder. No sooner done, however, than another Marine was struck in the face by shrapnel from a B-40 rocket or 60mm mortar round. Once again,

Corporal Meadows pulled the wounded man to the rear.

As soon as the third wounded Marine had been lowered down the fire escape, Meadows yelled down that he needed more 3.5-inch rockets, right away. Then he ran forward to find his radioman. He saw him, and was about to give him a message to relay, when the lights went out. Bob Meadows was engulfed in an RPG blast and knocked unconscious.

When Corporal Bob Meadows regained consciousness, it was late in the evening and he was aboard a medevac chopper bound for Phu Bai. Though he had sustained numerous shrapnel wounds in the head and back, he would be back with Hotel/2/5 within a week.

While the drama on the roof was unfolding, Private First Class Peter Murray, of Hotel/2/5's 2nd Platoon, was firing at the treasury from a window in the south corner of the university. As Murray and his comrades fired, Murray heard the racket of a Marine M-48 tank trundling up Truong Dinh Street. When the tank nosed out into Ly Thuong Kiet Street, its turret was hit by a hail of green .51-caliber tracer rounds. The tank stopped, and its turret turned toward the source of the fire. Then the tank commander's cupola-mounted .50-caliber machine gun spat a concise response in orange tracer. The NVA machine gun ceased firing, but a B-40 rocket streaked out of a building to the tank's right front, and it struck the tank obliquely on the thickly armored glacis plate, right in front of the driver. Momentarily cheered by the arrival of the tank and its deadly cool response to the NVA heavy machine gun, Private First Class Murray was disappointed to see the behemoth grind back up Truong Dinh in reverse.

As Private First Class Murray watched the tank recede, the lead fire team of his squad—part of Staff Sergeant Johnny Miller's 2nd Platoon—was already running across Ly Thuong Kiet. Murray wasn't sure what was going on, but he instinctively followed.

The nearest safe haven Murray spotted was a low masonry building he had watched throughout the previous night. Then, Murray had seen a number of people moving around inside the structure. Now, as he charged through the front door, he saw a dead civilian sprawled on the floor. The Marines ahead of Murray were already through the building, so he barreled down a hallway and charged out the back door. There was a shed in the yard, and Murray ducked into its doorway. From there, he fired three or four magazines at a building across a narrow side street, the Public Health Building itself. Murray's squad leader was firing his M-16 from a few meters away, and his fire team's M-79 grenadier was blooping out 40mm fragmentation grenades as fast as he could load and fire.

Murray had no idea if the other Marines had actually seen any targets; he was just following their lead. It was dawning on him that there was no return fire, when he felt like someone had punched him in the neck. Instantly, Murray realized that he had already heard a bullet strike the door frame in which he was standing, and another bullet had struck somewhere behind him. One of those bullets had ricocheted into Murray's neck. By then, Murray was sprawled on the lawn in front of the shed. Before he had sorted through the past second's events, his fire-team leader was helping him to his feet.

The next thing Murray knew, he was up and running around the corner of the shed. There he found a corpsman, who looked at the bruise on his neck. "There are probably some bullet fragments in there," the doc said, and he ordered Murray to return to the company aid station for treatment. Murray ran back through the house and dashed across the street to the university. When he reached the aid station, he found the docs treating about a dozen Marines, including the unconscious Corporal Bob Meadows and four members of Meadows's squad. When the company's senior doc finally got around to Murray, about twenty minutes later, he told the rifleman that he would have to return to Phu Bai for treatment. However, the doc said, the medevac choppers were reserved for men with serious wounds, so Murray would have to wait until a truck convoy returned to Phu Bai, probably in the morning. The neck wounds were cleaned and dressed, and Peter Murray was left to his own devices for the night.

Staff Sergeant Miller's 2nd Platoon pressed its dogged advance on the Public Health Building for nearly an hour against stiff NVA small-arms fire. The platoon actually entered the NVA stronghold at 1758 and had it cleared out by 1855. However, at 1924, the victory was negated by orders from Captain Christmas to return to the university. Fox/2/5 had failed to secure its objective, and, as a result, Miller's platoon could not risk spending the night in its advanced and insupportable position. Miller's troops reluctantly pulled back across Ly Thuong Kiet Street in the dark and helped man Hotel/2/5's night defensive position around the perimeter of the university.

Fox/2/5 had indeed failed to seize its objective, the massively built treasury building, but it certainly had given its all trying.

— 17 —

When Hotel/2/5 jumped off against the Public Health Complex at 1545, Captain Mike Downs's Fox/2/5 was still getting set in among the buildings and courtyards on the northeast side of Ly Thuong Kiet Street, facing the treasury and post office compounds. The plan was for Hotel/2/5 to get established on the southwest side of Ly Thuong Kiet before Fox/2/5 jumped off in its attack. However, when Hotel/2/5 was initially rebuffed and no solution seemed to be readily at hand, Fox/2/5 was ordered to cross the street whatever way it could.

The National Treasury was the place they kept the money. It was every bit as physically and psychologically imposing as anyone would imagine. From the northeast side of Ly Thuong Kiet Street, it looked as impregnable as a kid's fantasy of Fort Knox.

The objective was a flat-roofed structure of two-and-a-half stories. The building was set in behind a courtyard fronted by a knee-high masonry wall topped by a fence of upright wrought-iron stakes. The gate in the center of the front wall was also composed of wrought-iron stakes. NVA machine guns were set into several of the sandbagged windows in the top story and, apparently, in ventilation ports along the uppermost half story. No one could even guess how many NVA were inside the huge structure, nor what they had done to fortify the interior.

The tactical problems facing Fox/2/5 were many and complex. Except for the university, to the right, there were no high buildings northeast of Ly Thuong Kiet from which the Marines could fire down into the treasury courtyard. No one knew for certain what lay right behind the courtyard wall, but it was known that, whenever possible, NVA soldiers dug their neat little fighting holes right along the base of a wall. If Fox/2/5 Marines breached the courtyard and got as far as the front door, no one knew what they would face inside. No one had a diagram of the interior, but it was safe to assume that there would be built-in interior defenses designed specifically to thwart robbers.

On top of everything else, Fox/2/5's intentionally delayed attack across Ly Thuong Kiet Street revealed that at least one NVA .51-caliber machine gun in the Le Loi Primary School, to the company's left rear, had the street covered. Thus, any attack across the street would be made under observed fire from the well-hidden machine gun on the left flank. The farther out into the street the attackers got, the better targets they would become.

Lieutenant Donald Hausrath's 3rd Platoon was slated to lead the Fox/2/5 attack into the treasury. After leading the way out of MACV, the platoon had blown and blasted its way through a hotel and several small buildings until it came out into a courtyard directly facing the treasury gate. Fortunately for the men in the 3rd Platoon, a head-high masonry wall stopped the hail of small-arms fire that greeted the point fire team as it entered the courtyard.

The job looked impossible. There were NVA out there, but no one could see them. Before anyone was going to be willing to cross the street, the entire treasury complex would have to be softened up with whatever high-explosive ordnance Fox/2/5 could wangle. Over time, that amounted to a mere twenty 81mm mortar rounds fired from the university courtyard and another twenty 60mm mortar rounds fired directly from the 3rd Platoon's rear. The results of the mortar fire could not be observed, but there was no lessening in the NVA fire. In fact, in response to the Marine mortar fire, the NVA started working out with their own 60mm mortars.

Fox/2/5 Marines in second-story windows of the buildings facing the Treasury, which housed the Jeanne d'Arc chemistry lab and a music room, fired a preparation amounting to over thirty 3.5-inch rockets, fifteen LAAWs, fifty M-79 grenades, and thousands of 5.56mm and 7.62mm bullets from M-16 rifles and M-60 machine guns. The 3.5-inch rockets were the only weapons that seemed to do any real damage to the thick treasury walls. The LAAWs could punch through the walls, but they didn't have much effect beyond making holes. The M-79 grenades were about as effective as golf balls would have been; they had zero penetrating power. All the small-arms ammunition that was expended probably just made the Marines feel better.

As the 3rd Platoon's preparations mounted, Lieutenant Hausrath emerged from the chemistry building and told his troop leaders in the courtyard that Captain Downs wanted one man to cross the street to find out if there was any way into the treasury compound other than through the heavily defended front gate. Among the squad leaders listening to Hausrath was Lance Corporal Bernie Burnham.

Burnham was not your average lance corporal. He was thirty-one years old, three years older than Captain Downs, and a decade or more older than all the other men in his squad. He had been a Marine in the mid-1950s and had risen to sergeant. Then he had gotten out and found a high-paying job in the New York City area. He had never given any serious thought to returning to the Marine Corps until, less than a year earlier, he had become enraged over an antiwar protest in Central Park. On the spur of the moment, Burnham had reenlisted as a private and started on his way to Vietnam and Fox/2/5.

Intelligent and aggressive to a fault, Bernie Burnham felt his heart skip a beat when he heard Lieutenant Hausrath asking for a volunteer to cross the street.

Lance Corporal Burnham was well aware of the automatic-weapons fire streaming up Ly Thuong Kiet Street from the left flank. He looked at the wide-eyed youngsters in his squad; turned to his senior fire-team leader; and said, through abject fear, "It's your squad." To the others he said, "You guys give me some cover fire."

The courtyard wall of the chemistry building was fairly high, and Burnham knew better than to climb over it. So the courtyard was evacuated, and a 3.5-inch rocket was expended to create a fairly large sally port roughly in the center of the barrier. The dust had not yet cleared when Burnham stepped through the hole into Ly Thuong Kiet Street. He advanced all of three or four steps and was knocked on his butt by streams of rifle and machine-gun fire. His left foot was on fire where a bullet had gone through it, but he was otherwise unscathed—an authentic miracle. Instinctively, Burnham crawled through flying concrete and masonry chips and wedged himself beneath a truck parked just to the right of the hole in the wall. From there, he yelled back, "I'm hit!" Sergeant Willard Scott, the platoon guide, told him to hang on where he was.

Five minutes later, as Burnham was wondering how long he would have to hang on, a fire team from his squad, led by Lance Corporal Wayne Washburn, emerged onto the street from around the left side of the courtyard wall and made an oblique dash for the treasury gate. No sooner had Lance Corporal Burnham seen the four Marines than the NVA across the street poured a withering fire into them. Right in front of the gate, Lance Corporal Washburn was shot through the head, and at least two other Marines were also wounded.

Burnham saw his opportunity. While the NVA troops were occupied with Washburn's fire team, the wounded squad leader crawled out from beneath the truck and bolted through the hole in the wall, between Marines who were furiously firing at the treasury to suppress the NVA fire. Seconds later, the truck was demolished by a B-40 rocket.

The Marines inside the courtyard were doing everything they could to suppress the massive NVA fire, but the NVA had the upper hand. Staff Sergeant Jim McCoy, the 3rd Platoon's platoon sergeant, saw a B-40 rocket explode right in front of Lance Corporal Roger Warren's M-60 team. McCoy was sure that Warren and his assistant had been killed in the blast, but through the cloud of dust and debris McCoy heard someone cough. Then he heard Warren's voice saying, "Fuck this shit! We're not staying here anymore!" Both M-60 gunners had been injured. The assistant had to be evacuated, but Warren refused treatment.

Once inside the courtyard, Burnham learned that his entire squad had been sent out through another hole in the left side of the courtyard. A minute later, aided by intense covering fire from the rest of the platoon, everyone in Burnham's squad had returned to the courtyard—everyone except Lance Corporal Washburn, who had been in the forefront of the attack. He had fallen too far forward to be safely retrieved.

Lance Corporal Burnham waited to have the hole in his foot bound by one of the docs. A hulking, likable M-79 grenadier—Private Jerry Dankworth—was deposited next to him. Dankworth, whose only dream in life was to return home to become a preacher, had suffered what looked to Burnham like horrible, mutilating wounds in both legs. At least, as far as Burnham could see, the legs of Dankworth's trousers were shredded and bloody. Burnham was so stunned by Dankworth's apparent condition that he told the doc to skip his relatively minor wound and get to work on Dankworth. Unbelievably, Dankworth's injuries were superficial, and he was returned to duty as soon as they were treated.

As soon as Burnham left the aid station, he decided that it was time to retrieve Lance Corporal Washburn. Marines along the wall said they thought the fire-team leader was moving a little, so maybe his head wound had not been fatal. There was only one way to find out, but, before Bernie Burnham could squeeze through the hole in the wall, an amazing thing happened.

Private First Class William Barnes had joined Fox/2/5 only that day. He was one of the rear-area technicians who had volunteered or been pulled out of his job at Phu Bai to help restore 2/5's bloodied infantry companies. The luck of the draw had seen him assigned to Fox/2/5's 3rd Platoon. No one in the platoon knew Barnes when he arrived, and he knew no one in the platoon.

Yet before Bernie Burnham could go back out onto fire-swept Ly Thuong Kiet to retrieve his friend, Wayne Washburn, William Barnes beat him to it. The young mechanic, whose name nobody in the 3rd Platoon knew, rushed straight into the fire—and was shot from his feet several meters short of Washburn. Barnes was down, and he wasn't moving.

Now there were two dead or dying Marines in the street.

A pair of M-48 tanks was brought forward to fire target suppression at both the treasury and the Public Health Complex. Hotel/2/5 was stalled in its bid to breast the enemy fire coming from the Public Health Complex, and further efforts to rescue Lance Corporal Washburn and recover Private First Class Barnes were being stymied by the .51-caliber machine gun that could sweep Ly Thuong Kiet Street from Le Loi Primary School. The tanks were seen as the best weapons available for breaking both deadlocks.

The tank crews, by now, were getting the hang of city fighting. The plan was that, alternating turns, each would roll up to the head of Truong Dinh Street, the Fox/2/5-Hotel/2/5 boundary, fire their .50-caliber machine guns and 90mm main guns at either the Public Health Complex or Le Loi Primary, and then immediately withdraw. During its first sally, the first tank was struck on the glacis plate by a B-40 rocket, but the tank returned to action after the driver got the bells in his head to stop ringing. By then, Hotel/2/5's 2nd Platoon had crossed Ly Thuong Kiet.

The tanks expended a total of twenty rounds of 90mm and 400 rounds of .50-caliber ammunition against the treasury and Le Loi Primary, but without apparent effect. Two B-40 rockets struck one of the tanks and one B-40 rocket struck the other. After that, both tanks were withdrawn by their dazed crewmen.

Two 3rd Platoon Marines were still down in the street, only a few meters beyond Lance Corporal Bernie Burnham's reach. When the word arrived that the tanks were withdrawing, Burnham yelled "Cover me!" and headed right through the hole in the courtyard wall, right out into Ly Thuong Kiet Street again. Behind Burnham was Sergeant Willard Scott, the 3rd Platoon guide.

For some unfathomable reason, from some unknowable impulse, the NVA were merciful. Some fired at the two Marines, but most of them just watched. Burnham passed Private First Class Barnes's dead body and pulled Lance Corporal Washburn up over his shoulder. Then, as Scott covered him, he lumbered away to the right, toward the building next door to the courtyard in which the 3rd Platoon was holed up. Altogether, it was a fifty-meter run.

Once inside the building, Burnham and Scott tore a door loose from its hinges and placed Washburn on the door. The back of the wounded man's head had been blown out, and he was bleeding profusely, but Burnham was certain he was still alive. To Burnham he *felt* alive. With the help of several other Marines they pressed into service, Burnham and Scott carried the improvised litter through several buildings and open areas. When they emerged onto Highway 1, they commandeered a passing Mechanical Mule that was loaded with ammunition. They dumped the ammunition into the street and loaded Washburn aboard; he was driven to MACV. When Burnham and the others last saw him, the fire-team leader was still alive, but he died in Phu Bai the next day.

By the time Lance Corporal Burnham and Sergeant Scott returned to the courtyard across from the treasury, it was getting dark. To their chagrin, they learned that Private First Class Barnes's body was still in the middle of Ly Thuong Kiet Street. No one had even tried to retrieve it after Burnham and Scott had carried Wayne Washburn to safety. Scott settled the matter by assigning the job to four Marines he picked at random. One of the men he picked was Lance Corporal Ernie Weiss, who had helped to recover Sergeant John Maloney's body the previous evening. Sergeant Scott told him and the others to leave their rifles, web belts, helmets, and flak jackets in the courtyard. It was pitch dark by then, so speed was better than being armed or armored.

It took all of a minute. The Marines crept through the hole in the wall, grabbed Barnes's stiff corpse by the clothing, and dragged him back through the hole in the wall. It was too late and too dangerous to evacuate Barnes to MACV, so they placed his body beside the building and covered it with a poncho.

Late in the evening of February 3, a panicked Time-Life correspondent told Sergeant Scott and Lance Corporal Burnham that the NVA were going to mount a counterattack out of the treasury. How do you deal with a fantasyland newscast from the enemy camp? While rooting through the high school chemistry lab, Sergeant Scott had found a case of Carling Black Label beer. This he graciously shared with Lance Corporal Burnham while they stood watch together on the porch. As Burnham and Scott drank beer on the porch, a half dozen younger Marines played raucous, cacophonous music on a trove of band instruments they found in the music room.

Nothing at all happened that night. For Fox/2/5, the worst part of the dark hours was the damp, chilly air. The company had grounded its packs when it went into action on January 31 at Troi Bridge, and no one had seen his personal gear since. Some of the Marines had rain suits, but these didn't keep out the cold at all. Despite persistent rumors about NVA counterattacks, the troops were more concerned about the bone-chilling night air than about the danger from the enemy.

By the evening of February 3, the Marines in Fox/2/5 certainly knew something about waging war in a city, but the price of that knowledge had come very high. From Fox/2/5, several men had been wounded and medevacked, one man had been killed outright, and one would soon be dead. And all for no gain.

— 18 —

Fox/2/5 and Hotel/2/5 were slated to jump off across Ly Thuong Kiet Street once again at 0700, February 4. As before, Fox/2/5 was charged with seizing the treasury building, and Hotel/2/5's objective was the Public Health Complex. Though Hotel/2/5 had taken the complex the previous afternoon, it had had to withdraw its vanguard platoon after dark because Fox/2/5 had made no headway at all. There was every reason to believe that Hotel/2/5 could repeat the previous day's success, and everything that could be done to assist Fox/2/5 was being done.

During the night, Captain Ron Christmas had realized he had committed a grave tactical error in preparing for the February 3 afternoon attack. Rather than employing the company's M-60 machine guns to establish the strongest possible bases of fire, Christmas had allowed the M-60 teams to remain attached to the rifle platoons. The result was that the bush-trained machine gunners had employed their potent 7.62mm weapons as assault rifles rather than as medium machine guns. On the morning of February 4, Christmas repositioned most of the tripod-mounted M-60s, placing them on the roof and in the upper-story windows of the university, facing the Public Health Complex.

Adding appreciably to 2/5's firepower that morning was most of Golf/2/5. Elements of Golf/2/5 were posted with 3.5-inch rocket launchers and M-60 machine guns high up and along the southeast side of the university. Their primary target was the Le Loi Primary School, from which at least one NVA .51-caliber machine gun had fired on the attacking Hotel/2/5 Marines on February 3.

Another twist unique to city fighting had become apparent in the waning hours of February 3. Quite naturally, the 3.5-inch rocketmen had aimed their weapons *through* open windows of enemy-held buildings in the hope of killing the defenders inside. The success rate had been stunningly low. The rockets did not detonate until they hit something solid, and, when they did, the blast was in the direction the rocket was going—away from the NVA manning the windows. Late-night bull sessions resulted in new orders to all the rocketmen. On the morning of February 4, they fired their rockets around—rather than through—the windows from which the NVA were firing, counting on the blast to send masonry shards and shrapnel ricocheting around the room to cut down the men inside.

The Hotel/2/5 dawn attack jumped off under covering fire from M-60s, 3.5-inch rocket launchers, M-79 grenades, and LAAWs. The fire was augmented by twenty-five 81mm mortar rounds directed by Fox/2/5's 81mm forward observer. Firing the 81mm mortars was particularly nerve-racking because the nearest targets were actually within the minimum firing range of the weapons. The solution to this anomaly was provided by the mortar platoon commander, Gunnery Sergeant Lawrence Bargaheiser, a grizzled veteran and a superb mortarman. In the university courtyard, the six 81mm tubes were erected on their bipods at virtually vertical elevation, and the rounds were fired with minimum charges for the least possible range. As the rounds were lofted above the university roof, the steady southerly breeze off the Perfume River carried them just far enough to the southwest to tilt them into the NVA positions for which they were meant. Altogether, it was a masterful display of technical proficiency.

For all the fire support, however, Hotel/2/5's lead platoon—once again, Staff Sergeant Johnny Miller's 2nd—ran into exactly the sort of fire that had stymied the attacks of February 3. Once again, NVA in high buildings fired down into the street, and the heavy-machine-gun nest in Le Loi Primary cut the attack off at its knees. NVA, hidden in other positions west of Ly Thuong Kiet, blasted away at the University, forcing Marines in the windows to duck or die.

Hotel/2/5's attack across Ly Thuong Kiet was getting exactly nowhere until the lance corporal commanding one of the 106mm recoilless rifles approached Captain Christmas with an original idea. The 106 gunner pointed out that the deadliest fire was coming from way to the left, apparently from a .51-caliber in the basement of the Le Loi Primary School. He also pointed out that the backblast from his 106 could throw up enough debris to cover a rush across the street. The way the lance corporal had it figured, he and his assistant gunner could roll their 106 into the street on its Mechanical Mule and fire at Le Loi Primary to suppress or maybe even destroy the .51-caliber machine gun. As soon as the 106 fired, Captain Christmas could mount a platoon attack through the dust and debris thrown up by the backblast. The big advantage was that, unlike an attack through smoke, the NVA wouldn't know what was going on until it had already happened.

Christmas asked the lance corporal if he really understood what he was volunteering to do. "Sure," the gunner said, and he was eager to begin. With that, Captain Christmas alerted Staff Sergeant Miller's 2nd Platoon to cross Ly Thuong Kiet as soon as the 106 fired.

Lieutenant Colonel Ernie Cheatham got wind of the plan and decided to take a personal role in perfecting it. While the 106 crew was getting ready to go, Cheatham eased out a side door of the university and advanced up Truong Dinh Street to fire-swept Ly Thuong Kiet. There he tucked his six-foot four-inch frame behind a telephone pole. Cheatham peeked across Fox/2/5's front and toward Le Loi Primary. He saw the muzzle flash and the telltale green tracers of an NVA .51-caliber machine gun coming from a window right at street level.

The battalion commander got down in a kneeling position behind the telephone pole and watched for several moments. He noticed that when the NVA machine gun fired at targets on the southwest side of Ly Thuong Kiet—the side the treasury and Public Health complex were on—it fired low. However, as the gunner brought the barrel around to lay on targets on the northeast side of the street, the stream of tracer rose. It seemed as though the gun was obstructed by something. Cheatham became convinced that the gun fired so high to its right that there was no way he could be hit if he stepped into the street to mark the target for the 106 gunners.

Armed with this vital information, Cheatham went back into the university courtyard to lay out a plan of action with the 106 crew. The crew would bounce the Mechanical Mule down the front steps of the university, right out into Ly Thuong Kiet; he would mark the target with tracer rounds, the only type of ammunition he—and other senior Marine commanders—carried, precisely for situations like the one at hand.

Ernie Cheatham went back to the telephone pole and sighted in on the target. He couldn't quite get a round on it, so he leaned out for a better shot. His next round hit near the target, and the target tried to hit him. But, though the green tracer snapped and cracked right over his head, the .51-cal gunner could not hit the Marine battalion commander.

Then, exactly as planned, the Mechanical Mule bounced right down the front steps and into the middle of the street. Instantly, as the gunners turned the recoilless rifle to bear on Le Loi Primary, the NVA machine gun traversed to bear on them. The gunners were standing hip deep in green tracer.

Cheatham fired his M-16 marking rounds right at the target window; the 106 gunner squatted down behind the sight and twisted aiming wheels while the assistant gunner loaded a high-explosive round into the breech. "Fire the fifty," the gunner called, as if he were practicing gun drill on a Stateside range. "Fire the fifty," the assistant responded as he thumbed a half-inch tracer round into the .50-caliber single-shot spotting rifle set atop the 106mm barrel. As the world was blowing up around him, the gunner fired the tracer round and watched it strike near, but not on, the spot Ernie Cheatham's tracer was hitting.

The gunner corrected his aim. "Fire the fifty," he yelled. "Fire the fifty," the assistant gunner yelled back. The second marking round curved down along Ly Thuong Kiet and struck closer to the target, but not quite on it.

With the street around him awash in the light of green tracer, the 106 gunner corrected his aim once again. "Fire the fifty," he yelled for the third time. "Fire the fifty," the assistant gunner responded in a still resolute voice. The third .50-caliber tracer struck the northern face of Le Loi Primary right in among Lieutenant Colonel Cheatham's M-16 marking rounds.

Instantly the gunner yelled, "Fire the one-owe-six!" The assistant gunner responded, "Fire the one-owe-six!" And . . . *ba-ROOM*! The round roared down Ly Thuong Kiet Street toward the school. Meanwhile, a huge billow of debris and dust spread across the front of the university. As it did, the 106 gunners hauled ass back into the courtyard, and Staff Sergeant Miller's 2nd Platoon of Hotel/2/5 once again charged toward the low buildings fronting the Public Health Complex. The 106 round destroyed the NVA .51-caliber machine-gun position.

Two Hotel/2/5 Marines were wounded during the rush across Ly Thuong Kiet, but Miller's platoon once again established a strong toehold inside the Public Health Complex. The low buildings fronting the Public Health Building itself were cleared in a matter of minutes.

The main difference between the stalemated, bloody action of February 3 and the renewed assault on the morning of February 4 was the breadth of the Marine front. Unlike the day before, Fox/2/5's left flank was to be partially screened and secured on

February 4 by Lieutenant Colonel Mark Gravel's two-company 1/1.

Gravel's thin battalion had left MACV at dawn and begun working its way through the buildings on the city block from Highway 1 between Truong Dinh and Tran Cao Van streets. The 1/1 Marines had to blast their way from building to building to avoid attacking across open streets and other obvious avenues of approach. Near Highway 1, a Marine tank did the blasting with its 90mm main gun. Farther in, the job had to be done with 3.5-inch rocket launchers. Invariably, if the room on the other side of the blasted wall was occupied, NVA survivors picked up their gear and ran for safety, and alert Marines lying in wait outside the blast zone tried to pick off a few after each detonation. Slowly, very slowly, the main body of 2nd Lieutenant Ray Smith's Alpha/1/1 and 1st Lieutenant Gordon Matthews's Bravo/1/1 eased forward.

Corporal Herbert Watkins, who spent most of his time in the forefront of the Alpha/1/1 attack, popped up after one 3.5-inch detonation, just in time to shoot at three NVA he caught in the open. Two of the three ducked down behind a low wall. When Watkins stood up again to fire at them, hoping they would be in the open again, he found that one was waiting for him. The NVA soldier had a B-40 pointed right at Watkins. The Marine squad leader was still dropping to the ground when the wall he was using for cover exploded and fell back on him. When the dust settled, Corporal Watkins found that he was unable to move. Corporal Richard Pettit and another Marine cleared the rubble off Watkins's back, but Watkins was still unable to move. He told Pettit that he thought his back was broken, so he was gingerly carried back to MACV, full of shrapnel and masonry shards and racked by intense pain. As Watkins lay on a stretcher in the 1/1 battalion aid station, he watched the docs wrap Corporal Pettit's many wounds, until Pettit looked like a mummy. Watkins was sure Pettit was tagged for medevac, but when Watkins was loaded on a truck for medevac to Phu Bai later that morning, Pettit said good-bye and returned to the company.

Halfway through the block, 1/1 ran into a major NVA defensive sector centered on the huge square compound occupied by the Jeanne d'Arc Private Girls' High School. The Marines managed to enter the long building on the northeast side of the complex, but they were unable to advance across the huge exposed quadrangle or through the northwest and southeast wings. By 0900 the Marine advance was stopped, and both sides were exchanging small-arms fire, 3.5-inch rockets, LAAWs, and B-40s.

Sergeant Alfredo Gonzalez, the platoon sergeant of the 2nd Platoon of Alpha/1/1, was a young man who reveled in close combat. He was a fearless, ferocious fighter, more than willing to take responsibility for leading direct assaults on the enemy. Usually, when facing the enemy, the twenty-one-year-old Texan showed a huge, toothy grin. At about 0900, February 4, Sergeant Gonzalez collected an armload of LAAW rockets and climbed to the second floor of the Marine-held building in the Jeanne d'Arc complex. In an attempt to get NVA soldiers to reveal their positions and perhaps bolt into the open, Gonzalez moved from window to window, firing LAAWs into the enemy-held rooms facing the quadrangle. He was especially intent upon engaging RPG teams. While the NVA had their heads down, several of the Marines Gonzalez was supporting tried to attack across the open area, but the NVA recovered and threw the Marines back with intense fire. Sergeant Gonzalez went back to work on the NVA positions with his collections of LAAWs, but the NVA finally figured out what the Marine platoon sergeant had in mind. At 0905, a patient NVA RPG team caught him in one of the windows and fired a B-40 right at him. Sergeant Alfredo Gonzalez was struck squarely in the midriff and mortally wounded. In time, Sergeant Gonzalez would be awarded a posthumous Medal of Honor in recognition of all his singular acts of heroism on the way to and inside Hue.

Minutes after Sergeant Gonzalez was wounded, a handful of Alpha/1/1 Marines broke into an open area on the ground floor in the northwest of the building. The NVA caught the Marines in the open and poured in every bit of fire they could bring to bear. The Marines retreated, but the last of them went down with two AK-47 rounds in his back. Corporal Bill Stubbs and another Marine dropped back to drag the wounded man to safety. As they did, a B-40 detonated a few feet from them. Stubbs, who had weathered all but a few days of his one-year tour of duty in Vietnam, was painfully struck by glass and B-40 shrapnel in both legs. Though barely able to retain his stance, Bill Stubbs nevertheless helped drag the first wounded Marine to safety before he himself collapsed. Stubbs and the other Marine were helped back to MACV for treatment and eventual medevac.

And so it went.

Once across Ly Thuong Kiet Street and back in possession of the main building in the Public Health Complex, Staff Sergeant Johnny Miller's 2nd Platoon of Hotel/2/5 advanced into the buildings on the northeast side of Le Dinh Duong Street. There, as before, NVA soldiers in facing buildings were ready and waiting for the Marines to come out into the open.

The lead squad was Corporal Robert Elliott's, which had entered an abandoned private home immediately behind the Public Health Building. The squad settled in to await further orders. At about 1130 Corporal Elliott received word that they would move into the unsecured dwelling about seventy-five meters to the southeast and on the same side of Le Dinh Duong. To help the squad through the masonry wall surrounding the first house, an engineer demolitions team had set a satchel charge, filled with twenty pounds of C4 explosive, against the obstruction. The charge went off at 1141.

As had become their custom after only two days in Hue, Corporal Elliott and his Marines charged through the hole in the wall before the dust and rubble had settled. Plenty of fire came from the right, from across Le Dinh Duong, but the squad's momentum carried it into the next house. The NVA who had been occupying the structure evaporated as the Marines hit the door and fanned out to conduct their explosive house-clearing routine. As soon as the house had been scoured, the squad set in.

Corporal Robert Hedger's rocket squad was ordered to follow the same path and join Elliott's squad. Just before leaving, Corporal Hedger found two small crucifixes in the rubble of the first house. He placed one in the wide elastic band around his helmet and offered the second to Corporal Lyndol Wilson. Then

Hedger told his men to prepare to move out.

Corporal Hedger took the lead, a custom he would not break despite the heavy load of extra 3.5-inch rockets he insisted on humping to the new forward position. He crossed the first courtyard, ducked through the hole in the wall the engineers had blown, and started across the courtyard surrounding Corporal Elliott's house. As Hedger was ducking through the wall, NVA soldiers emplaced in buildings on the other side of Le Dinh Duong opened fire on him. Hedger was halfway across the open space when Corporal Lyndol Wilson saw him go down beside a pile of rubble. Wilson could not tell if Hedger had been hit or if he had simply taken cover, so he ran into the open and flopped down beside the rocket-squad leader.

"Are you hit?" Wilson asked. When Hedger replied that he was, Wilson dragged him behind a higher pile of rubble and yelled, "Corpsman, up!" However, as Wilson looked Hedger over, he saw neck and chest wounds he was sure would be mortal.

For all the 3.5-inch rockets Hedger and Wilson were carrying, neither corporal had the launcher. Hedger—a stable, devout, soft-spoken twenty-four-year-old—was the rocket squad's father figure, one of the best-beloved Marines in Hotel/2/5. Wilson was so enraged by the thought of Hedger's imminent death that he stood up and emptied his M-16 at the NVA across the street, even though he could not actually see any targets. When he used up the first magazine, he popped it out, rammed in another, and fired on full automatic. At length, Corporal Wilson fired all the 5.56mm rounds he was carrying, so he looted the magazines Corporal Hedger was carrying.

As Lyndol Wilson stood in full view of the NVA and fired his M-16 on full automatic, the rest of the rocket squad and Elliott's squad fired all their weapons—including a dozen 3.5-inch rockets—at the NVA-held buildings across Le Dinh Duong Street. When Corporal Wilson ran out of M-16 ammunition, he unholstered his .45-caliber pistol and emptied it at the NVA.

While the Marine infantrymen and rocketmen were firing, the pair of 106mm recoilless rifles attached to Hotel/2/5 reached one of the buildings fronting Le Dinh Duong. The 106 gunners slammed a total of eighteen of their highly lethal rounds into the NVA buildings across the street.

The 106s did the trick. As they were firing, the NVA had to keep their heads down, and that gave Corporal A. R. Briseno an opportunity to dash out from Elliott's house to help rescue Corporal Hedger. Briseno's arrival in the courtyard snapped Corporal Wilson back to Hedger's plight, and he helped Briseno carry the inert rocket-squad leader to the doorway of Elliott's house. There Briseno was shot through the leg.

As Elliott's squad and the 106s continued to pour fire across Le Dinh Duong, the remainder of the rocket squad charged through the hole in the wall and crossed the courtyard into Elliott's house. There Corporal Wilson assumed leadership of the rocket squad and began planning the evacuation of Corporal Hedger and Corporal Briseno. As expected, James Robert Hedger succumbed to his wounds that afternoon. Corporal Briseno was evacuated to Phu Bai. Corporal Lyndol Wilson was awarded a Silver Star for his stand in the courtyard.

— 19 —

The ferocity of the NVA resistance facing 1/1 in the Jeanne d'Arc complex ruined what had been conceived as a coordinated regimental assault by two Marine battalions. The attack quickly degenerated into two distinctly uncoordinated battalion assaults. However, the mere presence of Mark Gravel's thin battalion alleviated some of the pressure on 2/5, particularly Fox/2/5. Nevertheless, as long as the NVA prevented Gravel's companies from reaching Ly Thuong Kiet Street, Fox/2/5 was unable to advance.

Even after the machine-gun nest in the basement of Le Loi Primary was destroyed, Fox/2/5 got nowhere. The immensely strong treasury structure remained impervious to all the weapons the Marines could bring to bear, and Fox/2/5's lead platoon remained thwarted behind the facing courtyard wall, exchanging fire and sustaining more casualties for no discernible gains.

Corporal Forrest Towe, a fire-team leader with Fox/2/5's 3rd Platoon, had been firing his M-16 through a hole in the wall—without actually peeking out to look at the treasury. Around mid-morning Towe was leaning with his back to the wall, changing magazines and watching two Marines in the large first-story window fronting the house at the rear of the courtyard. Someone yelled, "B-Forty!" and Towe naturally jerked his eyes up. He saw the RPG as it came in over the wall, right over his head. It was so close, he thought he could reach up and touch it. But it passed him by in what felt like slow motion. Inscribing a smoky trail across the courtyard, it curved down into the window and detonated.

Corporal Towe was certain the two men in the window had been blown to bits, but he could not be sure. Marines were hurtling out a side door, through billowing dust and debris. There was nothing Towe could do to help. When he tried to move, he discovered that his right leg was twisted up behind his back and over his left shoulder. Towe straightened out the twisted leg and tried to pull out a long piece of shrapnel that was sticking out of the middle of his right shin, but it would not budge. The wound burned like hell, but there was no blood. The shrapnel had cauterized its own wound. At that moment, Sergeant Willard Scott, the 3rd Platoon guide, passed by. "Sergeant Scott," Towe called, "I've been wounded." Scott looked at Towe and said, "Ain't nothing we can do for you here," so Towe braced his back against the wall and stood up on one foot. As he tried to hop across the courtyard, enemy bullets from the treasury struck the ground around him. Dislocated leg and all, Towe ran into the building and right on through to the company aid station. From there, he was sent with several other walking wounded to Doc Lao Park for any available medevac.

And so it went, right through the morning.

The final collapse of the treasury compound began with an inauspicious event: the arrival in Hue of Major John Salvati, the 2/5 exec.

John Salvati was an especially aggressive type who, by virtue of his rank and bad fortune, had spent the first half of his tour in Vietnam without ever closing on the enemy. Just before 2/5 was transferred north to Thua Thien Province a week before Tet,

Above: U.S. Army twin-40mm Duster escorts Golf/2/5 convoy out of Phu Bai. January 31, 1968. *(Courtesy of Douglas Blayney)*

Below: Golf/2/5 Marines and convoy escorts take cover at the southern end of the cane field causeway in response to fire from NVA soldiers in and around the cane field. January 31, 1968. *(Courtesy of Jerome Nadolski)*

Above: As Marines from Fox/2/5's 2nd Platoon hunker down behind two Marine tanks and recover the bodies of their dead comrades from fire-swept Tran Cao Van Street, Lance Corporal Charles Campbell sprints to safety behind a dust cloud kicked up by one tank's 90mm main gun. February 1, 1968. *(UPI/Bettmann photo by Kyoichi Sawada)*

Below: The survivors of Fox/2/5's 2nd Platoon tend to their wounded and dead comrades along Highway 1 shortly after withdrawing from Tran Cao Van Street. February 1, 1968. *(UPI/Bettmann photo by Kyoichi Sawada)*

Above: A Hotel/2/5 M-60 team covers sweep-and-clear operations near Hue University. February 2, 1968. *(Official U.S. Marine Corps photo by Sgt W. F. Dickman)*

Below: One of 1/1's 106mm recoilless rifle teams sights in on a fortified NVA sniper position near the MACV Compound. February 2, 1968. *(Official U.S. Marine Corps photo)*

Above, left: An Alpha/1/1 rifleman moves through NVA fire during sweep-and-clear operations around the MACV Compound. February 2, 1968. *(Official U.S. Marine Corps photo by Sgt B. A. Atwell)*

Above, right: As a Marine M-48 tank advances up the center of Highway 1 toward the Nguyen Hoang Bridge, an Alpha/1/1 rifleman crouches behind a concrete electric-line pole to elude NVA sniper fire. February 2, 1968. *(Official U.S. Marine Corps photo by SSgt J. L. Harlan)*

Below: An M-48 tank covers Alpha/1/1 Marines converging on the traffic circle directly in front of the southern ramp of the Nguyen Hoang Bridge. February 2, 1968. *(Official U.S. Marine Corps photo)*

Above: Vietnamese civilians stream past a Marine M-48 tank as soon as the buildings in which they had taken refuge are liberated by Marine infantrymen. February 3, 1968. *(Official U.S. Marine Corps photo by Sgt W. F. Dickman)*

Below: A wounded Hotel/2/5 Marine is gingerly lowered from the roof of Hue University. February 3, 1968. *(Official U.S. Marine Corps photo by Sgt W. F. Dickman)*

Above: Marines from Hotel/2/5's 2nd Platoon break through into the Public Health Complex. February 4, 1968. *(Official U.S. Marine Corps photo by Sgt W. F. Dickman)*

Below: Once inside the Public Health Complex, Hotel/2/5 Marines advance cautiously in the face of stubborn resistance by NVA sniper teams. February 4, 1968. *(Official U.S. Marine Corps photo by Sgt W. F. Dickman)*

Above: A 2/5 106mm recoilless rifle team set up in a second-story window of Hue University prepares to fire across Ly Thuong Kiet Street to support Fox/2/5's final assault on the treasury building. When the 106 was fired, its backblast tore out the walls and brought down the ceiling. February 4, 1968. *(Official U.S. Marine Corps photo by Sgt W. F. Dickman)*

Below: A Hotel/2/5 rocketman (note 3.5-inch rocket on his hip) helps a Vietnamese child from a window of the building in which she had been taking refuge. February 4, 1968. *(Official U.S. Marine Corps photo by Sgt W. F. Dickman)*

Above, left: One of a mere handful of NVA prisoners taken by 2/5. February 5, 1968. *(Official U.S. Marine Corps photo by Sgt W. F. Dickman)*

Above, right: A 2/5 grenadier fires his M-79 grenade launcher to achieve a high-angle effect. *(Official U.S. Marine Corps photo)*

Below: Lance Corporal Bernie Burnham (*right center, without helmet*) briefs his squad of the 3rd Platoon, Fox/2/5, before leading an advance toward the hospital complex. February 5, 1968. *(Official U.S. Marine Corps photo)*

Above: Marines of Hotel/2/5 take a break while a platoon corpsman binds the wounds of a rifleman injured during the advance toward the Thua Thien provincial administrative complex. February 6, 1968. *(Official U.S. Marine Corps photo by Sgt W. F. Dickman)*

Below: A wounded Marine from the 3rd Platoon, Hotel/2/5, is unceremoniously dragged through a convenient opening during the advance toward the Thua Thien provincial administrative complex. February 6, 1968. *(Official U.S. Marine Corps photo by Sgt W. F. Dickman)*

Above, left: A Hotel/2/5 M-60 gunner delivers suppressive fire on an NVA position as fellow Marines advance toward the Thua Thien provincial administrative complex. February 6, 1968. *(Official U.S. Marine Corps photo by Sgt W. F. Dickman)*

Above, right: Alpha/1/1 riflemen attempt to locate NVA sniper positions. February 9, 1968. *(Official U.S. Marine Corps photo by Sgt B. A. Atwell)*

Below: An Alpha/1/1 rifleman gingerly checks for NVA snipers before leaving the relative safety of one of Hue's many churches. February 9, 1968. *(Official U.S. Marine Corps photo by Sgt B. A. Atwell)*

Above: The An Cuu Bridge across the Phu Cam Canal (looking south), after NVA sappers finally blew the span. February 10, 1968. *(Courtesy of Jerome Nadolski)*

Below: These eight NVA prisoners, taken by 1/1 and 2/5 south of the Perfume River, are about to be flown to rear detention facilities to be interrogated. February 11, 1968. *(Official U.S. Marine Corps photo)*

Above: An element of the Vietnamese Marine Corps's Battle Group Alpha boards an LCU in Doc Lao Park for a ride across the Perfume River to the Citadel. February 12, 1968. *(Courtesy of Ronald Ray)*

Below: A Charlie/1/5 M-60 team "works out" against an NVA fortified position in the Citadel. February 19, 1968. *(Official U.S. Marine Corps photo by J. Pennington)*

Above: The north corner of the Citadel wall after it fell to the 4th Vietnamese Marine Corps Battalion. This is a *cultivated* area honeycombed with bunkers and fighting holes like those shown in the center of this photograph. *(Courtesy of Ronald Ray)*

Below: A Marine Ontos 106mm recoilless-rifle carrier between fire-support missions inside the Citadel. *(Official U.S. Marine Corps photo)*

Above: Air and artillery attack along the Thon Que Chu treeline. This view is from the Thon Lieu Con Thuong treeline past the downed Cav Huey helicopter. *(Courtesy of Charles Baker)*

Below: During the 5/7 Cav's abortive February 12 attack, the battalion command group follows the action from behind the burial mounds halfway between Thon Lieu Coc Thuong and Thon Que Chu treeline. *(Courtesy of Charles Baker)*

Above, left: The NVA corner bunker taken by Company B, 5/7 Cav, troopers supported by the twin-40mm Duster. February 21, 1968. *(Courtesy of Charles Baker)*

Above, right: A 1/5 M-60 team duels an NVA strongpoint from a rooftop position in the shadow of the Citadel wall. *(Official U.S. Marine Corps photo)*

Below: A Marine sniper attached to Delta/1/5 takes aim at an NVA sniper opposing the Marine advance inside the Citadel. February 22, 1968. *(Official U.S. Marine Corps photo by J. Pennington)*

Above: The U.S. Army 0-1 Bird Dog observation plane dips low over the Perfume River as the Marine aerial observer aboard directs an air strike on the Citadel. February 23, 1968. *(Official U.S. Marine Corps photo by LCpl D. M. Messenger)*

Below: Delta/1/5 Marines move freely near the liberated Thuong Tu Gate. February 24, 1968. *(Official U.S. Marine Corps photo by SSgt J. L. Harlan)*

Salvati had been alerted that he was being routinely reassigned as 1st Marine Division headquarters commandant. That move, Salvati knew, would ensure his completing his tour without ever seeing combat. Extremely distraught, Major Salvati had approached his boss, Lieutenant Colonel Ernie Cheatham, to beg that he be taken along when Cheatham mounted out for Hue on February 3. Both knew well that the province of the battalion executive officer was "in the rear with the gear," and Cheatham knew that he would need a man of Salvati's character and drive at Phu Bai to push supplies and replacements forward against the tide of senior rear-area bureaucracies. But, in the end, Cheatham relented. A few days in Hue really would be John Salvati's last chance to see some action.

Major Salvati had been ready to mount out to Hue with Cheatham on February 3, but unfinished errands requiring the presence of a field-grade officer prevented him from going along. On the battalion commander's sworn promise of duty in Hue, Salvati agreed to remain in Phu Bai for one more day. By the morning of February 4, his tasks in Phu Bai had been completed. On radioed orders from Ernie Cheatham, Salvati gathered up every rear-area 2/5 Marine who could be spared and joined a convoy that left for Hue at 0910. He arrived at MACV at 1005. The only action on the way had been some desultory sniper fire along Highway 1 between the An Cuu Bridge across the Phu Cam Canal and a point about two blocks south of MACV.

Following directions he picked up at MACV, Major Salvati arrived at the 2/5's CP, in the university, at about the time the 106mm recoilless rifle was taking out the NVA .51-caliber machine gun in Le Loi Primary School. As soon as Salvati arrived, Lieutenant Colonel Cheatham detailed him to supervise the emplacement of another 106 in a top-floor window of the university. The 106 was to take out an NVA machine gun that could not be reached from the street.

The immensely heavy recoilless rifle had to be manhandled up a spiral staircase before it could be emplaced. Then the gunner adjusted his sights and fired a .50-caliber marking round at the target. During the time it took to fire several marking rounds, conversation in the crowded room naturally turned to the subject of the 106's deadly backblast. When the sights were correctly aligned, the platoon commander, Staff Sergeant James Long, rigged a remote firing device, and everyone evacuated the room. The 106 fired one round, and the room in which it was emplaced was demolished. Major Salvati, Staff Sergeant Long, the gun team, and sundry observers were covered in plaster dust, and the 106's tripod was severely damaged by falling masonry. The enemy machine gun had also been destroyed.

There wasn't much for a battalion executive officer to do in Hue without a staff armed with typewriters. So, after the 106 incident in the university, Lieutenant Colonel Cheatham invited Major Salvati to "check on the companies and see what they need." There is no telling how that open-ended assignment might have been undertaken by a less aggressive major. John Salvati took it to mean that he had carte blanche to mix it up with the enemy.

In very short order Major Salvati learned of Fox/2/5's thwarted attempts to cross Ly Thuong Kiet Street to the treasury. He decided to head to the Fox/2/5 CP to see what Captain Mike Downs was doing and to find out if he could be of any help. When Salvati first saw Downs, the major was reminded of a joke about a one-legged man in an ice-skating race. The NVA in the treasury were laying extremely heavy fire on Fox/2/5's positions, preventing Downs's Marines from jumping off. Downs was alternating conversations on the company radio with all three of his platoon commanders, trying to direct the company 60mm mortars against feasible targets, and yelling for ammunition.

When Major Salvati asked if there was anything he could do, Captain Downs asked him how he felt about training a 3.5-inch rocket team. Salvati agreed and took the two young Marines to a secure area behind several buildings. To his amazement, neither member of the rocket team had ever fired a rocket. Salvati ran them through the drill and asked them to expend a round on a three-story building just fifty meters away. The tyro rocketmen missed the massive structure entirely. There wasn't time to deal with it—Mike Downs was yelling for rocket fire—so John Salvati entered the fray as a rocket gunner. He got into a good position across from the treasury; placed the launcher on his shoulder; instructed one of the rocketmen on the intricacies of loading a rocket; and fired directly at a window on the treasury's second floor, from which he was certain the NVA were firing down on Fox/2/5.

Having provided his inexperienced gunners with brief but effective on-the-job training, Major Salvati returned to the Fox/2/5 CP. There he found Mike Downs as busy as ever; Fox/2/5 was still stalled on its side of Ly Thuong Kiet Street. Unencumbered by the responsibilities of command, John Salvati let his mind wander in search of a viable solution to Fox/2/5's bloody problem. He thought of using CS tear gas against the enemy position, but he knew the company would need a lot of it if its assault through the gas was to be effective.

Salvati's mind settled on the E-8 gas launcher, a pack-mounted device that was capable of firing sixty-four 35mm CS tear-gas projectiles in four five-second bursts of sixteen projectiles each. The E-8 was an area-saturation weapon, perfect for the situation Fox/2/5 was facing. Fortunately, Salvati knew, Lieutenant Colonel Cheatham had had the foresight to make certain that every member of 2/5 had or had access to a gas mask. So the only problem was locating one or more E-8s. By lucky coincidence, Salvati had seen several E-8s stacked against the wall of an ARVN compound adjacent to MACV. Without further ado, the battalion exec hopped into his jeep and ordered his driver to head straight for the E-8 cache.

It took much pointing and gesturing—and some serious threatening—to get the ARVN troops to go along, but Major Salvati and his driver managed to load four E-8 launchers into the jeep's trailer and head back to the battalion CP. There Salvati explained his idea to Ernie Cheatham, and the battalion commander readily assented. With that, Salvati drove down to the Fox/2/5 CP and laid out his plan for Mike Downs. Captain Downs jumped on the idea. He asked Major Salvati to set up the E-8 launchers in a nearby courtyard while Downs got his company ready to leap through the gas cloud and across Ly Thuong Kiet Street.

Second Lieutenant Donald Hausrath's 3rd Platoon of Fox/2/5 was still in the chemistry building and courtyard directly across Ly Thuong Kiet from the treasury, still assigned the lead-off position in the company assault on the objective. On the morning of February 4, Sergeant Chuck Ekker's squad moved to the courtyard wall, into the lead-off position. When Major Salvati launched the gas, Ekker's squad was to attack, with Corporal Arkie Allbritton's fire team in the vanguard.

Everything was set. Almost exactly at noon, the word came to Major John Salvati that Fox/2/5 was ready for him to activate the first E-8 gas launcher. Salvati personally pulled the lanyard—and nothing happened. The cord was rotted through, and it broke off in Salvati's hand. Fortunately, the E-8 could be fired with an electrical impulse. Second Lieutenant Dick Squires, a Marine engineer whose platoon of the 1st Engineer Battalion was attached to 2/5, somehow produced an old crank-operated field telephone. The phone was then rigged to the E-8 gas launcher. All Major Salvati had to do to produce an adequate electrical current was crank the phone vigorously. This he did. The first wave of sixteen gas projectiles was ejected from the launcher, followed in five seconds by sixteen more projectiles, and so forth, until sixty-four had been fired. The northeastern facade of the treasury building blossomed in detonations, which did little or no good. But several pellets fell through open windows, and that was the charm.

Unfortunately, in addition to causing the NVA no end of grief, the CS tear gas drifted southeast with the breeze off the Perfume River and caused much gagging and puking among dozens of unprepared 1/1 Marines. Lieutenant Colonel Mark Gravel gasped a protest direct to Lieutenant Colonel Ernie Cheatham, but there was nothing Cheatham could do except apologize.

As soon as the tear-gas canisters were launched, the treasury's wrought-iron front gate was blasted open by the 106mm recoilless rifle team that had earlier destroyed the NVA machine gun in the basement of Le Loi Primary School. Once again, the 106 gunners ran their mule-mounted 106 down the university steps, right out onto Ly Thuong Kiet. And, as before, they painstakingly aimed in on their target by firing the .50-caliber spotting rifle until the tracer rounds were perfectly placed.

As soon as the gas cloud started to spread across the front of the treasury building, Corporal Arkie Allbritton ducked through the hole in the courtyard wall and raced across Ly Thuong Kiet, straight for the treasury compound's blown gate. Right behind Allbritton were Lance Corporal Ray Stewart, Lance Corporal Ken Crysel, and Private First Class Hastings Rigollet. Behind Rigollet was the M-60 machine-gun team led by Lance Corporal Roger Warren. Behind the M-60 team were Sergeant Chuck Ekker and the rest of Ekker's squad. Staff Sergeant Jim McCoy, the 3rd Platoon's platoon sergeant, was with Ekker's squad and detailed with leading the fire team assigned to clear the treasury attic.

After passing through the front gate, Corporal Allbritton charged across the open courtyard—about twelve meters—and made it to the front door of the treasury building. The massive front door had been blown in moments before by a Marine tank, which was still firing its machine guns and 90mm main gun at windows all across the front of the building. Allbritton leaned against the door frame and chucked in a CS tear-gas grenade. Then Corporal Stewart tossed in an M-26 fragmentation grenade. When the M-26 went off, Arkie Allbritton stepped around the edge of the doorway, blindly spraying the foyer with his M-16.

Corporal Allbritton's orders were to seize the high ground—in this case, to find a way to the second story. In front of Allbritton, and to his left, was a counter topped by steel bars that ran to the ceiling. Clearly these were tellers' cages. To the right was the only doorway Allbritton could see, so he peered through it and saw that a long, narrow corridor stretched away to his left, toward the rear of the building. Directly across the hallway was an open door through which Allbritton could see a roomful of safes. To his left, back along the hallway, were three doors. The door farther back on the same side of the hallway as Allbritton's door was open. It seemed to lead behind the tellers' cages. A door directly opposite that door was closed, as was a door at the far rear of the hallway.

Allbritton reasoned that one of the closed doors led to the stairway, so he stepped into the hallway and began working his way to the nearest one. As Allbritton's fire team and the one behind it rapidly moved up the hallway, Staff Sergeant McCoy and the last of Sergeant Ekker's fire teams entered the smoke-filled foyer and immediately turned left. McCoy had been told that the stairway to the second floor was to the left, but he literally collided with the left-hand teller's cage when he went that way. Staff Sergeant McCoy collected the fire team he was leading and followed the rest of Sergeant Ekker's squad back through the doorway to the right of the main entrance.

Before Corporal Allbritton could consider opening either of the closed doors along the hallway, he heard Vietnamese voices behind the near one, coming from above. Apparently, several NVA were trying to evacuate the second floor.

Certain he had located the stairwell, Allbritton fired at the door, hoping he would kill or scare the men behind it. At the moment Allbritton opened fire, Lance Corporal Roger Warren arrived with his M-60 machine gun, and he also fired at the door.

When the firing ceased, Corporal Allbritton tried to open the door. It would not budge. It seemed to Allbritton that a body or some rubble was wedged in behind it. Corporal Ray Stewart and Lance Corporal Ken Crysel placed M-26 hand grenades at the base of the door, and everyone stepped into the rooms to the right and left. The grenades blew the door off its hinges. As Stewart and Crysel kicked the door out of the way, Allbritton passed between them, stepped over a pile of masonry rubble, and found himself confronted by a tightly enclosed stairwell. Opposite the door the Marines had just blown down was another door, which the NVA had clearly used to escape the M-16 and M-60 fire.

Hardly taking the time to let all the details sink in, Allbritton chucked the fragmentation grenade in his hand up to the landing to his right. Everyone flattened against the walls until it blew. With that, Corporal Stewart and Lance Corporal Crysel led the way up the stairs, through two turns. On the second floor, Allbritton's fire team and Lance Corporal Warren's gun team rushed to secure all the rooms. They were joined moments later by Staff Sergeant McCoy and another fire team from Sergeant Ekker's squad. Ekker and the last fire team were sweeping through the ground floor.

There was more tear gas on the second floor than there had been below, and the Marines' vision and hearing were restricted by their gas masks. The clearing operation, which would have been tense under any circumstances, was therefore especially scary because the Marines' two most important senses were handicapped. For all the terror, however, Allbritton's and Warren's teams found only one laggard NVA soldier. He turned up severely wounded after Corporal Stewart blindly tossed a grenade into a closet during routine clearing operations. The NVA soldier's wounds were treated on the spot by his captors, and he was later evacuated to MACV, the only prisoner to emerge from the treasury.

While searching for a way up to the half-story attic above the second story, Corporal Allbritton chanced to look through a steel-barred window facing back the way he had come, back across Ly Thuong Kiet. To his surprise, for he had heard no sounds of fighting below, Marines were dragging casualties back across the treasury courtyard.

At length, someone found a trapdoor leading to the attic. A ladder built into the wall was the only way up. The trapdoor was thrown back and fragmentation grenades were lofted through the opening before anyone attempted to climb up.

The deserted attic area was just one large open space. Ventilation holes the builders had cut into the foot-thick walls made perfect firing ports, and there were what amounted to individual bunkers built from masonry rubble around each aperture. While searching through the bunkers, Corporal Allbritton found just one 35mm tear-gas projectile. Apparently, it had been enough to force the NVA out of the attic. When Allbritton peered out through one of the firing ports, his heart nearly stopped. The NVA soldiers who had occupied the bunkers had enjoyed a flawless view of the courtyard in which Fox/2/5's 3rd Platoon had been bottled up for nearly a day and a half. The NVA fields of fire had been perfect.

Lance Corporal Bernie Burnham's squad was right behind Sergeant Ekker's. Just before jumping off through the hole in the courtyard wall, Burnham's Marines gripped hands. "Okay,"

Burnham said, "here we go." And they went.

After passing through the front door of the treasury build-ing and into the foyer, Burnham's squad followed Ekker's and went to the right, into the hallway first penetrated by Corporal Allbritton's fire team. By the time Lance Corporal Burnham entered the hallway, the noise of gunfire and exploding grenades was deafening. The dark interior of the building, tear-gas fumes, thick billows of gun smoke, and the narrow vistas afforded by gas-mask goggles combined to make it virtually impossible for Burnham to see where he was going, but he knew that he had to forge ahead—no matter what.

Ekker's squad had rushed ahead, chasing the fleeing NVA, but Burnham's squad had to go slowly, carefully searching the building for stragglers or intentional stay-behinds. Feeling their way through the smoky gloom, two-man teams from Burnham's squad cleared one room at a time in the by-then classic mode—a grenade through the doorway followed by both Marines entering simultaneously, hosing their M-16s around on full automatic.

Behind Burnham's squad was the last of the 3rd Platoon's three squads, Corporal Dave Theriault's. Lance Corporal Ernie Weiss saw the tellers' cages ahead and to his left as soon as he entered the treasury building through the front door. This had not quite registered when, through all the accumulated haze, Weiss saw the muzzle of an AK-47 appear over the top of the counter. He flung his body into reverse and came to rest outside the front door just as the NVA soldier, whom Weiss had not actually seen, opened fire.

No one was hit by the burst, and the NVA soldier ceased firing. Lance Corporal Weiss reentered the foyer on his hands and knees, crawled up to the counter, and pushed a fragmentation grenade between the bars of the teller's cage. When the grenade went off, Weiss stood up and opened fire. There was nothing behind the counter except a roomful of desks, so Weiss turned to his right and followed the rest of Corporal Theriault's squad through the door and down the hallway.

Somehow, Ernie Weiss found himself at the head of The-riault's squad as it moved rapidly toward a doorway at the end of the hallway. Burnham's squad had grenaded and blasted its way up the hallway already, so no one in Theriault's squad was checking the rooms on either side. Suddenly, a Chinese (Chicom) "potato masher" hand grenade was lofted into the hallway from a doorway at Weiss's left front. The Chicom bounced against the wall to Weiss's right and started rolling down the hall.

Weiss was transfixed. A live Chicom grenade was rolling down the hallway toward him, and he just stood there, staring. The only thing he could think of to say was, "Oh, shit!" With that, he jumped to the right, through another doorway. Corporal Dave Theriault yelled, "Grenade," but he was too late. The Chicom detonated, wounding about half the Marines in Theriault's squad, including Theriault himself. The wounded men had to be evacuated from the building with the help of all but two of their uninjured comrades.

While the wounded were being treated, Lance Corporal Weiss and Private First Class Mike Sowards charged into the room from which the Chicom had been thrown. The NVA soldier—probably the same man who had fired at Weiss from over the teller's counter—was long gone, but he or one of his comrades had left behind a radio pack. Weiss rifled through the pack and found an NVA battle flag, which he kept. From there, the two Marines eased through the door in back of the room and found themselves on a covered porch running the full width of the back of the treasury building. They worked to the left, down the covered porch, checking each room they encountered along the way. At the far end of each room was a teller's cage facing the front foyer of the building.

A few minutes later, Weiss and Sowards found themselves in a small side courtyard. When they entered the enclosed space, they discovered a wounded NVA soldier who was crawling very slowly on his belly. Weiss turned to Sowards and said, "Holy shit, it's a gook." It was the first enemy soldier he had ever seen up close, and he was not sure what he was supposed to do. Weiss looked around for a superior and saw a more experienced Marine passing only a few yards away. "Hey," Lance Corporal Weiss called, "we got a wounded gook over here."

The newcomer took one look at the wounded, pathetic NVA

soldier. He felt no spark of human kindness. All he saw in his mind's eye were the bloody bodies of Private First Class William Barnes, who had been shot dead in the middle of Ly Thuong Kiet the previous afternoon, and Lance Corporal Wayne Washburn, who had been carried to safety but had died nonetheless. The Marine wordlessly lowered the muzzle of his M-16 and fired several rounds into the crawling man. He knew he had done something wrong, but he could not make himself feel any remorse.

The rear section of the walled treasury compound was a broad, shallow courtyard containing several small outbuildings. As teams of Marines stepped into the open from the rear of the treasury building, an NVA soldier in one of the outbuildings opened fire on them. One Marine fell, wounded and unable to fend for himself.

Lance Corporal Roger Warren, the M-60 team leader, was also in the open. Rather than hit the dirt, Warren fired the M-60 from his hip and advanced to the side of the wounded Marine. The NVA soldier was still firing at the wounded man—and Lance Corporal Warren, who was also hit—but Warren continued to return the fire, using up two entire belts of M-60 ammunition before he and others quelled the NVA soldier's fire. The Marine Warren had been aiding was evacuated, but Warren ignored his own injuries. He had already been awarded two Purple Heart medals, and the rule was that he would be sent home to the States if he earned a third. There was no way Roger Warren was going home if he could still move under his own power.

Staff Sergeant Jim McCoy was checking through the building, making sure it was secure, when about thirty civilians emerged from nowhere. They all were well dressed in American-style clothing. McCoy radioed the 3rd Platoon commander, Lieutenant Donald Hausrath, to tell him about the civilians; Hausrath sent word that McCoy was to "handle it." McCoy found that one of the civilians spoke good English, so he told the man that the treasury compound was secure and that the danger had passed. With that, the civilians left. McCoy never found out who they were, where they had come from, or where they went.

While Staff Sergeant McCoy was tied up with the civilians, Lance Corporal Bernie Burnham radioed the Fox/2/5 CP and told Captain Mike Downs that the treasury building was secure. Downs said that he was coming right over with his CP group, but Burnham told him that it wasn't safe. This was not true, and Burnham knew it, but he had a plan to blow one of the safes. He knew he had erred as soon as he had told Downs the building was in Marine hands; Downs's quick arrival obviated the safe-blowing job. Burnham collected no booty, but, overnight, scores of Marines from Fox/2/5 and Hotel/2/5 helped themselves to currency and even thin leaves of gold they found in safes and vaults throughout the building.

In all, on February 4, eighteen Fox/2/5 Marines had been wounded trying to cross Ly Thuong Kiet Street or securing the treasury compound. About half were evacuated from Hue; several were treated and returned to duty; and several, like Lance Corporal Roger Warren, never bothered to turn themselves in for fear of being awarded a third Purple Heart and shipped home.

— 20 —

Altogether, February 4 was a pivotal day in the battle for Hue, for it marked the beginning of a regimental effort by U.S. Marines to recapture the southern portion of the city—a signal to the NVA that the Americans had placed Hue near the top of their list of nationwide priorities. For the Marines, the fall of the NVA strongpoint in the treasury building was of immense significance, for it served notice to the 4th NVA Regiment that in a matter of days the Americans had mastered the art of city combat. The Marines had captured the treasury with an improvised attack using available weapons—tear gas, tanks, 106mm recoilless rifles, mortars, and 3.5-inch rocket launchers—combined with tough infantry clearing tactics. That success demonstrated that they could probably seize any NVA strongpoint in the city.

Also of significance that afternoon was the arrival of the

U.S. Navy's guided-missile destroyer *Lynde McCormic*. From around 1700 on, 1st Marine Regiment and 1st ARVN Division units in need of direct fire support would be able to receive on-call assistance from *McCormic*'s 5-inch guns or from other U.S. Navy warships that were eventually deployed in the South China Sea east of the city.

Despite the fact that he was in hiding, Jim Bullington was better informed about events around South Vietnam than most Americans in Hue. Thanks to shortwave news broadcasts Bullington listened to all day on February 4, he knew that the Communist TCK-TKN plan was in ruins and that Communist forces were in retreat in all but a few locations, chiefly in Saigon, Hue, and Khe Sanh. Though his own fate was still in doubt, Bullington was elated by the good news.

Only a few blocks from Jim Bullington's hideout, the Than-Trong compound was bathed in despair. The family had a shortwave radio, but frequent visits by roving VC propaganda cadres and search teams prevented any listening. Also, the food was running out. The family had been forced to share its food with many NVA and VC, and about the only fare left was steamed rice with fish sauce, and even that was in short supply. On February 4, Tuy-Cam's mother oversaw the hiding of a 100-kilo sack of rice in the family bunker, where it might be mistaken by searching VC for a bag of sand. The big danger remained the discovery of Tuy-Cam's two servicemen brothers, who were still hiding in the attic. If things seemed to be going well elsewhere in Hue that day, February 4 was the day the Thán-Trong clan began to lose hope.

Attacks to expand the 1st ARVN Division's holdings inside the Citadel had continued. By the morning of February 4, it is probable that the ARVN force inside the Citadel actually outnumbered the NVA defending force. Most likely, the NVA force deployed inside the Citadel consisted of only the 6th NVA Regiment's 800th and 802nd NVA battalions and part of the 12th NVA Sapper Battalion. Though relatively small in numbers, the NVA occupied a massively fortified Japanese-built complex of bunkers and fighting positions. Facing them were the 4th Battalion, 2nd ARVN Regiment; a company of the 3rd Battalion, 1st ARVN Regiment; the 1st Battalion, 3rd ARVN Regiment; the 3rd Company, 7th ARVN Armored Cavalry Battalion; and the reinforced 1st ARVN Airborne Task Force—the 2nd, 7th, and 9th ARVN Airborne battalions.

The major event of February 4 for the 1st ARVN Division was the seizure of the An Hoa gate, at the western end of the Citadel's northwest wall, by the 1st Battalion, 3rd ARVN Regiment. The 4th Battalion, 2nd ARVN Regiment, also made good progress, advancing to a point about halfway down the Citadel's southeast wall.

Outside the Citadel, the 3rd ARVN Regiment's 2nd and 3rd battalions continued their dogged efforts to attack into the Citadel through the southwestern gates. Despite their persistence, however, the ARVN battalions made only negligible gains. Their main contribution was in keeping NVA units tied up along the north bank of the Perfume River while the ARVN units inside the Citadel mounted their attacks.

Also on February 4, the 4th Battalion, 3rd ARVN Regiment, broke through the main body of the 4th NVA Regiment's 804th NVA Battalion. In the end, however, only about 170 members of the ARVN unit, which had been surrounded and fighting desperately since the onset of the Communist offensive on January 31, fought through to the MACV Compound.

There were still an enormous number of loose ends to police up around MACV, and, throughout the day, 1st Marines commandeered small elements of 1/1 and 2/5 to undertake many of the missions. One such mission was an attempt to locate and retrieve two Alpha/1/1 Marines who had been killed and left behind during a patrol sweep several days earlier toward Tu Do Stadium, on Tran Cao Van Street northeast of MACV. Around mid-morning, 2nd Lieutenant Bill Donnelly was ordered out to find the bodies. With him went part of his 1st Platoon of Alpha/1/1 and an ad hoc platoon of Bravo/1/1 commanded by the Bravo/1/1 first sergeant. Since the area around the stadium was still held by most of the 804th NVA Battalion, Donnelly's patrol was bolstered with an Army M-42 twin-40mm Duster.

Lieutenant Donnelly and the Alpha/1/1 Marines with him had arrived in Hue only the day before, the last of their company to reach the city from Quang Tri. Similarly, the Bravo/1/1 Marines were new to the city. At least one of the new arrivals, Lance Corporal Ed Neas, an M-60 team leader who had been in Vietnam since August 1967, could not quite believe what he was seeing as the patrol shoved off from MACV. The first scene that set Neas's mind to wandering was a dead NVA soldier he saw hanging out a window. Nearby was another dead NVA who was leaning against a guard shack. That man's eyes were hanging from their sockets, and his testicles were swollen to the size of apples.

The image and smell of the dead NVA had not quite receded when several human forms jumped up from hiding places and ran into the center of the street. Instantly, the two keyed-up Marines on point dropped to their knees and opened fire, and the Duster's machine gunner followed suit. Only after the targets had been cut down was anyone able to identify them as civilians, who, unfortunately, had chosen the wrong bunch of Marines to help them to safety. Before the Marines could even begin to register any shock or grief, the Duster started forward again and unavoidably crushed the dead civilians beneath its tracks.

A block beyond the dead civilians, the patrol was fired on by several NVA soldiers holed up in a small house in the center of a field adjacent to the roadway. Other NVA in houses farther up the street also opened fire. The Marines halted, took cover, and returned the fire in both directions. The Duster pulled up beside Lance Corporal Neas's M-60 team, ranged in on the house in the field, and blew it to pieces. The unbelievably intense *thrum* of the 40mm guns, as they had fired right over Lance Corporal Neas's head, left his ears ringing for days afterward.

About fifty meters farther up the street, Marines at the head of the patrol column spotted the two dead Marines they had been sent to retrieve. It is possible that the NVA had staked the bodies out, confident that more Marines would eventually return to get them.

As the Marines opened fire, Lieutenant Donnelly and the

first sergeant of Bravo/1/1 worked their way up the street to the bodies. The NVA small-arms fire intensified, and several B-40s streaked out of the NVA-held houses. Lance Corporal Rick Mann, the M-60 squad leader, saw several figures dart out of one of the houses. He turned his machine gun on them, bowling them over. When the smoke cleared, Mann saw a dead baby in the street. He broke down, certain he had just shot the infant, but other Marines told him the baby had been lying there before they arrived. That calmed him down. Later Mann found where a bullet had gone right through a C-ration can he had attached to his M-60 to catch expended cartridge casings. The can was directly in front of Mann's face whenever he fired the M-60, but the bullet had somehow missed him.

Under intense covering fire, Lieutenant Donnelly and the first sergeant of Bravo/1/1 dragged the two dead Marines back down the street. The patrol disengaged from the firefight and withdrew to MACV, arriving at 1240.

Shortly after the patrol returned to MACV, the 1st Marines CP came under fire from the east by the 804th NVA Battalion. This intrusion drew the wrath of several of 2/5's 81mm mortars, at least two Marine M-48 tanks, several Army M-55 quad-.50 trucks, two M-42 dual-40mm Dusters, and Marine artillery located far from Hue. The NVA fire was throttled. One Marine was killed in the exchange, and three Marines had to be medevacked. Somehow, someone in the 1st Marines CP divined that eighteen NVA had been killed in the uneven exchange.

Early in the afternoon, Lieutenant Donnelly's Alpha/1/1 Marines and the platoon from Bravo/1/1 were sent across Highway 1 to join the 1/1 main body in clearing the Jeanne d'Arc complex.

Along Highway 1 through the day, trouble continued. The first Marine convoy to reach Hue from Phu Bai arrived at 1005, having met only minor sniper fire between the An Cuu Bridge and MACV. At 1150, on their return journey, the same trucks were engaged at medium range by heavy automatic-weapons fire near a small bridge about halfway to Phu Bai. The convoy stopped briefly, and the small security force deployed to return the enemy fire. The enemy was driven off and the convoy continued on into Phu Bai without further trouble. The most ominous aspect of the incident was its location. Hitherto, no convoy from Phu Bai had been molested that far south of Hue.

At about 1600 the second resupply convoy of the day set out from Phu Bai beneath a gray, overcast sky. The convoy trail officer was 2nd Lieutenant Terry Charbonneau, the Charlie Company, 1st Motor Transport Battalion, platoon commander who had led several convoys between Phu Bai and Camp Evans at the end of January.

The sudden onset of the Tet offensive, cutting Highway 1 north of Hue, had left Charbonneau's small January 31 convoy stranded in Camp Evans. After seeing his trucks wrecked when they were commandeered as mobile antimortar and antirocket revetments for 101st Airborne Division helicopters, Lieutenant Charbonneau had hitched a helicopter ride to Phu Bai on February 3 to see if anything could be done to evacuate his men. Finding no help there and with no way back to Camp Evans, on February 4 Charbonneau had volunteered to help oversee the afternoon convoy to Hue. He assumed he would be back in Phu Bai that evening or early the next morning.

The first thing that struck Charbonneau as odd about the afternoon convoy to Hue was that most of the Marine replacements in the trucks did not even have helmets. They told the lieutenant that there were not enough helmets left in Phu Bai to go around, but they had been assured of an ample supply in Hue—because of all the casualties. The replacements seemed a little somber, and maybe cheerful news like how much gear the casualties were leaving behind was at the heart of their mood. It certainly shocked Terry Charbonneau.

The last truck in the convoy was a 6 × 6 with a .50-caliber machine gun mounted on it. Following it was a brand-new wrecker that had just reached the 1st Motor Transport Battalion. Whenever possible, a wrecker was incorporated into a convoy along Highway 1 so at least one damaged vehicle could be towed to safety. However, Charbonneau noticed something strange about the new wrecker. Its lift was hydraulically operated. Even a raw second lieutenant like Terry Charbonneau knew that hydraulics could be knocked out by the tiniest piece of shrapnel, whereas the older mechanically operated lifts were impervious to anything less than a direct hit.

The villages along the way looked deserted, which was also something new for Lieutenant Charbonneau, who well remembered the throngs of Tet pilgrims he had encountered on his last trip, on January 31. To Charbonneau the silence and emptiness were downright eerie. At length he saw one little boy standing beside the road, waving at the passing trucks. A few of the Marines gave the boy thumbs-up signs in return, but most of the Americans stared at him in stony silence. Where children were involved, Charbonneau thought this was unusual behavior for his countrymen.

Close to Hue the convoy passed the big signal-intelligence station, marked by its three huge radio masts. When he saw men wearing American uniforms in the station compound, Lieutenant Charbonneau could not believe that the vulnerable installation, set in the middle of a huge field, had not been attacked. Perhaps, he thought, someone was paying the Communists to leave the place alone. How else to explain its inviolate status?

As the convoy slowed to cross the An Cuu Bridge, Terry Charbonneau suddenly felt like a duck in a shooting gallery. Sure enough, at that very moment, there was a huge explosion followed by the pop and crack of small-arms fire.

The commander of the twin-40mm Duster that constituted the convoy's main security tried to radio the captain in command of the convoy. There was no response, so he radioed Lieutenant Charbonneau and said simply, "You're in charge, Sir."

The convoy had stopped, and there was a great deal of shooting ahead, but Charbonneau could not see what was going on from his position in the rear of the convoy. He dismounted from his truck and started walking forward. Suddenly, the trucks ahead started to move forward rapidly. Charbonneau signaled the driver of his truck to start rolling. As the truck came abreast, the lieutenant hopped onto the running board and ordered the .50-cal gunner to lock and load. Then, after climbing into the back of the truck, Charbonneau radioed his position to Phu Bai and explained the situation.

Dead ahead, right across the An Cuu Bridge, Charbonneau saw the lead vehicle, a Mighty Mite cargo transporter. It was on fire, apparently after detonating an antivehicle mine. The convoy commander had been in the vehicle, but neither he nor his driver were anywhere to be seen.

Though the vehicles ahead of Lieutenant Charbonneau's truck were rapidly receding to the north, Charbonneau ordered his truck and the wrecker to stop beside the Mighty Mite so he could see if any Marines had been left behind. At first, he saw nobody. But just as Charbonneau was getting ready to leave, someone spotted the convoy commander and his driver next to a roadside building. As Charbonneau's .50-cal gunner sprayed a row of storefronts to the left, the wrecker pulled over and a corpsman jumped off to treat the wounded men. Meanwhile, Lieutenant Charbonneau ordered his driver to advance slowly so the .50-cal gunner could cover the evacuation. He assumed the wrecker would be along in a minute.

Moments later, when Charbonneau's truck reached the traffic circle, he was amazed to see that the Texaco station's huge glass windows were still intact. At that moment, several 60mm mortar rounds detonated around the rear cargo truck, which was several hundred meters ahead of Charbonneau's vehicle. Fortunately, the mortars missed, for the truck was loaded with ammunition and explosives.

Dead ahead was the raised causeway across the cane field. Charbonneau saw NVA soldiers hiding behind trees near the road. As the main body of trucks sped along the causeway, the Marines poured out a withering fire and inflicted many casualties. However, Charbonneau's truck ran the gauntlet at slow speed because the lieutenant wanted to allow the wrecker to catch up. On the way across the causeway, the .50-cal gunner swung his ominous weapon to the left and right at the NVA in the trees, but he did not fire. Neither did the NVA.

There were no further incidents as Lieutenant Charbonneau's truck rolled slowly into the urban area and on to MACV. However, the wrecker still had not caught up. The lieutenant ran up to the Duster and told the commander that they were going back to find the wrecker. The Army sergeant, whose face registered shock mixed with extreme dismay, blurted out, "But we're an antiaircraft weapon."

"Fine," Terry Charbonneau shot back, "if we see any Commie planes, you can shoot them down. Now, let's roll!"

Fortunately, as Charbonneau was climbing into the Duster, the wrecker came barreling up Highway 1 and screeched to a halt inside the MACV gate. The Mighty Mite driver had most of his foot blown off, and the motor-transport captain was full of tiny slivers of shrapnel. The Charlie Company gunny, who had been riding in the wrecker, had been hit beneath one eye by a ricochet, and the wrecker's hydraulic-fluid storage tank had been holed by many bullets, rendering the brand-new vehicle useless.

Terry Charbonneau's bullet-riddled convoy reached Hue at 1700. At 1940, before the trucks could be unloaded and repaired for the return journey to Phu Bai, word reached MACV that the NVA had finally blown the An Cuu Bridge into the Phu Cam Canal. Highway 1 between Phu Bai and Hue was closed.

Fox/2/5's seizure of the treasury complex, followed rapidly by the bloodless occupation of the adjacent post office complex, and Hotel/2/5's final seizure of the Public Health Complex brought 2/5 all the way to Le Dinh Duong Street by 1700, February 4. Though the battalion's morale was sky-high and there was adequate daylight left, it was decided that 2/5 was to halt along the northeast side of Le Dinh Duong and set in for the night. The reason: neither of 2/5's flanks was secure. To Fox/2/5's left, 1/1 had penetrated barely halfway into the Jeanne d'Arc complex, well short of Ly Thuong Kiet Street; on the right, Hotel/2/5's right flank was unprotected along the riverfront north of Le Loi Street.

The 1/1 Marines were unable to push through the Jeanne d'Arc complex that afternoon. The battalion's two companies were both understrength, and Lieutenant Colonel Mark Gravel did not have sufficient organic supporting arms at his disposal. Also, there are security advantages to be gained from having a dangling flank curve behind an advancing front line; it prevented the enemy from rolling up the main line by way of the open flank. So, it was decided to hold in place and renew the attack on the morning of February 5. However, only an hour after 2/5 had halted, some aggressive NVA provided the impetus for an unplanned attack.

At 1755, Hotel/2/5 Marines set in at the rear of the Public Health Complex were taken under intense fire by NVA small arms and machine guns emplaced inside the French Cultural Center, a two-story building in the riverfront parkland northwest of Le Loi Street and southwest of Le Dinh Duong Street. While most of Hotel/2/5 returned the NVA fire with even stronger fire, Captain Ron Christmas dispatched 2nd Lieutenant Leo Myers's 1st Platoon across Le Dinh Duong to occupy a substantially built two-story building from which flanking fire could be placed on the French Cultural Center.

The first two Marines to reach the objective were Private First Class Walter Kaczmarek and Lance Corporal Ron Walters. The two had been ordered to clear the building with grenades, at which point the rest of the platoon would charge inside. Kaczmarek and Walters reached the front door without incident, and each tossed a fragmentation grenade through the door, as ordered. However, Kaczmarek got a little carried away and threw in a second grenade. As soon as he did and before it blew, the first of his buddies passed him on his way in the door. Kaczmarek frantically grabbed the Marine and turned to block the thundering herd that was right on his heels. The second grenade blew, and then everyone entered the building and ran a classic clearing operation. No NVA were to be found, but around the northeast windows the floors were covered with expended cartridge casings. As usual, the NVA had "boogied."

The house Lieutenant Myers's platoon seized was clearly the home of a very rich and influential family—a physician's home, as it turned out. In addition to opulent furnishings, which included a stuffed tiger, the Marines found large cans of cottonseed oil and heavy sacks of rice, all with prominent USAID logos on their sides. Veterans who had scoured many a poor South Vietnamese village commented that they had never seen their nation's gifts in the hands of the poor.

At the same time Lieutenant Myers's Hotel/2/5 platoon was mounting its bloodless attack, a platoon of Golf/2/5 attacked southwest through the riverfront parkland. The platoon overran a one-story building southwest of Le Dinh Duong that stood directly in front of the cultural center. Outflanked and out-gunned, the NVA abandoned the French Cultural Center, which Lieutenant Myers's platoon occupied as soon as it was evident the NVA had fled.

The big surprise of the afternoon was the discovery that 175 civilians, including two Americans, were hiding inside the French Cultural Center. All were escorted to MACV along with the bodies of five NVA and a small cache of weapons and ammunition. Not one Marine was killed or even injured in the swiftly contrived and unimaginably successful response to the NVA's harassing fire.

At 1904, Fox/2/5's 2nd Platoon, commanded by Staff Sergeant Paul Tinson, was sitting around inside the post office complex when gunfire erupted from an underground bunker the Marines had not even known was there. Immediately, the Marines closest to the shelter's front entrance pumped in rifle fire, followed by five 3.5-inch rocket rounds and two CS tear-gas grenades. This produced a brief lull, and then a lone figure emerged from the bunker with his hands up. The man, who was immediately taken prisoner, was an NVA warrant officer.

Through gestures and obvious threats, the Marines got the warrant officer to try to talk his companions out peaceably. However, it was evident from the strident tenor of the shouted responses that at least a few of them did not want to surrender.

Gunnery Sergeant Ed Van Valkenburgh, the Fox/2/5 gunny, was standing at the edge of the crowd, just observing, when a Marine on the second floor of the post office called down, "They're going out the back!" Gunny Van Valkenburgh ran around to where he thought the unseen back exit might be and fired a few rounds at what he thought was a moving shadow. "No," the Marine upstairs called, "he's up against the building!" The gunny pivoted and fired two rounds at the nearest structure. A man yelped once and fell—dead, as it turned out. Instantly, another dark form emerged from the bunker and took off down the street. Van Valkenburgh fired, but he was sure he missed.

At that point, one of Staff Sergeant Tinson's Marines—bored with the exchanges or expecting the NVA to come out shooting—fired a LAAW rocket into the front entrance of the bunker.

To everyone's surprise, the detonation was followed by several powerful secondary explosions. No doubt, an ammunition cache inside the bunker had been set off. When the smoke cleared, Staff Sergeant Tinson's platoon, wearing gas masks, pulled twenty-four dead NVA from the bunker along with five AK-47 assault rifles, two SKS carbines, two old U.S. M-1 carbines, one RPD light machine gun, five B-40 rocket launchers, and three satchel charges. There were more dead NVA in the post office courtyard that evening than anyone in 2/5 had ever seen in one place at one time. In fact, even the oldest hands had not seen a total of twenty-five dead NVA until then.

On February 4, late in the afternoon, 2nd Lieutenant William Donnelly's 1st Platoon of Alpha/1/1 was sent from the Jeanne d'Arc complex to outpost 1/1's open left (south) flank from within the small walled compound of the Jeanne d'Arc Student Center. The Marines had no trouble securing the two-story L-shaped main building, which, though abandoned by the NVA, was strewn throughout with NVA rucksacks and crude explosive devices.

Shortly after setting in at around dusk, Lieutenant Donnelly requested tank support and 81mm illumination to help chase NVA hecklers from a hedgerow and a small building just to the south of the Student Center compound. A Marine M-48 tank arrived at 1950, and the illumination was layed on. The first 90mm round the tank fired caused four NVA soldiers to bolt from the building, toward the open field to the south.

From a second-story window Lieutenant Donnelly's platoon sergeant, Sergeant Joe Burghardt, was watching when the NVA bolted. Dropping the four NVA was a simple matter for Burghardt. They were in the open, with virtually no place to hide, and only thirty to forty-five meters away. Since Burghardt had already claimed shooter's rights to any NVA emerging from the door the four NVA had used, no one else in the Student Center was going to steal his targets unless he fouled up altogether. He simply raised his M-16, aimed in, and squeezed the trigger—four times. All four of the NVA were cut down.

From elsewhere in the building, Donnelly's Marines opened fire at NVA that gunfire from the tank had flushed from the hedgerow. After the fight, Donnelly's men counted twenty-two NVA corpses in the open field; one uninjured NVA lieutenant surrendered to the Marines.

Taken altogether, the achievements of the ARVN and U.S. Marine units on February 4 demonstrated that ejection of the 4th and 6th NVA regiments from Hue was only a matter of time. But, although the 1st ARVN Division and 1st Marine Regiment had seized the initiative in Hue, the NVA and VC forces they were facing were far from beaten and still able to inflict serious losses.

If the Marine and ARVN commanders could feel eventual victory within their grasp on February 4, the NVA's Tri-Thien-Hue Front's senior staff had evidence almost within sight of its own CP bunker that its forces were still able to win important victories. While the U.S. Marine and ARVN forces inside Hue were chalking up impressive results, a battalion of the U.S. 1st Cavalry Division was soundly defeated in its bid to advance— albeit unwittingly—into the NVA regional headquarters.

PART V

THON QUE CHU

Isolate the battlefield. According to classic military strategy for combat in a built-up area, all three of the major players in Hue should have been striving to cut off the city from the outside. In reality, none had managed it.

The NVA battle plan for the attack on Hue did show an awareness of the need to isolate it—the 806th Battalion had closed Highway 1 between Hue and PK 17, and the 804th Batallion had attacked ARVN troops east of the city. After these attacks, however, the NVA seemed to let chances for sealing Hue slip through their fingers.

ARVN troops did nothing to seal Hue. From the start, ARVN units aimed their efforts at breaking into the Citadel and clearing it.

All the U.S. Marine units dispatched to Hue through February 4 had wound up in the heart of the modern city, where they waged the battle from the inside out. No additional Marine units were available, so the Marines were in no position to seal the city from the outside.

From the time higher U.S. and ARVN headquarters had finally realized the scope of Communist intentions, it was clear that the only units capable of surrounding Hue and holding the approaches to it were the heliborne brigades of the 1st Cavalry and the 101st Airborne divisions. However, the need to respond to other Communist threats in northern I Corps and the need to redeploy U.S. units throughout I Corps left only one U.S. Army unit in any position to respond to the Hue emergency. That unit was the U.S. Army's I Corps reserve battalion and Camp Evans "palace guard"—Lieutenant Colonel Dick Sweet's 2nd Battalion, 12th Cavalry Regiment (2/12 Cav, "2nd of the 12th Cavalry"), an element of the 1st Cavalry Division's 3rd Brigade.

The Air Cav had been in-country since mid-1965, and it had honed its techniques to perfection in the Central Highlands of II

Corps. One airmobile brigade of the 101st Airborne Division, sent to Vietnam in mid-1965, had also served with distinction in II Corps. The remainder of the 101st Division had arrived in Vietnam in December 1967. After shaking down in II Corps, the untested 2nd Brigade had begun staging into northern I Corps immediately prior to the Tet offensive. It was not quite ready to begin combat operations when Tet broke.

On the morning of February 2, the reconnaissance element of the 3rd Brigade, 1st Cavalry Division—B Troop, 1st Squadron, 9th Cavalry Regiment (B/1/9 Cav)—was flying reconnaissance missions west of Hue from its LZ near Camp Evans. Deployed mainly in UH-1E Huey gunship and scoutship helicopters, the swift-moving cavalry reconnaissance troop quickly located a unit of NVA soldiers in the open only three kilometers west of the city. Sixteen of the NVA soldiers were killed in the first clash. Sightings throughout the rest of the day, followed by instantaneous assault from the air, resulted in claims of an additional twenty-two NVA killed by B/1/9 Cav.

Even before B/1/9 Cav had reported the first sighting of NVA west of Hue, however, Major General John Tolson, the 1st Cavalry Division commander, had directed Lieutenant Colonel Dick Sweet to turn the defense of Camp Evans over to headquarters and base troops. He ordered the 2/12 Cav to stage by air into a new LZ just south of PK 17. The move was completed during the afternoon.

Beginning on the morning of February 3, General Tolson ordered Lieutenant Colonel Sweet's four companies to mount an attack toward Hue, paralleling Highway 1. For the moment, Sweet's effort would be aimed less at sealing Hue's western flank than at feeling the enemy out and, hopefully, forcing him to deploy his reserves well away from the city.

The 2/12 Cav would not be able to conduct its assault aboard its helicopters. Even if there had been sufficient helicopters to lift the entire 2/12 Cav—and there were not—the helicopters could not have been adequately fueled or serviced. The 1st Cavalry Division was so new to the area that the bulk of its refueling and maintenance facilities were still back in II Corps, and all land routes for fuel and ammunition had been severed.

Also, the weather was lousy. Though the helicopters could certainly operate at low ceilings—B/1/9 Cav's reconnaissance forays on February 2 had proven as much—the NVA and VC in I Corps had already shown a surprising willingness to stand up to threatening helicopters and fire back. In light of the sparse helicopter resources, it was decided that the 650-man 2/12 Cav would walk.

To the 2/12 Cav's commander, that was no problem. Dick Sweet was an infantryman, pure and simple. He had fought on his feet in Korea and, more recently, had been a senior instructor at the Army's Infantry School, at Fort Benning, Georgia. He was used to leading an airmobile Air Cav unit, but, under the circumstances, he preferred meeting the enemy on foot.

For the 2/12 Cav, the mission at Hue was unusual in that all four of the battalion's letter companies (A, B, C, and D) would be operating together in the field. The Air Cav's high-mobility heliborne tactics virtually ensured the fragmentation of Air Cav battalions; it was unusual for an Air Cav battalion commander to have more than a company or two maneuvering on the ground at any time. On the morning of February 3, Lieutenant Colonel Dick Sweet was eager to test his mettle as the commander of a complete *infantry* battalion.

The 2/12 Cav's mission to Hue was Dick Sweet's dream mission. As the only U.S. Army unit thus far committed to the Hue emergency—and the only U.S. Army or ARVN unit deployed to the verges of the battlefield—the 2/12 Cav was assigned to cover a huge area of operations: everything on both sides of Highway 1 from PK 17 to the northwestern wall of the Hue Citadel and the north bank of the Perfume River. For all practical purposes, the 2/12 Cav's zone had no western limit. If Sweet's companies located any NVA units in the zone, Sweet was to deal with them as he saw fit, to the limit of his unit's capabilities. Other battalions of the 3rd Brigade, 1st Cavalry Division, and the virgin 2nd Brigade, 101st Airborne Division, would be committed as they became available. But, on February 3 and for the foreseeable future, the northwest quadrant outside Hue belonged to Dick Sweet.

At PK 17, late on the afternoon of February 2, Lieutenant Colonel Sweet stopped by the 3rd ARVN Regiment CP. The regimental commander told him that there was little his ARVN units could do to assist the 2/12 Cav. All four of his infantry battalions and numerous attached units were engaged to the hilt in and east of Hue, and the regimental forward CP had been ordered to move into the Citadel to direct clearing operations there. The only help the ARVN could provide, the commander said, would be support fire from two ARVN 105mm howitzers, which were to remain at PK 17. The ARVN artillery would be the only supporting arms at Sweet's disposal. His regularly assigned six-gun 105mm artillery battery was not scheduled to arrive at PK 17 for a day or two.

The intelligence summary Sweet received was incomplete and grim. An estimated sixteen to eighteen NVA battalions were believed to be active in and around Hue, with six to eight of them north and west of the city. No one could say how these figures had been divined, and staff officers in higher headquarters openly scoffed at the high count. For some reason, Dick Sweet's instincts were aroused. He believed the enemy order-of-battle estimates—which eventually proved to be accurate.

As preparations for the mission mounted throughout February 2, the unfamiliar requirements of a footborne infantry sweep resulted in considerable confusion. The Air Cav troopers were used to having their packs and other personal gear flown out to them aboard logistical transport helicopters ("log ships") each time they secured a new LZ. Somehow, the directive to leave their packs at Camp Evans was interpreted to include leaving extra ammunition, sleeping bags, and blanket rolls as well. That first night, the weather turned from overcast to cold and rainy, a portent of even worse weather to come. Extra clothing and bedding were beyond reach, and they would remain so for the duration of the operation.

Following a cold, drizzly night, the entire 2/12 Cav jumped off from PK 17 at 0700, February 3. Though the morning was overcast and foggy, many of the troopers could see the glow of fires to the southeast, from Hue.

Lieutenant Colonel Sweet arranged his companies in a classic diamond formation. Company A was on the point, heading southeast on the south side of and parallel to Highway 1. Company B was to the right (south) rear of the point company, and Company C was to the left (north) rear. The battalion command group was directly behind Company A, and Company D was behind the command group, acting as both rearguard and reserve. If the point company or either of the two flanking companies ran into trouble, the battalion would be able to orient itself in any direction with three companies on line, one in reserve, and the battalion command group in the ideal location to control the entire battalion.

Sweet selected Company A for the point position because of its commander, Captain Bob Helvey. Helvey had served in the area as an advisor to the 1st ARVN Division. He knew the terrain. Moreover, Helvey was a natural soldier. Sweet trusted Helvey's judgment and admired his business-as-usual attitude. If the 2/12 Cav met the enemy, Sweet wanted Helvey's Company A to be there first.

The terrain south of PK 17 along Highway 1 was open pretty much to the limit of visibility. Despite the exposed nature of the push, the battalion encountered no enemy resistance at first. At 0850, however, Company A's point platoon began receiving sporadic sniper fire. As was typical of most American combat units, the entire battalion halted in place as attempts were made to call in artillery support. However, the call for fire support came to nothing because of communications problems.

Since there was nothing to be done against the sniper—Lieutenant Colonel Sweet was not about to dispatch even a squad to find just one sniper—the battalion moved on. The sniper fired a few more ineffectual rounds, and then he quit.

At 0945, five kilometers southeast of PK 17, Company A reached Thon Lieu Coc Thuong, the first of several thickly wooded, heavily populated "islands" on the south side of Highway 1 between PK 17 and Hue. No opposition met the battalion as it started to move through the large hamlet, but evidence of recent enemy occupation was everywhere. There were freshly dug trenches and bunkers at every turn. Even more ominous was the desertion of the prosperous hamlet by its entire population.

After searching the empty village, the 2/12 Cav got back on the move. As soon as the point element of Company A stepped out of the treeline at the southern edge of Thon Lieu Coc Thuong, the troopers saw the backs of many civilians, who were fleeing across the cultivated fields to the next settled island to the southeast, Thon Que Chu. As the civilians disappeared into the Thon Que Chu treeline, NVA soldiers could be seen manning a trench line facing the Air Cav battalion. Company A instantly deployed just inside Thon Lieu Coc Thuong's southern treeline, and Company C drew abreast on its left to cover the battalion flank in the direction of Highway 1.

The 2/12 Cav command group and supporting-arms teams spent a full hour trying to bring in outside fire support against the fortified treeline. The two ARVN 105s at PK 17 could not be called because of the language barrier, no U.S. Army artillery was in range, and the ceiling was too low for fixed-wing air support. However, several of the 1st Cavalry Division's Huey helicopter gunships and CH-47 aerial rocket artillery (ARA) helicopters were finally brought in. The Hueys' machine-gun fire and the rockets from the ARA ships looked like they were doing some good. But later inspection revealed that the NVA had dug into a mass of trenches and deep one-man spider holes that employed living bamboo hedges and palm trees to excellent advantage as overhead cover. NVA casualties from the heliborne fire were probably negligible.

The air attacks ran for just under an hour, until a Huey shot up the wrong treeline, spraying Company A and killing one Company C trooper. At that point, Lieutenant Colonel Sweet decided to launch a direct assault against the NVA trench line.

The ground between Thon Lieu Coc Thuong and Thon Que Chu was open and flat, with no cover other than a tiny cemetery about midway across. There was a larger cemetery about 200 meters to the northeast, and a small thicket about 250 meters to the south.

The NVA were beginning to bring in 60mm and 82mm mortar rounds—and possibly a few 140mm rockets—against the Air Cav battalion's position. On command, Captain Robert Helvey's Company A jumped off into the open in three reinforced-platoon waves. The lead platoon crawled and ran past the small graveyard and advanced to within seventy-five meters of the NVA-fortified trench. Then it was stopped cold by heavy fire.

As the main body of Company A passed the small graveyard in its path, two platoons of 1st Lieutenant Michael Thompson's Company C jumped off from Company A's left (north) rear. The open area was wider in Thompson's zone and there was absolutely no cover between one treeline and the other, so Thompson left his 2nd and 4th (weapons) platoons in the treeline to lay down covering fire for the assaulting 1st and 3rd platoons.

Company C's assault had covered about half the distance to the enemy-held treeline when snipers directly ahead and within the large graveyard to the northeast began dropping individual American troopers with uncanny accuracy. The bulk of the kills, in fact, were from head shots. Compounding the problem were the high casualties among troopers who stopped to help their wounded comrades. Company C's two lead platoons had now lost their momentum and were pinned down in the middle of an open area under lethal fire.

At that moment Captain Helvey, the Company A commander, was set up among the burial mounds in the little graveyard. The Company A executive officer, 1st Lieutenant Anton Kalbli, was bringing the rear echelon forward. As Kalbli approached the graveyard, the intense NVA fire relaxed a bit. Helvey was already positioning his machine guns to lay a base of fire along the treeline, but if the stalled lead platoon did not advance quickly, Company A would lose its momentary fire superiority. Helvey ordered Kalbli to advance to the stalled vanguard platoon and lead it the rest of the way into the enemy-held treeline. Kalbli ran forward in the open and, through sheer force of will, got the lead platoon moving again despite a surge in enemy fire. By about 1230, Company A's lead platoon was in the enemy-held treeline, carving a niche for itself in the NVA trenches.

As soon as Company C's attack had bogged down on the battalion left, Lieutenant Colonel Sweet had ordered his reserve company, Captain Richard Kasparzyk's Company D, to attack the enemy trenchline through Company C. Captain Kasparzyk left his weapons platoon and one rifle platoon to man a base of fire and personally led his two remaining platoons into the open field.

Fortunately, a scoutship helicopter following the action from above was able to bring accurate machine-gun fire on the NVA trench line facing Company C and Company D. This allowed Captain Kasparzyk's two-platoon assault to get all the way into the enemy trench line. By 1330, the cavalry troopers had cleared the line in its entirety.

After reorganizing, Company A and Company D began pushing their way almost due south through Thon Que Chu. By then, with the aid of scoutship helicopters from C/1/9 Cav, Lieutenant Colonel Sweet had been able to lay on ample helicopter support. Employing the precise air-ground coordination that was the hallmark of the 1st Cavalry Division, observers with the advancing ground elements were able to direct the reconnaissance scoutships against pinpoint targets in the dense undergrowth and trees.

However, the gunships eventually ran out of fuel and ammunition and had to leave. Through the middle of the afternoon, the two cavalry companies pushed the NVA back an average of 300 meters before they linked up at a trail that bisected the hamlet.

By 1630, Company C, Company B, and the battalion command group had crossed the open area from Thon Lieu Coc Thuong to Thon Que Chu. During the late afternoon, while Company C and Company B mopped up bypassed NVA positions, the 2/12 Cav medevacked nine dead, forty-eight wounded, and three prisoners. The NVA threw in mortar rounds from time to time during the late afternoon, and snipers were active around the entire periphery of the American-held area. At 1800, in failing light, the ongoing attack by Company A and Company D was halted, and the troops set in a night defensive perimeter.

In the morning, the 2/12 Cav was to finish clearing Thon Que Chu and attack southward into the next hamlet, Thon La Chu. Unknown to Dick Sweet or any of his superiors, the Tri-Thien-Hue Front headquarters was in an American-built multi-story ferroconcrete bunker at the southern end of the village.

Thon La Chu was the main staging area and transit point for
NVA reinforcements and supplies bound for Hue. Most of the
5th NVA Regiment was guarding Thon La Chu. Indeed, the
2/12 Cav had engaged at least two battalions of the 5th NVA
Regiment in Thon Que Chu.

— 22 —

Lieutenant Colonel Dick Sweet's 2/12 Cav spent a relatively
uneventful night in Thon Que Chu. The NVA fired four 82mm
mortar rounds into the American battalion's perimeter at around
0300, but that was about it. For the many Air Cav troopers who
had left their sleeping bags and blanket rolls behind the previous
day, the worst aspect of the night was the cold, damp air.

At first light, the Air Cav battalion began preparing to
resume its attack southward through Thon Que Chu and on into
Thon La Chu. At 0710, as preparations mounted, the American
perimeter was subjected to a flurry of small-arms fire. In minutes, the fire became increasingly—then unbelievably—intense
and accurate. Company A snipers a few meters in front of the
perimeter were kept busy shooting at NVA soldiers moving later-
ally behind the NVA line. It became apparent that, in the dark,
many NVA soldiers had woven a tight cordon around most of the
2/12 Cav's perimeter and that much of their fire was coming
from within hand-grenade-throwing range.

The enemy fire was so intense and so accurate that the
battalion could not even begin to launch its attack; the 2/12 Cav
was pinned within its perimeter. The supply of enemy troops
seemed inexhaustible, as indeed, in relative terms, it was. Each
time an NVA soldier fell, more NVA soldiers arrived to drag him
to safety and replace him. As the hours passed, the enemy soldiers
inched perceptibly closer. The pressure increased noticeably with
each passing hour. By 1000, the American perimeter had been
struck by as many as sixty 82mm mortar rounds and countless
bullets, and twenty Air Cav troopers had been wounded.

The first successful attempt to medevac the wounded was

made at 1035, under a heavy mortar barrage. The one medevac chopper made it out with only three or four wounded.

The houses outside the American perimeter were of stone and relatively impervious to American fire. Even LAAW rounds had little effect. The NVA eventually set up a mortar in a stone house only forty meters from Company C's line—so close, in fact, that the Americans could not at first distinguish the noise of its discharge from the noise of their own weapons. The house was impervious to the M-79 grenades and LAAWs that the Americans fired at it. In the end, however, a trooper threw a hand grenade into one of the windows, and that silenced the mortar.

At 1135, two 122mm rockets impacted within the American perimeter. This was seen as a major escalation in the ongoing bombardment and small-arms barrage.

Around 1350, the Americans tried another medevac. As soon as the NVA heard the helicopter approach, they poured an immense volume of fire into the sky and against all possible LZs within the perimeter. The helicopter—the same one that had flown the earlier medevac—dropped off a resupply of desperately needed ammunition, picked up a handful of wounded, and took off at 1355. During the late afternoon, the same bird made several more trips, bringing in more ammunition and taking out dead and wounded troopers. The last flight left Thon Que Chu at 1651.

From the outset of the morning action, Lieutenant Colonel Dick Sweet had faced just three alternatives: he could continue his attack, he could stand and fight, or he could leave the ground to the enemy. The simple mathematics of attrition were clearly working against the 2/12 Cav. There were far more NVA soldiers than there were Air Cav troopers. It quickly became apparent that the 2/12 Cav could not advance against such vastly disproportionate odds, so that option was ruled out. As the day progressed, the steady attrition on Sweet's side clearly was not being matched on the other side, so standing and fighting ceased being a viable alternative. Moreover, the battalion's position, which was not on particularly defensible terrain, was not worth a do-or-die, last-stand effort. Sweet would have to withdraw, leaving Thon Que Chu to the NVA.

Having made his decision, Sweet faced several new alternatives, the most important of which was the timing of the 2/12 Cav's departure. Also, he had to decide where he was going and how he was going to get there.

Night movements of any sort were very rare for Americans in Vietnam. It was virtually an axiom that "the enemy ruled the night." However, Dick Sweet did not see things the way many other American commanders did. He had, after all, been a senior tactics instructor at The Infantry School. He knew his onions, and he found the idea of a night movement ideally matched to the 2/12 Cav's situation on February 4. Besides, Sweet had already led the battalion in several night moves during the three weeks since his arrival, and he knew what his officers and men could do.

So, where to go, when to go, and how to go—those were the variables. The first and obvious choice was a night move toward Thon Trieu Son Tay, a hamlet island astride Highway 1 about 2.5 kilometers east of the 2/12 Cav perimeter. Early in the afternoon, Sweet asked his forward air controller to lay on an observation mission over Thon Trieu Son Tay. This was accomplished to the accompaniment of powerful 37mm antiaircraft fire from the objective. Rule out Thon Trieu Son Tay; if the enemy had antiaircraft guns there, the place was powerfully held.

It was fairly certain that the route the battalion had covered between PK 17 and Thon Que Chu on February 3 was still open, but this route was not seen as an alternative. A withdrawal to PK 17 was, in reality, a retreat, and it was a point of honor that retreat was unthinkable except as a last resort.

At length, after carefully consulting his maps and discussing options with his officers, Dick Sweet arrived at a plan that, for him, had great appeal: an advance to a dominant piece of real estate deeper inside enemy territory.

Only a short distance to the southwest of Thon Que Chu, the coastal plain rose suddenly at the verge of the Annamite Cordillera. The nearest dominant high ground was right at the edge of the mountain chain, directly overlooking Provincial Route 554 and the Perfume River. If the 2/12 Cav could disengage in Thon Que Chu and march overland at night to the new objective, it would be in an ideal position to overlook and help interdict the only possible enemy infiltration route into Hue from the west. The high ground would also be an effective point from which to continue the 2/12 Cav's own attack toward Hue. As Sweet's mind settled on this alternative, he liked it more and more.

At a commanders' meeting at 1600, Lieutenant Colonel Sweet let his company commanders in on the plan, and he issued specific orders to each of them. Preparations would commence immediately for departure at 2000 hours. Discretion was of the utmost importance; the troopers must give no indication of the move. To the enemy, everything must appear as if the battalion intended to spend another night in its perimeter.

All the wounded who needed to be evacuated during the day had been flown out by 1651, but eleven dead Americans remained in the perimeter. They presented a major problem. It was anathema for U.S. units to leave their dead on the battlefield. In this case, however, carrying out the dead could only result in slowing the night march and adding to the chance of discovery. With extreme reluctance, the Americans decided to leave the dead behind in a temporary mass grave until an opportunity to recover them presented itself. Once the hard decision was made, the two engineer squads attached to the battalion converted an 81mm mortar pit into the grave site. Along with the bodies, all gear belonging to the dead and many medevac cases, some cumbersome ammunition, and other expendable gear were placed in the hole.

In preparing for the night move, the 2/12 Cav was indeed discreet. Many of the troopers were quite innovative in rigging dummies in their fighting holes. With the onset of darkness, the enemy fire died away, a sure indication that, for the moment at least, the NVA had been taken in.

When it came to issuing orders for the move itself, the men were briefed in very small groups. There was to be absolutely no talking, no cigarette smoking, no extraneous noise. If a single sniper was encountered, he was to be ignored. If a sizable enemy force was encountered, a base of fire was to be established and the affected unit was to attack swiftly through the enemy force. Becoming bogged down at any point could doom the mission. At the last moment, everyone—officers and troopers alike—was literally shaken to determine if anything on them rattled.

The Air Cav battalion was to move in a column of files, two companies abreast and two companies deep. If the enemy struck at any point, the battalion could deliver an immediate assault with two companies up and two back, a classic tactical formation.

As darkness settled in, the Cav 105mm howitzer battery newly emplaced at PK 17 fired individual smoke rounds in a pattern designed to thicken the fog in front of the 2/12 Cav's position, without alerting the NVA to Sweet's impending withdrawal. As the smoke drifted outward, Company A and Company D evacuated their sectors on the south side of the battalion perimeter. They passed through Company C and Company B and took the lead. The battalion command group followed the lead companies, and Company B and Company C followed the battalion command group. It was a moonless night, so dark that many troopers in the column had trouble seeing the next trooper ahead.

By 2020, the 500-meter-long American column was out of the Thon Que Chu perimeter, heading north into the open area it had fought across the previous day. On the battalion point was Private First Class Hector Camacho, a nerveless trooper who had excelled in earlier night operations. After Camacho marched 200 meters to the north, he turned toward his next checkpoint, a stream 350 meters to the southwest. There was enormous tension, and one fear-induced stop when Camacho heard what sounded like the *snick* of a machine-gun bolt being worked.

The vanguard troopers knew they were approaching the stream when they marched into soft, muddy ground. Camacho halted the long column, and tension mounted by the second as he searched for a suitable ford across the five-foot-deep, twenty-foot-wide stream. As Lieutenant Colonel Sweet waited, he became concerned that the battalion would not reach its objective before sunrise. At length, a shivering Camacho reappeared and reported that he had found a crossing. The troopers had to ford the stream in pairs, and two precious hours of darkness were used in the crossing. Around the midway point, timed demolitions packs left in the former battalion perimeter detonated in several huge balls of flame. Shortly, troopers in the rearguard reported seeing tripflares go off and hearing the chatter of small-arms fire.

The enemy attack on the empty perimeter had been foreseen. In an elegant flourish, Lieutenant Colonel Sweet ordered his artillery forward observer to call in a preregistered artillery fire mission on the enemy scouring the perimeter. The battery also fired smoke rounds to help reorient the battalion toward its objective.

The ground on the far side of the stream was rougher, and the troopers frequently lost contact with each other. The column often had to stop to wait for the rearguard to catch up.

As the march continued, the 2/12 Cav began to pass into exhaustion. Troopers who had been concealing wounds to avoid medevac gave in to shock and blood loss and had to be carried. Men who had been high on adrenaline for two days fell asleep on their feet. During one halt, a drowsy Company D trooper fired an M-79 round into the ground. Fortunately, the 40mm grenade did not detonate.

The company columns swung slightly to the southeast, and then due south. The battalion now had four kilometers of open ground—terraced rice paddies and unimproved pastureland—to cover before sunrise. Along the way, many of the troopers saw the flash of signal lights between villages. They assumed that such lights were part of an enemy navigational system, but they may instead have been the means by which the ever-suffering locals warned one another of the approach of all armies.

Wading through the paddies and climbing over the paddy dikes was cold, slow work. Somehow the 2/12 Cav maintained momentum.

But now a new danger threatened in the form of U.S. parachute flares. Friendly flareships were illuminating Hue, which was about five kilometers to the east of the 2/12 Cav. Borne by the steady breeze off the South China Sea, several flares drifted over the unit, spotlighting its position. Dick Sweet's request that the flareships douse the lights was passed up through the chain of command. The flare drops were discontinued.

The night march took eleven tense hours to complete. At 0710, the battalion rearguard reached the new high-ground position and began setting in under intermittent mortar fire. For most of the rest of the day, the 2/12 Cav troopers ate, smoked, and slept. The battalion executive officer, back at Camp Evans, arranged a major lift of ammunition, gear, and replacements.

Though the 2/12 Cav had been forced to retire from Thon Que Chu, the troopers who completed the night march had much to be proud of. It had been an epic effort for a significant payoff. For the next four days, as higher U.S. Army headquarters scrambled to lay on more pressure north and west of Hue, the 2/12 Cav observed the routes the NVA used to infiltrate soldiers and supplies into Hue from the west. Artillery and mortar fire called by observers in the 2/12 Cav perimeter entirely shut off the flow during the day. The enemy's access to the battlefield was far from being sealed, but thanks to the 2/12 Cav, NVA access was seriously reduced from February 5 onward.

PART VI

THE HOSPITAL

On February 5 the ARVN battalions inside and outside the Citadel continued their relentless attacks against the stoutly resistant but otherwise unaggressive battalions of the 6th NVA Regiment. The entire reinforced 1st ARVN Airborne Task Force redeployed along the northeast wall of the Citadel, and the 4th Battalion, 2nd ARVN Regiment, launched an attack to the southwest, along the airborne task force's left flank.

The badly understrength 4th Battalion, 3rd ARVN Regiment, left MACV at dawn and was ferried to the north bank of the Perfume River aboard a variety of riverboats and small naval vessels. Once ashore, the battalion launched a total of seven successive assaults aimed at gaining access to the Citadel's Thuong Tu Gate. When the battalion finally had to concede that the gate's defenses were impenetrable, it fought its way southwest along Highway 1 to link up with the 3rd ARVN Regiment's 2nd and 3rd battalions, which were still stalled between the river and the southeast wall.

On February 5 the 1st Marines regimental objective remained the same: 1/1 and 2/5 were to continue their attacks to secure the Thua Thien Provincial Prison and the provincial administrative complex. Four long blocks lay between the objectives and the line 2/5 had held during the night of February 4–5, and there was no reason to suspect that the 4th NVA Regiment soldiers holding the masonry buildings along the way would be any more willing to give them up than they had been willing to give up the treasury or the Public Health Complex.

Lieutenant Colonel Ernie Cheatham's 2/5 was ready to go on, but Lieutenant Colonel Mark Gravel's 1/1 had just about run out of steam. Despite being brought partly back to strength by the arrival of its officers and nearly a full platoon of stragglers, 2nd Lieutenant Ray Smith's Alpha/1/1 was used up. It had endured much and had suffered numerous casualties, particularly among its veteran enlisted leaders. Moreover, the entire 1st Platoon had been detached to outpost the battalion's southern flank. First Lieutenant Gordon Matthews's Bravo/1/1 was not even a standard infantry company. Composed mainly of pickup squads of headquarters technicians and weapons specialists, the company was not completely viable as a tactical unit. The Marines who remained operational in Gravel's demibattalion gave it their all, but the task of clearing the enormous Jeanne d'Arc complex was beyond their capabilities, and little progress had been made there on February 4.

On the other hand, Ernie Cheatham was a happy, incredulous man. The 2/5 commander had fully expected that Fox/2/5 would remain stymied in front of the treasury for some time. He was therefore surprised and gratified when Fox/2/5's Captain Mike Downs had reported that the treasury complex was secure. Even more gratifying was the late-afternoon exploitative attack by Hotel/2/5 and Golf/2/5. This attack had taken 2/5 across Le Dinh Duong Street and resulted in the bloodless occupation of the French Cultural Center, on the northwest side of Le Loi Street. That night, Cheatham hoped that these quick, cheap victories heralded a softening in the NVA's opposition.

For all Ernie Cheatham's hopes, however, there were ample indications that the NVA were preparing to defend the city blocks in front of 2/5 in considerable strength. During the evening of February 4, the trickle of civilian refugees arriving from the southwest had turned into a flood of several hundred Vietnamese citizens—and, mercifully, five American civilians, most of them teachers or medical workers. The Vietnamese civilians had been passed on to the Vietnamese civil authorities, but the Americans had been questioned at length in the hope of turning up possible leads regarding NVA intentions and plans. The news was grim. According to the American civilians, the NVA and VC had taken over Hue Central Hospital as a military hospital and were fortifying it. Scores of seriously wounded Communist soldiers were being treated in beds from which civilians had been forcibly evicted.

The day's fighting south of the Perfume kicked off at 0530,

on the south flank of 1/1 sector, where 2nd Lieutenant William Donnelly's 1st Platoon of Alpha/1/1 was outposting the Jeanne d'Arc Student Center. As Sergeant Joe Burghardt, Donnelly's platoon sergeant, was preparing the troops to move out, somebody yelled, "There's gooks outside!"

Sergeant Burghardt dropped what he was doing and ran toward the source of the shout. At a second-story window overlooking the Student Center courtyard, a Marine told Burghardt that at least three NVA soldiers were in a stand of palm trees inside the compound. Burghardt peeked out the window and saw the three NVA soldiers peeking back at him. The trees were only eight meters away from the building.

Burghardt ran down to a first-floor window in the opposite wing of the L-shaped building. From there he could see the NVA from their rear, without being seen by them. As Burghardt raised his M-16 to take aim at the nearest of the enemy soldiers, Marines in front of the NVA opened fire. The bases of the palm trees were wide enough for the enemy soldiers to hide behind, so they just hunkered down, out of danger from their front. However, Sergeant Burghardt nailed two of them from behind; someone else killed the third one.

Shortly after the shooting stopped, three Vietnamese women and a Vietnamese priest emerged from a tiny outbuilding on the far side of the courtyard. They told the Marines that they had been held captive by the NVA since January 31 and had just been released that morning. They had been debating the advisability of entering the Marine position when the three NVA filtered into the compound. As soon as the NVA soldiers were dead, the four frightened civilians decided that the moment to seek Marine refuge had definitely arrived.

Captain Ron Christmas's Hotel/2/5 led 2/5's efforts with a sweep to clear the area around the house its 1st Platoon had captured the previous afternoon. Hotel/2/5 accomplished this swiftly, against light opposition. Meanwhile, Fox/2/5 was once again scouring the area between the treasury and post office and Le Dinh Duong Street. When the area had been cleared to everyone's satisfaction, Fox/2/5 and Hotel/2/5 began advancing cautiously into new territory to the southwest.

At 0829, members of Fox/2/5's 3rd Platoon were checking out a building the NVA had given up without a fight when they discovered a handful of live U.S. Air Force officers and enlisted communicators who had been hiding there since the morning of January 31. In fact, this was the hostel and these were the men that Fox/2/5's 2nd Platoon had been sent to rescue as soon as it had arrived in Hue on February 1.

By 0834, Fox/2/5's 1st Platoon, on the company right, had advanced an entire block without opposition. The 1st Platoon occupied the neighborhood municipal police station, at the end of Truong Dinh Street.

By 0840, Captain Chuck Meadows's fully recommitted Golf/2/5 had progressed unimpeded through the riverfront parkland northwest of Le Loi Street. It had reached the Cercle Sportif, the high-class club that, in better days, had been the social center for Hue's French and Vietnamese upper classes. According to rumor, the Cercle Sportif complex was a nest of NVA and was heavily fortified. Golf/2/5 was ready for a bloody fight.

While trying to sneak into the Cercle Sportif complex, Golf/2/5's lead element—a cut-down squad—became pinned behind a knee-high stone wall at the entrance. They called for help, and a half dozen fellow Marines crawled forward.

As the entire group lay behind the fire-swept wall and prepared for the inevitable rush, Private First Class Doug Blayney saw someone crawling along the bank of the river, which was only a few meters to the right. Blayney assumed it was a fellow Marine until he saw that the man had a B-40 launcher strapped to his back. Carefully, Blayney centered the enemy soldier in the sights of his M-16 and fired three rounds. The NVA soldier slumped and lay motionless. However, Blayney's fire drew the wrath of an RPG gunner, who slammed an RPG into the wall behind which the Marines were hiding. The roar of the explosion was deafening, and several of the Marines were caught in the fallout. Blayney took a sliver of steel in the palm of his right hand.

The NVA fire remained intense, but a Marine M-60 team eventually worked its way up to the wall. A Marine who had been shot several times in the legs was dragged to the rear. Finally, a

106mm recoilless rifle was manhandled into position opposite the main building. Just one round from it caused an immediate abatement of the NVA fire. Golf/2/5 attacked in strength and entered the lavish sports center without further opposition.

The roof of the Cercle Sportif afforded Golf/2/5 a wonderful all-around view. The Perfume River was just to the north, and the Citadel, from which thick columns of smoke were rising, was in plain view. Also in plain view was 2/5's next objective, the multiblock warren of the Hue Central Hospital complex. But before the attack into the hospital could commence, Hotel/2/5 and Fox/2/5 had to fight their way abreast of Golf/2/5's advanced position.

Captain Christmas's Hotel/2/5 advanced down the narrow residential block in the center of the 2/5 zone. The 3rd Platoon and its commander, 2nd Lieutenant Mike Lambert, were chasing a covey of NVA when Lambert passed a Vietnamese girl lying face-down in a driveway. Her shiny black hair was neatly braided, and she wore a crisp white blouse and a blue plaid jumper. To Lambert, the clothing brought back memories of parochial-school girls he had known at home. In fact, the elegant two-story home outside of which she lay reminded the lieutenant strongly of similar homes in his native Atlanta. The girl looked to be about fourteen years old, and the congealing blood around her suggested that she had been shot only minutes before. It was plain to see that she was dead, but no one wanted to move her to be sure, because the NVA sometimes booby-trapped bodies. The dead girl was not the most grisly sight Lieutenant Lambert had witnessed or would witness in Hue, but her innocence and the random violence that had ended her young life affected him profoundly.

At 0850, Hotel/2/5's lead platoon entered the Hue University Library, directly between the Cercle Sportif and the municipal police station at the end of Truong Dinh Street. Thus, by 0900, 2/5 had taken its entire objective for the day—and with only minimal opposition. The whole battalion was now arrayed along Le Thanh Ton Street, an east-west thoroughfare that cut across the battalion front at a 45-degree angle between the river, on Golf/2/5's right, and Tran Cao Van Street, on Fox/2/5's left. Though Mark Gravel's 1/1 was stalled a full block to Fox/2/5's left rear, Ernie Cheatham decided to keep going for as long as he could. He felt he had the enemy on the run—this was certainly no time to wait for 1/1 to clear the opposition on its front and advance abreast. As soon as all three of his companies were in line along Le Thanh Ton, Cheatham ordered the entire battalion to advance into the vast network of buildings that made up the Hue Central Hospital complex.

— 24 —

By about 0900, February 5, the 4th NVA Regiment had conceded a complete city block to 2/5, but that was the limit of its largess. As soon as Captain Ron Christmas's Hotel/2/5 jumped off toward the Hue Central Hospital, NVA soldiers emplaced in buildings across the Marine company's front opened fire with small arms, machine guns, and B-40s.

Fox/2/5's advance into an empty triangle of parkland south of Le Thanh Ton was uncontested. But as soon as Captain Mike Downs's company pivoted back to the southwest to face the hospital across Nguyen Thai Street, it was stopped by the NVA who were already contesting Hotel/2/5's advance.

Fox/2/5 was further hampered by the need to watch its open left flank. By then 1/1 was several hundred meters to Fox/2/5's left rear, so Staff Sergeant Jim McCoy, the platoon sergeant of Fox/2/5's 3rd Platoon, was given Sergeant Chuck Ekker's squad and an M-60 team and ordered to seal the gap.

The outpost assignment was tantamount to giving Sergeant Ekker's squad the morning off. In fact, as soon as they had secured the second floor of the building, Ekker's Marines decided to take a break and chow down on some recently acquired booty—a large can of fruit cocktail mixed with a large can of chocolate syrup.

As they were dividing up the treat, one of the men called out to Corporal Arkie Allbritton and said he could see men in uniforms moving around on the flank. Allbritton looked out the window, but, by then, the men had disappeared. He asked the squad radioman to call back to the company CP to ask if any Marines were supposed to be out that way. The answer was "Negative. If it's got a uniform on, it's NVA."

Allbritton ordered the Marine lookout to fire a few rounds toward where he had last seen the intruders. Lance Corporal Roger Warren, the M-60 team leader, also opened fire. The Marine fire was answered instantly by B-40 rockets that blew out most of the upper-story wall of Staff Sergeant McCoy's building. When the dust settled, wounded Marines lay everywhere. When Lance Corporal Warren, the M-60 gunner, regained his senses, he found that the force of the blast had hurled him through an interior wall and into the next room.

Sergeant Ekker, Corporal Allbritton, and Staff Sergeant McCoy organized an evacuation of the wounded to the first floor. Everyone else in the building fired at the unseen targets. Among the shooters was Lance Corporal Warren, who, after being carried downstairs with painful wounds in both legs, had picked up a discarded M-16 and crawled to a window from which he could fire at the NVA.

Sergeant Ekker's squad was so badly riddled that it was replaced on the battalion flank by a squad of Fox/2/5's 1st Platoon. On the way out the door, Staff Sergeant McCoy warned the new arrivals to stay away from the southern windows, because of B-40 fire. He was hardly out of the building before he heard someone yell "There goes one of them now!" and the sound of an M-16 popping off through one of the southern windows. The NVA teams across the way started blasting the building anew, and more Marines were hurt.

Getting the casualties to the rear was a hair-raising venture. As the withdrawing Marines carried piggyback the nonambulatory wounded, NVA snipers made a game of firing into the ground at their feet. Enraged, Corporal Arkie Allbritton turned to Corporal Ray Stewart, who had sustained some shrapnel wounds, and said, "Stew, get rid of those guys for me, will you?" Stewart was carrying Lance Corporal Roger Warren's M-60 machine gun because Warren, despite his leg wounds, was hump-

ing another wounded Marine on his back. Stewart and Lance
Corporal Ken Crysel turned and stood in the open to engage the
NVA snipers, but the very first round misfired. Coolly, Corporal
Stewart cleared the jam and opened fire again. He knew he was
supposed to fire short bursts to keep the M-60 from jamming,
but he fired full tilt into the sniper's position, never releasing
pressure on the trigger until the NVA fire petered out. By that
time Lance Corporal Warren's borrowed M-60 was a dead loss;
its barrel was burned out and warped.

In all, twelve 3rd Platoon Marines had been hit, but only
eight were treated. Three were returned to duty that day, but
five—including a motor-transport mechanic who had joined
Fox/2/5 the previous evening—had to be evacuated to Phu Bai.
Since Corporal Ray Stewart had already received two Purple
Hearts, his shrapnel wounds were bound to get him shipped
home. Because the wounds were light and did not impair him, he
chose to ignore them and stay with his platoon. He was not
counted in the day's official casualty tally. Neither was Corporal
Allbritton, for the same reason.

And neither was Lance Corporal Roger Warren, who had
also already received two Purple Hearts. Warren had failed to
have a third set of serious wounds treated after he sustained them
while clearing the treasury on February 4, and he ignored the
painful leg wounds he had sustained on February 5. In the end,
Roger Warren's bravery and extreme devotion to his platoon
earned him a Navy Cross.

The NVA unit facing Hotel/2/5 and Golf/2/5 must have
been reinforced, because at 1030 NVA fire just about doubled. At
length, the 81mm mortar forward observer with Golf/2/5 called
a fire mission, and, under cover of the mortar barrage and
Golf/2/5's base of fire, the right-flank platoon of Hotel/2/5
rushed across Nguyen Thai Street and seized an NVA-held building. The rush cost the NVA eight killed against five Marines
wounded and evacuated and three Marines with minor wounds.

For the next two hours, 2/5 was stalemated, but there were
no casualties despite heavy exchanges of fire. Then, at 1240,
Communist RPG teams facing Golf/2/5 on the southwest side

of the Cercle Sportif launched five B-40s. The RPG blasts and an accompanying fusillade of machine-gun fire wounded six Marines. In response, Marine gunfire and three 3.5-inch rockets killed six NVA and opened the way for a flank attack by a squad from Hotel/2/5. This, in turn, opened the way for Hotel/2/5's seizure of an adjacent building. But the NVA in a nearby bunker stymied hot pursuit by firing eight B-40s and many automatic weapons. In retaliation, the Marines fired fifteen 3.5-inch rockets into the enemy bunker and followed up with an uncontested direct assault. Ten fresh NVA corpses were found in the ruins.

On 2/5's extreme left flank, Fox/2/5 was struck by intense small-arms fire and five B-40 rockets. The Marines returned the small-arms fire in kind, added a dozen M-79 fragmentation grenades, and called a thirty-round 60mm mortar mission. The fight turned into a standoff until a Marine Ontos worked its way forward. Lightly armored, the 106mm recoilless-rifle carrier was extremely vulnerable to small-arms fire, but the two-man crew managed to work it into a semicovered position from which it could fire its six 106mm ready rounds at the enemy-held building. As the Ontos fired its last round, the Fox/2/5 Marines were off and running toward the objective. The dazed NVA survivors were easily driven from the structure. Four freshly killed NVA were found in the rubble.

On February 4, after the fight inside the treasury complex, Lance Corporal Ernie Weiss had been elevated to the command of the remnants of his 3rd Platoon squad. The squad consisted of himself, one veteran rifleman, a veteran radioman without a radio, and three stranded truck drivers who had just arrived in Hue. Now, twenty-four hours later, Lance Corporal Weiss was marveling at an array of Bunsen burners and other esoteric equipment in a hospital laboratory. He decided to leave his squad inside the laboratory building and step out to the front porch to see what he could see.

Weiss had no sooner arrived on the porch than he saw an NVA soldier dart into the open, crossing an alleyway. The squad grenadier, who had followed Weiss out of the lab, dropped an M-79 fragmentation round right in front of the NVA soldier. The force of the blast struck the enemy in the chest and knocked him to the ground. Weiss raised his M-16 and fired once. The bullet hit the man in the temple.

There were other NVA firing on Weiss's position, so he fired the rest of his magazine and then knelt with his back against a wall so he could reload. A B-40 slammed into the wall less than a meter to Weiss's left, right where he had been standing when he shot the wounded NVA. Weiss emerged from the blast with a mouthful of dust and gravel, but he felt okay. However, as he tried to raise his rifle, he felt a burning sensation spread up and down his left arm and leg. With each beat of his heart, the burning intensified, and his limbs grew increasingly stiff. Still unable to grasp the fact that he had been wounded, Weiss picked up his left arm with his right hand and saw that the sleeve of his field jacket was shredded and oozing blood. So was the left leg of his trousers. "I'm hit," he yelled or thought, and he crawled back into the building.

Inside the building, Weiss saw Sergeant Willard Scott, the 3rd Platoon guide. "Scotty, they have a rocket team out there. They have us zeroed."

"Ho, Hoss," Scott responded, "we'll take care of it." And he turned to leave by the opposite door.

"Yo, Scotty," Weiss called after him, "do you think if I get to a corpsman I won't bleed to death?"

Scott turned on his heel, a puzzled expression on his face. He leaned down close to Weiss. He realized that Weiss had sustained dozens of tiny shrapnel and stone-fragment wounds along his left side. Scott called a corpsman, and Weiss began the long journey to Phu Bai. As a squad leader, he had lasted exactly twenty-four hours.

At 1300, on 2/5's left flank, the NVA hit Hotel/2/5 with rifle fire and two rounds from a captured M-79. The Marines returned fire and killed at least one NVA soldier. At the same time, the main body of Alpha/1/1, which was still mired in the Jeanne d'Arc complex, was engaged by NVA small-arms fire and two B-40 rockets. The Marines responded with everything from M-16s and M-60s to twenty 106mm recoilless rifle rounds. For good measure, a Marine tank supporting 1/1 struck the enemy position with fifteen rounds from its 90mm main gun. One Marine was killed in the exchange, and four Marines were wounded and evacuated. Later, four dead NVA were pulled from the fortified position at the focus of the Marine fire.

As the Marines advanced, scores of civilians emerged from the rubble of their homes and the many public buildings. At one point, a large group of teaching nuns entered Fox/2/5's position from their hiding place in the National Nurses' Training Center, just off 2/5's left flank. The constant stream of frightened civilians, many of them wounded, hampered the company commanders, who were forced to provide troops to escort the refugees out of the battle zone.

Shortly after 1300, 2/5 halted for two hours to reorganize and take on an ammunition resupply. Then, in some of the heaviest fighting of the day, Golf/2/5 attacked southward, across Hotel/2/5's front, right into one of the main hospital buildings. The objective was strongly defended, and Golf/2/5 became embroiled in a meter-by-meter, room-by-room battle of wills.

Private First Class Doug Blayney was helping to clear the first ward building the Marines had captured when he stopped to peer out into a narrow alleyway. It was his turn to go first. Another Marine stood by a window to cover the facing doors and windows. Blayney stepped into the open. As he ran to the opposite door, he heard the *crack-whiz* of a near miss, but he made it.

Propped in the doorway to provide cover for the next Marine, Blayney thought he saw a hint of movement in a second-story window. As he raised his M-16 to fire, he saw a muzzle flash in the window and felt something hit him. He was knocked down, and the M-16 in his hand was shattered. Too scared to move for fear of being shot again, Doug Blayney just lay in the doorway and prayed. All around him, men were shouting and shooting. Then he felt a tug at his flak jacket as someone he could not see pulled him out of the exposed doorway. It was Blayney's platoon sergeant, who asked if Blayney was okay and if he knew where the round that had hit him had come from. Blayney told him about the flash in the second-floor window, and the sergeant had a grenadier fire an M-79 round into the opening.

Piecing the action together later, Blayney realized that the AK-47 bullet had hit his M-16 just as he was raising it to sight in on the window. The M-16 prevented the bullet from hitting him square in the forehead. Instead, it had cut the M-16 in half, gone through his left index finger, and lodged in the meaty part of his left thumb. That ended Doug Blayney's involvement in Hue. He was evacuated to Phu Bai by helicopter that evening.

In most cases, whenever a new building or room in the hospital complex fell into Marine hands, the only signs of recent NVA occupation were little piles of spent brass AK-47 cartridges and, rarely, a blood trail. Civilian patients from medical wards silently indicated that NVA were close by, but they also made it clear with body language that they were not about to get involved.

At 1600, while waiting for Golf/2/5 to cross its front, Hotel/2/5 was struck by small-arms fire and RPGs from a position practically on top of the opposing Marine position. As was typical by then, the Hotel/2/5 Marines responded massively to the NVA challenge. They expended over 1,500 rounds from M-16s and M-60s, four 106mm recoilless rifle rounds, and six 3.5-inch rockets. For good measure, the Marines threw in a quick assault and secured the NVA position. In this exchange alone, seven Marines were wounded and evacuated, against eight NVA killed and one wounded NVA captured. In addition, the Marines captured two AK-47s, three M-1 carbines, and a pair of B-40 rocket launchers.

Also at 1600, on the 2/5 left flank, Fox/2/5 opened an attack on a building in a cultivated field to its left front. As the NVA resistance stiffened, the Marines softened the building up with intense small-arms fire supplemented with 106mm fire from an Ontos, 81mm mortar fire, and 3.5-inch rocket fire. Then the Marines attacked. The objective was seized at a loss of two Americans wounded against seven more NVA killed.

Golf/2/5 continued to inch forward into the hospital complex, toward its objective, until the NVA defenders finally broke and ran at 1632. By the end of the 92-minute assault—in which

Marine tanks, 106mm recoilless rifles, and 3.5-inch rocket launchers played pivotal roles—Captain Chuck Meadows's company had lost five more wounded. The Golf/2/5 Marines found four dead NVA inside the liberated portions of the objective and thirty wounded patients who were suspected of being NVA or VC soldiers. Trucks had to be called forward from MACV to transport the wounded prisoners and forty-two assorted NVA weapons to the rear.

A thorough search of the operating rooms in Marine hands revealed signs of heavy recent use. Mounds of bloody waste bandages and other discarded supplies revealed that scores, perhaps hundreds, of patients with all kinds of battle wounds had been treated as recently as a few hours earlier. The search also turned up several dozen insane patients who had been locked inside their ward with barely enough food and water to survive. These poor souls were evacuated to MACV on foot, as were numerous medical patients and other civilians who were obviously not NVA or VC.

At 1645, less than a quarter hour after Golf/2/5 seized its objective, Hotel/2/5 jumped off again, this time to seize a large building between its front and Golf/2/5's left flank. The defending NVA were between the proverbial rock and a hard place. Golf/2/5 was already holding the building behind them, and the only other escape route was covered by elements of Fox/2/5. Well dug in, the NVA fought like desperate men. They poured intense small-arms and B-40 fire on Hotel/2/5, and they would not budge.

In the face of such relentless resistance, the Hotel/2/5 cleanup attack quickly bogged down. Under pressure from the battalion CP to get his men moving again, Captain Ron Christmas ran forward across a thirty-five-meter open area to confer with the troop leaders and see for himself what could be done. After taking a good look around, Christmas decided that he needed help from the Marine M-48 tank that had accompanied Golf/2/5 to its objective.

To return to the company CP, Christmas braved the thirty-five-meter open stretch once more. He ordered his reserve platoon to work forward, into positions from which it could join the final rush. Then Christmas sprinted across another fire-swept open stretch—this one seventy meters wide—to the tank.

The desperate NVA poured heavy machine-gun fire in the direction of the tank, and both of the B-40 rockets they fired at the armored vehicle struck the frontal glacis plate as Captain Christmas was climbing up behind the turret. With Ron Christmas standing tall behind the turret, directing fire, the tank fired five 90mm rounds into the NVA-held building. With the tank and Marines providing a base of fire, the Hotel/2/5 reserve platoon swept in with CS gas grenades and quickly reduced the opposition. Three Marines were wounded in this phase of the assault, and the bodies of twelve NVA and many weapons were recovered. Captain Ron Christmas was awarded a Navy Cross for his outstanding display of leadership under fire.

As the Hotel/2/5 platoons scoured the objective, NVA soldiers manning what turned out to be underground bunkers on three sides of the building suddenly opened fire. The M-48 tank was brought up, and it fired its main gun and .50-caliber cupola machine gun into one bunker after another. The surviving NVA bolted from the last bunker, but they were cut down in the open as they sprinted across a street.

Dead NVA recovered from the bunkers and gathered in the open amounted to thirteen, for a total of twenty-five NVA killed in the one strongpoint. The position also produced the largest haul of NVA weapons captured to date, including many personal weapons, three B-40 launchers, and two Chinese-made RPD crew-served light machine guns.

At 1700, the main body of 2nd Lieutenant Ray Smith's Alpha/1/1 came under intense fire from several bunkers in the no-man's land southeast of the Jeanne d'Arc complex. For reasons that never became clear—for the NVA did not launch an assault—the enemy fired an estimated 2,500 rifle and machine-gun rounds and eight B-40s into the Alpha/1/1 lines.

The Marines responded with 3,000 rounds from M-16s and M-60s, and they directed the firing of twenty-two 90mm tank rounds, twenty-nine 81mm mortar rounds, and seventy-one eight-inch and two 105mm howitzer rounds. The artillery fire caused several violent secondary explosions in one NVA position.

In this fracas one Marine was killed and eight were wounded and evacuated. Alpha/1/1 claimed nine confirmed kills.

At 1815, capping a successful though costly day, Staff Sergeant Paul Tinson's 2nd Platoon of Fox/2/5 entered the southern portion of a hospital building in its sector. In addition to finding five dead NVA, the Marines took three prisoners. One of the prisoners, who was obviously a military man despite his hospital garb, claimed to be the mayor of Hue. The others alleged that they were his bodyguards. The Marines knew a wild claim when they heard one, so they spread-eagled all three captives against a wall and frisked them. When Captain Mike Downs entered the building, Staff Sergeant Tinson was terrorizing the captives, trying to elicit a credible story.

"What's going on, Staff Sergeant Tinson?" the company commander asked.

"Sir," Tinson replied, pointing to the eldest of the three, "this silly son of a bitch is trying to tell me he's the mayor of Hue."

"My God," Downs thought, "maybe he is!" So Downs turned to his two radiomen, who had both graduated from Vietnamese language school, and asked them to get the whole story.

The lengthy interrogation in Vietnamese revealed for a certainty that the eldest captive was indeed Lieutenant Colonel Pham Van Khoa, the mayor of Hue *and* the Thua Thien Province chief. He told the Marines that his wife and children had probably been captured by the VC and that he thought they were probably dead. What Khoa failed to tell his chastened audience was that, when he had bolted from his residence on the night of January 31, he had left his wife and children and most of his staff to fend for themselves in the face of an imminent Communist attack. Khoa and his two bodyguards had been hiding in the hospital, under the noses of the NVA, ever since. (Several days later, Khoa's entire family emerged from their nightmare alive. One of the children had sustained slight wounds, but, otherwise, all were in good condition.)

At 1715, the first Navy landing craft arrived at the Hue LCU ramp from Danang. With the An Cuu Bridge down, the only way to get supplies and reinforcements into Hue was via limited helicopter assets or by boat. The LCU was not molested, and it was offloaded by 1815. At 2015, a second craft arrived with a three-day supply of ammunition. Following this success, many other LCU sorties were scheduled for the days ahead.

At 1830, 2/5's three infantry companies stood down for the night and set in at the limit of the day's advances. When it halted, 2/5's most advanced element was little more than a block away from the 1st Marines regimental objectives, the prison and the provincial administration complex.

PART VII

PROVINCIAL HEADQUARTERS

At their nightly command conference, Lieutenant Colonel Ernie Cheatham and his company commanders laid out a sort of holy mission for 2/5 for the battalion's February 6 advance. From the first full day of battle in Hue, the flagpole in front of the Thua Thien Provincial Administrative Office had shown the colors of the National Liberation Front. Cheatham and his officers decided to take that as a personal affront that had to be expunged. They agreed that the NLF flag must be pulled down on February 6 and that the provincial headquarters complex had to be liberated. All 2/5 needed to do to accomplish that mission—which coincided exactly with the 1st Marines regimental operations order—was battle its way across one more street and through one more narrow block of NVA-held buildings.

On February 6, elements of the 4th NVA Regiment got an early start against 2/5. At 0425, positions manned by Captain Mike Downs's Fox/2/5, on the southeastern margin of the Hue Central Hospital complex, were struck by a volley of nine B-40 rockets. One Marine who was slightly injured was treated on the spot and returned to duty. Meantime, his comrades called for an immediate 81mm illumination mission and fired about 1,000 small-arms rounds and six 3.5-inch rockets into the suspected source of the B-40s. The RPG teams were gone long before the largely cathartic return fire even began.

All three companies of 2/5 jumped off at 0700 to clear the remainder of the hospital complex and develop a line of departure facing the Thua Thien Provincial Prison and the provincial headquarters complex. The NVA were out there, in front of the companies, but, initially, they put up only light resistance. The factor that slowed 2/5's early-morning advance the most was the caution of the Marines who had survived up to six days in Hue. The Marines wanted to see how serious the NVA were about defending their ground before they committed themselves.

The Marines gnawed away at the NVA, and the NVA gnawed back. At 0734, Marines from Captain Chuck Meadows's Golf/2/5 were engaged by snipers as they attacked the hospital's main administration building through a billow of tear gas from four CS grenades. The gas flushed two NVA soldiers, who were cut down as they fled out a back door. Two Marines were wounded and evacuated as a result of the fracas. An American-built radio was recovered from the building the snipers had been holding.

At 0741, Marines from Captain Ron Christmas's Hotel/2/5 were fired on by an automatic weapon set in about fifty meters southwest of the company front line. As Marines manning a base of fire responded with M-16s, M-79s, and LAAWs, another squad maneuvered toward the enemy position, delivered a volley of flanking fire, and attacked. The NVA had already retreated, leaving two of their comrades dead on the ground.

At 0815, while a Hotel/2/5 platoon was delivering preparatory fire on its next objective, two NVA bolted out the back door of the building. Both men were cut down by M-16 fire.

Due to Golf/2/5's attack across Hotel/2/5's front on the afternoon of February 5, Hotel/2/5 was on the right flank when it opened its attack at 0820, February 6. Against meager resistance, Captain Ron Christmas's Marines quickly captured the NVA forward position, where they found a cache of abandoned weapons, including a Chinese-manufactured submachine gun, five B-40 rocket rounds, five Chicom grenades, six M-26 grenades, 200 AK-47 rounds, and fifteen satchel charges.

The Hotel/2/5 Marines were waiting for orders to jump off into the provincial headquarters complex when a 6 × 6 truck carrying a load of fresh replacements chugged up the street. Before anyone could react, the truck passed right through the Hotel/2/5 line and proceeded on toward the company objective. It was halfway there when the NVA opened fire on it. The truck driver immediately threw the vehicle into reverse and backed down to safety, but two of the Marines riding in the rear were left wounded in the street.

As the veterans of 2nd Lieutenant Leo Myers's 1st Platoon

tried to figure out how to rescue the two Marines, one of the wounded men kicked himself on his back through a line of hedges. Immediately, the nearest Hotel/2/5 Marines grabbed him and brought him to the 1st Platoon CP. There the platoon corpsman went to work on a sucking chest wound from which blood bubbled and foamed as the wounded Marine gasped for air. The wound was sealed with cellophane, and the wounded man—nobody ever learned his name—started the long journey back to the rear.

Meantime, the second wounded Marine had managed to crawl out of the center of the street and was lying at the end of a driveway in front of the 1st Platoon's position. He was unable to move farther. Though the enemy fire was fierce, Lieutenant Myers called across the driveway to ask Private First Class Walter Kaczmarek to crawl out and drag the wounded man to safety.

Kaczmarek was scared, but he knew someone had to go. He started down the driveway on his belly. He had gone only a few meters when a bullet-chipped sliver of brick struck him beneath his left eye. It was sticking out like an arrowhead. Kaczmarek ducked back to safety, and another Marine pulled the brick chip out. After holding the sleeve of his field jacket against his bleeding cheek for a moment, Private First Class Kaczmarek allowed a corpsman to treat the wound. To Kaczmarek's dismay, the corpsman informed him that the wound was minor.

On Kaczmarek's next attempt, he crawled alongside the garage up to a metal-skinned driveway gate. As Kaczmarek pushed the gate shut so it would hide him, a bullet penetrated the sheet metal at the bottom, just above his hand. He was not hit, but his hand stung painfully for many minutes. Though Kaczmarek now knew that the gate could be penetrated by bullets, he crawled across the driveway behind it and on into the hedge bordering the street. The best he could hope for was that the NVA across the way would not be able to see him.

After crawling through the hedge to a point even with the wounded Marine, Kaczmarek rolled out of his web belt and other jettisonable gear and dashed out through the hedge, into the open street. All hell broke loose. Kaczmarek dropped down next to the wounded Marine. All the shooting stopped.

Every few moments, the wounded man yelled that he had been shot in the chest. Each time he yelled, he thrashed around. Each time he thrashed, the NVA opened fire until he stopped. Kaczmarek spoke to him in a calming voice, then grasped the man's arm, jumped up, and tried to yank him through the hedge. The victim screamed that Kaczmarek was tearing his arm off, so Kaczmarek, who was already in the hedge, let go and dropped down behind the thin cover. It became clear in Kaczmarek's mind that the wounded man had already been shot, and that he, Kaczmarek, had not. He was not going to go back out into the open.

From his hiding place inside the hedge, Private First Class Kaczmarek reached out and grabbed the collar of the wounded man's flak jacket. When he was set, he jumped up and heaved the man into the hedge with both hands. The NVA opened fire again, so Kaczmarek laid low for several moments.

As soon as the shooting died down again, Kaczmarek opened the wounded man's flak jacket to check on the wound. There were two holes in the collar of the flak jacket, but there was no blood. He opened the man's shirt. He still didn't see any blood. There were no holes in the skin. Kaczmarek felt his temper boil. He was so angry he grabbed the double-bit ax he carried on his web belt and was about to strike the wounded man with the flat of the blade when a corpsman arrived. The doc checked the wounded man and found that his collarbone had been shattered, no doubt when the bullet had gone into the collar of the flak jacket.

On the left flank, at 0828, Captain Mike Downs's Fox/2/5 was briefly held up by a pair of NVA who opened fire from the company objective. The Marines responded with their M-16s and two LAAWs and then overran the position. Two more dead NVA were found, along with an SKS carbine.

At 0905, elements of Golf/2/5, while attacking through a very light screen of NVA skirmishers, discovered and sent to the rear over 300 hospital patients and other civilian refugees. It appeared that the NVA had decided to concede the remainder of the hospital complex to 2/5.

Hotel/2/5 reopened its attack upon the provincial head-quarters complex at 0950. The company was immediately halted by intense enemy fire all along its front. As the Marines engaged the NVA strongpoint with small-arms and machine-gun fire, two M-48 tanks were called in, and a tripod-mounted 106mm recoilless rifle was manhandled to the front. One of the tanks was immediately hit by two B-40 rockets, but it remained in action. The NVA then moved a 75mm recoilless rifle to a position on Hotel/2/5's right front and fired six rounds that subdued the ardor of the attacking Marines. In their turn, the Marines called for 81mm mortar fire, and 100 rounds were dropped on various targets along Hotel/2/5's front.

As the provincial headquarters complex was blanketed with heavy fire, Major John Salvati, 2/5's sanguinary executive officer, oversaw the emplacement of several E-8 gas-launcher packs. As scores of tear-gas pellets were being fired, Hotel/2/5 Marines wearing gas masks launched a direct frontal assault into the objective. Unlike the gas attack at the treasury, the tear gas at the provincial headquarters was not effective. The area around the complex was more open, and the breeze off the Perfume River worked to the advantage of the NVA defenders.

Nevertheless, the Marines secured a fortified outbuilding inside the headquarters complex—at a cost of five wounded and evacuated. Twelve newly killed NVA were located in the strong-point.

The hospital complex, on the left flank of 2/5's zone, extended along the full city block southeast of and alongside the prison. As Fox/2/5 continued its sweep through the complex, it entered the Antituberculosis Center and, in so doing, began to outflank the prison's southeast wall.

At 1020, NVA resistance within the Antituberculosis Center suddenly stiffened. The NVA manning the prison must have realized what Fox/2/5's possession of their southeast flank would mean to them. The apparently reinforced NVA in the Antituberculosis Center put up such a stubborn fight that Fox/2/5's stymied 2nd Platoon had to call 81mm mortar fire to regain the initiative.

As the company attack recommenced, a B-40 rocket struck a wall along which a Marine squad was dispersed. The rocket literally blew up in the face of Lance Corporal Reginald Gautreau, whose wounds were ghastly. One of the docs had to push a tube down the Marine's throat to keep him from choking on his own blood, but Gautreau was clearly dying. At length, Gunnery Sergeant Ed Van Valkenburgh made the hard decision and told the doc to stop trying, that Gautreau was past saving.

Minutes later, from his position in a doorway facing out toward the prison, Captain Mike Downs could see Marines from Staff Sergeant Paul Tinson's 2nd Platoon working their way up a side lane running at a right angle to the prison wall. One of the Marines got inside a hospital-ward building. But, when Staff Sergeant Tinson and his platoon command group tried to follow him, alert NVA soldiers on the prison wall scaled the doorway with gunfire. Tinson backed off, led his men around to the other side of the building, and started looking for another way in. At that moment, NVA manning another position fired across Tinson's front. Tinson, who was in the lead, tried to backtrack, but the Marines behind him were crowding him as they came around the blind corner from the rear of the building. In no time, the 2nd Platoon command group got stalled in the open beside the hospital-ward building. Before Staff Sergeant Tinson could get the stacked-up Marines turned around, NVA soldiers manning yet another overlook position chopped them all down.

For Mike Downs, who had seen it all, it was a terrible moment—and it wasn't over yet.

Suddenly, before Captain Downs could act, NVA soldiers, who could see him and his command group in the doorway of the small building, opened fire on them. Downs ducked inside, his back against the wall to his right. At the same moment, the captain's battalion radioman stepped back to the left. Corporal James Violett, the company radioman, had nowhere to go. He fell flat, half in and half out of the open doorway. In the split second after Violett fell, Downs thought, quite clearly, that he should have fallen flat too—he knew that the incoming AK-47 rounds could penetrate the wall he was standing against. In that split second, however, Corporal Violett started flopping spastically on the ground.

Captain Downs reached out through the doorway and made a grab for anything he could use to pull Violett back indoors. He got a grip on something and pulled with all his might. The handset of Violett's radio came off in his hand. On the next try, Downs caught the packboard to which Violett's radio was secured, and he pulled the radioman indoors. But James Violett was dead. He had been shot three times in the head.

When Mike Downs's mind cleared a moment later, he asked for volunteers to accompany him in a dash across the street to a building from which they might be able to reach Staff Sergeant Tinson and the other fallen Marines. No one budged. "Do you mean to tell me," Captain Downs began, "that I can't get any of you to cross the street with me?" There was another moment of silence. Then Lance Corporal James Spencer, the 81mm forward observer assigned to Fox/2/5, stepped forward. "I'll go," Spencer said. A moment later, Private First Class George Blunt agreed to go, too.

Downs, Spencer, and Blunt crossed the street under fire and ran up against a locked door, which they had to batter down. From inside the building, they could see the fallen Marines, but there was no way to tell if any were still alive. Lance Corporal Spencer volunteered to crawl across the fire-swept alleyway to find out.

Downs and Blunt—a puny base of fire—fired their M-16s at the prison while Spencer went outside and crawled over to Staff Sergeant Tinson and the others. The news was grim. Staff Sergeant Paul Tinson was dead. So was Sergeant Alonzo Mayhall, Tinson's platoon sergeant. And so were Private First Class Jimmie Palmo, the 2nd Platoon radioman, and Hospitalman Charles Morrison, the 2nd Platoon corpsman. All had been shot dead where they stood. Four other 2nd Platoon Marines had been wounded.

As it had on two previous mornings, 1/1 attempted to expand its holdings around the complex. Progress had been slow, but gains had been made against an NVA force that was clearly being reinforced from the south and southwest, through 1/1's open left flank. At 0900, February 6, Alpha/1/1's main body was engaged by NVA soldiers occupying a church a half block south of the Jeanne d'Arc complex and a half block east of the 1st Platoon's position inside the Student Center. After a heavy fire-fight involving mortars, M-60s, and a 106mm recoilless rifle, the Alpha/1/1 Marines assaulted the church. Thirty dead NVA were recovered, a civilian man and a civilian woman were detained for questioning, and five rifles and one light machine gun were captured.

At 1100, the NVA precipitously pulled out of the Jeanne d'Arc complex, leaving seventeen dead in the rubble of the western half of the once beautiful Catholic high school. As soon as the Jeanne d'Arc complex had been scoured, Alpha/1/1 and Bravo/1/1 reorganized and attacked to the southwest to catch up with 2/5.

Less than an hour later, while rushing to catch up with 2/5, Alpha/1/1 was caught on the move by a barrage of twenty 82mm mortar rounds. Eight Marines were wounded and evacuated, and another dozen casualties were treated and returned to their platoons. The 1/1 attack continued, but at a much slower pace. The Marines encountered no further direct opposition until 1345. As it was easing its way along the southeastern edge of the hospital complex, Alpha/1/1 came under fire from a group of NVA soldiers armed with a .51-caliber machine gun. The Marines responded with small arms and 60mm mortars. Two Marines were lightly wounded in the exchange, during which the enemy position was bypassed and Alpha/1/1 pressed on to the southwest to close with 2/5.

In the 2/5 zone early that afternoon, Fox/2/5 was attacking yet another building southeast of the prison. Gunfire from within the building suddenly engulfed the assault element. The Marines stepped back and responded with intense small-arms fire of their own, which was supplemented with twenty 60mm mortar rounds. Fox/2/5 resumed the attack and overran the building. No dead NVA were turned up, and two Marines who had sustained minor injuries were treated and returned to duty.

At 1305, approximately two dozen NVA soldiers who had been resisting Fox/2/5's ongoing attacks southeast of the prison

suddenly disengaged and withdrew toward the prison itself. Fortunately, 2/5's 81mm Mortar Platoon was already registered on
the area, and fifty high-explosive rounds were fired at the retreating NVA in a matter of seconds. Twenty-three of the fleeing NVA
were killed in the open.

Golf/2/5, meanwhile, had driven out the few NVA remaining in its sector of the hospital complex. Thus, at 1405, Fox/2/5
was in secure positions on the southeastern flank of the prison,
Golf/2/5 was on line facing the prison from the northeast, and
Hotel/2/5 was in line on Golf/2/5's right, held up in its day-
long bid to break into the provincial headquarters complex.

The Marines of 2/5 knew that the battalion's key objective
was the stoutly defended provincial headquarters, on whose flagpole the NVA had unfurled the large NLF battle flag. But first
there was the prison. Behind its thick, imposing walls, a token
force of ARVN soldiers and Thua Thien provincial policemen had
held off a reinforced Communist battalion for three days. To the
hard-bitten survivors of 2/5, the prison looked like the toughest
nut they had yet encountered in Hue.

After nearly three hours of pounding by mortars and recoilless rifles, the NVA defending the prison just caved in. Supported
by a heavy base of fire provided by Fox/2/5, Golf/2/5 launched
its final assault at 1405. The prison's stout outer wall was
breached at 1415, and the entire prison complex was quickly
overrun at the cost of one Marine wounded and evacuated. Five
ARVN soldiers and two prison officials were liberated. Altogether, thirty-six dead NVA were found, two NVA soldiers surrendered, and six men who could not explain their presence were
detained. Left behind by the fleeing NVA was a motley collection
of captured booty and military relics. Golf/2/5 Marines scouring the fortress found one old French-made rifle, eleven SKS
carbines, four AK-47s, three U.S.-made M-1 carbines, six other
carbines, three U.S.-made M-3 "grease guns," two Chinese-made
RPD light machine guns, one U.S.-made Browning Automatic
Rifle, one B-40, one submachine gun, seven cases of 7.62mm
ammunition, eight Chicom grenades, four M-26 grenades, one
M-2 "pineapple" grenade, four cases of CS grenades, and twenty
assorted demolitions charges.

— 26 —

Hotel/2/5's progress through the provincial headquarters complex remained nil through the late morning and early afternoon. The NVA holed up in the warren of small office buildings were putting up a hell of a fight.

After firing the E-8 gas launchers in the morning and deciding that the gas blanket was more of a hindrance than an aid, Major John Salvati had joined up with a 3.5-inch rocket team. At one point Salvati and the rocketmen took up a position in a long, narrow hospital ward that had a window facing out on the provincial headquarters complex. As the rocketmen were getting set to fire, Salvati looked back into the ward to satisfy himself that the many Vietnamese civilians sprawled motionlessly on the floor were indeed dead, as they appeared to be. Then he selected a target and told the rocket gunner to fire. As the 3.5-inch rocket arced toward the target, the immense backblast blew all the bedding and many of the bodies into a great, twisted pile along the back wall of the room. To Salvati's shock, the many "corpses" slowly pulled themselves to their feet and, while hurling venomous epithets, hobbled from the building by way of the back door.

A squad from the 1st Platoon of Hotel/2/5 was holed up in a cookhouse across from the two-story provincial administration building. For hours all the Marines in the cookhouse had been able to do was harass the NVA in pretty much the same way the NVA were able to harass them—by firing randomly at windows in the buildings across the way.

From time to time, Marines whose jobs kept them in the company rear arrived to vent their spleens. One such visitor, Private Louis Denny, a 60mm ammo humper, had only just stepped up to the cookhouse window when an NVA bullet penetrated his helmet and ricocheted off his skull. Denny was knocked silly, but he was not badly hurt.

At length, a 106mm recoilless rifle was emplaced at the end of the driveway Private First Class Walter Kaczmarek had tried to crawl down to rescue the wounded replacement. The 106 was loaded and prepared to fire directly into the provincial administration building as soon as Gunnery Sergeant Frank Thomas, the Hotel/2/5 gunny, opened the gate.

Just as Gunny Thomas pulled the gate open by means of a brick affixed to a rope, Kaczmarek was stepping to the cookhouse window to take his turn at firing into the administration building. The 106 was fired without the usual "Fire in the hole" warning, and the backblast caught Kaczmarek in the chest. It threw him into the back wall of the cookhouse, and he was knocked unconscious for several minutes.

When Kaczmarek came to, his barely focused eyes told him that someone was leaning over him. It was the platoon doc, who was tagging Kaczmarek for evacuation. Still stunned by the concussion, Kaczmarek assumed that the NVA had blown the cookhouse with a satchel charge and were now collecting prisoners. He squeezed the trigger of his M-16, which was locked in his tight grip, and fired a burst of 5.56mm bullets into the cookhouse ceiling. He would have kept firing, but three or four of his buddies jumped on him, effectively pinning his shooting arm. When the last of the cobwebs lifted and Kaczmarek realized what he had done, he felt like an ass. But no one held him to blame. Under the circumstances, it was an error anyone could have made.

At 1425, while trying to jump-start the stalled assault on the provincial headquarters complex, Hotel/2/5 was hit with yet another barrage of intense fire from the objective, including one B-40 rocket and several 75mm recoilless rifle rounds. The assaulting Marines once again stood down where they were and called for heavy preparatory fire. Though a half dozen previous attempts to break into the complex had failed, the fresh barrage of one hundred 81mm mortar rounds and sixty 106mm recoilless rifle rounds broke the back of the defense.

During the barrage, word came down from Captain Ron Christmas that 2nd Lieutenant Leo Myers's 1st Platoon was to kick in the door. Myers selected Private First Class Alan McDonald's squad to lead the assault, and McDonald and his men drew straws to see who was going to be the first man out the cookhouse door. February 6 was definitely not Walter Kaczmarek's lucky day. He picked first, and he drew the short straw.

The 2/5 battalion chaplain, a priest, came forward to the cookhouse, and the Catholic Marines in McDonald's squad said the Rosary. No one was more fervent in his prayers than Walter Kaczmarek.

An E-8 gas launcher was fired, but Myers's platoon was called back because the men went the wrong way as they stepped out into the thick, roiling clouds of tear gas. As the platoon waited tensely for another E-8 pack to be set up and fired, Walter Kaczmarek used the reprieve to pray.

The second barrage of tear gas pellets was launched, and the assault was on. Noise came from all directions, and the gas and the limited view through the gas mask goggles only made things worse. However, if the attackers could not see through the gas, then perhaps the defenders could not, either.

A long board was thrown across the roll of concertina wire the NVA had erected around the administration building, and Private First Class Walter Kaczmarek led the way across. Kaczmarek had firm orders not to heave a fragmentation grenade through the front door because the Marines had heard that the walls were only plaster over lathe—too thin to contain the blast.

With his view restricted by the gas mask, Kaczmarek fell over some rubble on the wide stairway to the front porch. When he had crawled to the top of the stairs, he emptied a full M-16 magazine through the portal and scrambled into the foyer on his hands and knees. Then the rest of Lieutenant Myers's platoon thundered into the lobby, right over Kaczmarek, and spread out.

Walter Kaczmarek saw that there was a stairway to his left and a long hallway to his right that went the full width of the front of the building. NVA soldiers fleeing up the hallway were firing back as they went.

A barricade lay across the doorway leading to the stairwell. Lieutenant Myers dropped a fragmentation grenade over the top of the barricade, waited for it to detonate, and led an attack up the stairs. At the top of the stairs was another long hallway, which also ran the full width of the front of the building. Here, too, NVA fleeing up the hallway were firing back at the Marines. Undaunted, the Marines chased them down the hall, but most of the NVA had simply vanished. From a second-story window near

the end of the hall, Kaczmarek saw the backs of many NVA
soldiers as they fled across an alley. Before Kaczmarek could
bring up his M-16 to fire, an M-60 gunner was beside him,
firing full tilt into the retreating enemy.

There were so many rooms and buildings to clear inside the
provincial headquarters complex that every Marine who could be
spared from the company headquarters and 60mm mortar section
was sent forward to help. Private First Class Jim Hunter, a 60mm
ammo humper, was one of the first to arrive. Though Hunter had
been in Vietnam since November, he had never directly engaged
the enemy. His war had always been fought at relatively long
distance, even in Hue. He was scared when he formed up with a
handful of riflemen and entered the provincial administration
building. No sooner was Hunter in the front door than several
1st Platoon Marines prodded a North Vietnamese soldier outside
through the same door. Hunter's group was ordered upstairs to
join the room-clearing operation. Everywhere around him, hand
grenades were bursting as fellow Marines cleared each room the
easy way. Each grenade detonation was followed by a burst of
gunfire. In one large conference room, Jim Hunter saw a GVN
flag still hanging on the wall. As the room clearers were running
through that room, an NVA soldier in an adjacent building fired
a round through a window. The bullet struck and killed Private
Jerry Tillery, a 3.5-inch rocketman who, like Jim Hunter, had
been pressed into service to clear the building.

In all, the Hotel/2/5 Marines who cleared the administration building found four NVA bodies. They were still searching
the building when Jim Hunter heard a commotion outside, but he
was too busy to get the details. He thus missed a momentous
occasion.

As soon as Captain Ron Christmas received word that the
administration building was clear, the Hotel/2/5 commander
radioed Lieutenant Colonel Ernie Cheatham: "We have the building, Sir. We're going to run up the American flag."

Strictly speaking, Christmas's plan to hoist the U.S. colors
was illegal. Under numerous prior agreements, American troops
were forbidden to hoist the American flag on any liberated struc-

ture. Strictly speaking, Christmas should have turned the building over to an ARVN officer or a GVN official so the South Vietnamese colors could have been run up on the flagpole. But Ron Christmas was adamant: when American troops, particularly Marines, are triumphant on a field of battle, the U.S. colors, if available, are shown. Captain Christmas turned to Gunnery Sergeant Frank Thomas and said, "We've looked at that damn North Vietnamese flag all day, and now we are going to take it down. Let's go."

Gunny Thomas was all ready for the captain. He had realized early on that the NLF flag would have to be replaced and had put the word out that he was looking for a large American flag. When none could be found, two hard-bitten riflemen ran all the way back to MACV and pulled down—stole—the flag that was flying legally over that compound.

The company commander and company gunny were planning to lay on a proper flag ceremony, but two uninvited guests nearly knocked their plans askew. The moment Private First Class Walter Kaczmarek had laid eyes on the NLF flag, he had decided that it was his if he could grab it. He talked his squad leader, Private First Class Alan McDonald, into helping him lower the enemy banner. The two had just reached the flagpole when Gunny Thomas appeared, the Stars and Stripes tucked into the front of his flak jacket. The gunny had no idea what Kaczmarek and McDonald were up to, but they were there, so he pressed them into service.

At 1603, with Captain Christmas, Lieutenant Myers, several other Marines, one ARVN interpreter, and a camera crew from CBS News looking on, Kaczmarek and McDonald struck the wet, limp NLF colors; Gunny Thomas cut them free from the lanyard with his K-bar knife.

Then Old Glory was affixed to the lanyard. As bullets popped and cracked nearby, and as wisps of tear gas floated around them, Kaczmarek and McDonald, who had a cigarette dangling from his lips, ran their nation's colors up the pole to stand in history beside American flags another generation of filthy, tired Marines had run up over Guadalcanal, Tarawa, Saipan, Iwo Jima, and Seoul. There was no time to call the onlookers to attention, no one remembered to salute, and the lanyard became entangled for a few embarrassing moments, but there wasn't a dry eye in the crowd. Later, many of the onlookers sheepishly blamed their tears on the tear gas.

When Ernie Cheatham reported the fall of the provincial headquarters complex to Regiment, he told it like this: "Be advised we have taken the provincial headquarters. Somehow or other, an American flag is flying over there."

As soon as the deed was done, the CBS camera crew got a handful of the flag raisers together to hold up the deposed NLF banner and pose for pictures. All the time newsman Don Webster was giving his report to the camera, bullets popped and cracked in the background. As the correspondent wrapped up his report, Lieutenant Leo Myers's Oklahoma drawl overcame all the other noise: "Hey, you finished?" Myers asked. "We want to get the hell out of here." There was still a battle to be won, and being in a static crowd inside Hue bothered the lieutenant and, when he brought the subject up, everyone else who was there.

The crowd around the flagpole dispersed in a flash as Lieutenant Myers and Gunny Thomas led their Marines back into the clearing operation.

Moments after leaving the flagpole, Gunny Thomas noticed many distinctive square NVA fighting holes right along the inner edge of the head-high wall surrounding the administration building. Most of the holes were camouflaged, but some were not. Though the holes appeared to be empty, Gunny Thomas had survived too many harrowing episodes in Hue to take anything for granted.

Shotgun at the ready, Thomas stalked over to the nearest hole and, a moment later, yelled a warning that there was an NVA soldier in it. Without hesitation the gunny reached into the hole, grabbed the enemy soldier by the collar of his shirt, and dragged him halfway out. "This one's still alive," the gunny called as he leaned over the uniformed but limp rag doll of a man.

Most of the other holes were also occupied by NVA soldiers, some dead and others wounded. Those who looked like they had any fight in them were shot. One raised his hands before the

Marines could get to him, and he was spared. He was bound with a bandage, and blindfolded with another bandage, before being led off into captivity. His wounded comrades were treated and evacuated after all the wounded Marines had been cared for. The dead NVA were pulled from their fighting holes; searched head to foot; and, for the moment, left sprawled in the middle of the courtyard.

At 1800, Lieutenant Colonel Ernie Cheatham's victorious 2/5 set in at the limit of the day's advance. That evening, 2nd Lieutenant Ray Smith's Alpha/1/1 caught up with 2/5 and relieved Captain Mike Downs's Fox/2/5 of its positions in the Antituberculosis Center. Then, for the first time since it had entered Hue, Fox/2/5 went into reserve.

In four days of vicious combat, 2/5 had broken the backs of two and possibly three NVA infantry battalions and an unknown number of VC units attached to the 4th NVA Regiment. Thereafter, though the 4th NVA Regiment fought on against 2/5 and 1/1 for nearly three more weeks, it ceased to be a strategically relevant factor in the battle for Hue.

— 27 —

There were no celebrations on February 7, 1968. There was no cause for celebration. The battle for Hue was far from over. The loss of life continued.

At 0530, February 7, NVA sappers, who apparently had worked through the night, blew the two center spans of the Nguyen Hoang Bridge into the Perfume River. For the moment, the action was little more than a gesture, because no American or ARVN effort was aimed at the bridge. However, for anyone who cared to look, the demolition of the bridge and the resulting isolation of the 6th NVA Regiment from the 4th NVA Regiment symbolized that the NVA commanders had acknowledged the turning point in Hue. Though the Communist occupation of Hue was now pointless, three weeks of bloody street fighting remained to be endured.

Late in the morning, a large NVA force attacked the 4th Battalion, 3rd ARVN Regiment, which was holding a static fortified position in the vicinity of the Citadel's Chanh Tay Gate. The already much-battered ARVN battalion sustained numerous casualties and gave up communications equipment and weapons before finally fighting the attackers to a standstill.

Also on February 7, in the largest air strike to date over Hue, VNAF A-1 Skyraiders dropped twenty-four 500-pound bombs on NVA positions on the Citadel's southwest wall. ARVN observers on the ground credited the bombs with killing a large number of NVA soldiers. However, the NVA were well entrenched in bunkers and pillboxes within the wall and in masonry buildings of all types across the ARVN front. Even though the South Vietnamese force—with four infantry battalions, three airborne battalions, and numerous smaller combat units—was larger than the NVA force, the ARVN was unable to make measurable gains at all on February 7.

Hue stank of rotting corpses tinged with tear gas, and smoke from hundreds of untended fires. Countless dogs and barnyard animals were loose in the streets, gorging themselves on animal and human flesh. Desperate for food and water, thousands of defenseless civilians risked life and limb in often vain attempts to reach Marine or ARVN lines, where they knew they would be fed and could have their wounds treated.

In the course of a few days, the Hue University complex, liberated by Alpha/1/1 and 2/5 on February 2, became an overcrowded refugee relief center. By February 7, in the late morning, 5,000 homeless South Vietnamese civilians were being cared for and processed there. Though all the supplies the Marines consumed had to be lifted to Hue aboard helicopters or LCUs, a huge stockpile of foodstuffs and other disaster-relief items maintained by the GVN in Hue was more than adequate to meet the basic needs of the refugees who had sought sanctuary within the liberated blocks of the city.

One refugee, only a few short blocks from the Marine front, had to remain in hiding. Jim Bullington dared not dash to safety in the open streets. Bullington had not come close to being apprehended since his arrival on February 1 at the home of Father Cressonier and Father Poncet. This is not to say, however, that they had not had a close call or two. At 1000 on February 6, a shell—probably a Marine mortar round—had hit the house and demolished several rooms, but no one had been hurt. On the afternoon of February 7, they had heard savage bursts of small-arms fire nearby, to the northeast. In fact, 2/5 Marines were scouring the block adjacent to the municipal power station, at whose margin Bullington and the priests awaited their arrival.

The Marines' early-morning advance on February 7 fell into a vacuum. The NVA had withdrawn from 2/5's and 1/1's front, leaving the bodies of their dead, odd lots of military gear, and many untended weapons. Indeed, by noon, the Marines had advanced through buildings and compounds in an area two full city blocks wide and two blocks deep—all without encountering more than the odd sniper. As each building was scoured by the infantry companies, the 2/5 and 1/1 intelligence officers and scouts combed the area for booty and bodies from which documents and other intelligence matter could be retrieved. In the course of the morning, Marine infantry units and intelligence teams turned up the battlefield graves of sixty-two NVA or VC soldiers and catalogued the retrieval of sixty-one carbines of various types, four RPD light machine guns, four flare pistols, forty-five M-3 submachine guns, one heavy machine gun, two .30-caliber light machine guns, and a handful of oddly assorted weapons.

At 1245, Golf/2/5 Marines scouring the Directorate of Social Welfare compound, hard by the Phu Cam Canal, discovered the bodies of three Caucasian males who appeared to be Americans. The corpses were checked by an intelligence team and evacuated to MACV.

The first significant resistance to the February 7 Marine sweep came at 1530, when Golf/2/5 started closing on the Le Lai Military Camp, south of the prison and a block north of the Phu Cam Canal. In addition to armed NVA infantrymen holed up in buildings, the Marines were hit by four 60mm mortar rounds. As Golf/2/5 began deploying to attack the enemy position, an

81mm preparatory fire mission was called. The attack, which jumped off at 1600, overran the NVA strongpoint and produced eleven more NVA corpses. Nevertheless, the bulk of the military camp remained in enemy hands.

At 1746, two blocks southwest of the prison, elements of Hotel/2/5 were searching a building when four 82mm mortar rounds struck it. Ten Marines were wounded. An immediate countermortar mission fired by 2/5's 81mm mortars either silenced the NVA mortar or forced it to displace.

The only Marine killed in Hue on February 7 was 1st Lieutenant Gordon Matthews, the Bravo/1/1 commander. Relatively few were wounded. In the course of the day, 2/5 and 1/1 found that the NVA had abandoned, virtually without a fight, the entire triangular area between the Perfume River, the Phu Cam Canal, and a north-south line from the prison to the canal. NVA snipers and stragglers still infested the area, but it was as good as liberated.

February 8 was another pretty easy day for the Marines, though the NVA kicked it off with an 0530 wake-up call of ten 122mm rockets launched at MACV from sites south of the city. From its battery site near Nam Hoa, Bravo/1/1 fired its six 105mm howitzers at the telltale rocket-ignition flashes. The rocket fire stopped, but no results could be observed.

At 0547, Marines from Alpha/1/1 spotted a small NVA force moving into a building a block south of the Jeanne d'Arc Student Center. M-16 and M-60 fire dispersed the NVA soldiers. When a patrol from Alpha/1/1 searched the area later, it found six dead NVA and collected three carbines, an M-16, quite a bit of ammunition, and several M-26 and Chicom grenades.

The large numbers of NVA bodies, abandoned weapons, ammunition, and equipment found in the liberated buildings told the Marines that the NVA had suffered a major loss of discipline and spirit. For NVA units to leave their dead or very much gear on a battlefield was almost unheard of. As the body count and small-arms and equipment caches added up, it became evident that the demoralized 4th NVA Regiment was having command-and-control problems as well. Of the small number of prisoners taken, a large proportion were officers and senior sergeants.

Beginning at 0700, Hotel/2/5 and Fox/2/5 opened an attack to the south to close on the Phu Cam Canal. Once at the canal, 2/5 was to wheel to the east and attack in that direction as far as Highway 1.

Almost at once, Hotel/2/5 came under heavy machine-gun fire from a building on its left flank. A vigorous response with small arms and M-79 grenades, bolstered by an 81mm mortar barrage, forced the NVA from their position. Hotel/2/5 overran the objective.

Meanwhile, on Hotel/2/5's left (east), Fox/2/5 ran into sniper fire along its front. The enemy position was overcome with small-arms fire at the cost of two Marines wounded, two NVA killed, and one NVA soldier taken prisoner.

At 0944, Hotel/2/5 attacked the Le Lai Military Camp, from which Golf/2/5 had had to withdraw the previous evening to consolidate the 2/5 night defensive position. The camp was overrun again at around 1000, this time at the cost of one Marine killed, one Marine wounded, and one NVA soldier killed.

The biggest windfall of the day resulted from a routine search through the Le Lai Military Camp. While probing for more NVA, Hotel/2/5 Marines stumbled on the ARVN's main armory in Hue. Apparently, the store of weapons and munitions had not been discovered by the NVA, for, in addition to a huge stockpile of ammunition and military equipment, the Marines inventoried 1,500 rifles, carbines, and submachine guns; one hundred U.S.-made .30-caliber light machine guns; four 57mm recoilless rifles; fifteen M-113 APCs; and—get this—eight M-41 light tanks! After many Hotel/2/5 Marines had helped themselves to weapons—.45-caliber Thompson submachine guns went particularly fast—the armory was turned over to the Thua Thien Sector Advisor, a U.S. Army officer attached to MACV Advisory Team 3.

At 1000, two platoons of Bravo/1/1 were sweeping along Highway 1 from the northwest, in the direction of the An Cuu Bridge. They were accosted by NVA holed up in the Thua Thien Province Police Bureau, a walled compound halfway across the cane field causeway. The Marines—mostly cooks, bakers, and clerks pressed into infantry duty—returned the fire with even stronger fire. When the Marines maneuvered into the compound, they found three dead NVA, fourteen rifles of various types, a B-40 round, three 60mm mortar rounds, some detonation cord, and a police armory containing 2.5 tons of assorted arms and munitions.

While the infantry companies were active to the east, the engineer platoon attached to 2/5 was preparing the westernmost bridge across the Phu Cam Canal for demolition. NVA snipers south of the canal wounded three engineers, who could not be evacuated until Marine M-48 tanks arrived to cover the rescue effort with 90mm smoke rounds and fire on the enemy position with their .50- and .30-caliber machine guns.

Why the Marines were demolishing a bridge in a city they were liberating, and in the course of a battle they were winning, demands some explanation. The 4th NVA Regiment's intentions were then deeply cloaked in mystery. Marine commanders believed that a counterattack across the Phu Cam Canal was imminent, or at least possible. It was easier to demolish the bridge than to use limited troop resources to develop a strongpoint around it. The bridge in question—the westernmost of six that spanned the canal—was not militarily vital to the Marines and higher headquarters, which approved the bridge demolition in advance and judged that there were adequate resources in I Corps to replace all the canal bridges when needed.

Interestingly, plans were afoot to mount III MAF's 1st Marine Bridge Company out of Phu Bai the next day to replace the NVA-demolished An Cuu Bridge at the other end of the Phu Cam Canal. The bridge company, which was to be escorted by a platoon of the real Bravo/1/1 and all available replacements bound for 2/5, was to be met at the bridge site by Alpha/1/1 and the main body of the provisional Bravo/1/1.

February 8 was liberation day for Jim Bullington and his hosts, Father Pierre Poncet and Father Marie Cressonier. Early in the day, Bullington's friend, Albert Istvie, arrived from his home at the Hue Municipal Power Station with startling news: the NVA had gone. Still, Bullington and the priests remained indoors until, shortly after lunch, they heard American voices outside. Minutes later, from a second-story window, Bullington spotted several "real, honest-to-god U.S. Marines." The CORDS officer was about to shout a greeting to his countrymen, but one of the priests asked him to keep quiet until several of his Vietnamese neighbors had been escorted from sight. The priest was fearful that VC sympathizers might mark him for retaliation for harboring an American. Fifteen minutes later, Marines from 2nd Lieutenant Mike Lambert's 3rd Platoon, Hotel/2/5, reached the house. When Bullington introduced himself to a Marine sergeant, the sergeant matter-of-factly replied, "Oh yeah, they told us there might be some sort of VIPs hiding around here. I'd better tell the captain." Bullington was surprised to learn that he had been elevated to VIP status and that his deliverance had been anticipated.

When Captain Ron Christmas arrived a few minutes later, Bullington explained the priests' dilemma with the neighbors. After a moment's thought, Christmas had a corpsman wrap Bullington in a military blanket and escort him from the house. It was hoped that any onlookers would take Bullington for a wounded Marine.

When Jim Bullington arrived at MACV, he used the communications facilities there to announce his safe return to his superiors in Quang Tri City and to ask permission to remain in Hue until he had some word about the fate of his fiancée, Tuy-Cam. Permission was denied; Bullington was ordered to fly to Danang the next day.

At that moment, Tuy-Cam and her family were safe. They were at home, only a few hundred meters west of the priests' house, but on the wrong side of the Phu Cam Canal. The best assurance that Jim Bullington could get was that their neighborhood would be cleared as soon as important military objectives had been secured.

Father Poncet and Father Cressonier chose to remain at home, where they felt they could best help their neighbors restore their lives. Albert Istvie also opted to remain at his post at the power company; he wanted to get to work helping to restore electricity to the city. The next day, after Jim Bullington's intercession, Istvie's wife and two children, with Bullington, were flown to Danang aboard a Marine helicopter.

Sparring with NVA rearguard detachments and stragglers consumed most of the afternoon of February 8, and more NVA bodies, weapons, and gear fell into Marine hands.

At 1315, Golf/2/5 Marines entered the U.S. consul general's residence, on Ly Thuong Kiet Street, right across from Hue Cathedral, and only a half block west of the cane field that stretched out on both sides of Highway 1. Reaching the consular quarters brought Captain Chuck Meadows and the Golf/2/5 survivors full circle, for the first shots fired at them in the battle for Hue had come from an NVA machine gun set in near the cathedral.

As soon as the Marines entered the U.S. consul's residence, they turned up evidence that the compound had been used by the NVA as a field dispensary. Bloody bandages, other medical waste, and abandoned medical supplies abounded. In a search of the area, twenty hastily dug graves were discovered, and a total of twenty-five dead NVA soldiers were exhumed.

Late that afternoon, 2/5 established night defensive positions on both sides of Ly Thuong Kiet Street. The only action of the night was a brief mortar barrage at 1905, which wounded three Marines at the 2/5 CP.

Outside the battle zone on February 8, several LCUs arrived at the Hue LCU ramp. They were chock-full of ammunition and other useful gear and equipment. The last LCU to leave the ramp that afternoon was fired on heavily by small arms and mortars, but, undamaged, it ran the gauntlet to the South China Sea. The LCU lifts were extremely important because the continuously foul weather had halted helicopter resupply efforts.

On February 9, NVA gunners again started the day by terrorizing the MACV Compound. This time they fired six 60mm mortar rounds at it. The 1st Marines CP, which was inside the compound, arranged for counterbattery missions against the area southeast of the city, in which muzzle flashes had been observed. Against the one or two NVA light mortars, the Marines fired ten 81mm mortar rounds and, from Phu Bai, eight 155mm rounds. Once again, damage and casualties could not be assessed.

The task of securing the An Cuu Bridge site was given to Lieutenant Colonel Mark Gravel's 1/1, which was to attack from the north, down the northeast side of the cane field, from the vicinity of Tu Do Stadium. Lieutenant Colonel Ernie Cheatham's 2/5 was to secure the north side of the Phu Cam Canal all the way from the Perfume River to a battalion boundary line set just to the east of the An Cuu Bridge.

After clearing two city blocks, including Tu Do Stadium, without firing a shot, Alpha/1/1 suddenly ran into opposition. At 0820, as the company point pushed east from the stadium, four Marines on the point were wounded as they crossed a street. In the ensuing exchange, it took three 90mm rounds fired by the attached M-48 tank to get Alpha/1/1 across the street. At 0900, the NVA hit the tank with seven 57mm recoilless rifle rounds. The tank was set afire and abandoned on the spot by its crew, three of whom were burned and needed to be evacuated.

It is not surprising that 1/1 encountered such strong opposition in its new zone. Apparently, the Marine battalion was facing the main body of the 804th NVA Battalion, which the Marine clearing operation had not seriously engaged in the preceding week.

Shortly after the damaged M-48 tank was towed away, an ARVN major entered the Alpha/1/1 lines. He had been home for Tet leave when the battle started, and, in joining 1/1, he was leaving his house for the first time since January 31. The ARVN officer pinpointed his house on 2nd Lieutenant Ray Smith's map and told Smith that the building next door was the site of an NVA battalion CP—presumably the 804th NVA Battalion. Before being escorted to MACV, the ARVN major said that a Chinese advisor was stationed with the NVA command group. Lieutenant Smith passed these tidbits up the chain of command and requested permission to level the area around the enemy CP with some serious artillery fire. Permission was conditionally granted—if higher headquarters agreed.

At 1020, while pulling out of the line of the anticipated friendly fire, Alpha/1/1 was struck by an estimated 200 small-arms rounds and three B-40 rockets. The Marines returned fire with M-16s, M-60s, and six LAAWs. Three Marines were wounded and evacuated in the exchange, and two of eight NVA soldiers who sprinted into an open area were killed by a direct hit from one of the LAAWs.

At 1325, Bravo/1/1 was struck by yet another group of NVA. At the outset of the exchange, an accompanying Army M-55 quad-.50 truck was struck by a B-40 rocket and rendered inoperable. At the cost of one Marine wounded, the enemy strongpoint was silenced by a cloud of bullets, M-79 grenades, and LAAWs. Five minutes after the M-55 was damaged, the main body of Alpha/1/1 was struck by ten 60mm mortar rounds fired from north of Tu Do Stadium.

By then, higher headquarters had come back with permission for Lieutenant Smith to fire all available artillery at the 804th NVA Battalion CP and the battalion's zone south and east of Tu Do Stadium.

In the largest artillery barrage to strike Hue to date, Lieutenant Smith's artillery forward observer directed a total of about 250 8-inch howitzer rounds, nearly five hundred 155mm gun rounds, and all the rounds the 1/1 81mm Mortar Platoon could spare.

For all the artillery fire, it was painfully obvious by the middle of the afternoon that 1/1 was not going to be able to close on the An Cuu Bridge from the north that day. At 1515, the battalion attack was canceled, and Lieutenant Colonel Gravel's two thin infantry companies were ordered to consolidate a night defensive position at the limit of their advance. Harassed at 1515 by NVA snipers, who fired sixty rounds and wounded three Marines, the Marines responded, as usual, with M-16 and M-60 fire. This time, however, the small-arms fire was bolstered with 81mm mortar fire. Results could not be determined.

Five more Bravo/1/1 Marines were wounded and evacuated during another exchange at 1600, and yet another exchange at 1745 resulted in two Marines killed. A 105mm howitzer mission was placed on the source of the enemy fire, but that had no lasting effect. The only enemy fatality actually confirmed during the course of the day's action was chalked up at 1800, when a scout-sniper sent down to the Bravo/1/1 position from the 1st Marines CP shot an NVA soldier dead in the open. However, subsequent searches through the area fronting the Bravo/1/1 position turned up thirty-three enemy corpses and three weapons.

At 0828, February 9, Captain Chuck Meadows's Golf/2/5 turned up a cache of 600 tons of rice and one ARVN M-41 tank. After liberating hundreds of civilian refugees from several church buildings, Golf/2/5 continued to apply pressure on the NVA manning positions in and around the cane field southwest of Highway 1. At 1005, in Golf/2/5's only action of the morning, both Army M-42 Dusters attached to the Marine company were disabled when their fuel tanks were holed by NVA fire. One Marine was killed and two Marines were wounded in the exchange. Fortunately, neither Duster caught fire, and both were towed to the rear for repairs.

At 1820, as engineers accompanying Golf/2/5 were placing charges to drop the first bridge to the west of the An Cuu Bridge, NVA soldiers to the south put out an intense volley of small-arms and automatic-weapons fire. The NVA fire was quelled and the bridge was blown, but one Golf/2/5 Marine was killed and two others were wounded.

Altogether, throughout the day, in addition to recovering the rice and the ARVN tank, Golf/2/5 accounted for seventeen NVA killed. The unit captured five AK-47 assault rifles, two SKS carbines, one 60mm mortar, eight B-40 rockets, and twenty-eight 60mm mortar rounds. Golf/2/5's losses were two killed and five wounded.

At 1051, as the 3rd Platoon of Captain Ron Christmas's Hotel/2/5 moved east alongside the Phu Cam Canal, it was struck from south of the canal by small-arms fire. One Marine was killed. At 1220, a routine search by several Hotel/2/5 Marines turned up three Vietnamese men clad in civilian clothes and carrying a carbine, a submachine gun, and a B-40 round. At 1305, the company apprehended eight more civilian-garbed Vietnamese men who were monitoring a Marine artillery fire-control net on a transistor radio. The eight men and their radio were turned over to the 1st Marines CP. At 1720, after being prevented by NVA fire from demolishing the second Phu Cam bridge east of the An Cuu Bridge, Hotel/2/5 called in an 8-inch howitzer mission to drop the span. When the initial heavy-artillery rounds fell astride the target, they produced two large secondary explosions on the south side of the canal. A moment later, eight enemy soldiers were shot to death in the open as they attempted to flee from a strongpoint beside the bridge. No Marines were even scratched during the incident.

In its only action of the day, Captain Mike Downs's Fox/2/5 was harassed by a sniper at 1035 as it was clearing the built-up area at the western end of the Phu Cam Canal. The sniper was beyond reach, on the south side of the canal, so the Marines responded with small-arms fire, ten 106mm recoilless rifle rounds, and twenty-two 81mm mortar rounds. One Marine was wounded, and the sniper was claimed as a kill.

On February 9, 2/5 seized all but the eastern tip of the triangular area bordered by the Perfume River, the Phu Cam Canal, and Highway 1. Much of the newly liberated area still had to be searched carefully, but it was evident that the 4th NVA Regiment had been ejected from Hue's modern central area. The inability of 1/1 to break into the defensive sector held by the remnants of the 804th NVA Battalion necessitated a one-day delay in the deployment of the 1st Marine Bridge Company at the as-yet-unsecured An Cuu Bridge site.

Throughout February 10, 2/5's efforts went into mopping up NVA stragglers and collecting their discarded weapons and equipment from the built-up areas north of the Phu Cam Canal. Casualties were extremely light in all three companies—just three 2/5 Marines wounded all day in exchange for nine confirmed kills.

In the 1/1 zone, the attack toward the An Cuu Bridge was canceled. Instead, Alpha/1/1 and Bravo/1/1 were put to work clearing the 804th NVA Battalion out of the neighborhoods to the east and southeast of Tu Do Stadium.

In the only significant action of the day undertaken by 1/1,

Lieutenant Ray Smith's Alpha/1/1 fired an E-8 gas launcher and threw in a dawn attack against the reported site of the 804th NVA Battalion's CP. Marines searching through the rubble left by the previous afternoon's massive artillery strike found that the target building had indeed housed the CP, complete with tattered NVA battle flags. Several bodies were exhumed from the rubble, but large pools of congealing blood and numerous blood trails and drag marks indicated that many more dead and wounded enemy soldiers—hopefully including the Chinese advisor—had been dragged away during the night.

As in the 2/5 zone, the Marines made few contacts with the enemy through the remainder of the day; casualties were light. Though the 804th NVA Battalion had not quite given the area up, it did not put up much of a fight.

At 1235, February 10, the delayed bridge convoy, guarded by a platoon of the real Bravo/1/1 and about 150 replacements bound for 2/5, was ordered out of Phu Bai. When it arrived at the An Cuu Bridge site, the Marine engineers discovered that the condition of the span was far worse than they had been led to expect; their bridging materials were inadequate. The 1st Marine Bridge Company and all the trucks laden with supplies for 1/1 and 2/5 returned to Phu Bai, but nearly 200 fresh infantrymen crossed the shattered span on foot and walked to MACV, where they reported to the 1st Marines CP. The Bravo/1/1 platoon was turned over to 1/1, and the rest of the new arrivals were sent to the 2/5 CP for assignment to the letter companies. A number of the 2/5 replacements were among the first Marines to be returned to the battalion following earlier injury and evacuation in Hue.

For all practical purposes, the mission assigned to the 1st Marines by Task Force X-Ray on February 3 had been accomplished by the end of the day on February 10. The entire heart of modern Hue bounded by Highway 1, the Perfume River, and the Phu Cam Canal was free of organized NVA or VC opposition. Moreover, the 804th NVA Battalion's resistance in the built-up area east of Highway 1 and south of the Perfume appeared to be on the verge of collapse. In the days ahead, 1/1 would continue to clear the enemy from its zone around Tu Do Stadium, while, in the absence of firm orders from above, Lieutenant Colonel Ernie Cheatham would, on his own authority, ease elements of 2/5 into the built-up areas south of the Phu Cam Canal to see if they were strongly held.

The focus of the battle for Hue was about to shift to the symbolically meaningful effort to liberate the entire Citadel of Hue from the reinforced 6th NVA Regiment. To restart the 1st ARVN Division's and 1st Airborne Task Force's stalled drive inside the Citadel, the GVN decided to "send in the Marines."

PART VIII

THE CITADEL

Though it had been defeated, the 4th NVA Regiment had not been driven entirely from Hue. Indeed, from about February 10, it was reinforced by elements of two NVA regiments dispatched from around Khe Sanh following the collapse of the assault on the Marine combat base and possibly by other units from elsewhere in I Corps.

The 4th NVA Regiment had been ejected from southern Hue, but the 6th NVA Regiment—which was also to be reinforced by infantry units from other areas—was still strongly in possession of more than half the Citadel. In eleven days of heavy fighting, the 1st ARVN Airborne Task Force and up to four infantry battalions of the 1st ARVN Division had been fought to a complete standstill. By February 10, ARVN General Headquarters, in Saigon, was demanding the withdrawal of the three airborne battalions, which were part of the ARVN General Headquarters reserve. If the airborne battalions were indeed withdrawn and not replaced in kind or by a much stronger force, Brigadier General Ngo Quang Truong faced grim prospects in his struggle to clear the NVA and VC from the Citadel. Truong therefore requested that the airborne battalions be replaced with any available but comparably proficient units from anywhere outside the 1st ARVN Division's area of operations. In the end, the GVN's Joint General Staff (JGS) decided to throw in part of the JGS national strategic reserve—at least two of the six strong infantry battalions composing the Vietnamese Marine Corps (VNMC). Since no other South Vietnamese combat units were available, MACV finally persuaded the GVN to employ a U.S. Marine infantry battalion inside the Citadel.

The 1st Battalion, 5th Marines (1/5), had had a bad Tet. Charged with guarding Highway 1 south of Hai Van Pass, the battalion had found itself strung out in four widely dispersed bases on January 31, easy pickings for the aggressive Communist units operating in Quang Nam Province. Not only were elements of 1/5's dispersed infantry companies bombarded and harassed, the battalion's main encampment at Phu Loc was directly attacked by NVA or VC infantry. Further, 1/5 was hampered in defending itself by its missions to defend or rescue a number of Vietnamese units and Marine CAPs based in its area of operations. During one such mission, on February 1, the battalion commander was severely wounded and evacuated. His replacement, Major Bob Thompson, the III MAF embarkation officer, arrived in Phu Loc to assume command of 1/5 late the following day.

Between January 31 and February 6, 1/5 worked the area along Highway 1 in the vicinity of Phu Loc. The battalion sustained many casualties, but it and other ARVN and U.S. units in the area slowly gained the advantage. On February 7, the bulk of 1/5 moved north of the Hai Van Pass to clear NVA units that were still molesting the strategic Troi Bridge. When that one-day sweep had been completed, the entire battalion was again concentrated south of Hai Van Pass, once again in the vicinity of Phu Loc. Security for Troi Bridge was left to Echo/2/5, and the job of patrolling Highway 1 south of Phu Bai was turned over to a battalion of the U.S. Army's 101st Airborne Division.

Early on February 10, Alpha/1/5 was detached from its parent battalion and ordered to proceed via Phu Bai to the 1st Marines CP in Hue. At 1400, 1st Marines assumed operational control of Alpha/1/5, and, at 1430, the company proceeded by vehicle convoy to the damaged An Cuu Bridge. After dismounting from the trucks and crossing the span on foot, Alpha/1/5 proceeded without incident to MACV and set in for the night. Late in the day, two platoons of Bravo/1/5 were also detached from 1/5 and ordered to the 5th Marines CP, in Phu Bai.

At midnight that night, the 5th Marines CP contacted Major Thompson, who was hunkered down in a hole in the middle of an open, rain-swept field eight or nine kilometers from Phu Loc. Regiment told Thompson to pack up the rest of the battalion and proceed immediately to Phu Bai to take part in a new operation. Thompson later claimed he was so cold he could barely speak. But his operations officer, Major Len Wunderlich, was right in the hole with Thompson, and he thought that Thompson's words

were choked more by anger or exasperation than by the cold. In
any event, Thompson finally pieced together a reply that conveyed
to his superiors that elements of his battalion were in contact with
the enemy and that he thought a night disengagement would not
be a smart move. He said he would begin to disengage from the
contact at first light and get up to Phu Bai as soon as possible.
The regimental commander heard Thompson out, said he understood the basis of Thompson's objections, and told Thompson to
carry out his order anyway. With that, the main body of 1/5
began a night march through the wind and rain, across flooded
fields and freezing, swift-running streams, nearly nine kilometers
to Phu Loc.

At first light on February 11, 1/5's entire rear echelon was
ordered by 5th Marines to move immediately from Phu Loc to
Phu Bai. Also at first light, Major Thompson's main body arrived
back at Phu Loc. The battalion CP group, escorted by one infantry platoon, left for Phu Bai at 0810. At 0930, as soon as Major
Thompson reached the 5th Marines CP, 1/5 was officially
passed to the operational control of the 1st Marines for duty in
Hue.

When Bob Thompson and Major Len Wunderlich stopped
by the Task Force X-Ray CP for a quick check-in chat before
departing for Hue, they received a situation briefing that appears
to have been every bit as vague as those served up to Hue-bound
units on January 31, the first day of combat in Hue. In fact,
Brigadier General Foster LaHue, the Task Force X-Ray commander, frankly admitted that he knew little about the situation
in Hue; he even asked Thompson to "let me know what's going
on when you get there." Thus, when Thompson and Wunderlich
left for their battalion's new area of operations, they were supported more by vague rumor than by hard fact.

If Bob Thompson had learned little about conditions in Hue,
his Marines had learned plenty—perhaps too much—from members of 1/1 and 2/5 who were filtering through Phu Bai on a
score of different chores. Naturally, the old salts told the new
guys only the most lurid tales of life and death amid the rubble in
Hue. And, naturally, the 1/5 Marines both disbelieved the street-
fighting veterans and decided that their own bravery and profes-

sionalism were being questioned. In fact, as 2/5's and 1/1's maimed companies had learned, there was no way to prepare for the especially brutal brand of warfare the new guys would face in Hue. They could only learn by doing.

At 1045, February 11, Bravo/1/5 boarded Marine CH-46 helicopters at Phu Bai for a lift directly into the 1st ARVN Division CP compound, inside the Citadel. Within fifteen minutes of lift-off, Bravo/1/5 received its baptism in Hue. Small-arms fire rising to greet the Marine helicopters from the NVA-held portion of the Citadel wounded the pilot of the CH-46 carrying Bravo/1/5's 3rd Platoon. The copilot was obliged to return immediately to Phu Bai so the wounded officer could be treated.

At 1600, Bravo/1/5's 3rd Platoon departed Phu Bai again, this time as security for a road convoy charged with delivering the 1/5 battalion CP group to Hue. The convoy made the obligatory stop at the fallen An Cuu Bridge, and everyone piled out and crossed the Phu Cam Canal singlefile on a jury-rigged 2-inch-by-12-inch catwalk. On the way up Highway 1, Major Len Wunderlich was awestruck by the destruction he witnessed. Major Thompson conducted a methodical tactical advance along the rubble-choked highway even though many studiously incautious 2/5 and 1/1 Marines were out and about. Thus, it wasn't until after 1800, February 11, that he and Major Wunderlich reported to the 1st Marines forward CP at MACV to learn what was in store for themselves and their Marines.

Thompson and Wunderlich reported to Colonel Stan Hughes, the 1st Marines CO, who was to show them where 1/5 would operate inside the Citadel. Hughes pointed to the Citadel on his map and told Thompson that 1/5 would operate under orders only from 1st Marines, not from the 1st ARVN Division. That was all. When Thompson tried to outline a plan for using his companies in the attack, Hughes cut him off in mid-sentence and said, "Major, I'm not at all interested in what you do with your companies. That's your business."

As Major Thompson was finishing up with the regimental commander, Major Wunderlich went off to confer with the 1st Marines assistant operations officer, Major Bob Kerlich, an old and trusted friend. In the next few minutes, Kerlich told Wunderlich everything he had been able to pick up about how 2/5 and 1/1 had developed the use of tanks, Ontos, recoilless rifles, 3.5-inch rocket launchers, CS tear gas, and other weapons in clearing built-up areas. It was all news to Wunderlich, whose training in street fighting was rudimentary and long ago. The biggest problem Wunderlich faced was finding the equipment and ordnance his battalion lacked. Fortunately, while passing through Phu Bai, Wunderlich had been advised to take his battalion's 3.5-inch rocket launchers out of storage, and he had seen that it was done.

Late in the evening, as Major Thompson was arranging for the Perfume River crossing the next day, he was approached by a bespectacled, middle-aged U.S. Army major who, on second glance, proved to be a chaplain. The stranger introduced himself as Father Aloysius McGonigal, and he said right off that he had heard that 1/5 had come to Hue without a chaplain. Thompson confirmed the report, and the priest offered to accompany 1/5 into the Citadel and stay until the Navy sent a new chaplain to join the battalion. Thompson readily agreed, and they sealed the deal with a handshake. Little did either man know how profoundly their lives would be affected by their casual arrangement.

The plans to move 1/5 into the Citadel to take part in the final clearing operation were well advanced. As 1/5 was staging into Hue on February 11, the five M-48 gun tanks of the 1st Platoon of Alpha Company, 1st Tank Battalion, were on the move aboard Navy LCUs from Danang. In fact, the tanks were landed at a secure quay only a hundred meters east of the Truong Dinh Gate, the secure entrance into the Citadel's northern corner. All five of the tanks were inside the 1st ARVN Division CP compound by 1645. Less than an hour later, at 1730, Alpha/1/5 was picked up by LCUs at the Hue LCU ramp, ferried up the Perfume alongside the Citadel's northeast wall, and landed behind the five M-48 tanks. Thus, by nightfall on February 11, all of Alpha/1/5, two-thirds of Bravo/1/5, and five Marine M-48 tanks were inside the Citadel. Charlie/1/5 and Delta/1/5 were expected to report to Hue the next day, and Major Thompson, his CP group, and Bravo/1/5's 3rd Platoon expected to make the river journey from the Hue LCU ramp to the Citadel the next morning.

The plan for 1/5 was to launch its attack inside the Citadel on February 12, but delays in rebuilding the An Cuu Bridge and the shortage of transport combined to put Major Thompson's battalion a full day behind schedule. Then, on D-day itself, small-arms fire from NVA soldiers atop the Citadel's northwest wall, overlooking the river, seriously threatened the LCU ferry service. As a result, Major Thompson, his CP group, the Bravo/1/5 escort platoon, and Charlie/1/5 did not leave the Hue LCU ramp until late in the afternoon, with a flight of Huey helicopters overhead as surety against enemy fire.

When the CP group finally did land at the quay adjacent to the Citadel's northern corner, Major Thompson personally led it astray, southeast along the northwest wall. The Marines had already progressed several hundred yards in the wrong direction before several Vietnamese civilians came out and stopped them with cries of "*Beaucoup* VC!" The civilians got the Marines turned around and guided them to the Truong Dinh Gate, but the massive gate was closed and the guards refused to open the portal. They even demanded that Thompson disperse his force lest it draw mortar fire. Not quite the most patient soul in Hue, Bob Thompson reached the end of his fuse and icily informed the gate-guard commander that Charlie/1/5 would make a direct assault on the gate if it was not opened immediately. No sooner had the U.S. Marine battalion commander delivered his ultimatum than the gateway was thrown open. On the other side, the battalion CP group was greeted by the commanders of Alpha/1/5 and Bravo/1/5, which were already inside.

By the time Major Thompson reported to General Truong's CP, it was after 1800. However, in dribs and drabs, three U.S. Marine companies and the battalion CP were assembled within the 1st ARVN Division CP compound by late that evening. Not present was Delta/1/5, which had arrived in Hue intact but had been placed under the operational control of 2/5 for duty south of the Perfume.

Major Thompson was warmly welcomed by Brigadier General Truong outside the ARVN Tactical Operations Center. At the

ensuing meeting, which several of Truong's American advisors
attended, the ARVN division commander told the U.S. Marine
battalion commander, "Major, whatever you want to do, we'll
support. We are having a difficult time." Truong's cooperative
demeanor put Bob Thompson at his ease; he felt that he could
work with the scrappy Vietnamese general. Thompson told
Truong what he had in mind; and Truong quickly outlined the
deployment of the ARVN units inside the Citadel, his expecta-
tions for reinforcements, and how he planned to conduct his
renewed attack to clear the reinforced 6th NVA Regiment.

In a radio message at 2015, February 12, Major Thompson
informed the 1st Marines CP that

> Unless directed otherwise, [I] intend to commence at-
> tack at [0800, February 13] as directed by [the regi-
> mental operations order]. Two battalions of Vietnamese
> Marines assigned to conduct search-and-destroy oper-
> ations in northern sector of Hue on right flank of
> [1/5] have not arrived, and their time of arrival is
> unknown.

While 1/5 was moving toward Phu Bai and Hue, the
VNMC's Battle Group Alpha, commanded by Major Huong
Thong, was moving from Saigon to Hue. The entire VNMC—six
infantry battalions and one 105mm howitzer battalion—had
been embroiled in the battle to save Saigon. Though the battle
there was far from over, the situation had stabilized to the point
where two VNMC battalions, an artillery battery, and one of the
VNMC's two battle-group (brigade) headquarters were spared
for duty in Hue. Battle Group Alpha was to replace the 1st
ARVN Airborne Battle Group. Selected for duty in Hue were the
1st and 5th VNMC battalions and one six-gun 105mm howitzer
battery. The battle-group headquarters and the 1st VNMC Battalion were ordered to fly from Saigon to I Corps late on February 10, and the 5th VNMC Battalion was to follow as soon as
transport could be arranged.

It is emblematic of the slow progress toward normalcy in the
wake of TCK-TKN that the VNMC battle-group staff was unable

to learn from higher headquarters the precise nature of the situation in and around Hue and Phu Bai. Until he actually landed at peaceful Phu Bai, Captain Ron Ray, the temporary senior advisor assigned to VNMC Battle Group Alpha, had no idea that Phu Bai was secure. Indeed, he did not know he was in Phu Bai until after he had landed, for he had been told that his battalion would be transported directly into Hue's Tay Loc Airfield, inside the Citadel. At Phu Bai, however, liaison officers from Task Force X-Ray greeted the newly arrived VNMC units and provided maps and a briefing on the situation in northern I Corps.

Problems arose almost as soon as the meeting ended. The senior U.S. Marine officers representing Task Force X-Ray made it abundantly clear that they expected the leading half of the VNMC battle group to depart immediately for Hue. Major Thong, the VNMC battle-group commander, refused to be rushed. He wanted to wait until his entire task force had assembled at Phu Bai, by which time he hoped to have arranged for transportation and complete intelligence briefs. The U.S. Marine officers immediately began pressuring Major Thong, but Thong stuck to his guns.

Through the night, the U.S. Marine advisors assigned to VNMC Battle Group Alpha were hard at work trying to get better intelligence data and to arrange for helicopter, motor transport, or landing craft—whatever—to get the VNMC units to Hue. Though Task Force X-Ray wanted the Vietnamese Marines to mount out *now*, no one seemed willing to help them do so. At a minimum, the Vietnamese Marines needed field jackets to ward off the cold of northern I Corps, and all manner of weapons, gear, and ammunition that had not been replaced in the hurried departure from Saigon.

Toward dawn, February 11, the pot boiled over. Captain Ron Ray was inside the Task Force X-Ray CP, on the radio, trying to talk a U.S. Army helicopter unit into transporting the Vietnamese Marines to Hue. Ray had his back to the door when he heard a loud, authoritarian voice behind him erupt in a stream of derogatory language. Certain he was the target of the verbal abuse, Captain Ray spun on his heel and saw, live and in person, Lieutenant General Robert Cushman, the III MAF commanding general. Accompanying Cushman was Brigadier General Foster LaHue, commanding general of Task Force X-Ray. And behind the Marine generals were a U.S. Army major general Captain Ray did not know and an entourage of U.S. Marine and U.S. Army senior field-grade officers.

Captain Ray had no idea why General Cushman was berating him for not deploying "his" VNMC unit immediately. Ray had no authority over the Vietnamese Marines; he was just an advisor. The man to see was Ray's opposite number, Major Thong. But the young captain was not invited to speak, and he dared not do so. He took his dressing down like a good trooper, in silence, until General Cushman, a World War II Medal of Honor winner, wound down and finally followed General LaHue into LaHue's office for a ten-minute meeting. After General Cushman and his entourage left, General LaHue took Captain Ray aside and assured the younger officer that he, for one, understood the relationship of the advisor to his opposite number, and that he, LaHue, would do everything in his power to arrange for the VNMC battle group's needs.

General Cushman's extreme behavior was probably motivated by orders direct from the MACV commander, General William Westmoreland. The VNMC battle group was under pressure to get rolling because Westmoreland—and probably President Lyndon Johnson—wanted the NLF battle flag lowered from the southeast wall of the Citadel as soon as possible.

Major Thong stuck to his guns until the 5th VNMC Battalion arrived on February 11, and then until both VNMC battalions had been reequipped as completely as possible. Late in the day, Battle Group Alpha, aboard U.S. Marine trucks, mounted out of Phù Bai in the rain and cold. The Vietnamese Marines reached Hue without incident, but even the most battle-hardened veterans were stunned by the extensive destruction that greeted them there. Nothing in Saigon had prepared them for such damage. The VNMC units boarded U.S. Navy LCUs for a quick, uneventful trip up the Perfume River to the quay just east of the Truong Dinh Gate. By the late evening of February 12, the two VNMC infantry battalions, one six-gun 105mm howitzer battery, and battle-group headquarters were ready to jump off into the battle to liberate the Citadel.

As the plan for the final attack to liberate the Citadel from within evolved, Major Bob Thompson's 1/5 was assigned the relief of the entire 1st ARVN Airborne Battle Group, which was operating southeast of the 1st ARVN Division CP compound. Thus, the U.S. Marines would attack with their left flank along the Citadel's northwest wall in a zone from two to four blocks wide. The main body of Lieutenant Colonel Phan Ba Hoa's 3rd ARVN Regiment would continue to operate around the Citadel's western corner, and Major Huong Thong's VNMC Battle Group Alpha would be employed as needed, no doubt to replace the exhausted 1st ARVN Division infantry battalions around Tay Loc Airfield and the Chanh Tay Gate.

The plan of operations and deployment of U.S. and South Vietnamese assets within the Citadel had a strange aspect. Naturally, all the ARVN and VNMC units north of the Perfume were to operate under the direct control of Brigadier General Ngo Quang Truong's 1st ARVN Division. However, Major Bob Thompson's 1/5 would be directly controlled by the 1st Marines commander, Colonel Stan Hughes, despite the fact that the U.S. Marine battalion would be operating adjacent to and as an integral part of the ARVN/VNMC operation. In fact, before Thompson left MACV for the Citadel, he received express orders that he was to deploy 1/5 to deliver its attack to the southeast, with his left flank resting on the Citadel's northeast wall. To underscore the lines of command to which Thompson was to adhere, senior 1st Marines officers specifically enjoined him from obeying General Truong's orders if they were in any way contrary to those issued by his U.S. Marine superiors. Further underscoring 1/5's unique status and its unusual command relationship to 1st ARVN Division, General Truong personally ordered the direct attachment of the small 2nd Battalion, 3rd ARVN Regiment, to 1/5 for purposes of undertaking rear and flank security, mopping up, and civilian-control operations. The ARVN battalion commander would be subordinate to Major Thompson.

In a war in which U.S. units were ostensibly subordinate to the GVN forces, the operation to clear Hue's politically and culturally symbolic Citadel hardly seemed the place to register a tacit but clear misgiving about General Truong's ability to command a U.S. combat unit. Truong personally took no offense; he was happy to have all the help his American allies could provide, and he did everything in his power to facilitate 1/5's role in the Citadel. But, in the midst of the Vietnam War's penultimate political emergency, 1/5's command relationship with Truong was a strange way to deal with the unfailingly competent and aggressive 1st ARVN Division commanding general.

— 29 —

For Marines whose whole combat experience in Vietnam had been stomping the bush or occupying rural firebases and base camps, the Citadel was an eerie, confining place. Even during the slack evening hours of February 12 and through the dark, cold night, the sounds and sights of battle were somehow more intense, more troubling than anything these men had yet experienced in Vietnam. Many of Major Bob Thompson's Marines slept simply because they were exhausted, but many stayed awake that first night in the Citadel and worried about the possibility of violent death.

The U.S. Marine battalion's plan of action was simple and direct. According to General Truong's staff, the 1st ARVN Airborne Task Force was in possession of a solid line about halfway down the Citadel's northeast wall, a line that stretched southwest along Mai Thuc Loan Street, from the Dong Ba Gate to the northern corner of the Imperial Palace. Though it had suffered numerous Tet losses that had not yet been replaced, the truncated Marine battalion was still nearly as large as all three ARVN airborne battalions combined. Thus, at dawn, 1/5 would march out of the 1st ARVN Division CP compound in column of companies; deploy behind the ARVN line; and mount an immediate attack through the airborne units, directly into the NVA front line.

Leading the battalion tactical march would be Captain Jim Bowe's Alpha/1/5, followed by 1st Lieutenant Scott Nelson's Charlie/1/5. The battalion CP group would follow Nelson's company, and the reserve company—Captain Fern Jennings's

Bravo/1/5—would bring up the rear of the column.

At 0800 on February 13, 1/5 moved out of its bivouac area along the southeast wall of the 1st ARVN Division CP compound. Leading the way down Dinh Bo Linh Street was Corporal Vic Walker's squad of Alpha/1/5's 1st Platoon. The platoon's other two squads were in column behind Walker's, and the remainder of Alpha/1/5 and Charlie/1/5 were arrayed in similar fashion.

Corporal Walker did not like anything he had seen in Hue—least of all the uniformed NVA soldiers he could now see as they darted across the narrow street several blocks to his squad's front. Walker thought about firing on the enemy soldiers, but they seemed to be too far away, and he did not want to hold up progress. Three blocks southeast of the ARVN compound wall, Corporal Walker turned left up Tinh Tam Street and led his platoon toward the Citadel's northeast wall, which was marked by a prominent tower at the end of the street. The platoon to the rear of Walker's kept going down Dinh Bo Linh, and the rear platoon followed it. Thus, Alpha/1/5 would be approaching the ARVN line from the rear in two columns.

About 100 meters along Tinh Tam Street, just as Corporal Walker's squad was approaching the wall and the tower, a gaggle of ARVN soldiers climbed down from positions atop the wall. They were laughing and smiling as they passed the U.S. Marines, but none of them attempted to speak to Vic Walker or his men. Quickly, the ARVN soldiers passed Walker's squad in the opposite direction and disappeared from view.

When the Marine pointman reached the base of the tower, he turned right (southeast) and crossed in front of the tower entryway. The second man in the column also crossed in front of the entryway, but, as Corporal Walker was stepping across, it started raining Chicom grenades from atop the wall.

It was 0815, and the point squad of Alpha/1/5 was still over 200 meters northwest of the ARVN airborne's supposed front line.

Walker's pointman was hit by grenade shrapnel, and the concussion knocked him out. Walker took shrapnel in the hand, but it was not a serious wound, and he could use the hand. None of the Marines at the base of the wall or farther back could see the men dropping the Chicoms. The Marines fired blindly the whole time, but the cascade of deadly missiles never let up. The rain of grenades was constant for nearly fifteen minutes.

Several more of Walker's men were injured by shrapnel as they clung to the wall, which loomed a good seven meters over their heads. Finally, it was time to move the wounded men back. As several Marines stepped across the tower entryway to collect the unconscious pointman, the first NVA soldier anyone had seen atop the wall leaned over the edge and tried to shoot the fallen Marine and his two rescuers. Corporal Walker was ready for him. He emptied an entire M-16 magazine into the NVA soldier and rushed to the rear with the rest of his squad. Walker and the others took cover in several buildings on the southwest side of Nguyen Thanh Street, which ran parallel to the wall.

Corporal Walter Rosolie's squad moved up and tried to enter the gate portal. However, they too were turned back by the rain of Chicom grenades. As Rosolie's men pulled back, Walker's M-79 grenadier yelled from the building next door to Walker's that he could see into the tower and that he was going to shoot at an NVA soldier he could get his sights on. Before the grenadier could fire, Corporal Rosolie streaked across Nguyen Thanh Street alone. Instantly, every Marine opposite the tower poured blind suppressive fire into the structure. Rosolie made it to the tower entryway, disarmed an antipersonnel mine he found in the roadway, and lobbed one M-26 grenade after another into the tower and up along the top of the wall. Rosolie later reported that he had been able to see NVA soldiers run from the tower, along the wall, but he was unable to enter the structure because NVA inside were still firing back at him.

The Marines were stunned to have run into such strong opposition so far behind the 1st ARVN Airborne Task Force's front line. They tried to get some hard information. It soon became apparent that the ARVN airborne battalions were gone, that they had withdrawn from their advance positions during the night, and that elements of the 6th NVA Regiment had advanced into the vacuum. Alpha/1/5, completely surprised, had not even been in tactical formation when Corporal Walker's squad ran into the NVA. Walker believed that the ARVN soldiers who had passed him moments before the fireworks began were really NVA in captured ARVN uniforms, but it is more likely that they were the ARVN airborne rearguard. Whatever the case, the entire 1st ARVN Airborne Battle Group was gone, and about two-thirds of the liberated area to its rear had been reoccupied by the NVA.

Caught unaware, Alpha/1/5 suffered terrible losses. As the Marines groped to find weak spots in the enemy line across their front, the NVA brought more and larger weapons to bear. The Marines responded in kind. An M-48 tank was called forward, but as it neared the front, Corporal Vic Walker saw the telltale red streak of a B-40 rocket heading straight for it. The RPG missed the tank by inches, passed so close to Walker that the exhaust scorched his face, and landed in an alleyway amidst Walker's squad. Miraculously, the B-40 did not explode. The tank moved forward and pumped five 90mm rounds into the tower, but with no noticeable effect.

As Captain Jim Bowe searched for a solution and waited for Battalion to decide what to do next, an enemy RPG team sneaked into position opposite the Alpha/1/5 CP group and let fly one B-40 rocket. Captain Bowe, the company exec, the company gunny, and just about everyone around them was injured in the blast.

In all, in the morning engagement, two Alpha/1/5 Marines were killed and thirty-three were wounded, mostly from the 1st Platoon and the company CP group. Captain Jim Bowe, who had joined 1/5 only two days earlier, on the road between Phu Bai and Hue, was replaced by Alpha/1/5's senior platoon commander, an inexperienced second lieutenant.

Alpha/1/5, already understrength when it reached Hue, was so badly hurt that it had to be withdrawn from the battalion front line to reorganize. Major Thompson ordered Captain Fern Jennings's Bravo/1/5 forward from its reserve position. Once Jennings's company was in possession of the left (northeast) half of Alpha/1/5's line, it was to resume the attack to the southeast. As soon as Jennings jumped off, Lieutenant Scott Nelson's Charlie/1/5 was to launch a coordinated assault directly through the right half of Alpha/1/5 and also toward the former ARVN line, two blocks to the southeast.

While these preparations were under way—an hours-long job

because of enemy fire and unfamiliar conditions—Major Bob Thompson radioed the 1st Marines CP to request that Delta/1/5 be released from the control of 2/5 and shipped to the Citadel as soon as possible. Regiment said that it would honor the request but that it would be a full day before Delta/1/5 could reach the Citadel.

When Charlie/1/5 jumped off at 1255, it ran straight into NVA automatic-weapons fire bolstered by a shower of Chicom grenades and many B-40 rockets. The NVA had hurriedly but effectively entrenched themselves within and around many of the buildings facing the Marine company, and they were able to fire their weapons from virtually any angle into all parts of the fragmented platoon formations, including the rear.

Charlie/1/5 was barely able to inch forward as the Marines, novices at city fighting, trained on the run for a type of warfare none had ever faced. Devastating .51-caliber machine-gun crossfire was the most dangerous hurdle in the crowded streets, where reverberating echoes made it almost impossible for the Marines to locate the source of the enemy fire. Ricochets were as effective as direct hits, and flying masonry chips were as injurious as bullets.

Confused and inexperienced, Charlie/1/5 took heavy casualties, as had every Marine unit facing its first action in the city. But the survivors learned to shoot first and ask questions later, to clear rooms with grenades and heavy fire before stepping through doorways, and to blow entryways rather than step through doors or climb through windows. The lessons were painful and dearly bought, but they were immutable. One by one, the buildings down the first block facing Charlie/1/5 were reduced and scoured by the increasingly self-assured Marines.

Staff Sergeant John Mullan, the platoon sergeant of Charlie/1/5's 1st Platoon, was overseeing Lance Corporal Edward Estes's squad in the fragmented assault. One block into the attack, Estes's Marines entered a shattered building—and found three women and two young men hiding there. Staff Sergeant Mullan tried to interrogate them in his rudimentary Vietnamese, but all he could get out of them was "*Khong biet*," ["I don't know"] and screams of "No VC!" Stymied, Mullan sent a runner back to the company CP to say that he had prisoners. He could not wait there, so he left a rifleman and a corpsman with orders to cut the civilians down if they so much as moved.

Just as Mullan was about to leave the building, he heard a loud explosion in the street outside and cries of "Corpsman, up!" He ran out the front door and saw a store of some kind directly across the street. There were shelves and showcases, which Mullan thought he ought to check for souvenirs. A B-40 had exploded beside the store, which was being checked by Marines from Lance Corporal Estes's squad. A Marine had been caught in the open and sprayed with shrapnel in the face and arm. His flak jacket, which bore the brunt of the blast, undoubtedly saved his life. Staff Sergeant Mullan left cover to drag the wounded Marine into the store. As Mullan moved awkwardly in the open, he was struck by the fact that the NVA did not open fire on him. From the store, he dragged the wounded man back to the house with the prisoners because he knew the platoon corpsman was there.

The wounded Marine was mad as hell. As the corpsman dressed his wounds, he kept demanding to shoot the prisoners, but Staff Sergeant Mullan told him he could not and tried to calm him down. When Mullan was sure the wounded Marine was not going to attack the prisoners, he crossed back to the store. The Marines in there had not been hurt by the B-40 blast, but they had been shaken up a bit by the concussion.

The next building in Staff Sergeant Mullan's path was a boarded-up house behind the store. The NVA had the street covered with fire from the rooftops and from the windows of nearby buildings. The Marines had no means of blowing a hole in the objective, and the boarded-up doors and windows blocked direct entry. Mullan had no idea how his troops were going to enter the building, but he knew he could not wait where he was because the NVA were building up their line of resistance across his front. Sooner was better than later.

Mullan stepped to the doorway of the store for one last look at the objective. Lance Corporal Edward Estes was beside him, and the survivors of Estes's squad were behind the squad leader. Mullan drew in his breath so he could blow his whistle to signal the attack. Before he could blow, however, the lights went out.

The next time Staff Sergeant John Mullan opened his eyes—days later—he was aboard the hospital ship *Sanctuary*. His left eye was sewn shut and covered with a bandage (it eventually was saved), his broken jaw was wired shut, and most of his left ear was gone. He had numerous shrapnel wounds along his left side. For all that, John Mullan was a lucky man. Lance Corporal Edward Estes, who had been standing beside him when the RPG detonated, was killed in the blast.

Despite heavy and growing losses, Charlie/1/5 continued to press forward.

Though the NVA had opposed Alpha/1/5 along the company's left flank, along the Citadel wall Bravo/1/5's renewed attack, which jumped off at the end of the noon hour, met no opposition until it had advanced nearly two blocks. At that point, Bravo/1/5 was just seventy-five meters short of the former ARVN airborne line. Then, at 1330, several M-48 tanks rolling up in support of Bravo/1/5 became the targets of a salvo of B-40 rockets, several of which struck home. While the tanks pulled back so their crews could assess the damage, the Bravo/1/5 Marines halted in place. The damage to the tanks was minor: a broken gunsight on one, and a ruined radio on the other.

After a quarter-hour delay, two more tanks rolled up and Bravo/1/5 resumed the attack through moderate enemy fire. The heaviest resistance came from NVA soldiers manning the tower over the Dong Ba Gate, 1/5's assigned line of departure. The Marines overcame the resistance by firing three LAAW rockets and, from the tanks, four 90mm rounds and two hundred .50-caliber machine-gun rounds. As soon as the enemy resistance had ceased, Bravo/1/5 patrols scoured the area along the former ARVN airborne front line. No NVA were found, and no casualties were sustained.

In the meantime, Charlie/1/5 broke through the NVA who had been resisting along its front. Or, perhaps the NVA, who were flanked by Bravo/1/5, prudently withdrew. Thus, by 1445, 1/5's two assault companies were in possession of a continuous front along Mai Thuc Loan Street from the Citadel wall to the northern corner of the Imperial Palace.

At 1455, minutes after Major Thompson reported that 1/5 had finally reached its line of departure, Regiment ordered Thompson to stand down for the day and prepare to commence the battalion attack in the morning. Asked to submit a detailed plan by morning, Thompson replied in only five minutes. His plan was to continue the attack as soon as Regiment could lay on air and artillery—hopefully, 155mm and 8-inch fire from Phu Bai—as preparatory fire and on-call support. Thompson also requested that Regiment provide his battalion with CS tear gas.

During the rest of the afternoon, 1/5 improved its positions along Mai Thuc Loan Street and dispatched patrols to the south-west to try to locate friendly units reportedly operating on that flank.

Early on the morning of February 13, after nearly two weeks of subsisting on rice and rain water, the Than-Trong family heard small-arms fire coming from just east of the Phu Cam Canal. At first the women feared that the NVA and VC might be massac-ring civilians. But Tuy-Cam's officer brothers, who were still hiding in the attic, sent a message down that they could see ARVN soldiers on the other side of the canal.

Later that morning, the incessant, distant artillery fire sud-denly got closer and became more intense, and the racket of warplanes filled the sky. Eventually, the kitchen and a bedroom were blown up by an artillery or mortar round. Though no one was hurt in the blast, Tuy-Cam suggested that her brothers come down from their exposed attic hideout and join the rest of the family in the bunker.

Tuy-Cam's older brother, An, told the cowering family that he thought their liberation was imminent, since ARVN and American troops routinely shelled an area they meant to attack. If the Than-Trongs stayed where they were, it was a toss-up if the family would be killed by friendly artillery or NVA mortars. Though An and his VNAF-cadet brother, Long, had the most to lose if they were caught on the streets by the NVA or VC, they recommended that the family abandon their home and try to reach friendly lines. At that moment another shell struck the house, causing extensive damage. After that, there was no debate. The family decided to risk the 5.5-kilometer hike to the villa of Tuy-Cam's paternal grandfather.

The family and its retainers had been out of touch for many days, and, when they left the compound, everyone was amazed to find the streets choked with other refugees. The Than-Trongs were swept along by the throng. It seemed that as long as everyone stayed on the main street, there was no danger from the Communist troops in the area, but anyone who broke from the crowd was gunned down. American or ARVN artillery was pounding the area, and several rounds fell into the crowd—with terrible results. But there was nowhere to hide and no alternative but to continue.

The flow of the crowd carried the Than-Trongs along the south side of the Phu Cam Canal. At length, NVA soldiers ushered them and scores of others toward a prominent pagoda in which, as it turned out, the NVA had established a major field headquarters. In no time at all, a VC who had recently helped build an addition to the Than-Trong home identified An as an ARVN lieutenant who worked at the provincial headquarters. Long, too, was denounced. There was no way to deny the charges, so, to prevent reprisals against the rest of the family, the brothers allowed themselves to be blindfolded and led away without a struggle. Throughout the denunciation, Tuy-Cam's mother pleaded in vain. At the last moment, Tuy-Cam's sister, Tuy-Diep, gave An a blanket, and Tuy-Cam's grandmother gave her blanket to Long.

Inside the pagoda, which was crowded with refugees, Tuy-Cam was hidden by a monk who knew the family well. The monk knew that Tuy-Cam was in danger of being denounced by neighbors who knew she worked for the Americans in Danang.

Late that afternoon, the family reached a decision that death at home was preferable to death at the pagoda, among strangers and possible traitors. However, shortly after leaving the pagoda, the family encountered ARVN soldiers!

Joining hundreds of fellow refugees, the family followed the throng down a broad boulevard. Everywhere Tuy-Cam looked were shattered trees, shattered buildings, shattered vehicles, and shattered human corpses. The clan could not find enough places to bed down in the first refugee center, a school, so it went to another, and then a third before it found places.

Late that night, the houseboy, Cao Viet Chuong, learned from friends that Jim Bullington had been seen on February 8 as he was being driven from the priests' home near the municipal power plant. Later the rumor was confirmed by a friend of Tuy-Cam's who worked for the U.S. consulate in Hue, where Bullington had been stationed during his first tour in Vietnam.

It took all night for Jim Bullington to learn that Tuy-Cam had survived her ordeal. Though Bullington's boss denied his request to fly to Hue from Danang, Bullington arranged passage to Hue aboard a U.S. Army helicopter. He was dropped off the afternoon of February 14 at the riverside helo pad across Le Loi Street from the provincial administration complex. Thanks to help from Bullington's former colleague at the consulate, Tuy-Cam was there, right beside the helo pad, waiting for him. In fact, Tuy-Cam saw Jim before he saw her.

On February 15, while wrapping up many loose ends in Hue, Jim Bullington visited Albert Istvie, the manager of the municipal power station. The news Istvie had to share with Bullington was tragic. Two days after Bullington had been rescued from their home, Father Marie Cressonier and Father Pierre Poncet had left the house to conduct mass and comfort refugees at a nearby church. On the way home, their jeep was waylaid by armed men dressed in black pajamas, and both priests were shot and left dead beside the road. Albert Istvie had recovered their bodies and buried them.

Jim Bullington and Tuy-Cam were married in Danang on March 16, 1968. A few days later, at the conclusion of Bullington's tour, they flew to the United States.

The brothers, An and Long, were never seen again.

— 30 —

The situation facing the ARVN, VNMC, and U.S. Marine units inside the Citadel differed considerably from that 2/5 and 1/1 had faced south of the Perfume River. The primary difference was the compactness of the battlefield. Cheatham's and Gravel's battalions had had ample room for maneuver, but the units inside the Citadel were confined in their movement by a number of structures and features that could not be crossed or flanked. The largest and most troublesome of these was the Citadel wall, as many as seventy-five meters thick in places and honeycombed throughout by passages and bunkers excavated by the Japanese toward the end of World War II. As Alpha/1/5 had learned at the outset, the Citadel wall so dominated the terrain within the Citadel that the wall was a battlefield unto itself.

Another factor limiting Vietnamese and American units was the Imperial Palace, the citadel within the Citadel. For reasons of culture and politics, the palace was considered sacrosanct by the GVN forces and their allies. NVA and VC firing down from the palace walls could be engaged only by small arms. Moreover, the palace sat roughly in the center of the southeast half of the Citadel, channeling the attacking units into two distinct corridors that could not be mutually supported. In effect, in the southeastern half of the Citadel there were two distinct battlefields, isolated from one another and dominated by high walls on either flank.

Early on, another bizarre restriction came to light. Although the Americans did have the guns of the U.S. Navy in the South China Sea, and the ARVN 105mm battery at PK 17, all the U.S. Marine land-based artillery—105mm howitzers, 155mm and 175mm guns, and 8-inch howitzers—were to the south. To hit anything in Hue, all the tubes had to fire into the faces of the infantry they were supporting. Everyone involved knew how easy it was to fire artillery "over" the target. In an ideal scenario, the artillery fires from behind the troops it is supporting. In the second-best situation, the artillery fires across the front of the troops it is supporting, as it had when artillery based to the south supported 2/5's attack to the southwest. The close quarters of the battle in the Citadel and the fact that most of the available supporting artillery was firing toward the friendly front had a chilling effect when it came to using artillery in the Citadel. Though the artillery professionals had the skill to meet the challenge, no one was eager to bet the lives of the infantry on a bravura performance.

Air support might have made an enormous difference, picking up the slack where artillery could not be used. But there was little or no air support; flying conditions were too dangerous. The clouds were so low and the battlefield was so hot that airborne observers in light, slow spotter planes faced intense small-arms fire. Radar-equipped jet fighter–bombers were certainly capable of bombing through the cloud cover, but the radar-marking system could not achieve the pinpoint accuracy required. Massively armed American jets and VNAF Skyraiders were kept on station over or near Hue, but they could be used only when the pilots could see what they were bombing, rocketing, or strafing—and then only if there was adequate room between the target and friendly troops.

Despite the lack of adequate supporting arms, 1/5 nonetheless jumped off once again at 0800, February 14. On the battalion right, away from the Citadel wall, Lieutenant Scott Nelson's Charlie/1/5 faced relatively mild opposition and quickly advanced approximately 100 meters. On the left, the wall side of the battalion line, Captain Fern Jennings's Bravo/1/5 got nowhere fast. The NVA who had the previous morning followed the withdrawing ARVN airborne troops back to the northwest had had a full night to retrench around the Dong Ba Gate. They were immovable. Particularly heavy was the fire from the Dong Ba tower, which Jennings's troops had not quite been able to secure the preceding afternoon. NVA manning the tower completely dominated the two city blocks adjacent to the wall, and the small Marine company could not breast the uncannily accurate and intense fire. The Marines and NVA were so closely intermingled at street level that supporting arms—including tanks and 106mm recoilless rifles—could not be effectively employed where they would have mattered most, right along the front line paralleling Mai Thuc Loan Street.

The only reasonable alternative to a toe-to-toe struggle between infantry in the streets was a voluntary withdrawal by 1/5 so massive supporting arms could be employed. Major Bob Thompson and Major Len Wunderlich drew up a plan, got approval for it from Regiment, and began easing back from the fight along Mai Thuc Loan. The planned artillery and naval-gunfire bombardment could not be initiated until all friendly troops were clear of the impact zone, and that did not happen until the middle of the afternoon.

The bombardment began so late that the commanders decided to continue it through the night. Late in the afternoon, breaks in the cloud cover allowed several Marine and U.S. Air Force jet fighter-bombers to salvo bombs and rockets against known NVA positions along the northeast Citadel wall. The air support was effective, but it was limited. While the bombardment continued, 1/5 reorganized and consolidated its temporary positions for the night.

Late in the afternoon, Captain Myron Harrington's Delta/1/5 assembled at the Hue LCU ramp for a quick trip up the river to the Citadel. Problems arose at the outset. The LCUs were already crowded with loaded resupply trucks, ammunition, and gear—no one could see room for Harrington's Marines. But somehow, as the LCUs were casting off, space was found for Harrington, his company CP group, and one rifle squad.

The journey was about halfway over when the LCUs passed up the eastern side of a long, narrow island. Other landing craft had passed the island without being molested, but snipers opened fire this time. One Marine was wounded before the LCUs passed beyond range, a minor enough outcome. However, because of the threat implied by the snipers, the LCU commander refused to return to the Hue LCU ramp to pick up the rest of Delta/1/5.

Though the bulk of Delta/1/5 was temporarily stranded on the wrong side of the river, the company was assigned the task of leading the contemplated dawn assault on the Dong Ba tower. Everyone was sure that the rest of Harrington's company would be across in time.

Late in the day, after a good deal of hectoring from 1/5, the 1st Marines CP arranged to transport the balance of Delta/1/5 to the Citadel via a flotilla of three motorized patrol junks provided by the Republic of Vietnam Navy. The company main body arrived after 1700, just as Marine F-4 Phantom jets were dropping CS tear gas on the NVA-held portion of the Citadel. An unlucky last-minute shift in the wind carried the gas toward the motorized junks. Since most of the Delta/1/5 Marines had long ago discarded their gas masks, nearly all of about 100 Marines were severely sickened. Many hurled themselves into the river to escape the roiling fumes. Once ashore, the company main body drew fire from snipers manning positions along the outside of the northeast Citadel wall.

The selection of Harrington's company to lead the February 15 assault along the Citadel wall was a sound—perhaps an inspired—decision. Though Delta/1/5 mustered only about 100 Marines in Hue—a twenty-man platoon had been detached by higher headquarters for convoy security duty—it had not been traumatized by the February 13 battles inside the Citadel, as had all three of 1/5's other infantry companies. Nor did Delta/1/5 lack experience in Hue. It had spent two full days sweeping along the Perfume River, west of the Phu Cam Canal, as an attachment to Lieutenant Colonel Ernie Cheatham's 2/5. Delta/1/5 was thus the only U.S. Marine company to reach a front-line assault position in Hue with what amounted to an orientation course in city fighting under its belt.

For all that, the flap with the LCUs and the late arrival of the main body of Delta/1/5 prevented Captain Harrington and his officers and troop leaders from reconnoitering the ground over which their dawn attack was to be launched.

The situation on the northwest side of the Citadel, where ARVN units were locked in battle with stubborn NVA forces, required some sorting out. Elements of the 3rd ARVN Regiment, two battle-weakened troops of the 7th ARVN Armored Cavalry Battalion, the 1st ARVN Division's Hoc Bao Company, and the 1st ARVN Ordnance Company had been fought to a virtual standstill over a week before the arrival of VNMC Battle Group Alpha. The ARVN units had not been able to advance from the vicinity of Tay Loc Airfield, the ordnance company's armory, and the Chanh Tay Gate, but neither had the NVA units that were fighting for the same area. Each side had hurt the other, but neither had been able to gain the upper hand in what had become a battle of attrition. The two newly arrived VNMC battalions were to put things right and press the NVA back, particularly in the center, where the ordnance company was holding secure a store of 1,400 M-16 rifles and hundreds of other weapons.

Major Huong Thong, the VNMC battle-group commander, had expected to launch a two-battalion attack to the southeast, between the southwest Citadel wall and the Imperial Palace, as soon as he had arrived on February 12. But the situation in the 3rd ARVN Regiment zone was so chaotic that it took the Vietnamese Marines and their ARVN compatriots two full days to establish a line of departure. In fact, the NVA attacked the relatively weak 1st Battalion, 3rd ARVN Regiment, in such strength near the Chanh Tay Gate that the ARVN unit was surrounded and cut off. The Hoc Bao Company and an armored cavalry troop had to be diverted to attack through the enemy cordon in a battle that ultimately lasted two days.

The sum of all the line-straightening and the rescue operation was that the VNMC battle group was not in position to launch its two-battalion attack to the southeast until the evening of February 14. Even then, there were enemy troops to the rear—and no end of enemy troops to the front. Indeed, by then, unknown to GVN or American forces, the Tri-Thien-Hue Front had taken control of several NVA infantry battalions newly arrived from Khe Sanh, and elements of these units and fresh supplies were being infiltrated into the Citadel through the Huu Gate. As many reinforcements as General Truong could bring in, the NVA could see and raise.

— 31 —

While predawn artillery preparation raged against objectives all along 1/5's former front, Charlie/1/5 and Bravo/1/5 closed up to the right, and Delta/1/5 slid in between Bravo/1/5's left flank and the Citadel's northeast wall. At 0800, as soon as the preparatory fire lifted, all three U.S. Marine companies jumped off into the block northwest of Mai Thuc Loan Street. As expected, Charlie/1/5 and Bravo/1/5 quickly advanced through the twisted rubble and regained all of the ground they had given up the previous afternoon. As hoped, the NVA resistance on 1/5's center and right was noticeably weaker. For all that, however, Captain Myron Harrington's Delta/1/5 ran into a hornet's nest as it attempted to close on the Dong Ba tower.

Because Captain Harrington and his officers had been unable to reconnoiter the objective, Delta/1/5 was obliged to attack blindly, with no real knowledge of the ground or the location of enemy positions. The young lieutenant commanding Delta/1/5's 2nd Platoon advanced to a second-story balcony facing the Dong Ba tower, the better to control the fight. In a flash, the lieutenant, his platoon sergeant, his radio operator, and at least one of his platoon's squad leaders were injured by a B-40 rocket. As debilitating as the loss of the leaders was the loss of the precious platoon radio. The platoon remained in the fight, but Captain Harrington was unable to communicate quickly with the platoon guide, who was now in temporary command of the unit.

As Delta/1/5 learned, verbal communication of any sort was almost impossible in the din of gunfire echoing across the restricted masonry battlefield. Delta/1/5 had arrived in the Citadel confident of its experience in street combat, but the intense close-quarters battle the unit now faced made the company's two days with 2/5 seem like a walk in the sun.

Bravo/1/5 and Charlie/1/5 were able to fight their way back to Mai Thuc Loan Street primarily because the NVA conceded the ground. Delta/1/5 was fought to a standstill well short of Mai Thuc Loan and the Dong Ba tower because the NVA were unwilling to give up the high ground the tower and the wall represented.

The big break came at about 1400, when Captain Harrington resorted to the obvious. One infantry squad from the 1st Platoon climbed up onto the wall about 150 meters northwest of the Dong Ba tower and began a methodical sweep along the high ground. This was not a matter of running along a narrow rampart; the wall was up to seventy-five meters thick along the way, and every bit as heavily built up as the streets below. Advancing along the wall was much the same as advancing up a defended street, except the route was more predictable and thus more exposed.

As the squad on the wall registered modest gains against

stiffening opposition, Delta/1/5 Marines on the more lightly engaged company right began sending over scarce hand grenades in response to shouted appeals for what was proving to be the most effective weapon on the narrow high-ground battlefield.

In the toe-to-toe battle, the contribution of Private First Class Willie Smith was outstanding. Smith had been slightly wounded earlier in Hue. Though the wound hardly bled, it was Smith's third, and he rated a third Purple Heart and a trip home. Captain Harrington did not feel Smith's wound was that serious, however, and he decided to keep Smith with the company CP group until he could figure out what to do with him. On February 15, Smith was hanging around the CP when the first call for grenades came down from the wall. He had no part in the battle, so he went out into the street to collect the needed items and carried them to the men on the wall. Thereafter, without being told, Smith ran grenades, ammunition, radio batteries—whatever was needed—to the squad on the wall. He brought wounded Marines down, and he led replacements back up. If a job needed doing that day, Willie Smith was usually the one who did it—often at great peril to his life. Captain Harrington wrote Smith up for a Silver Star, and Smith, who ultimately refused his third Purple Heart, received the award.

Atop the wall and on the street, every available 3.5-inch rocket launcher was arrayed directly against the tower and the Japanese-built, NVA-held bunkers and pillboxes inside the wall adjacent to the Dong Ba Gate. Delta/1/5's 60mm mortars were also brought to bear on the gate and tower strongpoint, and they were fired at dangerously close range. It took as much in the way of guts for the gunners to fire the 60s as it did for the front-line infantrymen to call for the support.

Lieutenant Ron Morrison's platoon of M-48 gun tanks was also extremely effective. By a miracle of coincidence, the narrow streets inside the Citadel—they had no sidewalks—could accommodate the width of an M-48 tank with only inches to spare. While the other tanks and a pair of Ontos worked farther from the wall, Lieutenant Morrison gingerly guided his platoon's command tank in behind Delta/1/5's 1st Platoon and found a covered spot for it about twenty-five meters from the gate, just behind the building Captain Harrington was using for his company CP and observation post. At frequent intervals, Morrison's driver ran the lieutenant's M-48 right into Mai Thuc Loan. While Morrison personally fired his cupola-mounted .50-caliber machine gun to suppress the enemy RPG teams, the gunner brought the 90mm main gun around to a new target and fired right at the wall or the tower. Often as not, the gunner took his directions from Captain Harrington, who gave instructions via radio. Harrington was never more than a few meters away from the tank. At first, Harrington thought of using the field telephone that was affixed to one of the tank's rear fenders—a standard procedure— but the tank was raked by NVA bullets as soon as it appeared in the intersection so Harrington opted for the radio.

The U.S. tanks, rockets, and mortars were deadly accurate, but the NVA were bitterly determined to hold their strongpoint. The best NVA fighting positions were remanned as quickly as they were knocked out.

As Delta/1/5 struggled forward along the wall, Charlie/1/5's easy morning advance was stalled in the early afternoon by NVA machine guns at the northern corner of the Imperial Palace. Had they been located anywhere else in Hue, they would have been blasted to dust by Marine artillery, naval gunfire, or even 1/5's mortars. But American authorities had declared the Imperial Palace inviolate. The Charlie/1/5 Marines were permitted to return fire with M-16s and M-60s, but only ARVN or VNMC units were permitted to put explosives on the Imperial Palace. The only ARVN 105mm battery north of Hue was busy with other missions, and the VNMC battle group's 81mm mortars and 105mm howitzers were in hot action against the battle group's own objectives. In short, nothing could be done to help Charlie/1/5. When Charlie/1/5's February 15 advance bogged down, Major Bob Thompson ordered Lieutenant Scott Nelson, the Charlie/1/5 commander, to halt in place and re-fuse his right flank about 100 meters to prevent the NVA from infiltrating the 1/5 zone from that quarter. To help, Major Thompson sent Delta/1/5's 3rd Platoon, which had just arrived in Hue from a stint of convoy-escort duty to the south.

There were no ARVN or VNMC units for several hundred meters to Lieutenant Nelson's right, but there were plenty of NVA out there. The result was that it took most of the rest of the day for Charlie/1/5 to clear a buffer zone and emplace the Delta/1/5 platoon in a number of buildings back along the flank.

In the U.S. Marine battalion's center, Captain Fern Jennings's Bravo/1/5 had reached Mai Thuc Loan early. But the company had had to stop because Delta/1/5 could not come abreast on the left and because Charlie/1/5's advance had bogged down on the right. Thus, by the early afternoon of February 15, 1/5's three front-line companies were on or behind the line of departure that was supposed to have been passed and left behind on February 13.

Delta/1/5's squad on the wall—bolstered many times over by Marines replacing wounded Marines—reached the base of the Dong Ba tower at about 1600. By then, the tower was barely more than a higher pile of rubble, but it was still infested with NVA soldiers clearly intent upon defending it unto death.

Before the attack could bog down from sheer loss of momentum—a real possibility that late in the day—Captain Harrington engineered a quick final assault with troops readily at hand. Fortunately for Harrington, Delta/1/5 was reinforced at the last minute by a squad from the company's own newly arrived 3rd Platoon. The squad was led by the 3rd Platoon commander, Staff Sergeant Robert Thoms. The staff sergeant had undertaken the reinforcement on his own authority, as soon as members of Charlie/1/5 had told him about Delta/1/5's fight along the wall. Thoms, who had served as a lance corporal in 2nd Lieutenant Myron Harrington's infantry platoon in 1962, had arrived in Vietnam only a week earlier and had joined Delta/1/5's 3rd Platoon in Phu Bai just in time to be detached for convoy duty. February 15 was his first day in Hue and the first time he had ever faced combat. Captain Harrington sent Thoms and his 3rd Platoon squad up to the wall to bolster the 1st Platoon Marines already there.

At 1630, covered by a barrage of twenty 60mm mortar

rounds placed squarely atop the objective, the main body of 2nd
Lieutenant Jack Imlah's 1st Platoon jumped off from positions
just south of the tower that Imlah and his men had occupied
moments earlier. In a matter of only minutes, as Staff Sergeant
Thoms led the way into the tower strongpoint from the northwest, Lieutenant Imlah's force overran the Dong Ba Gate's archway and bridge at street level.

On February 15, 1/5 lost six Marines killed and thirty-three
Marines wounded and evacuated. The Marines pulled twenty-four
NVA and VC corpses from the rubble along with two AK-47s
and one SKS.

On the southwestern side of the battlefield, the 1st and 5th
VNMC battalions secured the 1st ARVN Ordnance Company's
armory and swung about to begin a two-column attack to the
southeast, paralleling 1/5's move. In their parallel zones, the
VNMC battalions faced pitiless resistance throughout the day,
and they sustained heavy losses. But, by day's end, they were in
possession of a line two blocks northwest of the Imperial Palace.
This line was separated from the 1/5 line by a no-man's-land
several hundred meters wide.

On February 15, the VNMC battle group counted thirty-
nine dead NVA soldiers and recovered twenty-two assorted infantry weapons, eighty 60mm mortar rounds, and ten Chicom grenades. It is possible that the Vietnamese Marines also killed a
high-ranking NVA officer, possibly the commander of the 6th
NVA Regiment.

As the Vietnamese Marines advanced deeper into what had
been enemy territory from the outset of the Tet Offensive in Hue,
they came upon increasing evidence that Communist hit squads
were hard at work alongside the retreating NVA Regulars. Fresh
civilian corpses bore execution-type gunshot wounds, and many
other civilian corpses were disinterred from graves in which they
had apparently been buried alive.

The 4th VNMC Battalion, which had just weathered two
weeks of bitter fighting in Saigon, arrived in Phu Bai by air late
on February 14. Major Bill Eshelman, the battalion's senior

advisor, made his way to the Task Force X-Ray CP and reported to Brigadier General Foster LaHue. The 4th VNMC Battalion mustered 700 effectives, including 200 new replacements assigned to the unit only two days earlier to make good the heavy losses sustained in Saigon. The battalion had only two jeeps, however. Eshelman guessed that General LaHue would be happy to accommodate the VNMC battalion's transportation needs.

Though the Tet emergency was almost over throughout most of I Corps, the demands upon U.S. Marine transport units were still overwhelming. Mustering enough trucks for the entire VNMC battalion took most of February 15. By then, it was too late to leave Phu Bai.

South Vietnamese and American commanders hoped that the addition of a third strong VNMC battalion to Battle Group Alpha would allow the Vietnamese and U.S. Marines to link up in the center of the Citadel battlefield and allow major elements of the reinforced 3rd ARVN Regiment to stand down and reorganize.

At about 0430, February 16, the NVA bombarded Delta/1/5's Dong Ba tower position with 82mm and 60mm mortars. Before anyone in the target area could react, a volley of Chicom grenades and B-40 rockets forced the five Delta/1/5 Marines in the tower to withdraw. In no time, the NVA opened fire from the tower, down upon the main body of Delta/1/5. Captain Myron Harrington led an instant counter-counterattack, using whatever troops were available. As Harrington fired his .45-caliber pistol at point-blank range, Marines who had regained a position at the base of the tower lobbed hand grenades at the NVA who were firing at them from above. LAAWs, M-79 grenades, and intense small-arms fire eventually turned the tide. The tower was retaken, but sporadic fighting continued around the Dong Ba Gate until dawn. When the NVA finally withdrew, they left two of their comrades dead in the tower. Delta/1/5 had lost one Marine killed and four Marines wounded.

— 32 —

February 16 dawned relatively fair and clear over Hue. For the first time since the struggle for Hue began, air support could be routinely scheduled into the morning's preparatory pounding, which also included naval gunfire from the east and heavy artillery from the south. The NVA responded with what they had. At 0655, Bravo/1/5 and Delta/1/5 were engaged by NVA small-arms fire and several B-40 rockets. The Marine infantrymen responded in kind and with 81mm mortars. Enemy casualties could not be estimated, but two Marines were killed and seven were wounded.

The U.S. Marine battalion jumped off at dawn. Delta/1/5, on the left, was the first company to cross Mai Thuc Loan Street. It immediately met stiff resistance along the wall, in an area that, for purposes of safety, could not be included in the morning's bombardment.

Captain Myron Harrington had reorganized his hard-hit company before it jumped off at 0800. The 2nd Platoon commander, his entire platoon headquarters, and one or two of his squad leaders had been severely injured at the outset of the preceding day's attack. As a result, the 2nd Platoon had been employed only sparingly on February 15. When the 3rd Platoon arrived late in the day from convoy-escort duty, it was led by Staff Sergeant Robert Thoms, and a sergeant was the platoon guide. Though Thoms was new to Vietnam, Captain Harrington knew him to be a strong leader, so he moved Thoms over to command the somewhat demoralized 2nd Platoon and moved the 3rd Platoon guide up to command the 3rd Platoon. When Delta/1/5 stepped off into the attack on February 16, Staff Sergeant Thoms's 2nd Platoon had replaced 2nd Lieutenant Jack Imlah's 1st Platoon along the Citadel wall.

Early in the attack, Staff Sergeant Thoms pulled Private First Class Jim Walsh aside and, though Walsh was a fire-team leader, armed him with an M-60 machine gun. Thoms explained that he had seen a sniper in a second-story window across the street; he wanted Walsh to help flush the man. The two broke away from the main body of the platoon and climbed to a half-story attic directly across from and slightly above the sniper's position. There was, however, no opening in the attic from which the sniper's position could be engaged. At Thoms's direction, Walsh fired the M-60 directly into the roof over the attic they were in, cutting a hole through the red clay tiles. Then Thoms and Walsh stepped forward into the open and ripped the sniper apart with their fire. When word of Staff Sergeant Thoms's personal role in that adventure got around the 2nd Platoon, his success as a platoon commander was ensured. From the get-go, the troops looked up to him.

Captain Fern Jennings's Bravo/1/5, in the battalion's center, ran into extremely stiff opposition. The area to the front of Bravo/1/5 had not been struck by the morning's preparatory bombardment, and the NVA remained well entrenched in a rat's nest of fighting holes, pillboxes, and bunkers set into the ruins of many masonry buildings. There was no way to conduct an orderly advance into the rubble.

On the far right, 1st Lieutenant Scott Nelson's Charlie/1/5 once again met light resistance and could have advanced deep into enemy territory, but the decision was made to keep its progress down to the pace of the two companies to its left. In addition, Charlie/1/5 was still responsible for screening 1/5's open and dangling right flank. As the tempo of the fighting increased in the adjacent Bravo/1/5 zone, more Charlie/1/5 troops were shifted toward the battalion center to support the struggling center company.

During one of Charlie/1/5's late-morning moves, a platoon of Marines was nailed by an NVA ambush as it crossed an open area toward a large building it had been assigned to seize. One Marine was killed and four others were wounded. The rest of the platoon was pinned down. Realizing the platoon's precarious situation, Corporal Paul Cheatwood knelt in an exposed position—the only place from which the enemy fire could be effectively answered—and suppressed the NVA position with coolly accurate fire while the platoon corpsman moved up to oversee the evacuation of the casualties. Two of the wounded Marines had been moved when the NVA fire suddenly abated, so Corporal Cheatwood moved forward to help treat and evacuate the remaining wounded Marines. No sooner done, however, than the NVA commenced firing again. Cheatwood again suppressed the NVA position, and then he crawled forward to try to render aid to the wounded Marines. As soon as the corpsman arrived to relieve him, Cheatwood maneuvered to the flank of the still-active NVA position and lobbed several hand grenades into the building. The NVA fire ceased altogether. A subsequent search of the building turned up two dead NVA.

Around the middle of the morning, Lance Corporal Tom Zwetow, a fire-team leader in Staff Sergeant Robert Thoms's 2nd Platoon of Delta/1/5, passed a little too close to a large window on the ground floor of a building his squad was scouring. Just as Zwetow exposed himself in the window, an NVA sniper who was apparently waiting for the opportunity, nailed him. Private First Class Jim Walsh saw the round strike Zwetow directly between the shoulder blades and slam him into the floor. There was no doubt in Walsh's mind that Zwetow had been killed.

"Corpsman, up," the Marines around Zwetow yelled. And everyone started trying to figure out a way to pull the motionless fire-team leader to safety without exposing themselves to the sniper.

Jim Walsh was devastated. Tom Zwetow was the only Marine he had allowed himself to get close to in Vietnam. Anytime the squad was involved in a fight, Zwetow's face was the first one Walsh looked for. If Tet had not overtaken 1/5, Walsh and Zwetow would have been winding up their R and R leave in Tokyo that very day. Now, a bullet had driven Tom Zwetow to the floor of this building in Hue's Citadel. He was motionless and probably dead.

Then Zwetow started talking. He just came back from the dead and started talking. Just like that. Two Marines leaned out into the danger zone and grabbed Zwetow's ankles. Then they leaned back and reeled him in out of the line of fire. They turned him over to assess the damage, but there was no blood. Zwetow complained about the pain, but there was no sign of a wound. Apparently, the SKS round had hit him square in the back, but it had not penetrated his flak jacket.

At noon, a fire team from Alpha/1/5's 3rd Platoon was patrolling the no-man's-land northwest of the Imperial Palace when it was struck by a volley of seven B-40 rounds. One Marine was wounded, but his comrades returned a heavy volume of small-arms fire and four LAAWs at the supposed source of the RPG attack. No results could be determined, however, and NVA small-arms fire pinned the patrol behind a masonry wall.

The cumulative effect of many such incidents and the heavy casualties—particularly among experienced, respected unit leaders—that Alpha/1/5 had sustained on February 14 had cut the heart out of the company. Alpha/1/5 was just about washed up as an effective fighting unit. Neither of the young lieutenants who had survived the rigors of the first day of combat in Hue was experienced or strong enough to get the company over its demoralization. Things were looking very grim when Battalion ordered the young lieutenant commanding Alpha/1/5 to send a reaction force to rescue the trapped patrol. The lieutenant was unable to coax any of his men into volunteering.

Fortunately for Alpha/1/5, there arrived at that precise moment an unattached young officer who had enormous presence and months of solid command experience. First Lieutenant Pat Polk had served as a platoon commander with Charlie/1/5 early in his tour, but he had been tabbed to serve as a junior liaison officer with the 2nd Korean Marine Brigade. Polk had just returned to 1/5's rear CP, in Phu Bai, to serve out the remainder of his tour as a junior assistant operations officer. That morning he had routinely escorted a mixed group of replacements and returning wounded to the 1/5 forward CP. He and his charges arrived at their destination just as the drama northwest of the Imperial Palace was unfolding.

As soon as Lieutenant Polk reported in, Major Bob Thompson took him aside and explained Alpha/1/5's situation and the plight of the patrol. He asked Polk if he wanted to take command of the company. Pat Polk was just days away from rotating home, and he did not have to agree. But he did.

When Polk reached the Alpha/1/5 CP, he tried to find volunteers willing to rescue their comrades. No one made a move, but Polk felt that a few could be persuaded if he set an example. He let it be known that he intended to lead the relief, and that netted him eight volunteers.

The little group of Marines jumped off and made rapid progress against no real opposition until it reached a masonry building twenty meters away from the trapped five-man patrol. From there, NVA, manning RPDs and protected by many riflemen, took Polk's relief party under fire. Among Polk's volunteers were Alpha/1/5's 81mm forward observer and his radioman. Rather than try to breast the enemy fire, which was now intense, Polk ordered an 81mm fire mission. The rounds dropped dangerously close—Polk was hit by a few tiny fragments—but the NVA ducked for cover. As soon as the NVA stopped firing, the relief party closed on the trapped patrol. By then, four of the five Marines in the patrol had been wounded.

Again calling on the 81mms for covering fire, Polk eased the patrol and the relief party out of the danger zone and back to the Alpha/1/5 CP. It took most of the afternoon because the four wounded men had to be carried in relays, but the move was accomplished without further loss.

After the news of Pat Polk's nerveless debut in Hue got around, Alpha/1/5 Marines began walking tall again. The company was sadly understrength, even after absorbing its share of the day's replacements, but its morale was restored and it would soon take its place again on the battalion front line.

Shortly after noon, Corporal Paul Cheatwood volunteered to lead a squad patrol to locate and destroy an NVA machine gun that had been sniping into the Charlie/1/5 zone. While searching through several suspect buildings, however, Cheatwood became separated from the rest of his patrol. Though he should have tried to locate the other Marines, he decided to go it alone. As he moved on through one building, he spotted eight NVA soldiers in an adjacent courtyard. Without giving the matter much thought, Cheatwood hurled several hand grenades into the courtyard and then fired his .45-caliber pistol at the surprised enemy soldiers. Several of the NVA were killed or wounded before the others pulled themselves together and returned fire. Though Cheatwood was painfully wounded, he kept firing his pistol and throwing grenades until the surviving NVA cleared out. Later he was brought to the battalion aid station, where he was treated and evacuated. Corporal Paul Cheatwood's performance on February 16 earned him a Navy Cross, the only such medal awarded to an enlisted member of 1/5 for combat in Hue.

Private First Class Jim Walsh was resting. He was standing on the second floor of a house, in a room with one window overlooking the side street. He thought he was completely concealed, but he was wrong. The muzzle of his M-16 extended all of a half inch past the window frame. An alert NVA sniper across the way saw the muzzle and put an SKS round through the wall beside the window. The impact spun Walsh away from the wall.

Jim Walsh could not catch his breath, and his vision was fogging over. At first, he thought the round had struck him in the chest, but it had not. It had punctured a CS tear gas canister dangling from his flak jacket. He felt the impact in his chest, but the loss of sight and breath was the result of being dusted with CS powder.

Walsh yelled for help, and his buddies led him out into the fresh air on a safe side of the house. They washed his eyes out with their drinking water and rubbed off as much of the CS powder as they could. When Walsh could see again, he undertook a body search to assure himself that he was whole. He was, but two of the three M-79 grenades he had been carrying for the squad grenadier had been nicked by the round that hit the gas grenade. As gingerly as possible, Walsh lifted the grenade bandoleer over his head and set it down out of the way. Then he took off his flak jacket and checked it. The bullet had grazed along the fabric shell, right at heart level. It had been deflected outward by the corner of an armor square, and that is how it came to hit the CS grenade and the M-79 rounds. When Walsh realized what had happened, he felt Death's hand lift from his shoulder.

But Walsh's combat debut in the Citadel was far from over. His squad emerged intact at the end of the first city block southeast of Mai Thuc Loan Street, but there was more ground to take ahead, and plenty more time to try.

As Delta/1/5's 2nd Platoon paused to reorganize, Staff Sergeant Robert Thoms arrived following a quick confab with Captain Harrington. It was the 2nd Platoon's turn to advance up on the wall.

Thoms led Jim Walsh's squad up a pile of rubble, right up to the top of the wall. The first twenty-five meters fell without a fight. Then the NVA recovered their wits, and all hell broke loose.

Jim Walsh found himself hugging a pile of rubble, out near the point of the squad. Staff Sergeant Thoms was right beside him. The rest of the squad was spread to their right, hard at work burrowing into the rubble for all they were worth. Walsh heard the air over his head singing with the cry of passing bullets. It was a colorful sight, as the red tracer from M-16s and M-60s crisscrossed with the green tracer from AK-47s and RPDs. Seeing so many green tracers coming from so many directions scared Walsh more than anything he had yet endured in Vietnam.

During a brief lull, Walsh peeked and saw that NVA soldiers were burrowed into the rubble less than ten meters to his front. Among the pieces of broken masonry, he could clearly see the smooth curve of the tops of their pith helmets. In no time, the Marines behind Walsh started lobbing hand grenades into the NVA position. At first, the canny NVA soldiers tossed back the armed M-26s, which detonated in the Marine line, but the Marines caught on and held onto their grenades longer before lofting them. After that, the NVA soldiers responded with a hail of their own Chicoms. Several of the weaker Chinese-made grenades detonated at once and lifted Jim Walsh into the air, leaving him momentarily stunned. When he glanced back to see how the rest of the squad was doing, he saw that several Marines were bleeding from their noses and ears—from concussion. By then, everyone in the squad had been wounded by grenade shrapnel or brick shards.

As Walsh later described it, "The NVA had our asses pinned royally." When that became evident, Staff Sergeant Thoms turned to Walsh and ordered him to climb the mound they were using for cover, and fire down into the NVA position.

Keeping as low as he could, Walsh had barely started scrabbling up the pile of loose brick rubble when his right leg was knocked out from beneath him. He lost his balance and rolled to the bottom of the mound.

At first Walsh could feel no pain. It took long seconds for him to figure out that he had been shot. As he lay at the foot of the rubble mound, intense pain overtook him. Walsh had seen many wounded men go into shock at the first sight of their wounds, so he kept his eyes averted and hoped that one of his buddies would move him if he had fallen into the line of fire. He had landed on top of his wounded leg—it was twisted up underneath his body—but he could not bring himself to touch the limb. He just lay back on it. Unexpectedly, the pain melted away to a dull, bearable throb.

Staff Sergeant Thoms had been looking right at Walsh when the bullet struck the fire-team leader just above the right knee. He knew Walsh's leg was broken. He asked Walsh if he was okay, and Walsh replied that he would be fine as long as he didn't have to look at the injury. Thoms nodded and told Walsh to just lie back; he would get him out of there as soon as possible.

Walsh had had one really close call that day, and now he had been shot. If the progression continued, he felt, he would be shot again, only worse. With every passing second, the feeling of gloom and doom deepened. His hands gripped the loose rubble beneath him in a spasmodic attempt to hold onto reality. He fished a cigarette from his pocket and lit it, then he began loading empty M-16 magazines from his spare bandoleers, trying to keep his mind off his fears.

Every once in a while he could hear someone call "Corpsman, up," but his squad was really cut off atop the wall. There was no way for a corpsman or reinforcements to get up there to help.

Hours passed. The Marines were getting low on ammunition, and the NVA appeared to be in similar straits. The firing continued, but with less intensity, at less frequent intervals.

Staff Sergeant Thoms's M-16 jammed, so Jim Walsh traded with the platoon commander and then occupied himself by trying to fix the jammed weapon. While he was working, Walsh saw an Asian-looking man in civilian clothing dart in and out of his line of sight. It turned out the man was Kyoichi Sawada, a United Press International photographer, intent upon recording the standoff. (Walsh later saw himself spread across a page of *Life* magazine.)

At long last, a corpsman and a Marine helper arrived atop the wall. They rushed straight up a pile of rubble during a lull and dropped in beside Jim Walsh. Immediately, one of them grabbed him under his arms while the other grabbed his legs. Everyone fired into the NVA position. Walsh's broken leg was badly jostled on the way down the wall, but he landed in a safe spot from which he could be carried farther to the rear. The doc examined the leg and told Walsh that he had acquired a million-dollar wound, a certain ticket home. Walsh took the news with mixed feelings. He had no problem with getting home, but he did not really want to leave his squad in the thick of battle, particularly a battle he felt the good guys were winning.

The doc cleaned the wound, applied a battle dressing, and gave Walsh a shot of morphine. The morphine conked him right out. When he came to—only a minute later—it was because the NVA were trying to finish the job on him with mortars. They were firing a preparation for an attack on Staff Sergeant Thoms and the rest of the squad.

Someone brought a stretcher for Walsh, and he was carried to the rear in lurching leaps between mortar salvos. Up on the wall, his fellow Marines fought for their lives against a direct assault that came very close to sweeping them away.

Private First Class Jim Walsh was flown to Phu Bai that night. Two weeks later, in a hospital in Japan, he ran into his friend, Lance Corporal Tom Zwetow. Unknown to Walsh, Zwetow had been the squad point when the February 16 fight on the wall erupted. He had taken cover in a makeshift bunker built by the NVA in the rubble, but the bunker had collapsed on top of him when a grenade rolled in and detonated. Zwetow was wounded and buried alive. He could not dig himself out. Fortunately, one Marine had seen him dive into the bunker, and that Marine survived the hours-long struggle. Zwetow was pulled from the collapsed bunker at dusk, treated, and evacuated.

On February 16, 1/5 lost twelve Marines killed, forty-five
Marines wounded and evacuated, and fifteen Marines wounded
and returned to duty. In return, the battalion turned in a claim
for twenty-six NVA confirmed killed, fourteen assorted weapons
taken, and the recapture of a Marine field radio.

Late in the morning on February 16, the 4th VNMC Battalion had arrived at the Hue LCU ramp. While the Vietnamese
Marines waited to be ferried across the Perfume River, Major Bill
Eshelman, the senior U.S. Marine advisor, made his way to
MACV in the hope of getting some reliable information from
fellow U.S. Marines. At MACV he found two trusted friends,
Major Frank Breth and Major Wayne Swenson, respectively the
3rd Marine Division and 1st Marine Division liaison officers to
the 1st ARVN Division. Breth and Swenson had been back and
forth between MACV and the 1st ARVN Division CP several
times, and they knew the score inside the Citadel. They wasted no
time telling Major Eshelman all they knew.

The trip across the river was painless, but not without a scare
or two from NVA or VC snipers on the island east of the Citadel.
The battalion mustered at the quay and marched straight into the
1st ARVN Division CP compound. No sooner had the battalion
arrived than it was sent into the attack to relieve pressure on the
1st Battalion, 3rd ARVN Regiment, which a superior NVA force
had pinned to positions around the Chanh Tay Gate for two days.
In effect, the 4th VNMC Battalion was being called upon to
clear a significant force of NVA from the 3rd ARVN Regiment
zone, which was northwest—in the rear—of the 1st and 5th
VNMC battalions.

Jumping off fairly late in the afternoon, the 4th VNMC
Battalion advanced cautiously, with its right-flank elements atop
the Citadel's northwest wall. The battalion had been in intense
city combat in Saigon for most of the preceding two weeks, but
the Citadel's close masonry structures in no way resembled Saigon's relatively open sprawl of less formidable buildings.

But it was not simple caution or unfamiliarity that slowed

the 4th VNMC Battalion. The NVA were out in force, sniping from the top of the wall and firing from within multistory buildings. The NVA were using small arms, B-40s, and .51-caliber heavy machine guns. One of the few weapons the Vietnamese Marines had that could punch through masonry walls was a few captured B-40s, so the only way for them to advance was to move up the streets. That, in the face of expertly sited .51-caliber fire, took guts.

At day's end, the 4th VNMC Battalion still had not reached the Citadel's western corner. Overnight, however, the NVA force defending the Chanh Tay Gate melted away. No doubt the pressure represented by a fresh 700-man VNMC battalion was enough to convince the Communist troops to leave the shattered 1st Battalion, 3rd ARVN Regiment, in peace.

At 2150, the 1/5 command group received mixed news from enemy sources. A message from the 1st Marines CP stated:

> Message, intercepted from . . . the commander of the enemy force inside Hue to his superior, states that original commander of the force inside Hue had been killed and that many others had either been killed or wounded. He recommended to withdraw. Senior officer ordered new commander of the force in Hue to remain in position and fight.

It was heartening to the Marines to learn that the enemy commander had been killed, but the fact that the new commander's request to withdraw had been denied was not good news at all. It smacked of a fanatical desire on the part of the Tri-Thien-Hue Front commander, for there was no doubt that the Communist forces would be driven from Hue. The only unknown factors were how long it would take and how many needless deaths it would cost. All this so the NLF flag could fly over the Citadel wall for a few days longer.

— 33 —

For 1/5, the February 17 action began at 0430, when Delta/1/5 was struck by a mortar barrage from an NVA-occupied but uncontested sector east of the Citadel, across the Perfume River. As the mortar barrage was lifting, NVA soldiers, dug in along the company's immediate front, opened fire with B-40 rockets and small arms. The Marines responded with M-16s, M-60s, M-79s, and LAAWs, and finally called an 8-inch howitzer mission for good measure. As the 8-inch shells were landing, the NVA broke contact. The result of the two-step wake-up call was one Marine killed, four Marines wounded and evacuated, and two NVA soldiers known dead.

The U.S. Marine battalion waded into the NVA defensive zone at 0700. The advance was slow but steady. As they had during 2/5's final sweep between the Perfume River and the Phu Cam Canal, the NVA were resorting to delaying tactics consisting of the unyielding defense of strongly fortified, mutually supporting strongpoints. Initially, this offered the ever-diminishing Marine companies, platoons, and squads more latitude for maneuver. Each strongpoint was reduced in turn, albeit at great expense in time and manpower. But, as the battalion advanced, it came under fire from NVA automatic weapons atop the northeast wall of the Imperial Palace. The Marines returned fire with their M-60s and M-16s, but they were not allowed to use explosive ordnance. ARVN and VNMC artillery fire against the Imperial Palace wall was limited in strength and duration; thus, such fire was of limited value.

By the middle of the afternoon, Charlie/1/5 was obliged to tie up one of its small platoons to cordon off the Imperial Palace wall. Meanwhile, the remainder of the battalion side-slipped a block away and bypassed the most active strongpoints along the top of the wall. The decision to use even eighteen or twenty Marines to man static positions nearly overtaxed 1/5's dwindling manpower. Nevertheless, by 1630, when 1/5 stopped for the day, its three front-line companies were arrayed along Han Thuyen Street, halfway down the Imperial Palace's northeastern wall and only three blocks from the Thuong Tu Gate, Golf/2/5's January 31 objective.

In response to 1/5's pleas for reinforcements, sixty-two replacements were helilifted into the Citadel between 1617 and 1640, February 17. The replacements hardly made a dent in the battalion's manpower shortage. In fact, the new men did not even make good that one day's losses. The cumulative results of the February 17 fighting alone amounted to twelve Marines killed and fifty-five Marines wounded and evacuated. Against this, 1/5 counted twenty-eight NVA soldiers confirmed killed.

Also on February 17, the 4th VNMC Battalion reached the Citadel's western corner against sporadic rearguard resistance—just enough to slow the clearing operation. After clearing the area around the Chanh Tay Gate, the VNMC battalion relieved the cut-up ARVN battalions that had been fighting there for several weeks. The battalion's orders were to continue mopping up around the Chanh Tay Gate on February 18. Then, if everything went well, it was to rejoin Battle Group Alpha on February 19 for the final assault toward the south corner of the Citadel.

Bob Thompson's U.S. Marine battalion could not continue its attack on February 18. Hampered by extremely cold and wet weather, 1/5 had run low on ammunition of all types. Moreover, each of its four infantry companies mustered fewer than 100 men. The battalion had been in contact with enemy forces for most of the past forty-five days, and it was badly disorganized. So critical was the shortage of supplies that the troops had not been fed adequately for the past two days; some of the men had not been fed at all. Compounding all those problems, the battalion's front line was only a few blocks from the Citadel's southeast wall—it was no longer possible to call on artillery or mortar support without seriously endangering the troops.

On February 18, the 1st ARVN Division's Brigadier General Truong partially alleviated 1/5's manpower shortage by dispatching the battle-weakened but formidable Hoc Bao Company and the 1st ARVN Division Reconnaissance Company to the U.S. Marine battalion's right flank, along the Imperial Palace wall. But Truong's gift was a two-edged sword. As soon as the tiger-suited Hoc Bao troopers reached the 1/5 CP, the company commander, Captain Tran Ngoc Hue, asked Major Bob Thompson to blow a hole in the palace's northeast gate so his soldiers could assault the citadel within the Citadel. Thompson admired the ARVN captain's courage, but he refused the request. Not even the elite Hoc Bao Company could survive such an attack, much less prevail. When Captain Hue insisted that he was under direct orders from General Truong to carry out the assault, Thompson radioed the 1st ARVN Division commander and begged him to rescind the order. Truong readily acceded to Thompson's request, but Truong decided then and there that the Hoc Bao Company would indeed liberate the Imperial Palace when the time was right.

On February 18, 1/5 remained rooted to its line along the northwest side of Han Thuyen. A day of small but intense fire-fights produced no significant gains but resulted in thirty-five NVA dead at a cost of four Marines killed, ten Marines wounded and evacuated, and another four Marines wounded and returned to duty.

A week earlier, as Major Bob Thompson had been preparing to leave MACV for the Citadel, Major Aloysius McGonigal, a forty-six-year-old Jesuit priest serving as a U.S. Army chaplain, had volunteered to accompany 1/5. From the moment 1/5 had jumped off into the attack, the diminutive, owlishly bespectacled Jesuit had stubbornly clung to the units at the forefront of the action. Whenever a Marine fell, there was a good chance that Father McGonigal would soon be at his side, administering last rites or words of consolation or just helping to carry him to safety. When there were no wounded Marines to console, Father McGonigal simply cheered the fire teams on to victory. To Major Bob Thompson, he seemed like a man possessed. Though Thompson considered the priest to be reckless and maybe even subconsciously suicidal, he was nevertheless inspired by Father McGonigal's many heroic acts. Many admiring Marines warned McGonigal to take care, but the priest never avoided a dangerous situation. Indeed, he seemed intent upon seeking out the hottest spots, eager to go wherever the danger was greatest.

McGonigal was present each evening for Major Thompson's command briefing, but he had failed to show up on February 17. It became evident that he was missing. In the morning, the

Marines began an all-out search of the rubble through which 1/5 had fought. At 1430, the bad news reached the battalion CP: Father McGonigal's body had been found in the rubble of a house two blocks behind the front line. No doubt, while on one of his countless errands of mercy, the priest had been caught in one of the mortar barrages the NVA fired into 1/5's rear every evening. Searching for Marines to tend and comfort, Father Aloysius McGonigal had died—alone and untended—killed by shrapnel that entered the back of his head. Marines and corpsmen of all faiths openly mourned their loss.

That day 1/5 had lost another brave and devoted man. From the beginning of the battalion's ordeal in the Citadel, the 106mm Recoilless Rifle Platoon's Mechanical Mule drivers had been at the forefront of the evacuation and resupply efforts. No evacuation mission was refused as being too dangerous. Tragically, at 1730, on February 18, one of the bravest of the drivers had missed Charlie/1/5's front line—everyone was hunkered down out of sight—and he was well into a contested but momentarily quiescent intersection before anyone could stop him. The NVA shot the driver right out of his seat. The Marines opened heavy suppressive fire, and the driver's helper was able to scramble back across Han Thuyen Street. But in the face of overwhelming NVA fire, it proved impossible to rescue the driver or recover the Mechanical Mule. Finally, long after dark, a few Marines crept out into the intersection and recovered the body.

Though the 1st and 5th VNMC battalions were each larger than 1/5, they were less well equipped and less acclimated to the bitter weather. Despite the best efforts of their officers and enlisted troop leaders to get them going, the Vietnamese Marines made only the most feeble efforts to advance.

Late in the afternoon, the equally wet and miserable 4th VNMC Battalion slid into position on Battle Group Alpha's right flank, along Thuy Quan Canal, and the 1st VNMC Battalion went into reserve. If the weather improved by the next morning, Battle Group Alpha would kick off what was expected to be the final assault to clear the southwest side of the Citadel. Overall, more than 1,200 Vietnamese Marine infantrymen—two 700-

man battalions, less casualties—were to attack an area no larger than that assigned to 1/5—a force of fewer than 400 Marines—and the Hoc Bao and 1st ARVN Division Reconnaissance companies, which together numbered fewer than 200 men.

February 19 was more of the same. Following a day of relative rest, 1/5's three hungry, exhausted front-line companies jumped off again, but feebly. The NVA had all the advantages of position and time, and may also have had the advantage in numbers.

The area held by the NVA was so compact that 1/5's attack was less the reduction of a built-up city area than an assault on a fortified position. Major Bob Thompson said later that the fighting during this period was more like that in Tarawa than that in Seoul. The whole objective was really one big strongpoint, complete with interlocking bands of fire from mutually supporting fortified positions. Moreover, the NVA defenders literally had their backs to a wall, so their fanatical resistance was the only alternative to annihilation. On the brink of defeat, the NVA soldiers facing 1/5 were first-rate combat veterans.

Even for fresh, experienced troops, the task facing the U.S. Marine battalion would have been formidable. As it was, 1/5 was understrength and diluted by inexperienced replacements. The troops were inadequately supplied and unable to take advantage of their supporting-arms superiority. Moreover, the only tactic available was the frontal assault, which was expensive in terms of men and equipment. With so much against it, 1/5 was simply unable to build up momentum.

Major Thompson considered the tanks and Ontos his most important assets. A tank was able to take a fair licking, but an Ontos was extremely vulnerable. For all that, the mobile 106mm recoilless rifles, fired in any combination from one to six, were easily the most effective weapons on the battlefield, superb for tackling the masonry houses the NVA were turning into bunkers. The trick was to get an Ontos into firing position—without getting it blown away. Lieutenant Ron Morrison, the tank-platoon commander, provided the solution. Quite simply, Morrison teamed one or two tanks with each Ontos. Then, at Major

Thompson's express order, whenever infantrymen came up against a target they thought was worth risking an Ontos to blow down, the infantry commander requested an Ontos via the battalion CP. The Ontos and tank commanders and the infantry commander would then conduct a personal reconnaissance of the target. If the target could be fired on without undue risk, the Ontos commander laid out the plan. Generally, the infantrymen fired all the suppression they could while the tank nosed up and fired its main gun and machine guns. While the NVA still had their heads down, the tank withdrew and the Ontos zipped up, fired all its 106s, and reversed through the dust and debris thrown up by the backblast. Every M-48 tank attached to 1/5 had taken ten or twelve hits apiece, and many tank crewmen had been wounded or killed. None of the Ontos supporting 1/5 had ever been hit, and none of the Ontos crewmen had been injured by enemy fire.

Perhaps the worst liability facing 1/5 was the prohibition against firing at NVA positions within the Imperial Palace. The Hoc Bao and 1st ARVN Division Reconnaissance companies were supposed to deal with opposition on that flank, but their efforts never amounted to anything because they did not have access to effective supporting arms. Thus, as long as NVA machine guns and snipers could fire into 1/5's rear and flanks with virtual impunity, 1/5 could not advance. This is not to say that the U.S. Marines honored the letter of the law—tanks and Ontos fired at the palace wall when there were clear targets—but the heavy artillery needed to blast enemy positions and their occupants to dust could not be employed.

Adding to the general craziness was the need to consider the safety of many hundreds of civilians who were crowding in behind the battalion, waiting to return to their homes—or what was left of their homes. Several sniping incidents behind 1/5 convinced Major Thompson that there were NVA and VC infiltrators among the refugees, but there was nothing he could do. There were too many people for his Marines to interrogate or even cordon off from the battlefield. In the end, Thompson assigned the 2nd Battalion, 3rd ARVN Regiment, to handle the refugees. (In Thompson's opinion the battalion wasn't much good for any other detail.) The U.S. Marines did their best to ignore the civilians, but the civilians were there and they were a factor.

The effect of all the mounting problems was that 1/5 made little progress on either February 19 or February 20. The U.S. Marines claimed the lives of many NVA soldiers, but they sustained casualties in kind. The Americans overran NVA strongpoints, but they could not find the key to breaking into and overcoming the NVA defensive sector. In two days of heavy fighting—and after sustaining heavy losses—1/5 had penetrated only one block farther into the NVA defensive zone.

At first the Marines thought they were battling a demoralized 6th NVA Regiment rearguard. Instead, documents taken from NVA bodies showed that the enemy ranks consisted of soldiers from the 5th NVA Regiment, the 324B NVA Division's 90th NVA Regiment, and the 325C NVA Division's 29th NVA Regiment. The U.S. Marines and their ARVN and VNMC allies suddenly found themselves facing a seemingly inexhaustible supply of fresh combat-experienced NVA soldiers.

By dusk on February 20, after a week's fighting, 1/5 had sustained a total of 47 Marines and corpsmen killed, 240 Marines and corpsmen wounded and evacuated, and 60 Marines and corpsmen wounded and returned to duty. Nobody knew how many Marines and corpsmen had simply kept their injuries hidden to avoid being transferred from their units. Among the casualties arriving back at the battalion aid station were many replacements who had completed their training in the States little more than a week earlier.

The casualty figures alone do not present a complete picture; attrition from other causes was also significant. In one of the maddest aspects of the Vietnam War, Marines who were due to be rotated home or who qualified for R and R could not be held with the battalion main body if they chose not to be. Many such Marines did stay, and some were killed or wounded. But many grabbed the opportunity to depart Hue. What is more, the miserably cold, damp weather, the inadequate diet, the focus on treating the wounded, the hazards of living in the rubble, and just plain slipping morale resulted in losses due to injuries and illnesses of all sorts.

By the end of February 20, Alpha/1/5 was down to around

seventy effectives and Bravo/1/5 was down to about eighty effectives. Charlie/1/5 and Delta/1/5 were not much better off. Only two rifle platoons in the entire battalion were commanded by officers, and all three of Bravo/1/5's platoons were being led by corporals. The troops had not been adequately fed in four days, and there was never enough of the right kinds of munitions.

Truth was, 1/5 was slipping. Major Thompson saw it happening, but he could do nothing beyond yelling at higher headquarters to get the help he needed: food, ammunition, replacements, permission to level the Imperial Palace walls, and some way to seal the city against the further infiltration of NVA reinforcements. Higher headquarters yelled back. At one point, Thompson became so fed up with prodding radio messages from seniors who had never deigned to visit in person that he asked one of them to find his replacement. The senior officer backed off, but Thompson had the clear impression that his days as 1/5's commanding officer were numbered if his tired battalion did not overcome the NVA right quick. (In fact, Lieutenant General Robert Cushman, the commanding general of III MAF, actually announced Thompson's relief to reporters. When Cushman ordered Colonel Stan Hughes, the 1st Marines commander, to effect the relief, however, Hughes replied that he would resign his own command before he relieved Bob Thompson. Cushman backed down. The first Thompson heard of the Cushman announcement to the press was several weeks later, in a letter of condolence from his wife.)

Compounding the pressure was Thompson's certain knowledge that the 5th Marines commander was going to do everything in his power to obstruct the relief of 1/5 by Marines from any other regiment. The 5th Marines commander did not want a battalion from another Marine regiment to go down in history as the liberators of the Citadel of Hue. Even higher Marine headquarters did not want any of the U.S. Army battalions then becoming available in I Corps to finish the job inside the Citadel. So, topping all their other priorities, Major Thompson and his hard-pressed staff found themselves saddled with the exigencies of making history.

The only bright news on Thompson's horizon was that the

5th Marines commander was trying to get a company of 3/5 moved up from southern I Corps to attach to 1/5. In fact, late on February 20, Lima/3/5 was alerted for the move, which was to commence in stages the next day. When the Lima/3/5 troops heard they were going to Hue, they thought it was for leave, a reward for doing a good job around Danang.

At 0430, February 19, the NVA struck the 5th VNMC Battalion sector with three hundred 82mm mortar rounds and many B-40 rockets. Then they launched a large, well-coordinated infantry assault. Only the effective use of the VNMC 105mm battery, which fired over 2,000 rounds (nearly its entire ready supply), prevented the NVA reserves from attacking through breaches ripped into the VNMC line. The NVA attack was beaten back with enormous losses—estimates put the number of NVA killed as high as 150. The 5th VNMC Battalion's line was fully restored. The 4th and 5th VNMC battalions resumed the Battle Group Alpha attack on schedule, but they made no progress.

Though the VNMC battle group did field its own direct-support 105mm howitzer battery, which fired constantly from within the 1st ARVN Division CP compound, they lacked supporting arms. The heaviest weapons available to the battalions were 60mm mortars; 57mm recoilless rifles; 81mm mortars; and, once in awhile, a few ARVN M-41 tanks.

Whereas 1/5 faced a sector of densely packed multistory commercial buildings, the terrain facing the VNMC line across Thuy Quan Canal was more open—it consisted of single-story homes with courtyards, vacant lots, parks, and gardens. At first glance, this appeared to give the VNMC companies more room to maneuver, more options. However, the added visibility cut in both directions; NVA snipers had more and wider vistas, and the many NVA machine guns could reach farther in the VNMC sector than they could in 1/5's.

As in the 1/5 sector, the NVA facing the VNMC battalions were competent veterans. They employed every trick in the book. For example, the NVA placed machine guns in sandbag or rubble bunkers built against the rear walls of masonry houses. They fired the guns through open front doorways, the better to obscure muzzle flashes and defy observation. They fired B-40 rockets, AK-47s, and SKSs from similarly covered positions. The only way to get a direct hit on an in-house bunker was to stand in the front doorway, exposed to fire from the target and from numerous spider holes covering every intersection and every opening between the houses. Before coming to Vietnam, the 4th VNMC Battalion's senior advisor, Major Bill Eshelman, had taught tactics to U.S. Marine lieutenants at The Basic School, in Quantico, Virginia. In his years at the school, Eshelman had never heard of an integrated defensive plan as comprehensive as what he saw on the ground in the Citadel. He was frankly awed by the professionalism of his adversaries, whom, he now realized, he had seriously underestimated.

The reinforced NVA units inside the Citadel had adequate reason to stall 1/5, but their primary goal was to humiliate the GVN troops fighting in the Citadel. Political goals aside, NVA reinforcement, resupply, and withdrawal required the availability of the Huu Gate. Therefore, the NVA naturally put most of their effort into stopping the VNMC advance to that gate.

For all the resistance the VNMC battalions encountered, all was not well with the NVA forces inside the Citadel. Beginning late in the day of February 19 and continuing into February 20, VNMC officers monitoring NVA radio frequencies reported that high-ranking NVA and VC military and political officers were disappearing from their command post inside the Imperial Palace. There were even indications that several NVA combat units had been ordered to clear out of the Citadel before the Huu Gate was sealed.

The South Vietnamese forces halted on February 20 so psychological warfare experts and their equipment could be brought to the forward lines. The development was surprising and maddening to most Americans on the scene, but it was entirely consistent with Vietnamese values. Sensing that they were standing on the brink of a major political victory, the GVN forces realized they could afford to be magnanimous to their enemies. In fact, they had much to gain by offering easy surrender terms. If the remaining NVA and VC gave up without a fight, more physical damage—particularly to the Imperial Palace—

would be prevented and lives would be saved. And the impact of the political victory would be increased many times over if the GVN could show off Communists and Communist sympathizers who had defected to the forces of freedom. What better way to bury TCK-TKN in Hue than to convert its militant proponents?

At this crucial juncture—as both 1/5 and the VNMC battle group faced either collapse or success—ongoing efforts by the 1st Cavalry Division's 3rd Brigade to seal Hue from the outside and capture the Tri-Thien-Hue Front headquarters had likewise reached a critical stage. Indeed, the Cav's efforts no doubt precipitated events inside the Citadel.

PART IX

T-T WOODS

While 1/5 and VNMC Battle Group Alpha had been struggling to prevail over Communist forces inside the Citadel, elements of the 3rd Brigade of the 1st Cavalry Division and the 2nd Brigade of the 101st Airborne Division had been trying to seal Hue from the outside.

On February 4, as Lieutenant Colonel Dick Sweet's 2/12 Cav was becoming mired in its no-win fight at Thon Que Chu, Lieutenant Colonel Jim Vaught's 5/7 Cav was moving into PK 17. Vaught's battalion was to guard the vital ARVN base and to establish a new base from which it could conduct patrols along Highway 1, south toward Hue. On the morning of February 5— by which time Sweet's 2/12 Cav had completed its night withdrawal from Thon Que Chu—the 5/7 Cav was ordered to turn over its positions in PK 17 to two companies of the 2nd Brigade, 101st Airborne Division's 2nd Battalion, 501st Airborne Infantry (2/501 Airborne) and move out toward Hue.

Mortar fire that had been striking PK 17 throughout the 5/7 Cav's brief stay there seemed to be originating from the hamlet of Thon Thuong, several kilometers to the southeast. As soon as the relief at PK 17 and several adjacent LZs and fire bases had been effected, Lieutenant Colonel Vaught formed his four Cav companies into a standard infantry box formation—two companies up and two companies back—and started moving directly toward the apparently fortified area. It was the first time in memory that the entire 5/7 Cav had operated as a unit. Vaught's orders from his brigade commander called for a movement to contact; the 5/7 Cav was to uncover and attack any enemy force that might be in its way. In case of trouble, Vaught would have direct artillery support from Charlie Battery, 1/21 Artillery, which had set in its six 105mm howitzers at a newly established fire base, LZ Sally, adjacent to PK 17. Because the 1st Cavalry Division was severely short of troop-carrying helicopters, Vaught's battalion would have to operate on foot. Vaught preferred it that way.

Jim Vaught was a premier infantryman, one of the best in the U.S. Army. Though only thirty-eight years old, the gruff South Carolinian had fought as a "mud soldier" at the end of World War II. After completing his schooling at The Citadel military academy in his native South Carolina, he had commanded troops in Korea, where he gained a reputation as a leader who loved to close with the enemy. When the 5/7 Cav jumped off from PK 17, Jim Vaught had been in command for only a week, but the battalion officers were already in awe of him, and the troopers loved his blunt, aggressive style. Instinctively, they all knew that there was nothing about field soldiering they could not learn from Jim Vaught.

As the 5/7 Cav advanced in box formation, the NVA holding Thon Thuong resisted with long-range sniper fire and 82mm mortars. In addition, they shot down a UH-1E Huey command-and-control helicopter that had strayed over the battlefield en-route to another Cav battalion. Lieutenant Colonel Vaught had to divert Company B and Company C to rescue the crew of the downed Huey. Meantime, through increasingly heavy sniper and mortar fire, Company D pressed on toward Thon Thuong, with Company A in reserve. Unfortunately, the 5/7 Cav ran out of daylight, so all the companies had to disengage and pull back to a battalion-size night-defensive position.

Early on February 6, the 5/7 Cav reopened its two-part attack toward the downed Huey and Thon Thuong. Contact with the NVA was quickly reestablished. Following a 1,000-meter advance, Company B located the downed command-and-control chopper. After securing the area around the wrecked Huey, the troopers conducted a thorough search. Company B got into a brief, intense fracas with a platoon of NVA, but the Communists withdrew. There were no signs of life or death around the helicopter. The crewmen might have evaded the NVA on their own, or they might have been captured; no one in the 5/7 Cav ever learned the outcome.

Lieutenant Colonel Vaught re-formed the battalion, and, following a 120-round 105mm artillery prep, the 5/7 Cav attacked into Thon Thuong. By then, the NVA holding the hamlet were long gone. Vaught's men found fighting positions, miles of communications wire, and other signs indicating that the NVA force that had been in residence was a strong one. A thorough search of the hamlet uncovered ample stocks of food, weapons, and ammunition—all in quantities far beyond the needs of even the large NVA force that had occupied the area. Lieutenant Colonel Vaught was convinced that he had discovered a major NVA supply depot. He suspected that it supported the forces fighting in Hue and, perhaps, was even to supply the volunteer battalions that were supposed to have rallied to the General Uprising in the city. If Vaught's assessment was right, the 5/7 Cav had already dealt the Tri-Thien-Hue Front a significant blow.

On February 7, the 5/7 Cav advanced 2,600 meters southward and encountered nothing more than an occasional harassing mortar round. As the battalion was regrouping in the open a little after noon, they saw a Huey log ship pass over the huge kilometer-wide rice paddy that separated the Cav battalion from Thon Que Chu. The NVA mounted a tremendous small-arms volley and shot down the chopper. Lieutenant Colonel Vaught had wanted to attack into Thon Que Chu from the southwest, but now he was obliged to turn ninety degrees and attack straight across open fields, for the log ship had fallen to earth in front of Thon Lieu Coc Thuong, the hamlet from which Sweet's 2/12 Cav had attacked Thon Que Chu on February 3. Thon Lieu Coc Thuong was just south of Highway 1 and about 300 meters northwest of the northern tip of Thon Que Chu. However, to get there, Vaught's battalion had to attack to the north-northeast, with the heavily wooded area of Thon La Chu and Thon Que Chu on its right flank.

A preparatory barrage of artillery and naval gunfire was hurriedly arranged, and the 5/7 Cav turned to its left and attacked into the flat, open rice-paddy area with Company A on the left and Company B on the right. Company C was screening the battalion right flank; Company D was in reserve, guarding everyone else's packs. Major Charlie Baker, the battalion operations officer, thought the battalion "looked grand" as it stepped off into the attack, "sort of like a Civil War scene, but with ten meters between our people." A huge wooded area—Thon Que Chu and adjacent Thon La Chu—loomed to the right as far as the eye could see, but 1,000 meters of absolutely flat, open ground separated the first file of Cav troopers from the downed log ship.

Nothing happened. The Cav battalion jumped off at 1320, but there was no resistance and there were no casualties. The crew of the downed Huey and all the supplies were recovered. Since there were no other helicopters available to recover the Huey, the Cav troopers stripped it of its machine guns and other useful equipment.

Civilians brought in for interrogation revealed that the NVA force that had been occupying Thon Lieu Coc Thuong had withdrawn to the north, across Highway 1, as soon as the artillery and naval gunfire began. The weather suddenly changed from moderately bad to thoroughly lousy—cold, rainy, and overcast—so the main body of the battalion set in for the night in Thon Lieu Coc Thuong. Company D was unable to come forward with the packs because no log ships were available. To play it safe, after sunset, Company D carried all the packs to a new location 400 meters away. The company was not molested, but sentries spotted the muzzle flashes of mortars in Thon Que Chu that were firing on PK 17. An artillery fire mission was called on target by the forward observer attached to Company D, and the NVA mortars shut down.

Following the bloodless attack on Thon Lieu Coc Thuong, Major Baker, the battalion operations officer, conducted a detailed inspection of the NVA defensive positions. What he found were about thirty NVA fighting holes—neatly squared-off excavations a little over a meter deep and covered over with thin roofs of native materials just strong enough to stop artillery air-burst fragments. The villagers had spoken of "many" enemy, but Major Baker found only enough fighting holes for an NVA platoon.

On February 8, the main body of the 5/7 Cav stayed put in Thon Lieu Coc Thuong and established mutually supporting company perimeters. Log ships remained unavailable, so Company D and the packs stayed where they were.

Early in the day, Lieutenant Colonel Vaught established an observation post in the trees at the northeast corner of the Thon

Lieu Coc Thuong "island." From there, careful observation of the enemy island revealed an inordinate amount of activity around what appeared to be a large concrete structure deep within the trees. By late morning, observers were certain that the bunker had an NLF battle flag flying over it. Lieutenant Colonel Vaught arranged for an artillery fire mission against the bunker, but the 105mm high-explosive rounds just bounced off the structure. It was not until later that Vaught learned that he was looking and firing at the American-built ferroconcrete bunker that the Tri-Thien-Hue Front was using as its headquarters. (In fact, the bunker, three stories high and two stories deep, had been proposed, designed, and built with American funds and supplies by a local contractor who was eventually unmasked as an NVA major with an engineering degree.)

After noon, Lieutenant Colonel Vaught decided to conduct a reconnaissance in force against Thon Que Chu. Two rifle platoons from Captain Howard Prince's Company B prepared to move out of Thon Lieu Coc Thuong's treeline and advance toward Thon Que Chu. Unknown to Lieutenant Colonel Vaught, Captain Prince, or anyone else in the 5/7 Cav, the two infantry platoons had been assigned a mission that Lieutenant Colonel Dick Sweet's entire 2/12 Cav had accomplished on February 3 only after a bloody day-long struggle.

Captain Prince arranged his force in a single column and, at 1600, pushed off into the stubbly, fallow paddyfield. Nothing happened as the Cav troopers moved across the open field, but, as soon as they entered the woods, the NVA ambushed them from three sides. The 1st Platoon was hit hardest, and every man in the lead squad was killed or wounded. The survivors were hopelessly outnumbered, but the NVA made no move to leave their positions and overwhelm them. As the battalion command group tried to assist from inside the Thon Lieu Coc Thuong perimeter, a single stream of .51-caliber machine-gun bullets from Thon Que Chu struck the side of a house just behind the battalion TOC hole. The machine-gun fire kept the battalion staff pinned down for about thirty minutes, and then it suddenly ceased.

Company A launched a feint around Company B's left flank, alleviating some of the pressure on the survivors. Even so, it took

three hours and a supreme effort for Captain Prince and his
troopers to disengage and withdraw with their six wounded
comrades. Artillery smoke rounds helped a great deal when it
came time for the two Company B platoons to pull back across
the 300-meter open space. About 1,500 high-explosive artillery
rounds and several dozen aerial rockets blotted out the NVA
positions. Despite incredible acts of bravery and devotion, however, all three of Company B's dead—the 1st Platoon point
element—had to be left where they fell, just inside the Thon Que
Chu treeline.

The wounded could not be medevacked until after dark,
because the NVA had most of Thon Lieu Coc Thuong zeroed in.
When the medevac birds finally arrived, the weather was so bad
that the crews could not find the strobe lights set out to mark the
day's LZ. Despite the inherent danger, the pilots turned on their
landing lights to mark their positions in the sky, and the helicopter ground team talked them down safely. Though the NVA
certainly could have driven off the medevac birds with machine
guns and mortars, they withheld their fire.

In the wee hours, an all-volunteer patrol crept back to Thon
Que Chu to collect the three KIAs who had been left behind.
Though the patrol could hear NVA soldiers talking, the troopers
were not attacked, and they brought back all three of the dead.

NVA mortars attacked the isolated Company D perimeter in
the middle of the night, and three troopers were wounded. Company C's 60mm mortars were able to lay on the NVA from within
the Thon Lieu Coc Thuong perimeter, and their fire shut off the
NVA fire.

By the next morning, the Thon Que Chu–Thon La Chu
island had a nickname known to everyone in the 5/7 Cav: T-T
Woods, or, in the vernacular of the day, Tough-Titty Woods.

On February 9, Lieutenant Colonel Dick Sweet's 2/12 Cav
left its high-ground position and attacked the defended hamlet of
Thon Bon Tri. The hamlet was right at the base of the Annamite
Cordillera, due south of Thon La Chu and astride Provincial
Route 554. The move down from the mountain was not con-
tested, but the NVA opened a fierce defensive fight as soon as the

Cav troopers approached Thon Bon Tri itself. There was a persistent shortage of artillery rounds in the U.S. Army fire bases north of Hue. Since 1,500 precious rounds had been expended in support of Company B, 5/7 Cav, on February 8, it took all the limited artillery available on February 9 to support Sweet's hard-pressed battalion. Nevertheless, by day's end, Sweet's thin companies were able to push 300 meters northward through the heavily built-up area. Against an unknown number of NVA casualties, Sweet's battalion lost two killed and fourteen wounded.

Throughout February 9, Vaught's 5/7 Cav remained inside Thon Lieu Coc Thuong, strengthening its defensive positions. The 5/7 Cav was mortared several times during the day, every time a helicopter flew over or tried to set down. By the late afternoon, the NVA mortars had the Company B and Company C positions zeroed in. In no time, Company B had sustained nine more wounded, including a platoon leader, and Company C had lost twelve wounded. Until medevacked after dark, one of the wounded men screamed so loudly that everyone within earshot just about ground their teeth to dust.

Since log ships from Camp Evans remained unavailable and the LZs inside the battalion position were too dangerous, Company D finally humped all the packs in its care north to Highway 1 and, at 1700, rejoined the battalion main body through the back door. The return of the packs greatly improved the battalion's morale.

On February 10, Sweet's 2/12 Cav remained largely inactive inside Thon Bon Tri, and Vaught's 5/7 Cav continued to improve its defensive posture in Thon Lieu Coc Thuong and observe the NVA across the way. In the afternoon—after Company A, 5/7 Cav, had swept Highway 1 for mines—a logistics convoy rolled in all the way from Camp Evans. Several Company B troopers who were firing a .50-caliber machine gun from beside the grounded Huey were blown out of their position after an hour's sniping by a twenty-round 82mm mortar barrage from Thon Que Chu. A trooper who went back to retrieve part of the machine gun that had been left behind was shot dead by an NVA sniper. That night, word came down from the brigade intelligence officer that the entire Communist effort around Hue seemed to be controlled from the headquarters bunker in Thon La Chu.

Nothing much happened on February 11. The weather was execrable. The 2/12 Cav remained in Thon Bon Tri, and the 5/7 Cav stayed close to Thon Lieu Coc Thuong. At 0830, three NVA 82mm mortar rounds fired from Thon Que Chu wounded thirteen more troopers from Company B, 5/7 Cav, including the company exec.

After line-company officers and noncoms advised the battalion staff of the obvious—that NVA snipers and mortars had the Company B and Company C positions in the treeline zeroed in—Lieutenant Colonel Vaught ordered the main body of the battalion to shrink back 200 meters into a tight, well-constructed defensive position around the center of Thon Lieu Coc Thuong. Only well-concealed observation posts would be manned at the edge of the woods.

In the center of the 5/7 Cav's new battalion perimeter were three deep bunkers—the battalion aid station, the battalion CP, and the battalion TOC. Each new fighting hole was large enough to accommodate three troopers, and each was manned around the clock by at least one of the troopers assigned to it. Machine guns were sited in mutually supporting bunkers all the way around the battalion perimeter, and all the 81mm and 60mm mortars were preregistered on a host of targets and approach routes. Altogether, it was an impressive, formidable position.

As the troopers were digging in, Lieutenant Colonel Vaught requested and quickly received permission to mount a battalion assault the next day against the NVA headquarters bunker in Thon La Chu. Ample artillery support was promised, as well as fixed-wing and helicopter-gunship air support if the weather cleared. A carefully crafted operations order was drawn up.

That night, Jim Vaught taught his battalion a great deal about fighting in the dark. In the dead of night, a tripflare was set off, and the troops heard a lot of moving-around noise out in front of the battalion perimeter. Instantly, the battalion TOC was besieged with requests for illumination. Lieutenant Colonel Vaught denied the requests and declared that no one had permission to fire rifles or machine guns. Vaught passed the word that M-79 grenade launchers could be fired—they had no muzzle flash—but that the grenadier had better be able to show the battalion commander a dead body come morning. The noise to the front persisted, and troopers popped off several M-79s at fleeting targets. At first light, the dead body the battalion commander was shown proved to be that of a village pig.

— 35 —

Major Charlie Baker worked on his plan of attack through the night; had it approved by Lieutenant Colonel Jim Vaught; and, at a dawn meeting on February 12, explained it to the company commanders and supporting-arms representatives. In its essentials, Baker's detailed plan differed little from the one the 2/12 Cav had executed on the run on February 3. In its initial phases, it was to cover much of the same ground. Two companies—A, on the left, and C, on the right—were to move to a line of departure tangent to the Thon Lieu Coc Thuong treeline. They would then assault across the open paddyfield area to two intermediate objectives: Company A would take the small wooded cemetery, and Company C would take Thon Phu O. Company A was then to re-form and, under cover of artillery smoke rounds, attack into the northern edge of Thon Que Chu—T-T Woods.

Once inside the treeline, Company A was to re-form once again and press south through Thon Que Chu and Thon La Chu toward the Tri-Thien-Hue Front headquarters bunker. At the same time, Company C was to launch a flank attack in the open, down the west side of T-T Woods and on into the NVA headquarters sector in Thon La Chu. Company D was to be the battalion reserve, ready to jump off at a moment's notice. During the initial phases, Company B was to man a base of fire in Thon Lieu Coc Thuong, alongside the battalion's 81mm mortars, one 106mm recoilless rifle, and the .50-caliber machine gun. It would move forward as the situation demanded. Brigade informed the 5/7 Cav that the 2/12 Cav was going to launch a simultaneous attack from Thon Bon Tri into southern Thon La Chu, but a patrol from Lieutenant Dick Sweet's battalion encountered unexpectedly strong opposition, and the 2/12 Cav's attack was canceled.

The 5/7 Cav's attack, set to begin shortly after daybreak, was delayed because artillery support was not available in the morning. According to the new schedule, the assault companies were to cross the line of departure at 1230. Company C stopped short of the line of departure to wait for the exact time, but Company A kept going. Later, Major Charlie Baker asked the lieutenant commanding Company A why he had not stopped. The lieutenant's explanation led Baker to realize that the young officer did not know what a line of departure was. Baker blamed himself.

Company C stepped over the line of departure to support Company A's premature advance. The fire-support plan came unglued because the assault companies were reaching targets before the support could be fired. Company B covered the attack with direct fire, and that helped. Company A advanced beyond the cemetery and then wheeled slightly to the left, toward Thon Que Chu. As soon as Company A eased left, many NVA manning positions within a facing bamboo thicket opened fire, forcing the Cav troopers to take cover behind a prominent paddy berm that ran from northwest to southeast. When Company A came under fire, Company C naturally stopped too. Company A had partial protection from the berm, but Company C went to ground in the open. Its only cover was the stubble in the paddyfield.

The Cav troopers came under increasingly intense small-arms fire from the bamboo thicket on Company A's left, while, 150 meters dead ahead of both companies, mortars and artillery were fired at the NVA—but without noticeable effect. Company D maneuvered to Company A's left, but it was pinned down in the paddyfield to the left of the cemetery.

As soon as the attack bogged down, Battalion requested ARA (aerial rocket artillery), an emergency ammunition resupply, and fixed-wing air support. The companies made no further progress, but the ARA ships arrived and attacked the enemy-held woods. Meanwhile, ammunition-laden Huey log ships landed, through intense fire, behind the berm and the cemetery, only 150 meters from the NVA's defense line. The first flight of Air Force jet attack bombers did not arrive until after

1400, but they attacked vigorously through broken cloud cover. Unfortunately, the spotter plane from which the jet strike was being coordinated had difficulty with low clouds and fired its marker rockets deep inside Thon Que Chu. Therefore, the effort was largely wasted. In the end, none of the outside support had much influence on restarting the ground attack, which had gone awry from the opening minutes.

The weather deteriorated through the middle and late afternoon, but Battalion kept requesting air support to fully prep the NVA-held treeline. Four separate jet strikes were unleashed upon the NVA. Coordination improved marginally following a tongue-lashing by Lieutenant Colonel Vaught, and the northernmost bamboo thicket and treeline facing the Cav battalion were reduced to kindling.

Throughout the hours-long softening-up process, Lieutenant Colonel Vaught peeked over the edge of a burial mound only fifteen meters behind the front line of Cav riflemen. Despite the incessant sound of gunfire and bombs, Major Charlie Baker heard a *whump* every time Vaught lifted his head. Baker realized that an NVA sniper had been attracted by the CP group's radio antennas. Fearing for Vaught's life, Baker finally said, "Sir, would you mind getting down here behind the mound with us? I think they have you spotted." Vaught just smiled and carried on. A short time later, Baker crawled to the left through sporadic sniper fire to alert Company D to its role in the upcoming attack.

Company D had moved out of Thon Lieu Coc Thuong and advanced with relative ease to the paddy dike that faced the northern tip of Thon Que Chu and extended at about a right angle from the dike Company A was using for cover. Thus, Company D was facing southeast toward the same bamboo thickets that the left half of Company A was facing from the west.

The three front-line companies of the 5/7 Cav jumped off at 1800 in a final assault against the bamboo thicket and treelines they were facing. The Americans hoped the defense had been pulverized by the ongoing artillery, mortar, and air attacks. If the attack went as planned, the frontal assault would breach the NVA line and carry the Cav companies all the way through Thon Que

Chu to the NVA CP bunker in Thon La Chu.

Once again the NVA let the U.S. Army battalion come on virtually without opposition. Then, as Company C entered the treeline on the right and Company D and Company A moved into the bamboo thickets, the world blew up in their faces. Since the Cav battalion had been preparing for the final assault for nearly four hours in plain view of the enemy, the element of surprise had been lost.

On the battalion right, Company C advanced all the way to its original initial objective, a dry streambed that ran between Thon Que Chu and Thon Phu O. Unfortunately, to secure Thon Phu O, Company C had to attack to its right rather than as called for by the original plan. Company C had insufficient manpower to cover its own front and Company A's open right flank. The result was a widening gap to Company C's left and the inevitable loss of lateral contact with Company A. As soon as Company C reached the streambed, it was stopped cold by many NVA soldiers manning a deep defensive sector inside the Thon Phu O treeline. The right Cav company had to go to ground north of the streambed.

Company A put the entire weight of its attack into the bamboo thicket that it now faced. The NVA let the company cross the narrow piece of open ground and enter the thicket. In fact, NVA manning a concealed line of spider holes allowed Company A to advance beyond their line, into the ville. As soon as the Cav troopers were between the spider holes and the next bamboo hedge within the ville, both NVA lines erupted. Caught in the middle, Company A was riddled by small-arms fire from the front and showered by Chicoms from the rear.

On the far left, Company D began attacking into the bamboo thicket—the first of several successive bamboo hedges the Vietnamese used as property markers. Like Company A, it passed through a line of concealed spider holes and then was engaged from front and rear by small arms and scores of Chicoms. Captain Frank Lambert, the Company D commander, had deployed his unit routinely, with two platoons up and one platoon back. When the NVA opened fire, the left platoon veered to the left to try to find a soft spot, and the right platoon did the same on its

side of the front. Both platoons were quickly pinned down, and
the reserve platoon was pinned down in the open before it could
move forward to plug the hole in the center. That left Captain
Lambert and his tiny command group pinned in the open, in
front of the reserve platoon and between the diverging assault
platoons. Captain Lambert noticed that the NVA were concentrating the bulk of their fire against the right platoon. He did not
realize at the time that, if it could ever get moving again, the
right platoon was in position to roll up the flank of the NVA
trenchline facing Company A. From Lambert's perspective—
gained by quick life-threatening peeks over a concealing clump of
grass—it was just a matter of time before the NVA riflemen and
machine gunners noticed the clump of antennas his radioman and
several supporting-arms teams were showing.

As the situation crystallized during the next few moments,
Lambert realized that the company's advance into the bamboo
thicket had placed a small NVA force to his left and left rear. That
force was manning a trench and holding the left platoon firmly in
place inside the bamboo. Lambert was thinking about ordering
the reserve platoon to try to breach the NVA trenchline when he
received word that the platoon leader had been killed. There was
no one else qualified to lead the platoon into action—the platoon
sergeant was on leave—so Lambert ordered the right platoon to
tighten up toward the center, the reserve platoon to advance into
the gap in the center, and his command group to pull back out of
the thicket.

In the midst of all the craziness, Lambert's company radioman stood up on his knees, opened fire with his M-16, and
yelled, "Sir, you get outta here." Lambert replied, "No, you go
first." A little argument ensued, incredible under the circumstances. Finally Lambert yelled, "Let's go," and led the way back
while the radioman stubbornly continued to cover everyone else.
That the various elements of Company D were able to move at all
was thanks to the crack 60mm mortar section, which walked
suppressive rounds up and down the NVA trenchlines—a masterful performance.

As soon as the late afternoon attack jumped off, it became

evident that the NVA were brilliantly deployed just inside the entire length of the Thon Phu O treeline facing Company C and in depth throughout the bamboo thicket fronting Thon Que Chu. In fact, they were manning multiple lines, each supported by interconnecting, mutually supporting trenches and strongpoints. Apparently, there were as many or more defenders as there were attackers. In addition to their own small arms and a limitless supply of hand grenades, the NVA controlled many mortars and, apparently, scores of captured American Claymore mines, which they blew off in the faces of the struggling U.S. troopers.

With all three Cav companies embroiled along their respective fronts, at least two NVA companies now counterattacked toward Company A's exposed right flank. Fortunately for Company A, the NVA were obliged to counterattack across the open rice paddy, where Company C was able to stun, then stop, and then turn them back.

As soon as the NVA counterattack was repulsed, Lieutenant Colonel Vaught and Major Baker agreed that pressing on was hopeless. At 1815, word went out to the three assault-company commanders to withdraw back to Thon Lieu Coc Thuong.

For Company A and Company C, disengaging was relatively easy, and the cemetery and the berm helped cover the withdrawal. Captain Frank Lambert's Company D, however, was boxed in between perpendicular and parallel NVA trenchlines. Unable to pull straight back toward the cemetery, Lambert ordered the company to side-slip to the left, where tall, thick bamboo hedges would screen it from the worst of the NVA fire. No sooner had the withdrawal order been screamed around the company position than Captain Lambert learned that a trooper had been wounded in an open paddy and that the NVA had him staked out. Lambert immediately left the relative safety of his trench and crawled straight out through enemy fire to retrieve the wounded man. The act earned him a Silver Star, not to mention the respect of his troops. Unfortunately, the company commander's example could not be followed elsewhere. When Company D held a nose count at Thon Lieu Coc Thuong that evening, it came up five men short, including the dead platoon commander.

On the night of February 12, after all the wounded had been

lifted out of Thon Lieu Coc Thuong, the 5/7 Cav's losses were tallied: Company A, two killed and twenty-four wounded; Company B, one wounded; Company C, two killed and eight wounded; Company D, five missing and three wounded. No one had any hope for the five MIAs. (A few nights later, Captain Frank Lambert personally led a team back to Thon Que Chu to recover the bodies of the five men. Just as the team found the disintegrating corpses, someone inside the battalion perimeter mistakenly ordered the artillery to fire an illumination round right over the bamboo thicket. Lambert's group froze stock-still until the light petered out. Then they withdrew, once again leaving their dead comrades where they had fallen.)

As to how many NVA had been killed or wounded at Thon Que Chu and Thon Phu O on February 12, the 5/7 Cav could only guess. Major Baker's official count was seven NVA killed and twenty-three NVA wounded. These were primarily the NVA that Company C had been able to account for during the late-afternoon counterattack in the open. But Baker estimated that the jets, artillery, ARA, and direct fire had killed and wounded many more.

It was clear to the men of the 5/7 Cav that they had encountered a major enemy position that the NVA intended to hold. With that in mind, Lieutenant Colonel Vaught, Major Baker, and the company commanders set to work focusing all their attention on finding a way to break into T-T Woods to capture the NVA command bunker in Thon La Chu.

— 36 —

The planning to seize T-T Woods began again in earnest almost as soon as the battered 5/7 Cav returned to its perimeter in Thon Lieu Coc Thuong. If nothing else, Lieutenant Colonel Jim Vaught and Major Charlie Baker knew one way it couldn't be done—by frontal attack.

High-level visits began shortly after noon on February 13, when Brigadier General Oscar Davis, one of the 1st Cavalry Division's two assistant commanders, dropped in by helicopter to confer with Jim Vaught. Davis was shown the scene of the previous day's battle, and then he departed. Major General Jack Tolson, the Cav division commander, arrived at 1400. After he was briefed, Tolson told Lieutenant Colonel Vaught and Major Baker that he hoped to mount a three-battalion assault on T-T Woods as soon as he could muster the forces. The Cav's 3rd Brigade was spread too thin for the job; the 5/7 Cav and 2/12 Cav were on opposite ends of T-T Woods, and the 1/7 Cav was the palace guard at Camp Evans. Following its reaction to the Communist coup de main at Quang Tri City, the 1st Brigade was still engaged in mop-up operations in Quang Tri Province. Tolson hoped that the impending arrival of the 2nd Brigade from central II Corps would free up the 1/7 Cav so it could help grab T-T Woods. Also, several companies of the 101st Airborne Division's 2nd Brigade were holding the area right around PK 17. If all went well, the entire airborne brigade would eventually be given a role along Highway 1. Capping his summary, General Tolson told Vaught that he hoped to secure the use of 8-inch howitzers and 155mm guns north of Hue and that he was trying to get an armored cavalry troop and some tanks attached to the 5/7 Cav for the final assault on T-T Woods and a follow-up drive on the Citadel's outer walls. General Tolson then departed, leaving Jim Vaught to grapple with what he actually had on hand: one 400-man Cav battalion and an objective too strongly held for that battalion to take.

The 5/7 Cav was modestly reinforced on February 13. A sniper specialist armed with a scoped M-14 rifle was dropped off in the battalion perimeter, and he later accounted for the only confirmed kill credited to the battalion that day. Late that night, a pair of tripflares fronting a Company C listening post were set off, and some wild shooting ensued. The troopers manning the post swore they had three or four NVA in their sights, and there was indeed someone out there shooting back and throwing Chicoms. But the only known result of the fracas was two lightly wounded Cav troopers.

General Tolson's promises began to bear fruit on February 15, in the form of upscaled 105mm fire-support resources. Only two modest jet strikes were mounted on T-T Woods during the day, but Vaught was assured from above that more would be laid on as the time to renew the ground assault approached. In fact things were looking up—until 1800, when Major Baker learned that no 8-inch or 155mm artillery were available for the projected ground attack.

Therefore, planning took a new tack. On February 15, the 3rd Brigade commander informed Lieutenant Colonel Vaught that Lieutenant Colonel Dick Sweet's 2/12 Cav would definitely be taking part in the ground assault on T-T Woods. According to Brigade, the 2/12 Cav would be airlifted from its position south of Thon La Chu to an LZ behind Thon Lieu Coc Thuong in time to assault T-T Woods on the 5/7 Cav's left flank. There was some talk of providing a battery of quad-.50 trucks and twin-40mm Dusters for a base of fire. That was well and good if it actually happened, but by then Jim Vaught and Charlie Baker were well along in formulating a radically different plan for a one-battalion attack through T-T Woods. Troopers were being trained in demo-litions work and were already constructing pole charges and makeshift bangalore torpedoes, and squads within each company were training to use them in the assault. The battalion supply section was directed to acquire flamethrowers and as many wire cutters as it could beg, borrow, or steal. Hoping for a two-battalion assault but relying only on his own battalion, Major Baker planned to use jet-delivered napalm and 1,000-pound bombs in the closing moments of the preassault bombardment. When naval gunfire became available on February 16, Baker amended his plan so it could incorporate the naval guns in the final assault.

Activity beyond planning was minor. Company D, 2/501 Airborne, was placed under the 5/7 Cav's operational control on February 15. That day, while patrolling Provincial Route 554 east of Thon Thuong, the company was engaged by an NVA force amounting to at least two companies. Artillery was called and ARA ships were dispatched, but the airborne company remained hard-pressed until Company B and Company C of the 5/7 Cav rushed to the scene on foot. Fighting was at very close quarters. Captain Howard Prince, the Company B commander, called in fire from helicopter gunships, directed ARA to within twenty-five meters of his own troops, and adjusted 105mm howitzers to within fifty meters, taking shrapnel in the process. The NVA stood and fought the U.S. Army companies to a standstill, but broke contact late in the afternoon. Fifty-eight NVA corpses were counted on the battlefield. It was later established that the NVA units to which they belonged had marched to the Hue area from Khe Sanh, the first indication that the Tri-Thien-Hue Front was beefing up the three NVA infantry regiments already accounted for in and around Hue.

The systematic destruction of the northern end of T-T Woods began in earnest on February 16. Land-based artillery fired 1,000 high-explosive rounds into T-T Woods, the Navy delivered 4,000 high-explosive rounds, and Air Force jets delivered 35 tons of assorted high-explosive bombs and 10,000 pounds of napalm.

On February 17, Major Baker flew by helicopter to Quang Tri to board an O-1 spotter plane for a reconnaissance flight over T-T Woods. Baker drew a detailed sketch of the bamboo thickets and treelines, but he was unused to observing from a fixed-wing airplane and could not make out the precise location of the NVA fighting positions. Baker explained this to the pilot, who had previously flown over the objective, and the pilot went into a steep dive and fired marker rockets to point out the NVA positions. The dive made Baker throw up, but the maneuver did help him get a better mental image of the enemy bastion. On the way out of the third or fourth dive, the O-1 drew fire from a .51-caliber machine gun, and Baker decided to call it a day.

Aggressive patrol activities, ongoing from the beginning, heated up closer to T-T Woods on February 19. Most of the 5/7 Cav participated in a sweep from Thon Lieu Coc Thuong northward a short distance across Highway 1. An NVA force entrenched inside a large cemetery just north of the highway engaged the Cav force at long range, but Cav forward observers brought in an artillery fire mission while the troopers returned to Thon Lieu Coc Thuong. No one wanted to get into a big fracas in that direction.

While the 5/7 Cav was patrolling to the north, two 2/12 Cav patrols operating east of Thon Bon Tri were engaged by separate squad-size NVA patrols. Both 2/12 Cav patrols responded with artillery and withdrew. Finally, a 2/501 Airborne patrol probing southeast from PK 17 crossed Provincial Route 554 north of Thon Bon Tri and contacted an NVA holding force that did not break contact until sunset.

Also on February 19—two days before the anticipated third assault on T-T Woods—the 2/501 Airborne was formally attached to the 1st Cavalry Division's 3rd Brigade, and the 1/7 Cav was relieved of palace-guard duty at Camp Evans and returned to the operational control of the 3rd Brigade.

The periods between the attacks on T-T Woods were not without tragedies. Patrol contact and aggressive NVA activity steadily whittled away at the battalion's strength. Every time a helicopter flew anywhere near Thon Lieu Coc Thuong, NVA mortars fired at it or simply at the large stationary target in the center of the American-occupied hamlet.

Many of the Cav troopers had come to Thon Lieu Coc Thuong with lousy flak-jacket discipline. Mounting losses cured them of that ill, but not before scores had been wounded or killed. Any disdain the troopers held for the enemy—most of the troopers, before heading north to I Corps, had only faced part-time VC fighters in II Corps—was erased long before the 5/7 Cav completed preparations for the third attack on T-T Woods.

The NVA kept the pressure up with unnerving harassment. At night, when they weren't probing around the outpost line or dropping in a few random 82mm mortar rounds, the NVA blew whistles and sounded bugles. Unable to guess what evil the noise augured, many troopers remained awake and tense—all to the detriment of the battalion's efficiency. It was a great mind game, and the NVA had the upper hand.

With four battalions now available for the February 21 assault on T-T Woods, the 3rd Brigade operations staff developed a plan at the last minute. The 5/7 Cav would conduct its long-planned attack from Thon Lieu Coc Thuong by way of Thon Phu O and the bamboo thickets at the north end of Thon Que Chu; the 2/501 Airborne would advance from the center, due east through Thon An Do, which was southwest of Thon Que Chu; two companies of the 2/12 Cav would advance northward directly into Thon La Chu from Thon Bon Tri; and the 1/7 Cav would support the 5/7 Cav on the north side. The two unengaged companies of the 2/12 Cav would be the brigade reserve. Most of the noninfantry reinforcements and support Major General Jack Tolson had promised to get for Vaught had not been delivered, but Vaught had no problem with that; he knew Tolson had done his best. As for being part of a four-battalion assault, Vaught gave it not one thought. His troopers had personal scores to settle in T-T Woods. Even though the 2/12 Cav and the 2/501 Airborne had been given better shots at the NVA command bunker in Thon La Chu, Vaught's final assault plan envisaged its capture by the 5/7 Cav.

Captain Howard Prince's Company B was to lead the 5/7 Cav's attack into the bamboo thicket at dawn on February 21, an ominous prospect to many of the young troopers who would be in the forefront. In fact, the inexperienced lieutenant commanding the vanguard platoon anxiously told Captain Prince that his troopers were cursing and threatening to refuse to go back to T-T Woods the next morning. Prince personally talked with the troopers and learned that they simply did not understand the tactics they were expected to employ. The company commander did his best to allay their fears, but the men were acting as if they were under a death sentence. Tempers flared in the Company B sector for the rest of the evening and on into the night, a sure sign that morale was coming unglued. As the hours passed, Prince decided that he should check back with the man who had written the plan, Major Charlie Baker. Prince told Baker that the troops were grumbling over the complexity of the plan. Prince did not say so, but Baker had the feeling that the company commander was trying to warn him that the troopers might not jump off at H-hour.

Baker's final plan *was* complex and, for that battalion at that time, quite radical. It called for Company C to lead the battalion out of Thon Lieu Coc Thuong in single file, and to seize Thon Phu O in the dark. As soon as that was done, still in the dark,

Company B was to assume the battalion vanguard position and cross the paddyfield east of Thon Phu O as far as the berm on which Company A had become stalled during the initial February 12 attack. At first light, right after a brief but massive artillery and naval-gunfire barrage, Company B would attack in single file down the left side of a bamboo hedge that jutted out from Thon Que Chu. Then, still in single file, Company B was to turn north (left) to secure the entire length of the outer NVA-held trenchline. At the same time, Company D was to advance down the right side of the jutting bamboo hedge, penetrate into Thon Que Chu, and turn left up the second interior NVA-held trenchline, which the bamboo thicket concealed and protected.

The idea was not to overwhelm the entire NVA line at once, but to surprise the NVA, penetrate into the southern end of their trenchlines, and roll their defenses up from one flank to the other, one emplacement at a time. To support the trench assault, Company A would man a base of fire around the downed Huey log bird. From there, Company A and the one Duster attached to the 5/7 Cav would foil large-scale reinforcement and suppress NVA mortars. As soon as the trenchlines in the bamboo thicket had been rolled up from south to north, Company B and Company D, with Company C in close support and Company A in reserve, would re-form inside Thon Que Chu and attack south through T-T Woods, perhaps all the way down to the NVA headquarters bunker.

To help breach NVA bunkers and other fighting positions, many of the troopers were to be equipped with field-expedient bangalore torpedoes—bamboo stalks filled with explosives—and pole charges. Company B's objections stemmed from the plan to attack in single file and to use unfamiliar weapons. Both were beyond the experience of the troopers, who were already edgy despite a week of careful squad-by-squad dry-run training.

Major Baker tried to rebuild flagging confidence by going over the plan's advantages once again, but even he could not find the right words of encouragement. He had no idea if things would work out. He knew that he had put together the best plan he could, given his resources, but he could not know if it was an effective plan until it had been executed. No one could.

In the wee hours of February 21, Lieutenant Colonel Jim Vaught positioned his CP at the southwest corner of Thon Lieu Coc Thuong, right on the battalion line of departure, to control the egress of their companies in the dark. As planned, Company C moved off the line of departure in single file and crossed the 500-meter paddyfield separating Thon Lieu Coc Thuong from Thon Phu O. The first objective was seized without a hitch. No NVA were found by Company C as it fanned out through the village, and not a shot was fired.

Long before Thon Phu O had been completely scoured, Captain Howard Prince's Company B turned left and advanced about 150 meters to the northeast-southwest berm fronting the west side of the bamboo thicket. The troopers had regained control of their fears, and there was not so much as a squawk from them; discipline was perfect. As soon as the tail of the Company B file cleared Thon Phu O, Captain Frank Lambert's Company D followed, also in single file. Finding the berm was a snap. The dry streambed running between the hamlets was the perfect guidepost.

The move across the paddyfield was a little behind schedule, probably because everyone involved in the attack was carrying a huge load of ammunition, explosives, LAAWs, and medical supplies. It was hot and humid long before sunup, and the blind trek across the flat, open paddyfield was physically and emotionally exhausting. Company B completed the move in the dark, but the rear elements of Company D were still on the move as the first hint of dawn appeared. There was a brief, final flurry of radio exchanges, and then Company D was ready to go. The assault companies tucked in while a withering artillery and naval gunfire barrage rained down on the defenders.

The NVA responded far more quickly than anyone thought possible. No wonder; the 5th NVA Regiment was a crack unit. As soon as the Company B point entered the bamboo, explosions erupted just to its front. The lead platoon commander reported back to Captain Prince that he could not see the source of the resistance and did not know if he was being attacked with mortars or hand grenades. The attack bogged down.

Captain Prince's command group was right behind the lead

platoon. As soon as the movement to his front stalled, Prince moved ahead into the bamboo to contact the lead platoon commander. Just as the captain dropped down beside the lieutenant, an 82mm mortar round fell in on top of them. Captain Prince, Company B's artillery forward observer, and their radiomen were injured; the lieutenant, the only other officer in Company B, was spared.

Captain Prince was conscious but stunned. The only wound he could see was to his right index finger, which was dangling from the knuckle, but he was actually riddled with shrapnel. Struggling mightily to remain conscious, Prince crawled back to the main body of the company before he passed out.

Back at Thon Lieu Coc Thuong, Major Charlie Baker was only partway through a silent litany of self-congratulation when his radioman picked up a frantic call from the Company B command radioman: Captain Prince was down, wounded in a snap mortar barrage.

When he overheard the news that Howard Prince was down, Lieutenant Colonel Jim Vaught reacted instantly. He knew that Company B had only one officer left, the young lieutenant without command experience. "Charlie," Vaught said in a dead-calm voice to Baker, "I want you to go over there and take command of Company B." Baker nodded; said "Yes, Sir"; and took off toward the berm. It was full daylight as Baker jogged across 400 meters of open ground. He heard some firing from within the bamboo hedge along the dry streambed, but not much. There were no visible signs of combat.

When Baker reached the berm, he squatted in front of Captain Prince, who was unconscious. Nearby, two or three wounded troopers were stretched out behind the berm. No one was working on Prince's or the other troopers' injuries. Baker realized that most of Company B was huddled down behind the berm. Inside the bamboo hedge, back along the stream, Company D seemed to be in the same state, hunkered down and immobile, waiting for Company B to recover itself. Everyone seemed to be stunned.

Baker passed behind most of Company B, to the bamboo hedge along the streambed. He cursed at several immobile medics. By the time Baker had the medics at work, he found that a medevac bird was hovering just off the ground, only ten meters behind the berm. He turned his attention to getting Captain Prince and the other wounded men loaded aboard the helicopter.

Next, Baker radioed the Company B lieutenant, who was under cover in the bamboo bordering the streambed, only a few meters forward. The lieutenant's voice was edged with panic; he reported that he was pinned down and asked for permission to withdraw. In fact, there was hardly any gunfire. Baker spoke to the young officer in what he hoped were reassuring tones: "Calm down, Lieutenant. Get organized and report back to me with clear facts." Baker waited in vain for a few minutes, then called the lieutenant again. There was no answer. Baker tried again, got no answer again, and started cursing into the mike. The company radioman tapped the major on the back and pointed to a handful of troopers who were running across the rear of the company. "Sir," the radioman offered, "the lieutenant's back there." With that, Baker told the radioman to tell the lieutenant to go back to Thon Lieu Coc Thuong and organize the flow of ammunition to the company. Company B was now Charlie Baker's problem.

While Baker was taking control, NVA mortar rounds began falling into the woods. Baker noticed that a stream of 40mm tracer was flying down the paddyfield to his rear, from north to south. It turned out that the crew of the Duster, which was set in near the downed log bird back at Thon Lieu Coc Thuong, had gotten a fix on the NVA mortars' muzzle flashes. A few moments later, the NVA mortars, which were set in about 200 meters south of the streambed, stopped firing. The 5/7 Cav was not molested by NVA mortars for the rest of the day.

When all the reports were in, it was apparent that Company B and Company D had stepped off right into heavy fire from a stout bunker that the NVA had had built since February 12. The structure was at the intersection of the bamboo thicket the two Cav companies were using to enter the NVA position and the bamboo thicket that formed the NVA outer defense line. From inside it, the defenders could see—and cover—the open area between the berm and their main line. The NVA were not doing much firing, but they had the advantage if they felt threatened.

Time was lost getting the .50-caliber machine gun moved across the paddyfield to the berm. During the wait, Major Baker called a platoon sergeants' meeting and asked for suggestions. Sergeant First Class Harold Klein, Company B's senior noncom, who was acting as a platoon leader, suggested getting the Duster moved into the paddy behind the berm so it could suppress the NVA trenchline from close in. While this brilliant solution was implemented, Baker told the platoon sergeants that he still thought his original attack plan could work. He asked for a volunteer to lead the point platoon. There was a brief, pregnant silence, and then Staff Sergeant Broom said he would do it.

By radio, Major Baker updated Captain Frank Lambert, and Lambert said that Company D would be ready to go as soon as the Duster started shooting. As the Duster opened fire under the direction of Sergeant First Class Klein, Private First Class Albert Rocha, the Company D pointman, crawled forward to take out the bunker with a pole charge. An NVA soldier inside the bunker fired at Rocha. The bullet hit the handguard of the trooper's M-16, but Rocha kept going. The Company D exec, 1st Lieutenant Frederick Krupa, crawled forward to help him. When the two reached the nearest firing aperture, Rocha fired his M-16 into the structure. Then Krupa jammed the ten-pound pole charge through the breach—and held it there while NVA soldiers inside stopped shooting and frantically tried to push it back out. After the charge detonated, one NVA soldier hurtled out through the back exit. Rocha shot him dead.

The destruction of the bunker broke the back of the NVA defense and reinvigorated the 5/7 Cav assault. Company D filed past the bunker to the second bamboo hedge and secured Company B's rear and right flank. At the same time, Company B's Staff Sergeant Broom led his troopers through the bamboo hedge, turned left, and began securing the forward NVA trenchline. Once in the bamboo thicket, Broom's platoon rolled into the NVA trenchline and advanced northward in single file. From behind the berm, the rest of Company B used gunfire to cover and support the vanguard platoon's advance. Company A covered both trenchlines from Thon Lieu Coc Thuong.

Whenever Company B platoon's rotating point elements encountered NVA, they radioed Sergeant First Class Klein, who was standing upright beside the Duster, and asked him to direct the Duster crew. Then the pointman would pop a smoke grenade to mark himself, and the Duster would pound fifteen to twenty 40mm rounds into the bamboo ten to fifteen meters to the left of the smoke. The method worked fine the first half-dozen times, but the Company B point eventually ran into a bunker the 40mm rounds could not penetrate. A Huey helicopter gunship arrived on station and was directed to fire into the position from above. In addition, Major Baker sent the flamethrower team forward. The flamethrower operator advanced upright, stopped only a few meters away from the bunker, and torched it. An NVA soldier raced out the back exit, but no one fired at him as he turned the corner and disappeared, because the flamethrower operator was in the way of the troopers watching from behind the berm.

It was just after noon, and that was the end of the battle for the bamboo thicket. Any organized NVA units that might have been left in there, withdrew. A 2/12 Cav trooper attached to the 5/7 Cav led a graves registration team to the former 81mm mortar pit in which eleven of his comrades had been interred on the night of February 4. And all five of the troopers Company D had left in front of the thicket on February 12 were recovered. Several NVA stragglers hiding in the bamboo thicket were rooted out, and there was much booty to collect and analyze. On February 21, the 5/7 Cav had reduced about seventy reinforced bunkers and numerous smaller positions, though few had been strongly defended. The 5/7 Cav advanced through Thon Que Chu but not into Thon La Chu. The battalion never entered the Tri-Thien-Hue Front command bunker.

As planned, the 2/501 Airborne attacked into T-T Woods at the Thon Que Chu–Thon La Chu line, and the two companies of the 2/12 Cav advanced into Thon La Chu from the south. The main force of NVA was gone; the Americans contacted only a desultory rearguard effort. The Tri-Thien-Hue Front headquarters bunker had been abandoned and fell without a fight. The 1/7 Cav, pushing along Highway 1 across the north side of T-T Woods, encountered only minor rearguard opposition when it jumped off at 0520.

By day's end, February 21, Thon Que Chu and Thon La Chu had been well scoured, and the 1/7 Cav was wrapped around the eastern side of T-T Woods, only five kilometers from the Citadel's western corner. For all practical purposes, the NVA's access to Hue had been sealed. Strategically, the battle for Hue was over. The bitter fighting that occurred thereafter mainly involved NVA and VC units and individuals trying to save themselves from being captured or annihilated.

PART X

THE FLAGPOLE

At 1/5's nightly commanders' meeting on February 20, Major Bob Thompson asked his company commanders if they felt their troops were up to launching a night attack—about the only tactic 1/5 had not yet attempted in its week-long Citadel ordeal. Three of the four company commanders thought their troops would be too tired to stay awake for a whole night after a full day of fighting. However, 1st Lieutenant Pat Polk's Alpha/1/5 had been in reserve for most of the week, so Thompson asked Polk if he wanted to give it a go. Polk said he would.

What Thompson's idea finally boiled down to was the infiltration by Alpha/1/5's minuscule 2nd Platoon of the area around the Thuong Tu Gate. Personally led by Pat Polk, the patrol—for that's what it really was—began the night move across the NVA line beginning at 2300, February 20.

Lieutenant Polk reported at 0330 that his Marines were safely ensconced in several multistory buildings on either side of the Thuong Tu Gate. They had encountered no NVA soldiers on the way.

At about 0600, members of the patrol interrogated an elderly Vietnamese man and two children. The captives were obviously innocent civilians with no information to offer, so they were released.

At 0800, patrol members manning observation posts inside the buildings spotted two NVA units gathering in the open, one on either side of the Marine-held enclave. The 81mm forward observer, who had accompanied the patrol—he was the main reason for its being there—ordered a tear gas mission from a section of 4.2-inch mortars established some days earlier at MACV. The CS gas caused the NVA to disperse. Then a scout-sniper team used the confusion triggered by the CS gas to pick off targets, without drawing undue attention. Four NVA soldiers were reported killed at that time, and many others died later as a result of the unique application of bushcraft to city warfare. The patrol's position was never compromised.

When news of the foray got around—Major Thompson had insisted that the other companies tune into Alpha/1/5's company net—the entire battalion became suffused with enthusiasm. As senior officers were quick to point out, here was an object lesson that Marines could be as skilled in infiltration tactics as the mythical NVA supermen.

Throughout the day the NVA facing the main body of 1/5 did most of its resisting at long range, with machine guns and rifles. U.S. Marines attacking toward the southeast wall saw few enemy soldiers, but they felt the sting of their presence. Captain Myron Harrington's dwindling Delta/1/5 tried time and again to advance along the top of the northeast wall to the Citadel's eastern corner, but their efforts resulted in no net gains. Bravo/1/5 and Delta/1/5 jumped off into a renewed assault late in the morning, but both companies were held to minimal gains. Toward the end of the day, Charlie/1/5 was boresighted by many NVA weapons, particularly atop the southeast wall, and it was driven to ground by the intense fire.

On February 21, the cumulative losses of 1/5 were three Marine infantrymen killed, fourteen wounded and evacuated, and five wounded and returned to duty. Against these totals, the Marines counted sixteen NVA or VC confirmed killed, one NVA soldier surrendered, and five enemy personal weapons captured. At day's end, for all the stiff resistance, elements of 1/5 were within a block of the Citadel's southeast wall.

Through the day and into a second night, Lieutenant Pat Polk's Alpha/1/5 patrol remained in the buildings it had occupied around the Thuong Tu Gate.

The next morning, February 21, Captain John Niotis's Lima/3/5 was attached to the 1st Marines. At 1435, the company was formally assigned to 1/5 for use in the Citadel. Immediately, the relatively fresh company was ordered to Doc Lao Park for a helilift into the 1st ARVN Division CP compound. The first lift was fired on by NVA machine guns, as was a subsequent lift. The operation became so hazardous that the effort was called off, leaving the last forty-five members of Lima/3/5 stranded at MACV for the night.

Major Huong Thong's VNMC Battle Group Alpha remained stalled behind Thuy Quan Canal, only halfway along the Citadel's southwest wall. Impeded by the canal, which ran the full length of the VNMC front, Thong's battalions were forced to channel their attack across two bridges, both of which were dominated by NVA machine guns on the Citadel wall. When the Vietnamese Marines tried to teargas the defenders, the NVA used cloth to make field-expedient gas masks that countered the effects of the CS. A VNMC ground assault in the wake of the gas attack was beaten back at great cost to Thong's battalions. Later, NVA 122mm rockets from the high hills to the west fell into the VNMC zone, inflicting additional casualties.

Clearly the NVA were exerting their major effort against the VNMC battle group. The Huu Gate was the 6th NVA Regiment's last escape route through the Citadel wall, and there were still many soldiers, sympathizers, and members of the proposed government to evacuate. Moreover, the terrain lent itself to the type of defense at which the NVA were most skilled. The ground facing the 4th VNMC Battalion, for example, was parkland dotted with homes and temples—ideal for the defender, particularly since the high Citadel wall prevented the 4th VNMC Battalion from maneuvering around the 1,000-meter-deep NVA defended area.

On their side, however, the VNMC battalions had almost more artillery support than they could use. Though Bob Thompson's 1/5 could not call much more than mortars to hit the restricted zone to its front, the Vietnamese Marines had access to their own 105mm howitzer battery, all manner of U.S. heavy artillery, and even U.S. naval gunfire. So, though the VNMC battalions could not advance, they controlled the Huu Gate and were positioned to kill any NVA or Communist refugees who attempted to escape. Moreover, by day's end, it was obvious that the four U.S. Army battalions northwest of Hue, around T-T Woods, could seal off the Communist evacuation and reinforcement routes from outside the Citadel.

Major Bill Eshelman placed part of the blame for the day's failure on the battle-group commander, Major Huong Thong. For some reason, Thong refused to resupply the 4th VNMC

Battalion with 81mm mortar ammunition. Since the 4th VNMC Battalion was down to just twenty-one 81mm rounds, the battalion commander, Captain Do Dinh Vuong, refused to deplete his remaining supply. When Eshelman queried the ammunition-supply figures through advisor channels, he learned that the battle-group supply people had more than they were letting on. So, while the American 8-inch and VNMC 105mm artillery were pummeling the NVA sector, the VNMC Marines on the front line were unable to fire their 81mm mortars at the pinpoint targets that blocked their advance. When two ARVN M-41 tanks joined the 4th VNMC Battalion late in the day, Captain Vuong and Major Eshelman were elated. But their high hopes were short-lived. The tanks' 76mm main guns lacked the punch needed to penetrate Hue's masonry buildings.

The resulting stalemate was so frustrating that Captain Vuong finally asked Major Eshelman, "What do we do next?" Eshelman could not believe his ears. Throughout their relationship, the proud, stoic Vuong had steadfastly refused Eshelman's advice; he considered his U.S. Marine counterpart to be, not an advisor, but an expediter of fire-support coordination. Now Vuong was asking Eshelman what he thought. Eshelman did indeed unburden himself of whatever advice he had to offer, and Captain Vuong listened intently. But the only real solace Eshelman could offer was a promise from the 1st Marines to make one or two Ontos available to the VNMC battle group as soon as 1/5 had secured its objective—in a day or two, it was hoped. However, Major Eshelman knew that the key to breaking through the Communist line was air support, and that depended on improvement in the weather.

In addition to the pressure the U.S. Army battalions were bound to provide from the outside, the generally favorable situation throughout I Corps had allowed the ARVN corps commander, Lieutenant General Hoang Xuan Lam, to act on Brigadier General Ngo Quang Truong's repeated requests for additional reinforcements. On February 21, General Lam agreed to ship the hitherto embattled 21st and 39th ARVN Ranger battalions—part of the I Corps reserve—to Hue. Both battalions moved to Hue via PK 17 that night, and the 1st ARVN Division assigned them the task of clearing VC cadres out of the built-up areas on the east bank of the Perfume River. Cadres in that sector had been conducting a campaign of terror, and VC snipers were still firing on passing patrol boats and landing craft.

By the evening of February 21, everyone in the know was saying that Hue would be liberated "in a matter of time," or "a few days, at most." It only remained to be seen how many more lives would be lost before the Communists acknowledged the obvious.

— 38 —

The NVA opened the February 22 fighting in the Citadel with a mortar barrage at 0330 that targeted Bravo/1/5 and Charlie/1/5. At least twenty 82mm mortar rounds fell on the Marine positions, killing four and wounding four. The Marines responded with their mortars, but no results could be observed.

Also before dawn on February 22, the VNMC battle group was struck by a vicious 122mm rocket barrage. Major Bill Eshelman, the 4th VNMC Battalion senior advisor, knew in his heart that the barrage was the consequence of lax radio discipline. He was certain the NVA had monitored radio conversations the previous evening in which the plans for February 22 had been openly discussed. It was all part of the show, however; the ARVN and VNMC units in Hue regularly listened in on NVA broadcasts.

At 0930, 1/5 moved into the attack again, but the NVA were packed solidly into their defensive zone and all three U.S. Marine front-line companies were out of steam. The attack degenerated into a desultory long-range exchange. The American and North Vietnamese troops seemed to have arrived at a modus vivendi.

At about noon, word arrived at the 1/5 CP that Lima/3/5 was at full strength and ready to join the fight. Major Bob Thompson decided to relieve particularly hard-hit Bravo/1/5 and send its fifty to sixty survivors back to Phu Bai to recuperate.

At 1300, 1st Lieutenant Pat Polk's Alpha/1/5 patrol crept out of the buildings it had been occupying next to the Thuong Tu Gate. The patrol made its way without opposition to the wall at the Citadel's eastern corner. There, Corporal James Avella pulled a small American flag from his pack. The implication was clear. With Lieutenant Polk's tacit approval, Avella wired the flag to a thin metal pipe, climbed to the roof of a tin shed, and affixed the pipe to a telegraph pole. For the second time, a U.S. Marine had hoisted Old Glory to a position of prominence over Hue.

At 1330, Lima/3/5 arrived. Supported by several Marine M-48 tanks, it attacked as soon as it reached the 1/5 front line. Fueled by the valor of the uninitiated, the company swept forward into strongpoints the scarred 1/5 Marines would not have dreamed of approaching in broad daylight. As the lead platoon rushed across a bridge in its path to the Citadel wall, hitherto quiescent NVA snipers concealed throughout the area initiated a devastating crossfire. A handful of the Lima/3/5 Marines were cut down, and many of the survivors were pinned in place.

Observing Lima/3/5's Hue baptism from a nearby observation post were Captain John Niotis and Staff Sergeant Wally Loucks, the company gunny. As soon as the Marines on the far side of the bridge went down, Loucks hurtled across the bridge through a hail of NVA bullets. The gunny checked the wounded men and picked up the Marine he felt was in the worst shape. He hoisted the man over his shoulder and trotted to the rear. The Marine arrived safely at the 1/5 battalion aid station, but he eventually died there. Meantime, Wally Loucks crossed the bridge again and single-handedly pulled the remaining wounded Marines under cover. When the Lima/3/5 attack resumed, Staff Sergeant Loucks helped get all the wounded to the rear.

At 1400, Major Ray Latall and Major John Van Es were on strip alert, sitting in the cockpits of their Marine Attack Squadron 211 A-4 Skyhawk light attack bombers at the Chu Lai Marine Corps Air Base. They had been warned that they might be launched to fly up to Hue to take advantage of clearing weather conditions over the city. Each jet was armed with eight 300-pound Snakeye high-drag high-explosive bombs, two 500-pound napalm bombs, and a full load of 20mm cannon rounds. As the Marine Air Group 12 intelligence officer, Major Latall knew that it had been at least days, probably weeks, since Marine jets had been in action over Hue. The weather at Chu Lai was clear, but in Hue the cloud cover was still low.

The two-plane flight, whose call sign was Helborne 513, was ordered to launch at 1430. After checking in with the Direct Air Support Control center at Hue–Phu Bai, Helborne 513 was instructed to orbit at 20,000 feet twenty miles east of Hue. When the A-4s arrived on station, the tops of the clouds were only 1,500 feet beneath their orbit altitude.

To a Marine rifleman fighting his way toward the Citadel's eastern corner, the preparations by the two A-4 pilots would have seemed inordinately relaxed and unhurried. While orbiting, Major Latall and Major Van Es checked and set their gunsights and arming switches for a low-level bombing run. Then, as they awaited clearance into the target area, they continued to orbit and listen to the strike channel to monitor a mission that was in progress; an Army O-1 spotter plane was directing two other Marine A-4s against a target beside the Citadel. The exchanges between the O-1 and the A-4 pilots revealed that the ragged cloud cover began only 1,000 feet above the ground and that the margin was rapidly deteriorating. Latall and Van Es also learned that the other flight—the third strike of the afternoon—had received hostile fire during its run on the target.

Hue–Phu Bai contacted Latall and Van Es and discussed the need to divert Helborne 513 to another target. The minimum ceiling and visibility standards for an "emergency" mission—a 1,000-foot ceiling with a three-mile visibility—had been breached. Major Latall and Major Van Es decided, however, that they would hit Hue if they could get someone to guide them onto a target right away, before the weather deteriorated further. Latall radioed Hue–Phu Bai with the offer and suggested they make the mission "mandatory" to skirt the weather minimums. At 1500, Hue–Phu Bai warned him that Helborne 513 was about to be assigned a close-support mission that was mandatory in precedence—an unheard-of level.

With weather restrictions effectively lifted, the A-4 pilots joined up, extended their speed brakes, throttled back, and, on instruments, began their descent over the South China Sea. The pilots had no clear idea where they were going to belly through the clouds. While the jets were descending, they were turned over to Benchmark 15, an O-1 flown by an Army pilot and manned by a Marine aerial observer, Captain Bob Laramy.

The A-4s completed their letdown over the water and found the bottom of the overcast at a mere 400 feet. They commenced a turn to port and slowed down as much as they could, as they turned back toward Hue. They were over the city before either jet pilot actually saw Benchmark 15 for the first time. The dark-green O-1 was barely visible, and, to A-4 pilots flying along at 350 knots, it appeared to be standing still one mile ahead and to the right. Just an instant after Major Latall first saw the O-1, Captain Laramy radioed that he could see the A-4s.

As Laramy was describing the target, Latall pulled back off Van Es's wing, but not as far back as he would have liked. The A-4s were painted light gray, just about the same color as the clouds they were skipping through. If Latall had let Van Es get too far ahead, he would have lost sight of him.

Latall was impressed with Laramy's target description. Benchmark 15 sounded like a good, sharp controller, an important bonus in the dark, closed-in sky over Hue. Bob Laramy *was* a sharp controller. In addition, he had been over Hue every day since January 31, mostly to no avail because of the weather.

Captain Laramy said he would mark the target with green smoke, an imperative in that weather. The Army O-1, the only one available to guide Helborne 513, was fitted out as a medevac bird; it had none of the smoke rockets the spotter planes usually carried. To deliver a green-smoke *grenade*, Captain Laramy had to ask the pilot to fly low and slow over the target, an extremely hazardous enterprise. It was then that Laramy learned that the pilot was making his combat debut; this was his very first mission over Vietnam. The pilot was game for the effort, but his inexperience severely complicated a really tricky situation.

The jets' final approach to the target was scary. Flying too low and too slowly with very heavy ordnance loads, both pilots were acutely aware of the many high radio towers that dotted

Hue. They could see none of them clearly and had no real sense of the positions of the towers relative to their flight paths. A broad column of oily smoke from an LCU burning in the river, towering dust clouds from heavy-artillery detonations, and rain impeded visibility and competed for attention. There were even reports that helicopters were in the air nearby.

Benchmark 15 commenced his marking run over the target—the section of the Citadel's southeast wall directly in front of Major Bob Thompson's 1/5. As the green smoke billowed up, both pilots reported from their loose orbit that they could see it—*and* another green-smoke source. Neither of the jet pilots had any idea which was the one marking their target. Clearly, the NVA were monitoring the tactical-air frequency, for only they could have set off the second green-smoke grenade. No problem. Captain Laramy knew which was the right marker, and he talked the A-4s into their target.

Major Van Es made a dummy run to confirm that he knew where the target was, and Major Latall followed. It was worth the extra risk. Neither pilot knew precisely how close to fellow Marines they would be dropping their bombs, but they knew it would be close. There was no margin for error.

Captain Laramy confirmed that the A-4s were on target. The NVA on the ground also confirmed—by firing several machine guns at the Marine jets.

The jet pilots had the option of dropping everything they were carrying on one run, but Van Es and Latall knew they were going to be the last flight of the day; the weather ensured that. Latall and Van Es decided to drop two bombs per run, to be sure the Marines on the ground would get the full benefit of the mission.

They went in at 100 feet, in dead level runs at 350 knots. Latall lost sight of Van Es during the first run, but the leader's first drop was superb. As he pulled off the target, Van Es radioed that the run had been "hot," meaning that he had released ordnance and that he had taken fire. Benchmark 15 gave Latall a slight correction so a broader area could be covered. Latall saw tracers coming at him, and he heard the *thumk-thumk* as several rounds struck his airplane. Despite the distractions, Latall made a perfect drop. Major Bob Thompson later reported in a letter of commendation that the first four napalm canisters had detonated only fifty meters in front of the battalion front line. Thompson had felt their heat.

On the next run, Major Van Es put a pair of 300-pound Snakeyes right on the target. Latall turned in to do the same. By then, the black smoke from the napalm and familiar landmarks made finding the target a snap. The overcast was lower—200 feet—and the NVA machine guns fired again. Latall continued toward the target, taking care that the O-1 was not in his way. He glanced down and was shocked to note that, in jet-jock terms, he was eyeball-to-eyeball with thousands of people—fleeing civilians carrying their valuables on their backs. At the release point, Latall again saw and felt rounds impacting his A-4. He pulled up slightly after releasing his bombs so he could check the jet's flight controls. Everything was running fine, but there were holes in the fuselage near his feet and cockpit pressurization had been lost. Latall also determined that his navigation equipment had been shot out.

On the way back to the target, Latall passed Benchmark 15. The O-1 was to his left, flying straight and level, going in the same direction. However, as Latall was returning downwind to position himself for another bombing run, his earphones rang with the warning, "Benchmark One Five! Pull up! Pull up!" Fearing that he was somehow on a collision course with the O-1, Latall pushed his airplane's nose down and dropped to only fifty feet. But the frantic call was repeated. By then Latall knew that he was nowhere near the O-1. It dawned on Latall that Captain Laramy had not described his last hits on the target.

Latall throttled back as much as he dared, to get a better look around. Over his left shoulder he saw the O-1 staggering from left rear to right rear. There was no smoke or flame, but Latall could clearly see orange fluid streaming from the O-1's nose. It was obvious that Benchmark 15 was going to crash or crash-land. Major Van Es broadcast that Helborne 513 was available for a rescue combat air patrol—that is, ready to orbit over the O-1 until a rescue helicopter could get there.

By then, both A-4s had used more than their allotted fuel for the mission. Any further flying over Hue would endanger their return to Chu Lai. Nevertheless, the A-4 pilots decided to stay longer. The O-1 broke out of its glide toward the Perfume River. Its nose pitched up, and the airplane fell to earth.

As the O-1 fell, Latall once again came in over the target. He did not feel he could drop bombs blindly, however, so he turned off his master armament switch and made a dummy run. If nothing else, the dummy run would put NVA heads down, thus affording the infantry some small respite.

Latall was coming off the dummy run when someone called on the radio to report that a ground rescue party was on the way to the crash scene. Helborne 513 was directed to drop the remaining bombs on the target and head home.

The A-4 pilots ignored these instructions and radioed that they were remaining over Hue. They made several more dummy runs over the target and passes over the O-1, discouraging both NVA movement against 1/5 and any enemy efforts to get to the downed spotter plane. Before the A-4s could drop any more bombs, Hue–Phu Bai firmly ordered them to fly home because the weather was nearly solid from the ground to 20,000 feet. Latall happened to catch sight of Van Es at the last minute, and he joined on the lead A-4, which was important because of Latall's nonfunctioning navigation equipment. They climbed out on instruments. On the way home, Latall notified Van Es that fuel was leaking from a hole in Van Es's main fuel cell.

Though both arrived with very little fuel, the A-4s made it back to Chu Lai without further difficulty. Major Van Es's bomber had been hit in the main fuel cell, port wingtip, and port landing-gear door; Latall's had sustained hits from the aft section of the nose on back to the rudder and elevator. Calls from Chu Lai that evening revealed that the Army O-1 pilot had been shot and killed as Major Latall was making his second hot pass. Captain Bob Laramy, a Marine infantry officer, had received rudimentary pilot training. He tried to fly the airplane, but the controls had failed and the O-1 had crashed. Captain Laramy walked into an ARVN position, but he had been critically burned in the crash and, eventually, was medically retired. The next day, Major John Van Es and Major Ray Latall heard that they had been credited with killing seventy-three NVA within 150 meters of the Citadel wall.

The battle in the VNMC zone on February 22 began at 0645, when NVA soldiers manning positions atop and within the Citadel wall opened fire with machine guns and rifles. Mortars set in farther to the southeast just added to the mayhem. Casualties began mounting noticeably. At 0830, an NVA counterattack pushed part of a battalion of the 3rd ARVN Regiment out of a schoolhouse it had been holding for days in the zone between the VNMC battle group and the U.S. Marine sector.

The VNMC battle group was again supported by creeping 8-inch howitzer barrages from the south. The 8-inch registration rounds for each fire mission were placed on a line 300 meters to the southeast of the VNMC line. The subsequent all-out barrage was drawn closer in small increments until Vietnamese Marines on the front line sent word that they were receiving shrapnel in their positions. Then, following each barrage, ARVN loudspeakers were brought up and the NVA and VC facing the VNMC battle group were given an opportunity to surrender. Most of the Communist fighters remained in their bunkers and fighting holes, but they allowed hundreds of civilians to cross into the VNMC lines. No doubt, some NVA and VC fighters escaped in civilian disguise, but several were captured after flunking interrogation or after being turned in by civilians loyal to the GVN.

For all the good the artillery and propaganda barrages did, the 4th and 5th VNMC battalions made no forward progress on February 22. The NVA and VC holding the Huu Gate open were, if anything, more determined then ever.

Victory was in the air in the 1/5 zone of action. Alpha/1/5's 2nd Platoon had spent the night of February 22 atop the wall at the Citadel's eastern corner, and the NVA in the area had made no hostile moves in its direction. At 0800, February 23, Captain Myron Harrington's Delta/1/5 attacked from its line a block from the southeast wall and punched through to the objective against sporadic sniper fire. Two Marines were wounded in the final assault, and one dead NVA soldier was discovered as the thin little company spread out to scour the area in its sector.

When Delta/1/5 went into the attack toward the wall, Captain John Niotis's much larger Lima/3/5 pivoted to the southwest to attack toward the Imperial Palace's eastern corner. There were not many NVA facing the company, but those that were put up remarkably strong resistance. Initial progress was slow, no doubt partly because the men of Lima/3/5, veterans of only one day's city fighting, were playing it safe.

One of the two or three M-48 tanks supporting Captain Niotis's company was struck at 0945 by a B-40 rocket. One crewman was killed, one crewman was slightly injured, and the heavily damaged tank had to be driven to the rear.

Sensing that the end of NVA resistance was near at hand, Major Bob Thompson and Major Len Wunderlich left the 1/5 CP and moved forward to the porch of a masonry building from which they could observe and direct their battalion's final maneuvers. By then, Lima/3/5 had found its stride. As Bob Thompson observed from his new CP, he thought it was the most beautiful attack he had ever witnessed—better even than the many rehearsed demonstrations he had observed or taken part in at Quantico. The sky had been clear at dawn, so there were plenty of Marine jets overhead, their pilots able and eager to deliver bombs, napalm, and rockets to within 100 meters of the advancing 1/5 front. Once it got over its early-morning caution, Lima/3/5 moved forward like a well-oiled machine. And the two or three surviving tanks and two Ontos were right on the money, attacking in perfect harmony with the infantry. In the course of the initial phase of the attack, the long-sought Thuong Tu Gate finally fell into U.S. Marine hands.

At about 1000, the tank platoon sergeant or his gunner apparently saw movement in the 1/5 CP building, which had only just been occupied by Major Thompson, Major Wunderlich, and their CP group. The tank crewmen jumped to the conclusion that the building was in enemy hands. For their part, the two majors were certain that they had front-row seats for the inevitable destruction of an NVA position somewhere behind the CP. They were thoroughly enjoying the show until they realized that they were staring straight down the 90mm gun's barrel. At what felt like the last instant, the gun barrel went up and the turret traversed. The gunner had seen a better target. The tank fired several rounds over the CP, toward the Imperial Palace wall, but then the gun was traversed back on the battalion CP. Bob Thompson saw a little puff of smoke and then—BOOM—a 90mm round tore into the CP building. Fortunately, Major Thompson, Major Wunderlich, and all their assorted radiomen were already sprawled on the deck when the tank round detonated on the concrete archway over the porch. As if that were not enough, the tank commander raked the porch with his .50-caliber cupola machine gun. Major Thompson instinctively headed for the door so he could get inside the masonry building, but his brand-new bodyguard threw Thompson to the ground and covered his body with his own. Thompson was amazed. His former bodyguard had been shot dead the day before, and the new bodyguard had been selected at random by the battalion sergeant major. Thompson did not even know the new kid's name, and he was sure the lance corporal knew him only as "Major." Then, compounding Thompson's amazement, a dead calm Len Wunderlich grabbed the handset from the battalion radioman and in uncharacteristically vulgar language ordered the tank platoon sergeant to cease fire. Miraculously, beyond damage to Major Thompson's equanimity, the tank attack had caused no harm.

A short time later, one of the tanks supporting Lima/3/5 was struck by several B-40s fired from the Imperial Palace wall. Three of the tank crewmen were wounded. A minute later, as the damaged tank was pulling back, it was struck by three more B-40s. Lima/3/5 Marines who spotted the source of the RPGs fired their M-16s and M-60s while calling for a 60mm mortar mission. The NVA returned fire at the Lima/3/5 Marines, but the mortars quickly blotted out the NVA position. The tank completed its withdrawal unmolested, but one Lima/3/5 Marine was killed, six were wounded and evacuated, and five sustained minor wounds in the exchange.

At 1020, the main body of Alpha/1/5 was struck by three 82mm mortar rounds as it inched its way along outside the Imperial Palace's northeast wall. Four Marines were wounded and evacuated; one Marine, who was lightly injured, stayed with the company.

Early in the afternoon, Delta/1/5 was attacking to the southwest, mainly clearing NVA-held bunkers and passages within the southeast wall. At length the company's lead element ran into a large NVA force holed up in a series of interconnecting, mutually supporting bunkers and pillboxes. Heavy fire from NVA rifles, machine guns, and RPGs threatened to stop the Delta/1/5 drive, but Captain Myron Harrington was not in the mood to let anything stand between him and final victory. Harrington moved forward with a pair of teams armed with 3.5-inch rockets and directed them against what he perceived as the cornerstone of the NVA defensive sector. Then Harrington darted from front-line position to front-line position, pinpointing objectives for his troops and directing suppressive small-arms fire. As Harrington personally called artillery and mortar fire down to within twenty-five meters of his own position, four NVA positions were overrun. As the NVA defensive sector started to crack, Harrington worked his way forward, rallied his company's point elements, and personally led an assault on yet another NVA position. At that point, Delta/1/5 began to make headway through the crumbling NVA defenses. When the attack finally routed the NVA force, Harrington's Marines counted twenty-five dead NVA soldiers within the strongpoint. Captain Myron Harrington was awarded a Navy Cross for his role in leading the attack.

As soon as Major Bob Thompson was certain that the NVA defenses all across 1/5's front were finally crumbling, he asked the commander of the 2nd Battalion, 3rd ARVN Regiment, to join him in the 1/5 CP. The ARVN captain, a rather dandified individual, had been asking Thompson for days to be allowed to mount the final attack on the flagpole from which the giant NLF banner remained flying over the center of the Citadel's southeast wall. Thompson kept telling the ARVN battalion commander that any such attempt would be suicidal until the Citadel's eastern corner was in friendly hands. During the afternoon of February 23, Thompson told the ARVN captain that the 2nd Battalion, 3rd ARVN Regiment, could probably seize the flagpole right then and there. Thompson expected the ARVN officer to jump at the opportunity, but the ARVN battalion commander just replied, "Maybe you better take it."

It was out of the question for 1/5 to seize the flagpole. Higher headquarters had made it abundantly clear that, no matter what it was *able* to accomplish, the U.S. Marine battalion was not *permitted* to strike the NLF colors from the Citadel's main flagpole, nor was it permitted to enter the Imperial Palace grounds. In deference to South Vietnamese national pride, only ARVN or VNMC units would be permitted to seize those two ultimate political objectives.

Given the restrictions, 1/5 ended the day in possession of all the objectives it was allowed. Except for straightening its front line and mopping up throughout its rear, there was nothing left for 1/5 to do inside the Citadel of Hue.

On February 23, the 4th and 5th VNMC battalions began their attack at 1100. An immense early-morning air and artillery bombardment had been promised all along their front, but hours had passed and no such support had appeared. Lacking support even from their own 81mm mortars, for which there was still no ammunition, each battalion simply attacked with three companies abreast. Once again, the Vietnamese Marines were unable to get across Thuy Quan Canal. Despite repeated efforts by officers and staff noncommissioned officers to motivate the troops, it was clear that the VNMC battle group was going to get nowhere that day.

By day's end, morale in the 4th and 5th VNMC battalions had taken a nose dive. An air of sullenness swept through the ranks, an unprecedented turn of events among the elite ranks of the stoic VNMC.

Apparently, the commander of the 2nd Battalion, 3rd ARVN Regiment, was prevailed upon by higher authority—General Truong, no doubt—to advance with his entire unit along the top of the Citadel's southeast wall from the Delta/1/5 line to the flagpole. The ARVN troops moved forward in the darkness before dawn, and the final assault was mounted at 0500. They easily overran the NVA unit holding the objective, killing thirty-one of the enemy soldiers.

At dawn the huge NLF banner that had taunted and haunted South Vietnam's and America's political leaders since January 31 was hauled down by the triumphant ARVN soldiers. Moments later, it was replaced with an equally large flag displaying the colors of South Vietnam.

At 0730, its morale revitalized by this moment of glory, the main body of the 3rd ARVN Regiment, bolstered by a troop of the 7th ARVN Armored Cavalry Battalion, advanced against spotty resistance to the outer walls of the Imperial Palace. For most of the next three hours, a circus atmosphere prevailed inside the Citadel. To the accompaniment of patriotic music broadcast over loudspeakers, the ARVN soldiers thoroughly shot up the palace wall and hurled hand grenades over the top. By 1025, the last shred of hostile fire had been subdued. General Truong ordered the Hoc Bao Company, the 1st ARVN Division Reconnaissance Company, and the 2nd Battalion, 3rd ARVN Regiment, to kick open the Imperial Palace's Ngo Mon Gate and secure the interior. More preparatory gunfire and grenade-throwing ensued, and the attack finally got underway at 1515. At 1700, the Imperial Palace was declared secure.

Throughout the morning, the VNMC battle group tried once again to breach the NVA defenses. As soon as the attack jumped off, it became obvious that many of the NVA had been withdrawn or had simply abandoned their positions. Before noon, two companies of the 4th VNMC Battalion had secured the vital Huu Gate, and the two-battalion attack quickly advanced beyond it. Any NVA or VC remaining inside the Citadel were now trapped there. The Vietnamese Marines were unable to complete the attack to the Citadel's south corner by sunset, but they jumped off again at 0500 the next day. At last, on February 25, with the help of two U.S. Marine Ontos, the south corner fell.

Epilogue

The city of Hue was declared secure by I ARVN Corps headquarters on February 26, 1968, one day after the liberation of the Imperial Palace. Though official communiques celebrated the end of the battle, bloody combat operations in and around Hue continued against stubborn Communist units and stragglers for the next three weeks.

Of the three U.S. Marine battalions committed to combat in Hue, Lieutenant Colonel Mark Gravel's 1/1 continued to run security patrols in the area east of MACV until it was relieved in early March. By the end of February, Lieutenant Colonel Ernie Cheatham's 2/5, which by February 10 had liberated the modern city center as far as the Phu Cam Canal, had just about destroyed the main body of the 4th NVA Regiment in aggressive sweep-and-pursuit operations south of the canal. During the first few days of March, Cheatham's 2/5 and Major Bob Thompson's 1/5 conducted sweep-and-security operations between the Perfume River and the South China Sea. Task Force X-Ray declared the end of Operation Hue City on March 2. On March 4, 1/5 was returned to the 5th Marines and ordered to Phu Bai to refit. On March 5, Colonel Stan Hughes and his regimental staff left MACV and returned to Phu Bai. On March 8, 2/5 began moving south to begin a new operation under the direction of the 5th Marines.

Following the fall of the Citadel, the 2nd Brigade of the 101st Airborne Division and the 3rd Brigade of the 1st Cavalry Division continued to sweep toward the city from the north and west. They and other elements of both U.S. Army divisions crossed the Perfume River and conducted mop-up operations for several days. Then the U.S. Army units were withdrawn to begin new operations that had been planned before the Tet emergency broke.

VNMC Battle Group Alpha also remained in contact with Communist units and stragglers in and around Hue. When it was withdrawn in early March, the three battalions were returned to their southern cantonments to reequip and train replacements for the hundreds of Vietnamese Marines killed and wounded in Saigon and Hue.

The 1st ARVN Division, which was headquartered in Hue, continued to mop up in and around the city, but it slowly went back to its previous routine of sweeping around and across northern I Corps. It took many months for the division to regain its pre-Tet strength, and months longer for it to absorb and train new conscripts. Yet, as long as the division benefited from the stalwart leadership of Brigadier General Ngo Quang Truong, it remained one of the best of the ARVN combat divisions.

In the end, beautiful Hue lay in ruins. Years of rebuilding lay ahead, and the task was far from completion when the Republic of Vietnam fell before the final NVA offensive in 1975. However, the real tragedy of the battle for Hue lay, not in the physical damage or even in the loss of national treasures, but in the deaths of many hundreds of Hue's citizens—the random deaths and maimings in the battles to liberate the city, and in the nearly 2,000 documented cases of mass murder and execution that claimed the lives of many of the nation's leading businessmen, government workers, politicians, theologians, foreign missionaries and doctors, intellectuals, and teachers. From this brutal human toll—discovered in many unmarked individual and mass graves found over a period of months and years—neither the city nor the nation ever rebounded. In a way, the unified nation of Vietnam is still paying a colossal price for the irredeemable acts of the Communist hit squads.

Bibliography

BOOKS

Davidson, Phillip B. *Vietnam at War: The History, 1946-1975*. Novato, CA: Presidio Press, 1988.

———. *Secrets of the Vietnam War*. Novato, CA: Presidio Press, 1990.

Nolan, Keith William. *Battle for Hue: Tet 1968*. Novato, CA: Presidio Press, 1983.

Oberdorfer, Don. *Tet!: The Turning Point in the Vietnam War*. New York: Doubleday & Company, 1971.

Palmer, Dave Richard. *Summons of the Trumpet: U.S.-Vietnam in Perspective*. Novato, CA: Presidio Press, 1978.

Phan Van Son. *The Viet Cong Tet Offensive (1968)*. Saigon: Republic of Vietnam Armed Forces, 1969.

Pike, Douglas. *PAVN: People's Army of Vietnam*. Novato, CA: Presidio Press, 1986.

Stanton, Shelby L. *Anatomy of a Division: 1st Cav in Vietnam*. Novato, CA: Presidio Press, 1987.

———. *Vietnam Order of Battle*. New York: U.S. News and World Report, Inc., 1981.

Tolson, Major General John J., 3rd. *Airmobility: 1961-1971*. Washington, D.C.: Department of the Army, 1973.

Westmoreland, General William C. *A Soldier Reports*. Garden City, NY: Doubleday & Company, 1976.

PERIODICALS

Bullington, James R. "And Here, See Hue," *Foreign Service Journal*, November 1968.

Christmas, G. R. "A Company Commander Reflects on Operation Hue City," *Marine Corps Gazette*, April 1971.

———. "A Company Commander Remembers the Battle for Hue," *Marine Corps Gazette*, February 1977.

Harkanson, John, and Charles McMahon. "USMC & Tet '68: There's a Little Trouble in Hue . . . ," *Vietnam Combat*, Winter 1985.

———. "Tet '68/USMC in Hue: The Grunts' War," *Vietnam Combat*, Spring 1986.

———. "Tet '68/USMC in Hue: The Second Week," *Vietnam Combat*, Summer 1986.

———. "The Last Days of Tet '68: Hard, Hungry, Horrible," *Vietnam Combat*, Winter 1986.

Smith, Captain George W., USA. "The Battle of Hue," *Infantry*, July-August 1968.

Truong Sinh. "The Fight to Liberate the City of Hue During Mau Than Tet (1969)," *Hoc Tap*, December 1974.

OFFICIAL SOURCES

Many official documents were used to piece this story together. Among them were the Command Chronologies and After Action Reports submitted by Task Force X-Ray; the 1st Marine Regiment; the 1st Battalion, 1st Marines; the 1st Battalion, 5th Marines; and the 2nd Battalion, 5th Marines. The operations of elements of the 1st Cavalry Division's 3rd Brigade are covered in several detailed narrative reports written soon after the events by the 14th Military History Detachment.

PRIVATE SOURCES

The preponderance of details contained in this narrative were gleaned from voluminous taped and written exchanges between the author and ninety-one survivors of the Hue fighting. An enormous amount of effort and energy went into verifying details with other survivors and matching events described by individuals with events described, usually quite tersely, in the official records. In every case, inevitably, exact matches could not be made. And, though most details were satisfactorily verified, disputes over others still rage between and among groups of eyewitnesses. Judging the efficacy of thousands of details, from both private and official sources, the results of disputes between sources, and, the verity of individuals is the stock and trade of the narrative historian. To the degree that doing so is a science, it is an inexact science. To the degree that doing so is an art, it is a very satisfying art.

Acknowledgments

I have written more than a dozen books, and it still amazes me how many strangers step forward willingly to give of their time, energy, and sleepless nights. Unfortunately, it is sometimes impossible to write a readable book using so much information, so some stories are not used. Here, then, are the names of all the men, and one woman, who provided information, whether it was used or not:

Joseph E. Abodeely (1st Cavalry Division), George O. Adkisson, Jr. (MACV), Danny J. Allbritton (2/5), Alfred G. Alvarez (1st Cavalry Division), Charles R. Baker (5/7 Cavalry), Barney W. Barnes (2/5), Gordon D. Batcheller (1/1), Roger B. Bergeron (1/5), Douglas E. Blayney (2/5), Frank Breth (MACV), Chris Brown (2/5), Jeff Brown (2/5), James R. Bullington, Tuy-Cam Bullington, Josef Burghardt (1/1), Thomas R. Burnham (2/5), Edward B. Burrow, Jr. (1/5), Hugh L. Buzzell (1st Cavalry Division), Terry Charbonneau (1st Motor Transport Battalion), Ernest C. Cheatham, Jr. (2/5), George R. Christmas (2/5), Joseph T. Dawson (2/5), Michael P. Downs (2/5), William P. Eshelman (4th VNMC Battalion), Michael L. Ferguson (1st ARVN Division), F. Fernandez Folio (1/5), Dennis J. Gillem (2/501 Airborne), Curtis D. Godfrey (1/1), Marcus J. Gravel (1/1), Robert A. Gross (2/5), Patrick Haley (2/5), Myron C. Harrington (1/5), Michael O. Harris (2/5), Robert L. Helvey (2/12 Cavalry), James P. Hunter (2/5), Steven M. Johnson (2/12 Cavalry), Thomas R. Johnson (Marine Attack Squadron 311), Walter Kaczmarek (2/5), James A. Kennedy (5/7 Cavalry), Kenneth Kromer (2/5), Donald H. LaJeunesse (2/5), Franklin P. Lambert (5/7 Cavalry), Michael T. Lambert (2/5), W. Roger Lansbury (2/5), Raymond F. Latall (Marine Air Group 12), Jack R. Lofland (Combined Action Platoon Alpha-2), Burdette W. Loucks (Lima/3/5), James H. McCoy (2/5), Charles McMahon (2/5), Charles L. Meadows (2/5), Robert L. Meadows (2/5), James M. Mueller, Jr. (MACV), John A. Mullan (1/5), Peter A. Murray (2/5), Jerome Nadolski (1st Motor Transport Battalion), Edward F. Neas (1/1), Jack E. Phillips (1/5), Carnell Poole (2/5), Daniel J. Powers (2/5), Ray

E. Poynter (101st Airborne Division), Howard T. Prince, II (5/7 Cavalry), Ronald D. Ray (VNMC Battle Group Alpha), Patrick Reilly (2/5), William L. Rogers, III (2/5), R. John Salvati (2/5), Scott Sampietro (2/5), Robert Scott (101st Airborne Division), Ray Stewart (2/5), Bill Stubbs (1/1), Dennis Studenny (2/5), Richard S. Sweet (2/12 Cavalry), William Tant (2/5), Ronald Taylor (1/11), Robert H. Thompson (1/5), Forrest Towe (2/5), Jeffrey N. Tressler (Lima/3/5), Ngo Quang Truong (1st ARVN Division), Michael Turley (1/5), Edward Van Valkenburgh (2/5), James B. Vaught (5/7 Cavalry), Frederick J. Vogel (1st Reconnaissance Battalion), Vic Walker (1/5), James P. Walsh (1/5), Herbert Watkins, Jr. (1/1), Ernest Weiss (2/5), Raymond G. Wojda (2/5), Leonard A. Wunderlich (1/5), James Yates (2/5), Donald C. Young (1/5), T. L. Youngman (2/5), Valente U. Yruegas (2/5).

Thank you, one and all!

Index